THE FUTURE OF MONEY

THE FUTURE OF MONEY

Benjamin J. Cohen

PRINCETON UNIVERSITY PRESS   PRINCETON AND OXFORD

Copyright © 2004 by Princeton University Press
Published by Princeton University Press, 41 William Street, Princeton, New Jersey 08540
In the United Kingdom: Princeton University Press, 3 Market Place,
   Woodstock, Oxfordshire OX20 1SY

All Rights Reserved

Library of Congress Cataloging-in-Publication Data
Cohen, Benjamin J.
   The future of money/Benjamin J. Cohen.
p.   cm.

Includes bibliographical references and index.

ISBN 0-691-11665-2 (alk. paper)

1. International finance. 2. Monetary policy. 3. Monetary unions. 4. Money. I. Title.

HG3881.C5854 2004
332'.042—dc21
2003045983

British Library Cataloging-in-Publication Data is available
This book has been composed in Sabon

Printed on acid-free paper. ∞

www.pupress.princeton.edu
Printed in the United States of America

10 9 8 7 6 5 4 3 2 1

For Jane, WHO IS THE PRESENT AND
For Christel, WHO IS THE FUTURE

Contents

List of Illustrations

ix

Acknowledgments

xi

Introduction

xiii

Abbreviations

xxi

One
The Changing Geography of Money

1

Two
Four Directions

33

Appendix: Tables

62

Three
Life at the Peak

67

Four
The Art of Survival

99

Five
Follow the Leader

123

Six
Hanging Together

153

Seven
New Frontiers

179

Eight
Governing the New Geography

203

Notes

223

References

247

Index

285

List of Illustrations _____

Figures

Figure 1. Choice Diagram   52

Tables

Table 1. Fully Dollarized Countries   62
Table 2. Near-Dollarized Countries   62
Table 3. Currency Boards   63
Table 4. Bimonetary Countries   63
Table 5. Monetary Unions   64
Table 6. Dependent Territories   65

Acknowledgments _____

THIS BOOK may be regarded as the third volume of a trilogy that began with *Organizing the World's Money*, published in 1977, and continued with *The Geography of Money* (1998). With *Organizing the World's Money*, I started a systematic exploration of the political economy of global monetary relations, past and present, that now culminates with this attempt to peer as clearly as possible into the mists of the future. In *Organizing the World's Money*, the analysis was almost exclusively state-centric, reflecting the reality of a time when international financial markets had barely begun their postwar resurrection (Cohen 1996). In *The Geography of Money*, by contrast, markets took center stage as major determinants of the configuration of currency space. Finally, here in *The Future of Money*, I focus once again on state behavior but in a context that is heavily influenced by the logic of market competition.

Despite its close connections to its intellectual antecedents, however, this book is by no means merely a new spin on old themes. It is, rather, an entirely new piece of work addressing critical questions left unanswered by its immediate predecessor. *The Future of Money* builds on *The Geography of Money* but does not repeat it. Where *The Geography of Money* emphasized the past and present—the origins and implications of today's market-driven process of currency competition—*The Future of Money*, as its title implies, is more forward-looking, aiming to help understand what can be expected to happen tomorrow and the day after. The inquiry is fresh and, as I hope to demonstrate, can make significant claims to originality. Both the perspective and the analytical model are novel.

Much of the volume draws on papers written since *The Geography of Money* was published. The only exception is chapter 1, which, but for the final few pages, is essentially a summary of the key arguments of the earlier book. The remaining chapters all build on a diversity of new work. Much of chapter 2 is based on Cohen 2003b, and much of chapter 3 on Cohen 2000b and 2002b. Chapter 4 draws in part from Cohen 2000c, 2000d, 2000f, 2001c, 2002a, and 2003a. Chapters 5 and 6 make much use of Cohen 2000a, 2000e, 2001a, and 2003c. Chapter 7 relies greatly on Cohen 1999 and 2001b. Versions of all of these papers were initially presented at conferences or professional meetings in the United States and elsewhere, and all benefited from the insightful comments and suggestions that I received from many colleagues around the world. Too numerous to identify individually by name, they are all thanked collectively in one comprehensive and sincere expression of gratitude.

The full penultimate version of this manuscript was read by seven outstanding scholars: Dave Andrews, Eric Helleiner, Peter Kenen, Kate McNamara, John Odell, Lou Pauly, and Randy Henning. I am indebted to them all for their extraordinarily useful commentaries, which have helped improve the final product enormously. The research assistance of my talented graduate student Tom Knecht is also gratefully acknowledged.

Finally, this book is dedicated to the two most important females in my life. First is my wife Jane Sherron De Hart, a talented historian and—deservedly—the only award-winning author in our family. And second is Christel Vidal Villela, our beloved goddaughter, who spent a good part of her early years doing her best to divert me from this project to the far more vital task of helping her with her jigsaw puzzles and coloring books. Without these two delights, my life would be impoverished.

Introduction _____

WHAT IS THE FUTURE of money in an increasingly globalized world economy? The question is critical. Though seemingly technical in nature, the management of money in fact is anything but neutral in its implications for the distribution of wealth and power across the globe. Whoever controls money gains access to real resources—goods and services of all kinds—which in turn are key to attaining economic and political advantage. For the citizens of any country, it matters greatly whether currency will be governed by recognized state authorities or by others, by friend or by foe, at home or abroad. Will the privilege that money represents be handled responsibly or exploitatively? Will currency be a source of prosperity or conflict? The future of money affects us all. It is our future.

For many monetary specialists, the answer to the question is clear. The future will see a dramatic reduction in the number of currencies in circulation, greatly simplifying the management of money around the world. I call this the Contraction Contention. But the Contraction Contention is utterly wrong. In reality, the global population of currencies is set to expand greatly, not contract, making monetary governance more difficult rather than less. We will all have to learn how to cope with an increasingly complex currency environment.

At issue is a breakdown of the neat territorial monopolies that national governments have historically claimed in the management of money—a process that in an earlier volume, *The Geography of Money* (1998), I described as the *deterritorialization* of money. Along with increasing globalization of the world economy has come direct competition among currencies across political borders. State authorities are no longer able to exercise supreme control over the circulation and use of money within their own frontiers; and this in turn is leading to fundamental changes in the way money is governed. Deterritorialization may not account for every recent development in international monetary relations, but it is central to determining what governments are able to do in response. The stakes could not be higher. As I wrote in *The Geography of Money*, accelerating currency competition transforms the role of the state in monetary governance, threatening a major crisis of legitimacy in this vital realm of political economy.

The aim of the present book is to take up where *The Geography of Money* left off. The earlier book highlighted the nature of today's challenge to monetary governance and outlined the principal policy responses available to governments. Left unanswered were the critical questions of what factors might determine state choices and how those choices in turn, interacting with market forces, will shape the monetary environment of the future. In *The Geography of Money*, the focus was on the emergence of new structures of power in global monetary relations. In this book I show where those new structures of power are leading us—toward a world far more complex, and far more difficult to govern, than commonly predicted. The novelty of the book lies both in the forward-looking perspective of the inquiry and in the innovative approach to analysis.

The book begins, in chapter 1, with a brief summary of the main conclusions of its predecessor. The geography of money refers to the spatial organization of currency relations. Monetary geography is rapidly changing as a direct result of the spread of competition between currencies. The population of the monetary universe is becoming ever more stratified, assuming the appearance of a vast Currency Pyramid: narrow at the top, where the strongest monies dominate; and increasingly broad below, reflecting varying degrees of competitive inferiority. As deterritorialization accelerates, power is being radically redistributed. Where once existed *monopoly*, we now find something more like *oligopoly*—a finite number of autonomous suppliers, national governments, all vying ceaselessly to shape and manage demand for their respective currencies. Monetary governance, at its most basic, has become a political contest for market share, posing difficult choices for policymakers. *The Geography of Money* ended with a question: Can public policy cope? *The Future of Money* offers an answer.

One possibility, of course, is that under the pressure of accelerating competition, many countries will simply quit the contest altogether. That is the Contraction Contention, now rapidly gaining popularity among specialists. The logic of the Contraction Contention stems from the power of economies of scale in monetary use. The reasoning is clear. From the point of view of market actors, whose concern is to minimize transactions costs, the fewer the currencies the better. Economies of scale will be maximized.

The Contraction Contention, however, is shortsighted. It reckons without the supply side of the market, where preferences can be expected to run very much the other way—toward preservation and even a proliferation of currencies around the globe. On the supply side, two sets of actors must be considered: states, of course, traditionally the core producers of money; but also the private sector, which is equally capable of creating viable, competitive currencies. The role of government is taken up in chapters 2 through 6, focusing on the alternative choices still available to state authorities in today's increasingly deterritorialized monetary geography. Analysis suggests that far fewer national currencies are apt to disappear than is commonly predicted. The role of the private sector, in turn, is taken up in chapter 7, emphasizing new opportunities and incentives for monetary production by a diverse range of nonstate actors. For a variety of reasons, the chapter concludes, the number of privately issued currencies in the world can be expected to multiply dramatically, adding even more to the complexity of money's future. What all this means for the future of monetary governance, finally, is explored in chapter 8.

The analytical heart of the book is outlined in chapter 2, where I lay out an innovative model for understanding the strategic preferences of states, as each government is driven to develop a winning strategy in the oligopolistic struggle among monies. In principle, four strategies might be possible. These are:

1. *Market leadership*: an aggressive unilateralist policy intended to promote use of the national money, analogous to predatory price leadership in an oligopoly.

2. *Market preservation*: a unilateralist status-quo policy intended to defend, rather than augment, a previously acquired market position for the home currency.

3. *Market followership*: an acquiescent policy of subordinating monetary sovereignty to a stronger foreign currency, analogous to passive price followership in an oligopoly.

4. *Market alliance*: a collusive policy of sharing monetary sovereignty in a monetary union of some kind, analogous to a tacit or explicit cartel.

In practice, even that list exaggerates the range of available choice, since at least one of the four possible strategies—market leadership—is generally beyond the capacities of most governments. Only a privileged few states with the most widely circulated currencies, such as the U.S. dollar, Europe's new euro (succeeding Germany's deutsche mark), and the Japanese yen, can realistically aspire to a unilateralist leadership strategy. For the vast majority of states with less competitive monies, policy options really are limited just to the remaining three—a tricky choice indeed. The analytical model developed in chapter 2 concentrates on the reciprocal relationship among these three strategies of preservation, followership, or alliance.

The essence of the choice can be easily stated. Should policymakers seek to defend their traditional monetary sovereignty, or should they delegate some or all of their formal authority elsewhere, either to a dominant foreign power or to the joint institutions of a currency partnership? Delegation of authority elsewhere necessarily implies a degree of regional consolidation in currency relations, either vertical regionalization (followership) or horizontal regionalization (alliance). Scholars are only beginning to address the question of what such a new regional geography of money might look like. My model offers two broad advances over the existing literature.

First, while it is true that numerous discussions already exist analyzing the advantages or disadvantages of one or another of the available choices, most scholarly work, almost without exception, is confined to evaluating the advantages and disadvantages of options *individually* or in comparison to just one other alternative. Few consider all three possible strategies in direct relation to one another. One claim to originality in the approach developed here lies in my emphasis on the *three-dimensional* nature of the decisions involved. The choice is inherently *tripartite*. The key to understanding state preferences is to be found in the relationship among all three elements of the choice, not in the pros and cons of any one option alone or of any single pair of options.

The second claim to originality lies in my emphasis on *degrees* of regionalization as a central determinant of state preferences. Scholars, of course, have long acknowledged that regional currencies may come in many shapes and sizes. But again, almost without exception, formal analysis tends parsimoniously to reduce state choice to starkly contrasting polar alternatives in order to highlight crucial differences. In fact, there is no substitute for more fine-grained exploration, since policymakers can be expected to vary greatly in the importance they attach to particular gains or losses depending on each country's unique circumstances.

Closer analysis of state preferences begins in chapter 3, with a look first at the prospects for the market leaders. At the peak of today's Currency Pyramid we find the Big Three—the dollar, euro, and yen. The logic of competition suggests that among currencies in circulation today, there seems no candidate with even the remotest chance in the foreseeable future of challenging the Big Three's top rank. Among the Big Three, however, there seems a very real chance of significant shifts in relative standing. The euro, in particular, is poised to increase market share at the expense of the dollar, though in key respects the competitive advantages of America's greenback will persist. The yen, by contrast, appears to have peaked as an international currency and may well be entering a period of long, painful decline. Much will depend, however, on how the governing authorities of the Big Three respond to prospective market developments. That is a matter of state preferences.

There are reasons to assume that a unilateralist strategy to maintain or enhance market position will be the preferred choice of each of the market leaders. Rational policymakers are hardly likely to turn their back on the considerable benefits to be derived from broader use of their currency. On the contrary, the Big Three can be expected to do all they can to sustain the underlying competitiveness of their currencies, with the objective of defending or promoting widespread use by *market* actors. Rivalry for market share, what I call *informal* leadership, is natural in an oligopoly. It is less evident, however, that governments will be motivated to go a step further, to seek to influence the behavior of other *state* actors, lending support to national strategies of followership. That would imply sponsoring formation of organized currency blocs, what I call *formal* leadership.

For its part the United States, at the top of the Currency Pyramid, will take no such initiative unless seriously challenged for formal leadership by either Europe or Japan. For their part, neither the Europeans nor the Japanese appear to have any appetite for overt currency conflict with Washington. None of the Big Three, therefore, is likely to offer direct inducements of any significance to alter the incentive structures facing other governments (with the possible exception of Japan in East Asia). In thinking about the tricky choice they face among the options of monetary preservation, followership, or alliance, most other states will find themselves more or less on their own.

The key issues involved in that difficult tripartite choice are explored in chapters 4 through 6, beginning with the option of preservation in chapter 4. Monetary sovereignty can be defended by tactics of either persuasion and coercion. Persuasion entails trying to sustain demand for a currency by buttressing its reputation—above all, by a public commitment to credible policies of "sound" monetary management. Coercion means applying the formal regulatory powers of the state to avert any significant shift by users to a more popular foreign money. Both approaches may be regarded as legitimate uses of political authority for the purpose of monetary governance; and both may be effective, at least for a time, in preserving market share. Neither, however, is without cost. As cross-border competition continues to accelerate, the cost of a preservation strategy is being pushed ever upwards, possibly making the alternative options of either followership or alliance relatively more appealing—or, at least, less unappealing. By no means does this mean that governments thus will *necessarily* delegate some or all of their monetary authority elsewhere. But it does mean that the decision cannot be evaded. Policymakers must consciously address the merits of regionalization in some form, as compared with the rising cost of a strictly national currency.

The option of vertical integration is addressed in chapter 5. Followership may take many forms—from the least demanding version, simple bimonetarism, where a popular foreign currency is granted legal-tender status to circulate alongside national money; to some form of currency board, where domestic money supply is firmly linked to the availability of a designated foreign currency; to the highest degree of vertical regionalization, what is typically called full "dollarization," where a strong foreign currency (such as the U.S. dollar) wholly replaces the existing national money. Because the cost of a followership strategy rises with the degree of subordination involved, relatively few states—apart from the special case of nations aspiring to membership in the European Union—are apt to be comfortable with the idea of full replacement of national money. Some governments in Latin America or elsewhere may go this route, adopting the greenback, but probably only when the cost of a strategy of market preservation becomes simply too high to bear—say, in the midst of a financial or political crisis. Dollarization will be pursued more as a refuge than a privilege. For other governments, the more appealing option will be one of compromise between preservation and follower-ship—a more diluted form of vertical regionalization that, hopefully, might ease the disadvantages of holding onto an uncompetitive national currency while retaining at least a few of the advantages of monetary sovereignty. In practical terms, this means some version of a currency board or bimonetarism. The monetary world will include a growing number of followers, but most will resist surrendering their formal authority unconditionally to a market leader.

The option of horizontal integration is taken up in chapter 6. Alliances also may take many forms, depending on the degree of formal authority to be delegated to joint institutions. As compared with any form of dollarization, an alliance strategy offers the critical advantage that monetary sovereignty is shared rather than subordinated or surrendered. But sharing necessarily implies some measure of collective action in the production and management of money, which is difficult to organize. An alliance requires allies—other states with similar preferences and a disposition to act cooperatively. In practice, willing partners are not all that plentiful. Analysis of past experience suggests that the necessary degree of cooperation requires at least one of two conditions—either a locally dominant state committed to using its influence to keep a monetary alliance functioning effectively on terms agreeable to all; or else a genuine sense of solidarity among the nations involved backed by a well-developed set of institutional linkages. In few parts of the globe today can the requisite conditions be found. Prospects for full new monetary unions, therefore, do not appear bright, despite active discussion in a variety of regions. Much more likely are less demanding forms of alliance that allow for some compromise between pooling and preserving monetary sovereignty. The monetary world will also include a growing number of joint ventures but few, if any, new joint currencies.

Turning from states to nonstate actors, chapter 7 takes up the role of the private sector, which is rapidly emerging as an alternative source of money, further complicating the strategic calculations of governments. Beyond the landscape defined by state preferences lie new frontiers, populated by an increasing number of privately issued currencies—new species of money capable of competing directly with existing national currencies. Controversially, the chapter argues that the growing proliferation of private monies represents a direct threat to the traditional authority of states. Within national borders, governmental control is being eroded by the spread of local currency systems, each determined to devolve a share of the power of monetary governance back down to the level of the community or subnational region. Across national borders, state-sanctioned monies face the prospect of multiple versions of electronic currency, each capable of diffusing authority outward to the emerging universe of cyberspace. Most governments have already lost their traditional territorial monopolies in the geography of money owing to the widening of choice on the demand side of the market. Now, contrary to the view of many respected economists, I contend that they risk losing dominance of the supply side as well—a development that will intensify even more the contest for market share.

Chapter 8, finally, asks what can be done about this increasingly complex currency environment. How will the new geography of money be governed? *Can* it be governed? With the global population of currencies increasing rather than decreasing, the chances of instability or monetary conflict will grow ever greater. The challenge is to minimize the risks of currency competition while preserving its acknowledged benefits. At the domestic level, I argue, this will require a resurrection of fiscal policy as a core tool of macroeconomic management, to offset the steady erosion that is occurring in the effectiveness of monetary policy. At the international level it will require a combination of cooperation among the market leaders and more active mediation by the International Monetary Fund, to provide a measure of coordination to the decentralized decisions of individual governments. None of these reforms, regrettably, can offer a foolproof antidote to prospective difficulties. But each, in its way, would make it easier for us all to live with the growing decentralization of power in monetary affairs. The future of money will be perilous, but it need not be chaotic.

Abbreviations

AMF	Asian Monetary Fund (proposed)
AMU	Asian Monetary Union (proposed)
ANZAC dollar	Australia-New Zealand dollar (proposed)
ASEAN	Association of Southeast Asian Nations
ASEAN + 3	Members of ASEAN plus China, Japan, and South Korea
BCEAO	Banque Central des Etats de l'Afrique de l'Ouest
BIS	Bank for International Settlements
BLEU	Belgium-Luxembourg Economic Union
CAEMC	Central African Economic and Monetary Community
CARICOM	Caribbean Community and Common Market
CER	Closer Economic Relations Agreement
CF	Comorian franc
CFA	*Communauté Financière Africaine* (African Financial Community)
CMA	Common Monetary Area
CMU	Caribbean Monetary Union (proposed)
DL	dollarization
DM	deutsche mark
EC	European Community
ECB	European Central Bank
ECCB	Eastern Caribbean Central Bank
ECCU	Eastern Caribbean Currency Union
ECOWAS	Economic Community of West African States
e-money	electronic money
EMS	European Monetary System
EMU	Economic and Monetary Union
ERM 1	Exchange-Rate Mechanism (part of EMS)
ERM 2	Exchange-Rate Mechanism (part of EMU)
EU	European Union
GCC	Gulf Cooperation Council
GDP	Gross Domestic Product
IMF	International Monetary Fund
IMFC	International Monetary and Financial Committee (formerly, Interim Committee)
LETS	Local-Exchange Trading System
LMU	Latin Monetary Union
LOLR	lender of last resort
MA	monetary alliance

Mercosur	*Mercado Común del Sur* (Common Market of the South)
NAFTA	North American Free Trade Agreement
NAMU	North American Monetary Union (proposed)
NC	national currency
OCA	optimum currency area
SMU	Scandinavian Monetary Union
Two S's	Subordination or Sharing (of monetary sovereignty)
URR	unremunerated reserve requirement
U.S.	United States
WAEMU	West African Economic and Monetary Union
Zac	Australia-New Zealand dollar (proposed)

THE FUTURE OF MONEY

One

The Changing Geography of Money

THE GEOGRAPHY of money is changing. Once upon a time it was not inaccurate to think of monetary spaces in simple territorial terms. Many currencies existed, but for the most part each circulated separately within the political frontiers of a single nation-state. Each government was in charge of its own sanctioned money. Today, however, the world's monetary landscape is being rapidly transformed under the impact of accelerating competition among currencies across national borders. Money is becoming increasingly *deterritorialized*, no longer the instrument of an exclusive national sovereignty.

What will the geography of money look like tomorrow? The prospect, according to many popular predictions, is for a radical shrinkage in the number of currencies in circulation, greatly simplifying the management of money around the world. I call this the Contraction Contention. But the Contraction Contention, I contend, is utterly wrong. The central argument of this book is that the population of the world's monies is more likely to expand, not contract, both in number and diversity. The future of money will be one of persistently growing complexity, posing increasingly difficult challenges for state authorities.

Revival of Currency Competition

The geography of money refers to the spatial organization of currency relations—the functional domains within which each currency serves the three traditional functions of money: medium of exchange, unit of account, and store of value. As a medium of exchange, money is synonymous with the circulating means of payment. In this role, its key attribute is its general acceptability to satisfy contractual obligations. As a unit of account, money provides a common denominator, or *numéraire*, for the valuation of diverse goods, services, and assets. Here, its key attribute is its ability to convey pricing information both reliably and expeditiously. As a store of value, money offers a convenient means for holding wealth. In this role, its key attribute is its ability to store purchasing power, bridging the interval, however transitory, between receipts from sales and payments for purchases The overall configuration of currency domains comprises global monetary geography.

The invention of money was one of the most important steps in the evolution of human civilization—"comparable," as one source has suggested, "with the domestication of animals, the cultivation of the land, and the harnessing of power" (Morgan 1965, 11). Gertrude Stein said that "the thing that differentiates animals and man is money."[1] Before money there was only barter, the archetypical economic transaction, which required an inverse double coincidence of wants for exchange to occur. Each of two parties had to desire what the other was prepared to offer—a manifestly inefficient system of trade, since much time had to be devoted to the necessary processes of searching and bargaining. With the introduction of money, the single transaction of barter split into two separate parts, sale and purchase, reducing transactions costs—the expenses associated with searching, bargaining, uncertainty, and the enforcement of contracts. Instead of goods or services for immediate delivery, a seller can accept money, hold it until needed for a purchase, and in the meantime use it to judge value in the marketplace. As a consequence, exchange is facilitated, promoting specialization in production and an increasingly efficient division of labor. Money, in effect, multilateralizes barter.

The magnitude of the cost saving afforded by monetary exchange, in lieu of primitive bilateral barter, is directly related to the size of a given money's transactional network: the number of actors with sufficient confidence in the instrument's future value and reusability to accept its present validity for both payment and accounting purposes. The larger the size of a money's transactional network, the greater will be the economies of scale to be derived from its use—what theorists call money's "network externalities" (Dowd and Greenaway 1993). Transactional networks define the functional domains of individual currencies, encompassing the range of their effective use.

It is conventional to identify currency domains with the nation-state, the basic unit of world politics. Just as in political geography we have long been conditioned to see the world's surface in terms of fixed and mutually exclusive entities called states, so we are conditioned to think of monetary geography in terms of the separate sovereign jurisdictions in which currencies originate. With few exceptions, each state is assumed to have its own unique money. Inside the nation's frontiers, that currency alone is expected to circulate freely. Money, in short, is thought to be effectively *territorial*—One Nation/One Money—with monetary governance exercised monopolistically by each national government. Nothing could be simpler.

But neither could anything be more misleading. In fact the notion of exclusive national currencies is of very recent historical origin, dating, in actual practice, back no further than the nineteenth century. Monetary geography in earlier eras was far more complex, involving varying degrees of competition among currencies; and even in the last two centuries, the principle of One Nation/One Money was as frequently compromised as respected. Today currency competition is reviving, causing the functional domains of individual monies to diverge more and more sharply from the legal jurisdictions of issuing governments. As in the more distant past, currency is once again becoming deterritorialized and monetary geography is once again growing more complex, with implications for monetary governance that are only beginning to be understood.

The Distant Past

Modern money began with the practice of sovereign coinage, whose origins go back to the very dawn of civilization. In the Western world, coins first appeared in the Greek city-states of Asia Minor (in Western Turkey) during the eighth and seventh centuries B.C.E. and were to be found everywhere in the eastern Mediterranean by 500 B.C.E. In the Far East, the oldest known coins originated even earlier, during the Chou dynasty that commenced in 1022 B.C.E. Previously all kinds of commodities, from salt and rice to cattle and tobacco, had been used in one place or another for standard monetary purposes (Weatherford 1997, ch. 1). But once invented, coins quickly came to dominate all other available instruments.

Before the nineteenth century, however, the sovereign right of coinage was hardly ever interpreted in exclusively territorial terms. Few rulers expected—or even, in principle, claimed—a monopoly for their coins within their own frontiers. Quite the contrary, in fact. The accepted norm was that coins could circulate everywhere, regardless of borders. Foreign coins could be used interchangeably with local money, and restrictions were only rarely imposed on what could be offered or accepted in market transactions. Choice was virtually unlimited. Currencies were effectively deterritorialized, and cross-border competition was the rule, not the exception. The system was heterogeneous and multiform, a veritable mosaic of money.

Not every currency circulated everywhere, of course. Most coins were of the small, fractional variety—"petty" coins generated for use in strictly local transactions. Minted of base metals like copper or bronze alloy, with a metallic content of little intrinsic value, these tokens were not often accepted and so were rarely found outside the limited area where they were issued. Widespread circulation was mainly restricted to bigger "full-bodied" coins of silver or gold ("specie")—monies whose usefulness as a medium of exchange or store of value could be more readily assured.

Among these full-bodied monies competition for the allegiance of users was keen, for two reasons. On the one hand there was the possibility of debasement: depreciation of the intrinsic value of coinage, accidental or otherwise, through erosion of weight or fineness. On the other hand, there was also a possibility of a shift in the commodity price of gold or silver, which would alter the relative attractiveness of coins minted from either metal. From these contingencies arose the famous proposition known as Gresham's Law—"Bad money drives out good"—named after a sixteenth-century English businessman who, among other accomplishments, was a financial adviser to Queen Elizabeth I. Gresham's Law predicted that where the intrinsic values of individual monies, as determined by market forces, diverge from their nominal values, the money of higher intrinsic value will be withdrawn from circulation and hoarded in anticipation of a rise of price. No one wanted to give up a coin that was likely to be worth more in the future.

Over time, however, as everyone sought the same "good" money, market favorites tended to develop, creating a hierarchy among full-bodied currencies—a kind of Gresham's-Law-in-reverse. "Good" money would drive out "bad" coins whose intrinsic value could not be maintained. Typically just one coin would eventually emerge as the dominant international money, the winner in a demand-driven process of natural selection. This Darwinian favorite would be used widely beyond the formal jurisdiction of the entity that issued it. Other monies would then offer the ultimate flattery—imitation—patterning themselves on the principal features of the dominant coin. Examples of dominant international coins down through the ages included the silver drachma of ancient Athens, the Byzantine gold solidus (later known, under Italian influence, as the bezant), the florin of Florence, the ducat of Venice, the Spanish-Mexican silver peso (later called the Mexican silver dollar), and the Dutch guilder.

Still, whatever money happened to dominate at any particular time, and however faithful its imitation by others, many other coins remained in circulation with diverse features and uncertain rates of exchange. In principle, this motley mosaic should have caused confusion—not to say chaos—in commercial and financial markets. How could one judge the meaning of prices with so many currencies in circulation? In practice, however, many difficulties, though by no means all, were resolved by the more or less spontaneous emergence of so-called imaginary or ghost monies—abstract units of account that could be used to compare the values of real currencies in actual use. Most popular in Europe were diverse variations on the silver pound unit, such as the livre (French), lire (Italian), peso (Spanish), and pfund (German) as well as of course the British pound sterling. In effect, a distinction was created between two of the functions of money: the medium of exchange and the unit of account. Any number of coins could pass from hand to hand in daily transactions. Ghost monies simplified transactions in a world of competing currencies.

The Era of Territorial Money

Truly fundamental changes in the geography of money did not occur until well into the nineteenth century, as national governments, eager to consolidate their emerging powers, started to assert greater control over the creation and management of money. For the first time in history, the goal of an exclusive national currency—One Nation/One Money—came to seem both legitimate and attainable. Once begun, the transformation of currency space took hold quickly and spread rapidly. Even before the century's end it was clear that a new age, the era of territorial money, had arrived.[2]

Monopoly over monetary powers was a natural corollary of broader trends in global politics at the time. The nineteenth century was a period of rising nationalism and a general centralization of political authority within state borders, greatly inspired by the Peace of Westphalia of 1648. Westphalia has long been recognized as a major watershed event in world politics, for the first time establishing the principle of absolute sovereignty based on exclusive territoriality. The treaty's ostensible purpose was to end the Thirty Years War. Its provisions addressed a number of contentious issues, including various dynastic claims, divisions of territory, religious practice, and the constitution of the Holy Roman Empire. But the Peace is most remembered for its assertion of the norm of sovereignty for each state within its own geographical frontiers, in effect formally establishing territoriality as the sole basis for Europe's—and, by extension, the world's—political map. Henceforth power was to be embodied in the independent, autonomous state, and global politics was to be conceived in terms of the now familiar state system.

Over the course of the nineteenth century the norm of sovereignty achieved a new level of tangible expression as governments undertook systematically to suppress all threats to their rule, whether from powers abroad or rivals at home. Their goal was to build up the nation, as far as possible, as a unified economic and political community led by a strong central authority. Monopolization of control over money was simply a logical part of the process. The territorial state came to be generally accepted as the basic unit of monetary authority as well—what in *The Geography of Money* I called the Westphalian Model of monetary geography.

Creating new territorial currencies was not easy. In fact, an enormous and sustained governmental effort was required to overcome market forces and centuries of monetary tradition. Control was implemented in two principal ways—first, by promoting the development of a robust national money; and second, by limiting the role of rival foreign currencies.

On the one hand, governments sought to consolidate and unify the domestic monetary order. Standardization was promoted, not only in coinage, but also in the new paper banknotes that were then just coming onto the scene. In addition, all forms of internal money were now fixed in relation to one another and tied to a uniform metallic standard, eliminating the need for ghost monies. The national unit of account now corresponded directly to tangible money in circulation. And ultimate authority over the supply of money was firmly lodged in a government-sponsored central bank, newly created or empowered to sustain both currency convertibility and the well being of the banking system.

On the other hand, increasingly prohibitive restrictions were imposed on the free circulation of foreign currencies. Most prominent were new legal-tender laws and public-receivability provisions. Legal tender is any money that a creditor is obligated to accept in payment of a debt. Public receivability refers to what currency may be used for remittance of taxes or to satisfy other contractual obligations to the state. As the nineteenth century progressed, coins that previously had been permitted, or even specifically authorized, to serve as legal tender had that privilege gradually withdrawn. At the same time, public receivability was gradually confined to domestic money alone. Also, and with increasing frequency, governments curtailed or suspended their commitment to accept foreign coins freely for conversion at the national mint. And ultimately, in most countries, the circulation of foreign currency was banned altogether, at least formally.

The experience of the United States was typical. Until the middle of the nineteenth century, the Mexican silver dollar and several other foreign currencies (including the gold coins of Britain, France, Portugal, and Brazil) not only circulated widely in the United States, but were even explicitly protected by federal legislation dating back to 1793. During the 1850s, however, when new U.S. silver and copper coins were introduced to ease a growing currency shortage, the opportunity was seized to eliminate all foreign elements from the money supply. In 1857 rates were fixed at which, for a limited time, the Treasury would accept foreign money for reminting into U.S. coinage. After 1861 the dollar became the country's sole legal tender, although it was to be another half-century before paper money would be standardized with the creation of the Federal Reserve System, America's own central bank.

In Britain the process started even earlier, with coinage reforms enacted after the Napoleonic Wars and later with the Bank Charter Act of 1844, which finally consolidated the central position of the Bank of England in the national financial system. Fully fledged territorial currencies also began to emerge elsewhere in Europe, as well as in Japan, during the second half of the century; and later, in the 1900s, in the British Empire and throughout Latin America. By the middle of the twentieth century, the exclusive monetary authority of national governments had become universally recognized and enshrined in international law. When the great wave of decolonization got under way after World War II, ultimately bringing scores of new states onto the global stage, few even questioned the assumption that each nation might legitimately aspire to create its own central bank and territorial money.

Back to the Future

In historical terms the Westphalian Model of monetary geography enjoyed a remarkably short life. From its beginnings in the nineteenth century, it reached its apogee during the Great Depression of the 1930s and the years following World War II, when newly invented limitations on cross-border transactions—exchange restrictions and capital controls—were widely employed to reinforce the exclusive role of each state's money within its own territory. Never before had governments come so close to absolute monopoly in the governance of monetary affairs. But the privilege was not to last as, in more recent years and under the pressure of market forces, competition among currencies has gradually re-emerged and intensified.

Even during its heyday, the Westphalian Model was never absolute. The broad norm of state sovereignty, as Stephen Krasner (1999) has accurately observed, has always been subject to compromise, depending on circumstances—"widely recognized but also frequently violated," as he writes (8). "Talk and action do not coincide." Currency was as much a matter of "organized hypocrisy," to borrow Krasner's phrase, as any other element of global politics. Though the norm of One Nation/One Money prevailed in principle, reflecting the logic of the territorial state, it was not necessarily expected to prevail everywhere in actual practice. Not all governments had the economic or political capacity to exercise the full powers of monetary monopoly; nor were all currencies successfully insulated from competition by more attractive foreign rivals. For many states, there seemed little choice but to accept some degree of compromise of policy authority. Two broad options were possible, either *subordination* or *sharing* of monetary sovereignty—what, in *The Geography of Money*, I called the Two S's.

Subordination, embodying a vertical hierarchy among states, most frequently took the form of a bilateral exchange-rate peg, whereby the price of the home currency was tied more or less firmly to that of a dominant foreign money, typically labeled the anchor currency or reserve currency. Exchange stability was promoted, but at the cost of a higher degree of sensitivity to the foreign money's market power or to the policy preferences of its issuing government. A stronger version of an exchange-rate peg is a currency board, which encompasses not only a fixed-price relationship but also unrestricted convertibility into the anchor currency and full foreign-currency backing for new issues of domestic money. In extremis, subordination meant simply adopting a foreign money in lieu of one's own—a total abnegation of authority in a process that, in contemporary parlance, has come to be known generically as full or formal dollarization.[3]

Sharing, by contrast, embodied a horizontal alliance among states—a *pooling* rather than a *surrender* of sovereignty. A monetary alliance could be achieved by freezing mutual exchange rates or by replacing existing monies with a joint currency. Common terms for such pooling arrangements include exchange-rate union, currency union, and monetary union. Both subordination and sharing were understood to loosen the tight bond between political nationalism and money. But both were regarded essentially as exceptions to the general rule of monetary territoriality.

More recently, however, exceptions have multiplied as national currency systems have become increasingly interpenetrated. The stage was set, starting soon after World War II, by an increased volume of trade, which, in combination with technological and institutional innovation in financial practice, greatly facilitated cross-border monetary flows, gradually expanding the range of choice among monies. Over time, currency competition has intensified under the pressure of market demand. In many countries, market agents are no longer restricted to using the national money alone, despite governmental efforts to preserve the exclusivity of their currencies. Now selected foreign monies may also be adopted for a variety of uses, competing directly with the state's own monetary issue for the favor of transactors and investors.

As deterritorialization spreads, encompassing more and more states, the world's monetary landscape is being fundamentally transformed. Today, as in the more distant past, currency choice is becoming less restricted, and cross-border competition is once again becoming the rule. Indeed, taking a long view, these developments can be seen as a sort of closing of a circle following what was, in historical terms, a relatively brief interlude of national monetary monopolies. Monetary geography is rapidly harking back to the deterritorialized model that prevailed prior to the Westphalian era—"back to the future," as one source (Craig 1996) has quipped, alluding to the popular film of the same name.[4] Another new age has arrived.

Accentuating Currency Hierarchy

Currencies, if attractive enough, may be employed outside their country of origin for either of two purposes: for transactions either between nations or within foreign states. The former is conventionally referred to as *international* currency use or currency *internationalization*; the latter is described as *currency substitution* and can be referred to as *foreign-domestic* use. Currency internationalization alters monetary geography by accentuating the hierarchical relationship among currencies, expanding the domains of a few popular monies well beyond the jurisdictions of the countries that issue them. Currency substitution is significant because it represents a direct invasion of traditional territorial domains, diminishing the use of many less popular currencies. Both are a product of the same sort of Gresham's-Law-in-reverse that gave rise to dominant international monies in the past—a Darwinian process of natural selection, driven above all by the force of market demand.

Today it is monies such as the U.S. dollar, Europe's euro, and the Japanese yen that have come to prevail over others for various commercial or financial purposes. The dollar and yen have long been popular for cross-border use. The euro, which was first introduced in 1999 in electronic form (a "virtual" currency) with notes and coins following in 2002, inherited its role from the deutsche mark, Germany's old DM. The euro has replaced the currencies of twelve of the 15 members of the European Union (EU)—all but Britain, Denmark, and Sweden, the notoriously reluctant trio that have opted, at least for now, to retain their traditional national monies.

Motivations

Neither currency internationalization nor currency substitution is an irrational form of behavior. On the contrary, each may be regarded as a quite natural response to prevailing market structures and incentives.

Analytically, the motivations for each type can be easily appreciated. Internationalization derives from the economies of scale, or reduced transactions costs, to be gained from concentrating cross-border activities in just one or at most a few currencies with broad transactional networks. To do business in each country in a separate money is analogous to barter and clearly inefficient. Just as monetary exchange, rather than barter, reduces the expenses associated with searching and bargaining within a single national economy, so costs of transactions between states are narrowed by making use of one or just a few currencies rather than many. The greater the volume of transactions that can be done via a single "vehicle" currency, the smaller are the costs of gathering information and converting from one money to another.[5]

In fact, currency internationalization improves the usefulness of money in each of its principal functions. A vehicle role enhances a currency's value both as a commercial medium of exchange and as a unit of account for invoicing; and these effects in turn also broaden its appeal as a store of value, by facilitating accumulation of wealth in assets of more universal purchasing power. At a minimum, it will pay market agents to hold some level of working balances in a popular international currency. Depending on cross-border variations of interest rates and exchange-rate expectations, it will pay them to use it for longer-term investment purposes, too. Moreover, once a money comes to be widely used by private actors, it is more likely to be employed by governments, as well—as a reserve currency, intervention medium, and peg for exchange rates. Public actors also can benefit from the economies of scale offered by a broad transactional network.

The motivation for currency substitution, typically, is a high or accelerating inflation rate, which erodes a local money's purchasing power both at home and, through exchange depreciation, for transactions abroad. Residents of a high-inflation economy, accordingly, have an incentive to turn to some more stable foreign currency as a preferred store of value—an inflation "hedge" for their savings—and perhaps even as a unit of account and medium of exchange. Foreign money, in effect, becomes the public's financial refuge, a convenient defense against the destructive power of rising prices. As one source (Calvo and Vegh 1993, 34) has suggested: "Like a crippling disease that leaves no part of the organism untouched, high inflation severely hinders the ability of a currency to perform its basic functions. . . . [But] unlike an organism that is unique and cannot be replaced, substitutes for a sick currency are easy to come by. . . . Not surprisingly, then, the public turns to a foreign money in its quest for a healthy currency."

Who would not choose inoculation against a crippling disease if a cure is so easy to find?

Choices

What determines which currencies will prevail in the Darwinian struggle? The principal qualities required for competitive success are familiar to specialists and hardly controversial. Demand is shaped by three essential attributes.

First, at least during the initial stages of a currency's cross-border use, is widespread confidence in a money's future value, backed by political stability in the country of origin. Essentially, this means a proven track record of relatively low inflation and inflation variability. High and fluctuating inflation rates increase the cost of acquiring information and performing price calculations. No currency is apt to be willingly adopted for cross-border purposes if its purchasing power cannot be forecast with some degree of assurance.

Second are the qualities of "exchange convenience" and "capital certainty"—a high degree of transactional liquidity and reasonable predictability of asset value. The key to both is a set of well developed financial markets, sufficiently open to ensure full access by nonresidents. Markets must not be encumbered by high transactions costs or formal or informal barriers to entry. They must also be broad, with a large assortment of instruments available for temporary or longer-term forms of investment. And they must be deep and resilient, with fully operating secondary markets for most if not all financial claims.

Finally, and most important of all, a money must promise a broad transactional network, since nothing enhances a currency's acceptability more than the prospect of acceptability by others. Historically, this factor has usually meant an economy that is large in absolute size and well integrated into world markets. A large economy creates a naturally ample constituency for a currency; economies of scale are further enhanced if the issuing country is also a major player in world trade. No money has ever risen to a position of international pre-eminence that was not initially backed by a leading national economy. The greater the volume of transactions conducted in or with a country, the greater are the potential network externalities to be derived from use of its money.

None of these attributes is a constant, however, as history amply demonstrates. Quite the contrary, in fact. Every one of a currency's attractions is subject to erosion with time, particularly if an issuing government imprudently abuses the privilege of its monetary monopoly. Hence market preferences, which determine the outcome of the competitive process, are also likely to change substantially from one period to the next. Shakespeare's words are as apt for money as they are for monarchs: "Uneasy lies the head that wears the crown." No currency has ever enjoyed a permanent dominance for either international or foreign-domestic use.

Orders of Magnitude

Though cross-border use is known to be accelerating rapidly, its full dimensions cannot be measured precisely in the absence of comprehensive statistics on global currency circulation. Partial indicators, however, may be gleaned from a variety of sources to underscore the impressive orders of magnitude involved.

The clearest signal of the rapid growth of currency internationalization is sent by the global foreign-exchange market where, according to the Bank for International Settlements (2002), average daily turnover accelerated greatly over the course of the 1990s, from $590 billion in 1989 (the first year for which such data are available) to nearly $1.5 trillion in 1998—a rate of increase in excess of 25 percent per annum—before declining to $1.2 trillion in 2001. Even allowing for the fact that much of this activity is accounted for by interdealer trading, the pace of expansion was impressive. The drop after 1998 was accounted for by several special factors, including notably the introduction of the euro in 1999, which eliminated trading among its constituent currencies (Galati 2001). In terms of currency composition, the U.S. dollar is the most favored vehicle for currency exchange worldwide, appearing on one side or the other of some 90 percent of all transactions in 2001 (unchanged from its share in 1989). The euro entered on one side of 38 percent of all transactions— higher than the share of its popular predecessor, the deutsche mark, which had appeared in 30 percent of transactions in 1998, but lower than that of all the euro's constituent currencies taken together in 1998 (53 percent). The yen's share in 2001 was just under 23 percent, up slightly from three years earlier.[6]

America's greenback is also the most favored vehicle for the invoicing of international trade, where it has been estimated to account for nearly half of all world exports (Hartmann 1998)—more than double the U.S. share of world exports. The DM's share of invoicing in its last years, prior to its replacement by the euro, was 15 percent, roughly equivalent to Germany's proportion of world exports; preliminary evidence from the European Central Bank (2001, 18) suggests that this share was maintained by the euro after its introduction in 1999. The yen's share has hovered at about 5 percent, significantly less than Japan's proportion of world exports.

A parallel story is evident in international markets for financial claims, including bank deposits and loans as well as bonds and stocks, all of which have grown at double-digit rates for years. Using data from a variety of sources, Thygesen et al. (1995) calculated what they call "global financial wealth": the world's total portfolio of private international investments. From just over $1 trillion in 1981, aggregate cross-border holdings quadrupled to more than $4.5 trillion by 1993—an expansion far faster than that of world output or trade in goods and services. Again the dollar dominated, accounting for nearly three-fifths of foreign-currency deposits and close to two-fifths of international bonds. The DM accounted for 14 percent of deposits and 10 percent of bonds; the yen, 4 percent of deposits and 14 percent of bonds. More recently, the International Monetary Fund (IMF 1999c) put the total of international portfolio investments (including equities, long- and short-term debt securities, and financial derivatives) at just over $6 trillion in 1997.

The clearest signal of the rapid growth of currency substitution is sent by the swift increase in physical circulation of the most popular currencies outside their country of origin, for purposes both legitimate and criminal. Most impressive is the widespread use of the dollar, mostly in the form of $100 bills. Authoritative studies by the Federal Reserve and Treasury put the value of all Federal Reserve notes in circulation abroad at between 50 and 70 percent of the total outstanding stock—equivalent in 2000 to roughly $275 billion to $375 billion in all.[7] Estimates also suggest that as much as three-quarters of the annual increase of U.S. notes now goes directly abroad, up from less than one-half in the 1980s and under one-third in the 1970s. By the end of the 1990s, as much as 90 percent of all $100 notes issued by the Federal Reserve were going directly abroad to satisfy foreign demand (Lambert and Stanton 2001). Appetite for the greenback appears to be not only strong but growing.

Along similar lines, Germany's central bank, the Bundesbank (1995), estimated deutsche mark circulation outside Germany at end-1994, mainly in East-Central Europe and the Balkans, at about 30 to 40 percent of total stock, equivalent to some DM 65–90 billion ($45–65 billion).[8] The deutsche mark's successor, the euro, took over the DM's role in foreign-domestic use after euro notes entered circulation in 2002 and in time is confidently expected even to cut into the dollar's market share. Similarly, on the other side of the world, Bank of Japan officials have been privately reported to believe that of the total supply of yen bank notes, amounting to some $370 billion in 1993, as much as 10 percent was located in neighboring countries.[9] In addition, smaller amounts of several other currencies are also known to be in foreign circulation, including the Swiss franc in East-Central Europe,[10] the South African rand in southern Africa, and the Australian dollar in the Pacific. Combining diverse estimates suggests a minimum foreign circulation of the top currencies at the end of the 1990s of at least $350–400 billion (Rogoff 1998: 279)—by no means an inconsiderable sum and, judging from available evidence, apparently continuing to rise rapidly. According to another source (Krueger and Ha 1996), as much as one-quarter to one-third of the world's paper money was, by the mid-1990s, already located outside its country of issue.

Deterritorialization is by no means universal, of course—at least, not yet. But it is remarkably widespread. Krueger and Ha (1996) estimate that foreign currency notes in the mid-1990s accounted for 20 percent or more of the local money stock in as many as three dozen nations inhabited by at least one-third of the world's population. Most currency substitution is concentrated in Latin America and the Caribbean, the Middle East, parts of Southeast Asia, and republics of the former Soviet Union, where the dollar is favored; or in East-Central Europe and the Balkans,

Germany's historical hinterland, where the DM traditionally predominated before the arrival of the euro. By a different measure, focusing on foreign-currency deposits rather than paper money, the IMF (Baliño et al. 1999) identifies some eighteen nations where by the mid-1990s a foreign currency accounted for at least 30 percent of broad money supply.[11] The most extreme cases, with ratios above 50 percent, included Azerbaijan, Bolivia, Cambodia, Croatia, Nicaragua, Peru, and Uruguay. Another thirty-nine economies had ratios approaching 30 percent, indicating "moderate" penetration. These trends have of course persisted into the new millennium.[12]

The Currency Pyramid

How can we best visualize money's emerging geography? The key characteristic of the new age, as in the more distant past, is the prevalence of cross-border competition, which naturally gives rise to a hierarchy among currencies. The use and influence of a few popular monies, such as the dollar or euro, now reach far beyond the legal jurisdictions of their issuing authorities, spanning large parts of the globe, while the effective domains of many other currencies are being sharply shrunk, sometimes dramatically. As a result the population of the monetary universe is becoming ever more stratified, assuming an appearance like nothing so much as a vast pyramid: narrow at the top, where the strongest currencies dominate; and increasingly broad below, reflecting varying degrees of competitive inferiority. I call this the Currency Pyramid.

Though difficult to operationalize for analytical purposes, the image of the Currency Pyramid is nonetheless useful to convey the rich diversity of money's competitive relationships while at the same time not exaggerating the degree of refinement that we can bring to the exercise. The labels for each stratum, though slightly tongue-in-cheek, are meant to accentuate the steeply vertical imagery appropriate to an accurate mapping of today's monetary geography.

The seven categories are as follows:

TOP CURRENCY

This rarified rank is reserved only for the most esteemed of international currencies—those whose use dominates for most if not all types of cross-border purposes and whose popularity is more or less universal, not limited to any particular geographic region.[13] During the era of territorial money, just two currencies could truly be said to have qualified for this exalted status: Britain's pound sterling before World War I and the U.S. dollar after World War II. In principle more than one Top Currency might be in favor simultaneously, as were both the pound and dollar during the interwar period, when sterling first went into what proved to be a long irreversible decline (Cohen 1971). Today, however, the greenback alone occupies the highest stratum of the Currency Pyramid. "The Yankee dollar is king of the world," exclaims one journalist (Hampson 2001), "the world's bedrock currency."

PATRICIAN CURRENCY

Just below the top rank we find currencies whose use for various cross-border purposes, while substantial, is something less than dominant and/or whose popularity, while widespread, is something less than universal. Obviously included in this category today would be the euro, as natural successor to the DM; most observers would still also include the yen, despite some recent loss of popularity. Both are patricians among the world's currencies. Neither, however, can claim a domain as extensive as that of the dollar. Each remains secondary to the greenback for most cross-border functions, and each has an attraction that is largely limited to a single region or subset of cross-border transactions.

ELITE CURRENCY

In this category belong currencies of sufficient attractiveness to qualify for some degree of international use but of insufficient weight to carry much direct influence beyond their own national frontiers. Here we find the more peripheral of the international currencies, a list that today would include inter alia Britain's pound (no longer a Top Currency or even Patrician Currency), the Swiss franc, and the Australian dollar.

PLEBIAN CURRENCY

One step further down from the elite category are Plebian Currencies—more modest monies of very limited international use. Here we find the currencies of the smaller industrial states, such as Norway or Sweden, along with some middle-income emerging-market economies (e.g., Israel, South Korea, and Taiwan) and the wealthier oil-exporters (e.g., Kuwait, Saudi Arabia, and the United Arab Emirates). Internally, Plebian Currencies retain a more or less exclusive claim to all the traditional functions of money, but externally they carry little weight (like the plebs, or common folk, of ancient Rome). They tend to attract little cross-border use except perhaps for a certain amount of trade invoicing.

PERMEATED CURRENCY

Included in this category are monies whose competitiveness is effectively compromised even at home, through currency substitution. Although nominal monetary sovereignty continues to reside with the issuing government, foreign currency supersedes the domestic alternative as a store of value, accentuating the local money's degree of inferiority. Permeated Currencies confront what amounts to a competitive invasion from abroad. Judging from available evidence, it appears that the range of Permeated Currencies today is in fact quite broad, encompassing perhaps a majority of the economies of the developing world, particularly in Latin America, the former Soviet bloc, and Southeast Asia.

QUASI-CURRENCY

One step further down are currencies that are superseded not only as a store of value but, to a significant extent, as a unit of account and medium of exchange, as well. Quasi-Currencies are monies that retain nominal sovereignty but are largely rejected in practice for most purposes. Their domain is more juridical than empirical. Available evidence suggests that some approximation of this intensified degree of inferiority has indeed been reached in a number of fragile economies around the globe, including the likes of Azerbaijan, Bolivia, Cambodia, Laos, and Peru.

PSEUDO-CURRENCY

Finally, we come to the bottom rank of the pyramid, where currencies exist in name only—Pseudo-Currencies. The most obvious examples of Pseudo-Currencies are token monies like the Panamanian balboa, found in countries where a stronger foreign currency such as the dollar is the preferred legal tender.

Implications for Monetary Governance

The labels in this illustrative sketch of the Currency Pyramid may be fanciful, even whimsical, but the geography they describe is not. Money is serious business, directly affecting authority relationships both within and among states. The campaign to establish exclusive territorial currencies that began in the nineteenth century gave governments enormous powers within their own borders, privileging the public sector in relation to societal actors. Ever since, policymakers have relied on the advantages derived from formal monetary monopoly to promote their conception of national interest. Now, however, all that is changing. As currency deterritorialization accelerates, power is being radically redistributed, fundamentally transforming the role of the state in monetary governance.

Benefits of Territorial Money

It is easy to see why the Westphalian Model of monetary geography came to be favored by governments. Five main benefits are derived from a strictly territorial currency: first, a potential reduction of domestic transactions costs to promote economic growth; second, a powerful instrument to manage the macroeconomic performance of the economy; third, a possible source of revenue to underwrite public expenditures; fourth, a potent political symbol to promote a sense of national identity; and finally, a practical means to insulate the nation from foreign influence or constraint. All five can be expected to be valued highly by policymakers.

A reduction of domestic transactions costs is perhaps the most fundamental benefit of a territorial currency and is shared by the public sector and societal actors alike. Just as the early invention of money meant greater exchange efficiency as compared with barter, the later creation of a single money for each country was bound to reduce local transactions costs even further as compared with the confusion of the pre-Westphalian world's competing coins and ghost monies. Historically, currency territorialization facilitated the emergence of an integrated and coherent national market, an essential ingredient in the project of state construction (Helleiner 2003a). One exclusive money maximizes the potential for network externalities within the nation's frontiers.

All the other benefits of a territorial currency contribute directly to the effective power of government. One such gain derives from money's potential impact on "real" economic performance—aggregate output and employment—as well as prices. So long as governments can maintain control of monetary supply within their own territory, they have the capacity, in principle at least, to influence and perhaps even manage the overall pace of market activity. This is what is generally referred to as *monetary policy*, which may be used to promote the broad prosperity and strength of the state as well as the government's own narrowly drawn fiscal requirements. Two policy instruments become available. First is the stock of money itself, which can be manipulated to increase or decrease levels of expenditure by residents. The second is the exchange rate—the price of home currency in terms of foreign currency—which can be adjusted to increase or decrease spending in the national economy through induced shifts between home and foreign goods. Neither instrument is infallible, of course; nor is either likely to attain a sustained impact on economic activity over the proverbial long term. Most economists agree that over a truly long time-horizon, monetary policy controls little other than the price level. But as John Maynard Keynes famously said, in the long run we are all dead. Most economists also concede that over the shorter time-horizons that are of most interest to public officials, monetary and exchange-rate policies can manifest substantial influence as tools for macroeconomic management.

Admittedly, the power that derives from an autonomous monetary policy may be, and often has been, abused, generating persistent price instability or even hyperinflation. In such circumstances, many might see a government's control of the money supply and exchange rate as more disadvantageous than advantageous, preferring instead to tie the hands of policymakers in one way or another. But only rarely does that sentiment tend to be shared by policymakers themselves, who may normally be expected to put a high premium on preserving a degree of flexibility to promote their conception of the national interest. Most governments, it is safe to assume, at most times will regard a capacity for independent macroeconomic management as a privilege not to be surrendered lightly.

A second well-known benefit for government is *seigniorage*—the capacity a monetary monopoly gives governments to augment public spending at will. Technically defined as the excess of the nominal value of a currency over its cost of production, seigniorage can be understood as an alternative source of revenue for the state, beyond what can be raised via taxation or by borrowing from financial markets. Public spending financed by money creation in effect appropriates real resources at the expense of the private sector, whose purchasing power is correspondingly reduced by the ensuing increase of inflation—a privilege for government if there ever was one. Because of the inflationary implications involved, the process is also known popularly as the "inflation tax," underscoring how this, too, is a power that can be, and often has been, abused. Yet despite the economic disadvantages associated with inflation, the privilege of seigniorage makes sense from a political perspective as a kind of insurance policy against risk—a "revenue of last resort," as one source has called it (Goodhart 1995, 452). Seigniorage is in fact the single most flexible instrument of taxation available to policymakers to mobilize resources in the event of a sudden crisis or threat to national security. This, too, is a capacity that most governments at most times would be disinclined to surrender lightly.

A third benefit for government is the vital *symbolic role* that a territorial currency can play for rulers wary of internal division or dissent. Centralization of political authority is facilitated insofar as citizens all feel themselves bound together as members of a single social unit—all part of the same "imagined community" (Anderson 1991). Cultural anthropologists stress that states are made not just through force but through loyalty, a voluntary commitment to a joint identity. The critical distinction between "us" and "them" can be heightened by all manner of tangible symbols: flags, anthems, postage stamps, public architecture, even national sports teams. And among the most potent of these tokens is money, as Eric Helleiner (1998b, 2003a) has insightfully emphasized. A state-sanctioned currency, Helleiner argues, can serve to enhance a sense of national identity in at least four ways—providing a vehicle for nationalist imagery that helps build a sense of collective tradition and memory; acting as a common medium of social communication; fostering a sense of trust in the state and nation; and contributing to a sense of popular sovereignty. Because it is issued by the government or its central bank, a national money acts as a daily reminder to citizens of their connection to the state and oneness with it. Likewise, by virtue of its universal use on a daily basis, the currency underscores the fact that everyone is part of the same social entity—a role not unlike that of a single national language, which many governments also actively promote for nationalistic reasons. A common money helps to homogenize diverse and often antagonistic social groups.

Finally, an important benefit is derived in a negative sense—from the enhanced ability a territorial money gives government to *avoid dependence* on some other provenance for this critical economic resource. Currency territoriality draws a clear economic boundary between the state and the rest of the world, promoting political authority. The nearer government is able to come to achieving an absolute monetary monopoly, the better equipped it will be to insulate itself from outside influence or constraint in formulating and implementing policy. The point is simple: If you want political independence, don't rely on someone else's money.

Winners and Losers

Thus we should not be surprised that states cling so resolutely to the idea of monetary sovereignty. What matters, though, is not formal principle but actual practice—and that depends not just on the supply of money but also on demand, over which governments today have decreasingly firm control. States exercise direct jurisdiction only over the stock of national currency and its exchange rate. With increasing deterritorialization, not even the most authoritarian government can assure that its money will always be preferred to currencies originating elsewhere.

Deterritorialization thus is bound to alter the distribution of power in monetary affairs, both between governments and between the public and private sectors. Clearly, critical shifts occur in the balance of influence among states. Less obviously, but no less importantly, decisive changes ensue in the reciprocal interaction between governments and markets— changes that can have a profound impact on effective political authority in every state, whatever the competitiveness of its currency. All four of a monetary monopoly's benefits for government are affected, though in ways that may not always be easily predicted.

MACROECONOMIC MANAGEMENT

Impacts on a government's capacity for macroeconomic management, for instance, will vary considerably, depending on the competitiveness of individual monies as well as the interaction of official policies with market preferences. The main impact is felt in the mechanism for balance-of-payments financing.

Economists have long contrasted the relative ease of adjustment to interregional imbalances *within* countries with the frequently greater difficulties associated with payments adjustments *between* countries. One major difference is the greater scope for equilibrating capital flows within an individual country in the event of transitory disturbances, owing to the existence of a stock of "generalized" short-term financial claims that can be readily traded between surplus and deficit regions. The development of these generalized claims, in turn, has traditionally been attributed to the existence of a single national currency, which of course removes all exchange risk.

Such reasoning is obviously based on the conventional assumption of an exclusive national money. The same logic applies, however, even if that assumption is relaxed in recognition of the accelerating pace of cross-border currency use. The broader the functional domain of a given money, the greater will be the effective range for equilibrating capital flows, taking the form of purchases and sales of generalized claims denominated in that single currency. Other things being equal, therefore, these flows should ease the constraint of the balance of payments on national policy, reducing the costs of adjustment for countries with the most competitive monies. Their macroeconomic policy flexibility should be enhanced. Countries with weaker currencies, by contrast, will find themselves less able to rely on equilibrating capital flows in the adjustment process. With confidence in their money lacking, the constraint exercised by the balance of payments will be reinforced, not eased, and their room for maneuver will be correspondingly reduced.

Consequences for neither class of country, however, are entirely unambiguous. For top-ranked states, domestic monetary policy could conceivably be aimed at a misleading target, since a large but indeterminate part of the money stock is in circulation abroad. Policy might also be destabilized periodically by unanticipated variations of foreign demand for the domestic currency or by a crisis threatening a weaker client currency. The gain of policy flexibility is by no means costless. Likewise, for lower-ranked countries, implications vary depending on how governments choose to respond to the reduction of their room for maneuver. Little economic control is gained, and much financial stability may be lost, if efforts to preserve an independent monetary policy are not regarded as credible by market actors. On the other hand, a much healthier economic performance might be attained, with lower costs of adjustment, if governments in effect submit their nominal sovereignty, at least in part, to the strict discipline of the marketplace. At a minimum, such states are obliged to take due account of market sentiment in framing macroeconomic policy.

SEIGNIORAGE

Much the same can also be said about a government's seigniorage privilege. Here, too, state power will be affected in all countries, and here, too, much will depend on how official policies interact with market preferences. For less competitive currencies, a government's capacity to appropriate resources via money creation is plainly compromised insofar as a convenient substitute for domestic currency becomes readily available from abroad. In effect, the base for levying an inflation tax is shrunk. As a consequence, state power to cope with unexpected contingencies is undoubtedly constrained.

But is state power correspondingly augmented for countries with more competitive monies? At first glance there seems no doubt. The broader a currency' functional domain, the easier it should be for its issuing government to exploit the fiscal benefits of seigniorage. Not only is the domestic monetary monopoly protected, but now foreigners, too, can be turned into a source of revenue to the extent that they are willing to hold the money or use it outside the country of origin. Expanded cross-border circulation generates the equivalent of a subsidized or interest-free loan from abroad—an implicit transfer that represents a real-resource gain for the economy as a whole. Economists refer to this as *international* seigniorage, in order to distinguish it clearly from the more traditional domestic variety. International seigniorage can be quite considerable in practice, as the historical experiences of both the pound sterling and dollar have amply demonstrated. But international seigniorage can be exploited only so long as a currency retains its competitive superiority in the marketplace—an advantage that can never be permanently guaranteed. In practice, therefore, the issuing state's seigniorage capacity may in time actually be decreased rather than increased.

The problem can be simply stated. As overseas circulation grows, foreigners may legitimately worry more about the possibility of future devaluation or even restrictions on the usability of their holdings. Hence, over time, the issuing government will have to pay increasing attention to competition from other international currencies and to curb its appetite for the inflation tax accordingly. At a minimum, interest rates may have to be raised significantly to maintain the money's attractiveness. Ultimately, national policies will almost certainly be inhibited by the need to discourage sudden or substantial conversions into more popular rivals.

In short, the power derived from the seigniorage privilege may be constrained for all countries, whatever the competitiveness of their currencies. In a world of accelerating cross-border use, no government can afford to ignore the preferences of market actors when reckoning how to finance its expenditures.

POLITICAL SYMBOLISM

Impacts on the role of money as a political symbol will also vary. If a territorial currency acts to cultivate a sense of national identity, deterritorialization might logically be expected to have more or less the reverse effect, loosening ties of loyalty to the state. In fact, however, consequences are rather more complex. In some cases, identification with the imagined community may actually be reinforced rather than reduced by an erosion of monetary insularity. Governments may gain as well as lose, depending not only on the outcome of the Darwinian struggle among currencies, but also on how official policies interact with the preferences of market actors.

Deterritorialization clearly does dilute the symbolic value of money for governments with relatively uncompetitive currencies: monies whose home space is successfully invaded by more popular rivals from abroad. The more a foreign currency comes to be used domestically in lieu of national money as a result of excessive inflation or perceived devaluation risk, the less citizens feel inherently connected to the state or part of the same social entity. The critical distinction between "us" and "them" is gradually eroded. Worse, an instrument that was intended to symbolize the power and nobility of the nation becomes instead a daily reminder of inadequacy and impotence—not sound currency but "funny money," an object of derision and disrespect. Governments that issue such monies are not apt to command much respect, either.

Looking to the most competitive currencies, by contrast, deterritorialization appears more likely to enhance than dilute a money's symbolic value. A position of prominence in the hierarchy of currencies plainly promotes the issuing state's overall reputation in world affairs. Broad international circulation tends to become an important source of status and prestige—a highly visible sign of elevated rank in the community of nations. What people would not take pride when greater esteem is accorded one of its most tangible symbols?

Matters get more complicated, however, when governments attempt to intervene to modify or control market preferences. A weak currency, for instance, might also become a source of strength if a government is determined to do something—or, at least, to give the appearance of doing something—about a competitive challenge from abroad. In effect, currency policy may be transformed into an exercise in political symbolism. A market-driven invasion of foreign money can be treated as the equivalent of an overt act of military aggression. Defense of the national currency may thus be promoted as the equivalent of a glorious stand on behalf of the imagined community—the ultimate expression of *amor patriae*.

Conversely, a strong currency might also become a source of weakness, particularly if a government attempts to preserve an international role for a money whose popularity has begun to fade. No currency, as I have said, has ever enjoyed a permanent dominance in cross-border use. Once gained, though, the prestige of great-currency status—whether Top, Patrican, or Elite—might quite understandably be difficult to surrender, even apart from any material benefits that may accrue. But just as a determined defense against an invading currency at home can inspire renewed confidence in a government, fruitless efforts to revive a national money's fortunes abroad may well have the reverse effect, encouraging skepticism and even ridicule. A prime example was provided by the British government's protracted, but ultimately futile, fight after World War II to prevent dissolution of the once far-reaching sterling area (Cohen 1971). The response of the British public was best summarized in the bitingly satirical words of television celebrity David Frost: "It's a shame to see what has happened to sterling. Once, a note issued by the Bank of England proudly read: 'I promise to pay the bearer on demand the sum of one pound.' Now it simply reads: WATCH THIS SPACE."[14] Efforts to manipulate market demand to preserve great-currency status are not always fated to succeed.

MONETARY INSULATION

The story is also much the same when we come to the fourth benefit of a monetary monopoly: insulation from external influence. In this respect, too, states with the most popular monies would appear to gain disproportionately, insofar as expansion of a currency's functional domain offers a potential means for coercing others. Political power should be enhanced at the expense of lower-ranked countries that become correspondingly more dependent on a foreign money. But in this connection also results are highly sensitive to the interplay of official policies and market preferences.

That hierarchy among currencies might influence the distribution of power between states is clear. The very notion of hierarchy is political in nature, suggesting varying degrees of reciprocal influence—differential impacts on the ability of governments to achieve goals at home or abroad. Internationally, the issuer of a widely circulated currency is in a position to exercise influence over others through its control of access to financial resources, directly or indirectly.

Jonathan Kirshner (1995) lists as many as four ways in which currency dependency may be coercively exploited by a top-ranked state: (1) enforcement—manipulation of standing rules or threat of sanctions; (2) expulsion—suspension or termination of privileges; (3) extraction—use of a relationship to appropriate real resources; and (4) entrapment—transformation of a dependent state's interests. Domestically, the country should be better insulated from outside influence in formulating and implementing policy.

Here, too, however, leverage can be exploited only so long as the currency in question retains its competitive superiority in the marketplace. Once rival monies begin to emerge, the issuing country will find that its ability to manipulate the dependency of others may in fact be compromised. Prospective outcomes will very much depend on the reactions of market agents, who may either reinforce or nullify the impact of overtly coercive measures. The exercise of power, therefore, will increasingly demand a systematic cultivation of market sentiment. Equilibrating capital flows may continue to provide an extra degree of policy flexibility to deal with transitory shocks. Over time, however, state behavior will be increasingly constrained by the need to discourage sudden or substantial conversions into other currencies. Ultimately effective political power, on balance, may well be decreased rather than increased.

SUMMARY

In brief some individual governments, particularly those with the most widely accepted monies, clearly benefit from deterritorialization, at least for a time. Moreover, as their gains come at the expense of states with less competitive currencies, the inter-state balance of power manifestly shifts in their favor. But not even the most top-ranked countries are immune from market pressures. Over time, all the advantages of broad acceptability are subject to erosion by the force of demand-driven competition. In comparative terms, therefore, it seems evident that some of the biggest winners are not governments at all, however popular their currencies may be, but rather a select set of private societal actors—specifically, those in the marketplace with the capacity and opportunity to choose among alternative monies. In the relationship between state and society, it is plainly the latter that is more favored by deterritorialization. Governments everywhere are privileged less than they once were, elements of the private sector more than in the past.

In purely material terms, societal actors attain a significant measure of efficiency gains: an improvement in the usefulness of money for all its principal functions. Cross-border substitutability also provides an effective refuge against abuse of the seigniorage privilege or misguided macroeconomic management. Politically, the private sector achieves a degree of leverage over public policy that is unprecedented in modern times. The power of the state is clearly diminished.

The State as Oligopolist

That does not mean, however, that where once governments exercised monetary sovereignty, the private sector now categorically rules—not so long as states remain the principal *source* of the currencies that today compete so vigorously across national frontiers. The Darwinian struggle may be intense, but it is a struggle that, for now at least, is limited on the supply side almost exclusively to monies officially sanctioned by the state. Governments thus continue to play a role, albeit a lessened one, in the management of monetary affairs. The power of the state may be diminished, but it has not yet been extinguished.

With deterritorialization, governments have been deprived of the monopoly control they once claimed over demand. This is as true for countries at the top of the Currency Pyramid as it is for those at the bottom. Because many transactors and investors now have the happy option of currency choice, fewer states are in a position to *enforce* an exclusive role for their own money within established political frontiers. So far, however, governments still dominate the supply side of the market, retaining jurisdiction over the creation of the principal monies presently in use. Hence they are in a position still to *influence* demand insofar as they can successfully compete, inside and across borders, for the allegiance of market agents. Power is retained to the extent that user preferences can be swayed.

In essence, therefore, the role of states today has become not unlike that of competing enterprises in an oligopolistic industry—the state as oligopolist—and no one has ever accused oligopolists of a lack of practical authority. In a world of increasingly interpenetrated currency systems, all governments find themselves driven to join the competitive fray, to preserve or promote market share for their product. Like oligopolistic enterprises, governments assert influence by doing what they can, consciously or unconsciously, to shape and manage demand.

Commercial rivalry between states is nothing new, of course. Governments have always contended with one another for markets and resources as part of the great game of world politics. What is different about currency competition is that the state participates directly, as the still dominant actor on one side of the marketplace—the supply side. It is the government's own creation, its own sanctioned money, that must be promoted.

The analogy with oligopoly is not perfect, of course. Money, as a generally accepted unit of account and medium of exchange, has public-good characteristics that are not typically shared by the products of private enterprise. Moreover states, as the embodiment of legitimized coercion, have policy options at their disposal not generally available to commercial oligopolists. Nonetheless, the analogy is apt because of the direct relevance of oligopoly's two key structural features: interdependence and uncertainty. Both are inherent features of the traditional state system, as well.

As in an oligopolistic industry, states are sufficiently few in number so that the behavior of any one has an appreciable impact on at least some of its competitors; in turn, the actions and reactions of other actors cannot be predicted with assurance. The result is a mutuality of decision making that compels all states, like rival enterprises, to be noticeably preoccupied with considerations of long-term strategy. In this sense, producers of currency are really no different from producers of cars or computers. Moreover, like producers of cars or computers, governments are forced to implement their strategies via efforts to manage the demand side of the market—in effect, to "sell" their product. Their targets are the users of money, at home or abroad. Their aim is to sustain or enhance a currency's domain, almost as if monies were like goods to be sold under registered trademarks. Monetary governance, at its most basic, has become a political contest for market loyalty.

The Contraction Contention

The question is: How will the contest turn out? The outlook cannot be predicted with certainty, of course. Forecasting the future of money is like looking into a misty landscape, where only the broadest topographical features may be perceived, dimly, on the horizon. Yet even through the mist it is possible to see the outlines of the new geography that is developing.

As in any market, outcomes ultimately will be determined by the interactions of demand and supply. On the demand side, efficiency considerations suggest a preference for as small a population of monies as possible, leading many informed observers to predict a radical shrinkage in the number of currencies in circulation. That is the Contraction Contention. On the supply side, however, considerations suggest very much the reverse, casting such predictions into doubt. In fact, the prospect is for more rather than less complexity in money's spatial organization. This development will further challenge state authority in the governance of monetary affairs.

The Demand Side

While it is clear that governments have good reason to prefer the old Westphalian Model, defining currency spaces in strictly territorial terms, it is also evident that if efficiency alone mattered, the number of separate monies would be far less than policymakers favor. At present there are more than 150 state-sanctioned currencies in circulation around the world,[15] from the U.S. dollar and other popular monies at the top of the Currency Pyramid to the many small Quasi-Currencies and Pseudo-Currencies at the bottom—what one source scornfully dismisses as mere "junk currencies" (Harris 2001, 35). All these diverse monies are caught up in an intense Darwinian struggle for survival. Can anyone believe that such a crowded population represents a truly efficient equilibrium?

At issue is the size of what economists call the "optimum currency area" (OCA)—the most efficient scale of a currency space. By definition, the larger the size of an OCA for individual currencies, the smaller will be the equilibrium population of monies for the world as a whole. The OCA issue has been debated extensively in the specialist literature since a pioneering article by Nobel laureate Robert Mundell more than four decades ago (Mundell 1961). As the theory of OCAs has developed, analysts have come to focus on the material gains and losses, as seen from a single country's point of view, from participation in a common currency area or its equivalent.[16] Against the advantages of a more useful money, governments are assumed to compare the disadvantages of the corresponding surrender of monetary autonomy: the potential costs of having to adjust to domestic or external disturbances without the option of changing either the money supply or the exchange rate. Because of the considerable complexity of the calculus involved, little consensus has ever been reached on just how big an OCA might be. But few economists doubt that it would be significantly bigger than the cramped domains characteristic of many national currencies today. That would imply a much less crowded monetary population than exists at present.

Certainly the profusion of monies we have now—including large numbers of small currencies with very limited circulation—would not be the preference of the many market actors who have an interest in transactions or investments across national borders or who simply seek a safe store of value for their savings. As another economist (von Furstenberg 2000b, 112) remarks, "small really is not beautiful in matters of money." In fact, if the outcome were left solely to cost-conscious market actors, the force of demand would undoubtedly shrink the total number of currencies dramatically, in order to lower the expense of transactions and maximize the material benefits of money. Fewer monies, as the late Rudi Dornbusch (2001a) put it, would mean better monies. The reason is simple: the overwhelming power of economies of scale in monetary use. The only question is: How low might that number go?

Transactions costs, as indicated, are inversely related to the number of market agents willing to accept a given money in payment. The appeal of each currency, therefore, can be assumed to be a direct function of the size and economic importance of its transactional network. The larger the size and importance of a money's transactional network, the greater will be the economies of scale to be derived from its use—its network externalities. Hence, the greater will be the incentive to reduce rather than increase the total number of currencies in use.

Indeed, if scale economies were the *only* consideration of concern to users, the equilibrium number of currencies would eventually shrink to just one, a single universal money—the ultimate manifestation of Gresham's-Law-in-reverse. This view is widely shared among economists. Mundell himself, the pioneer of OCA theory, today quips that the optimum number of currencies is like the optimum number of gods—"an odd number, preferably less than three."[17] Representative are the words of German economist Roland Vaubel (1977, 437, 440), an ardent exponent of free currency competition: "Ultimately, currency competition destroys itself because the use of money is subject to very sizable economies of scale. The money-industry must be viewed as a (permanently) declining-cost industry. i.e., as a "natural monopoly". . . . The only lasting result will be . . . the survival of the fittest currency."

As a practical matter, the natural-monopoly argument goes too far, since scale economies, though undeniably important, are *not* the only consideration of concern to market agents. Also salient, at a minimum, are considerations of stability and credibility, as modern network theory teaches, suggesting that the optimum number of monies in reality is likely to be something greater than one. In network theory, not one but two distinct structures are recognized in the organization of spatial relations: the "infrastructure," which is the functional basis of a network; and the "infostructure," which provides needed management and control services. Economies of scale, by reducing transactions costs, obviously do promote a consolidation of networks at the level of infrastructure, as the natural-monopoly argument suggests. At the infostructure level, by contrast, the optimal configuration tends to be more decentralized and competitive, to maximize producer responsibility. Some finite number of rival networks will counter the negative effects of absolute monopoly, which frequently leads to weakened control by users and incentives for exploitation by producers. In matters of money, this means that market agents must weigh the risk of possible inflationary abuse of monopoly privilege on the supply side against the advantages of a large transactional network on the demand side. Rational calculus thus suggests a preference for a degree of diversification rather than complete centralization—a smallish population of currencies rather than one universal money.

A multiplicity of monies is also promoted by the persistent inertias that are an inherent characteristic of monetary behavior. Two sources of inertia can be identified. First is the pre-existence of already well established transactional networks. The same network externalities that are responsible for the scale economies emphasized in the natural-monopoly argument are also responsible for a well-documented stickiness in user preferences—what specialists call "hysteresis" or "ratchet effects." In effect, prior use confers a certain natural advantage of incumbency. Switching from one currency to another is costly, involving an expensive process of financial adaptation, as numerous authors have emphasized.[18] Considerable effort must be invested in creating and learning to use new instruments and institutions, with much riding on what other market agents may be expected to do at the same time. Hence as attractive as a given money may seem, adoption will not prove cost-effective unless others appear likely to make extensive use of it, too. In the words of economists Kevin Dowd and David Greenaway (1993, 1180): "Changing currencies is costly—we must learn to reckon in the new currency, we must change the units in which we quote prices, we might have to change our records, and so on. . . . [This] explains why agents are often reluctant to switch currencies, even when the currency they are using appears to be manifestly inferior to some other."

Inertia is promoted as well by the exceptionally high level of uncertainty that is inherent in any choice among alternative monies. Uncertainty encourages a tendency toward what psychologists call "mimesis": the rational impulse of risk-averse actors, in conditions of contingency, to minimize anxiety by imitative behavior based on past experience. Once a currency gains a degree of acceptance, its use is apt to be perpetuated— even after the appearance of powerful new competitors—simply by regular repetition of previous practice. In effect, a conservative bias is inherent in the dynamics of the marketplace. As one source has argued, "imitation leads to the emergence of a convention [wherein] emphasis is placed on a certain 'conformism' or even hermeticism in financial circles" (Orléan 1989, 81–83).

Finally, there is the simple matter of the laws of probability. The greater the number of possible monies to choose from, the lower the chance that diverse market actors all will settle uniquely on the same asset. As Dowd (2001, 472) writes: "It would be fortuitous if agents happened to converge on one single money. . . . If agents have a choice of n assets, we get possible equilibria in which any of the n assets, or any combination of the n assets, circulate as money. . . . The outcome depends on agents' expectations, and yet there is no obvious way in which expectations can be coordinated."

In practice, therefore, spontaneous emergence of a single universal money, driven by the force of demand, would be highly unlikely despite the power of economies of scale in use. As much was acknowledged even by the influential Austrian economist Friedrich Hayek—like Mundell, also a Nobel laureate—who until his death was the best known advocate of unrestricted currency competition. Beginning with a noted public lecture in 1975, published shortly thereafter under the title *Choice in Currency* (1976), and continuing through three editions of his widely read *Denationalisation of Money* (1990),[19] Hayek decried the inflationary consequences of the monopoly privilege enjoyed by central banks. The solution to the problem of inflation, he argued, was not just to afford users maximum choice among currencies, effectively deterritorializing money. More importantly, it was to cede the right of production to the private sector—to "denationalize" it. Commercial banks should be the main suppliers of money, competing for the favor of transactors and investors. Inflation would be forestalled because rival issuers would have a strong inducement to limit quantity in order to promote market confidence in their product.[20] Yet by no means, he conceded, would this mean eventually a single universal money. Quite the contrary, in fact. "I believe," he wrote (1990, 126), "that, once the system had fully established itself and competition had eliminated a number of unsuccessful ventures, there would remain in the free world several extensively used and very similar currencies." Even earlier, economist Benjamin Klein (1974) had predicted that with unrestricted currency competition, the most likely outcome would be "multiple monies" linked by a common unit of account—not unlike the role played by so-called ghost monies prior to the emergence of territorial currency. And even Vaubel, in his later writings (1984, 1990), cast doubt on whether the supply of money is truly a natural monopoly.

No one number of currencies can be identified, a priori, as a precise optimum. In markets for money, as in other organized asset markets, preferences are highly sensitive to the strategic interdependencies of decision making by money's many users. Much more likely is the possibility of multiple equilibria—an inference consistent with other recent approaches to the analysis of international money.[21] As Barry Eichengreen has written (1996, 19): "As is so often the case when expectations are introduced, multiple equilibria are possible."

Still, the implication is unmistakable. Whatever the precise number of currencies that might be left in circulation, it would not be great—if users had their way, certainly nowhere near as great as the crowded population we observe today. Scale economies may not be the whole story, but their influence would certainly be strong enough to eliminate many less attractive monies at the bottom of the Currency Pyramid. As in any Darwinian struggle, ultimately only the strong would survive the pressure of accelerating demand-driven competition.

Given this logic, therefore, it should not be surprising that many informed observers today predict that the number of currencies in the world will soon contract. The Contraction Contention is widely shared, especially among economists, and is rapidly gaining in popularity.[22] Typical is the prediction of Michel Camdessus (2000, 35), former managing director of the IMF, who suggests that "in the long run, we are moving toward a world of fewer currencies." Dornbusch (2001a, 9), before his untimely death, was even blunter. "Convergence on regional monies," he asserted, "is a no-brainer." Even Krugman, who is otherwise inclined to dismiss the idea as "an intellectual fad, not a deep insight" (1999b, 3), accepts that today's crowded population of monies could very well shrink dramatically. "I say let a hundred currencies bloom," he writes. "Well, maybe twenty or thirty."

The Supply Side

The Contraction Contention, however, is seriously misleading. Whatever the power of scale economies for monetary use, they shape preferences on just one side of market—the demand side. In practice, the future of money will be influenced by considerations on the supply side, as well, interacting with demand; and on the supply side, preferences can be expected to run very much the other way, toward the preservation and even proliferation of monies in circulation around the globe. Many more than a hundred currencies may well bloom.

To begin, the Contraction Contention reckons without the power of the state, which as indicated remains considerable even in an increasingly deterritorialized monetary geography. Opposing the logic of market demand is the well-entrenched principle of national sovereignty. However much market actors may prefer a shrinkage of the population of currencies, not all governments are apt to concede the benefits of a money of their own without a struggle. The various choices available to governments will be examined in detail in chapters 2 through 6. Analysis suggests that far fewer national currencies are apt to disappear than is commonly predicted.

Additionally, the Contraction Contention discounts the role of the private sector as an alternative source of money. Though governments presently dominate the supply side of the market, that may not always be the case. Chapter 7 explores prospects for new issues of nonstate monies in the future that might complement or replace existing state-sanctioned currencies. For a variety of reasons, the number of privately issued monies in the world can actually be expected to multiply dramatically in years to come.

In short, the power of scale economies notwithstanding, monetary geography appears set to become more, not less, complex—more than ever like the heterogeneous, multiform mosaic that existed prior to the era of territorial money. The future of money will by no means be simple. What this will mean for monetary governance in years to come will be considered in chapter 8.

Two

Four Directions

IF MONEY'S changing geography is diminishing the power of the state, what can governments do in response? Four basic policy strategies, we shall see, are possible—four directions, as it were, to move through the mists of the monetary landscape. Each of the four strategies carries its own calculus of potential costs and benefits, which can be expected to vary considerably depending on the circumstances of individual countries. A priori, only a few broad generalizations about state preferences are possible in the absence of more detailed exploration of each alternative route.

The Perspective of Macroeconomics

At issue is the challenge that currency competition poses for state authority in the governance of monetary affairs. For specialists in open-economy macroeconomics, the significance of money's accelerating deterritorialization lies mainly in implications for the choice of exchange-rate regime. Regrettably, such an approach only scratches the surface of the policy issues involved.

In conventional macroeconomic analysis, the core of the issue, going back to the familiar Mundell-Fleming model, is thought to be best summarized by what I have elsewhere called the "Unholy Trinity" (Cohen 1993)—the intrinsic incompatibility of currency stability, capital mobility, and autonomy of national monetary policy. The dilemma for governments, it is said, is to fashion an exchange-rate regime that will neither encourage adverse speculation nor compromise management of the domestic economy. Much depends on how the choice of regime is framed.

In earlier years, the choice was cast in simple binary terms: fixed versus flexible exchange rates. A country could adopt some form of peg for its currency or it could float. Pegs might be anchored on a single currency or a basket of currencies; they might be formally irrevocable or based on a more contingent rule; they might crawl or take the form of a target zone. Floating rates, conversely, might be managed (a "dirty" float) or else just left to the interplay of market supply and demand (a "clean" float).

More recently, as international capital mobility has grown, the issue has been recast—from fixed versus flexible exchange rates to a choice between, on the one hand, contingent rules of any kind ("soft pegs") and, on the other hand, the so-called corner solutions of either floating or some form of monetary union ("hard pegs"). Today, according to an increasingly fashionable argument known as the "bipolar" view or "two-corner" solution, no intermediate regime can be regarded as tenable.[1] Owing to the development of huge masses of mobile wealth capable of switching between currencies at a moment's notice, governments can no longer hope to defend policy rules designed to hit explicit exchange-rate targets. The middle ground of contingent rules has in effect been "hollowed out," as Barry Eichengreen (1994) memorably put it.

In practice, of course, contingent rules are not truly discredited, for the simple reason that in an imperfect world there is no perfect solution. The bipolar view implicitly assumes that governments will be unwilling under any circumstances to pay the price of coping with occasional speculative crises. In effect, no trade-off is considered possible between currency stability and other objectives of policy. But that is a political judgment—and highly dubious, at best. The reality is that such trade-offs are made all the time when exchange-rate policy is decided. No option is ruled out a priori. As Jeffrey Frankel (1999, 2) has written: "Neither pure floating nor a currency board sweeps away all the problems that come with modern globalized financial markets. . . . Optimization often . . . involves an 'interior' solution."[2]

Optimization of course implies politics, a dimension of exchange-rate policy that tends to be discounted in conventional economic discourse. The closest that standard analysis comes to addressing the political dimension is in the now familiar theory of optimum currency areas, which directly considers the policy interests of government in alternative regimes. Efficiency benefits of a hard peg or equivalent are compared with the potential costs of doing without either an autonomous monetary policy or a flexible exchange rate. A diverse range of variables is identified, representing economic characteristics of countries, that might arguably affect the magnitude of prospective losses through their influence on either the severity of payments disturbances or the ease of needed adjustments. Included among these so-called country characteristics are wage and price flexibility, labor and capital mobility, commodity diversification, geographic trade patterns, size and openness of economies, levels of development, inflation trends, and the nature, source, and timing of potential economic shocks. Politics in this context, however, takes on an extraordinarily narrow meaning, since policymakers are assumed to be concerned with little more than maximizing output and minimizing inflation in an open national economy. Broader political considerations are most notable for their absence.

In fact, broader political considerations enter in two ways. First, as Jeffry Frieden (1993, 140) has noted, "domestic distributional considerations are also central to the choice of exchange rate regimes." The policy calculus is obviously affected by domestic politics—the tug and pull of organized interest groups of every kind, whether sectoral, regional, or partisan. The critical issue is familiar: Who wins and who loses? The material interests of specific constituencies are systematically influenced by what a government decides to do with its money. Policy strategies are bound to be sensitive to the interplay among domestic political forces as well as to the institutional structures through which interest-group preferences are mediated.

Second, the utility function of policymakers obviously includes more than just macroeconomic performance. As a practical matter, sovereign governments also worry about many other things—not least, about their own policy autonomy; that is, their scope for discretion to pursue diverse objectives in the event of unforeseen developments, up to and including war. Key here is seigniorage—the government's "revenue of last resort." The more tightly a currency is pegged, the less room policymakers have to resort at will to money creation to augment public expenditures. Monetary firmness is gained, but at a loss of fiscal flexibility. Certainly it is not wrong to attach importance to a reduction of exchange-rate uncertainty in hopes of promoting higher trade and investment and perhaps lower interest rates. But in an insecure world, governments may be forgiven for attaching importance to currency flexibility, too, as a defense against *political* uncertainty. Policy strategies are bound to be sensitive to the interplay among such considerations, as well.

In fact, the political dimension is central. Conventional economic discourse discounts the political dimension because analysis typically focuses narrowly on capital mobility alone—the phenomenon of asset exchanges in integrated financial markets. There is no question that capital mobility has grown enormously in recent decades, generating a scale of international flows unequaled since the glory days of the nineteenth-century gold standard. But these flows are no more than part of the story of money's changing geography. Capital mobility, expanding the functional domains of a few popular currencies, highlights just one of the standard roles of money: its use as a medium for private investment. As noted in the previous chapter, however, the reconfiguration of monetary spaces today has come to be far more extensive than that, in fact involving *all* the roles of money—not only a currency's function as store of value, but also its use as medium of exchange and unit of account for transactions of every kind, domestic as well as international. Cross-border competition means more than just currency *internationalization*, in the form of capital mobility. Even more critically, it means accelerating currency *substitution*—increased foreign-domestic use for all purposes, directly compromising many traditional territorial domains. Much more is involved, therefore, than a simple choice of exchange-rate regime.

A Political-Economy Perspective

At its most fundamental, what is really involved is nothing less than a challenge to the long-standing convention of national monetary sovereignty. Once we look beyond capital mobility alone to the full dimensions of currency competition, we see the extent to which, in many areas of the world today, the traditional dividing lines between separate national monies are becoming less and less distinct. The setting, as indicated, is now akin to an oligopoly, where each government is forced to battle on behalf of its individual brand of money. Monetary authority must now be exercised in fundamentally different ways from in the past. Effective strategies must be developed to shape and manage demand.

Available Strategies

What strategies are available? Broadly speaking, oligopolistic market theory distinguishes between two contrasting approaches to the formulation of competitive strategy by firms in a setting of interdependence and uncertainty. Behavior can be either defensive or offensive: that is, designed either to build defenses against existing competitive forces; or, alternatively, to attack existing conditions in order to enhance market position. The former seeks to match the firm's strengths and weaknesses to its environment, taking the structure of the industry as given. The latter seeks to improve the firm's position in relation to its environment by actively influencing the balance of forces in the marketplace. Currency policy, too, can be either defensive or offensive, aiming either to preserve or promote market share.

In turn, each approach may be pursued either unilaterally or collusively, yielding a total of four possible broad strategies. These are:

1. *Market Leadership*: an *aggressive unilateralist policy* intended to promote use of the national money, analogous to predatory price leadership in an oligopoly.

2. *Market preservation*: a *unilateralist status-quo policy* intended to defend, rather than augment, a previously acquired market position for the home currency.

3. *Market followership*: an *acquiescent policy* of subordinating monetary sovereignty (one of the Two S's) to a stronger foreign currency, analogous to passive price followership in an oligopoly.

4. *Market alliance*: a *collusive policy* of sharing monetary sovereignty (the other of the Two S's) in an exchange-rate union or monetary union of some kind, analogous to a tacit or explicit cartel.[3]

Of these four strategies, market leadership is of course generally available only to governments with the most widely circulated currencies, such as the dollar, euro (succeeding the DM), or yen. For the vast majority of states with less competitive monies, decision making is limited to the remaining three—a tricky tripartite choice that will be fundamental to determining the monetary geography of the future.

Market Leaders

For the privileged few suppliers with monies at the very peak of the Currency Pyramid—a Top Currency like the dollar or Patrician Currencies like the euro and yen—there is little reason to doubt that under normal circumstances a unilateralist strategy to sustain or enhance market position would be the preferred choice. The reason is simple. Much is at stake.

Though minimized by some (e.g., Wyplosz 1999, 97–100), the benefits of leadership in currency affairs can in fact be considerable. Economists tend to focus primarily on the potential for international seigniorage: the implicit transfer, equivalent to an interest-free loan, that goes to a state whose money is widely used and held abroad. But that is only a part of the story, as we know from chapter 1. Three other gains may also be anticipated. First is the increased flexibility of macroeconomic policy that is afforded by the privilege of being able to rely on one's own money to help finance external deficits. Second is the status and prestige that goes with market dominance. Foreign publics cannot help but be impressed when another nation's money successfully penetrates the domestic currency system and gains widespread acceptance. And third is the political power that derives from the monetary dependence of others. Not only is the issuing country better insulated from outside influence or coercion in the domestic policy arena. It is also better positioned to pursue foreign objectives without constraint or even to exercise a degree of influence or coercion internationally.

Admittedly there are limits to these benefits, as we also know from chapter 1. All are likely to be greatest in the early stages of cross-border use, when confidence in a money is at a peak. Later on, as external liabilities accumulate increasing supply relative to demand, gains may be eroded, particularly if an attractive alternative becomes available. The market leader's autonomy may eventually be constrained, to a degree, by a need to discourage sudden or substantial conversions through the exchange market. An obvious case in point is Britain, which after World War II found itself in an increasingly uncomfortable policy straitjacket once sterling began its long decline.

It must also be admitted that there can be exceptions among market leaders, where an aggressive unilateralist strategy may turn out *not* to be the preferred choice, at least for a time. Certainly this was the case with both Germany and Japan in the earlier decades of the postwar period, when the DM and yen first began to rise toward the top of the Currency Pyramid. With sterling's example weighing heavily on their minds, German and Japanese policymakers were initially ambivalent, resisting wider use of their currencies for fear of compromising their domestic policy autonomy—though, eventually, attitudes changed in each country. Japan in particular, as we shall see in the next chapter, has fundamentally reversed its position, now actively promoting a leadership role for its money and perhaps even the establishment of a formal yen bloc.

The German case is especially interesting. For decades after World War II, once currency convertibility was restored, Germany enjoyed unchallenged monetary dominance inside the European region. With absorption of the former East Germany in 1990, creating by far the most powerful economy in Europe, reunified Germany was unquestionably in a position to consolidate its regional currency leadership. Yet instead the Federal Republic voluntarily opted for a strategy of market alliance, abandoning its own beloved deutsche mark for the newborn euro. The country's circumstances, however, could hardly be regarded as normal. Given the historical legacy of the previous century, successive German governments long felt compelled to reconfirm their European credentials in every way possible, including—despite considerable domestic resistance—a commitment to monetary integration in the EU.[4] In the oft-repeated words of Helmut Kohl, the chancellor who presided over Germany's reunification, what was needed was "a European Germany, not a German Europe." In order to be seen as good Europeans, German policymakers were prepared to sacrifice even their country's monetary independence. Few other market leaders are apt to find themselves in similar circumstances.

Even admitting such limits and exceptions, though, it seems clear that on balance there are advantages here worth defending, as numerous sources acknowledge.[5] The benefits of market leadership provide more than enough incentive to motivate policymakers. I will have more to say on this subject in the next chapter.

All the Rest

But what about all the rest? In a landscape dominated by the market leaders, the basic challenge for most other governments is plain. Should monetary sovereignty be defended, shared, or subordinated? Should policymakers seek, above all, to preserve their traditional monetary sovereignty (market preservation)? Or, alternatively, should they countenance one of the Two S's, delegating some or all of their formal authority elsewhere, either to a dominant foreign power (market followership) or to the joint institutions of a currency partnership (market alliance)? Involved is what one scholar (Litfin 1997) calls a "sovereignty bargain"—a voluntary agreement to accept certain limitations on national authority in exchange for anticipated benefits.[6] Monetary sovereignty is either *surrendered* or *pooled*, wholly or in part.[7] A former president of the Argentine central bank put the point bluntly (Pou 1999, 244): "Should a [country] produce its own money, or should it buy it from a more efficient producer?" Economists Patrick Honohan and Philip Lane (2001, 324) call it "outsourcing" monetary policy. Outsourcing to a more efficient producer necessarily implies a degree of regionalization in currency relations, either *vertical* regionalization (followership) or *horizontal* regionalization (alliance).

Most governments, given a choice, would instinctively prefer to continue producing their own money, avoiding regionalization of any kind, vertical or horizontal. They would want to keep the national currency alive no matter how uncompetitive it might be. Monetary sovereignty can be defended by tactics of either persuasion and coercion. Persuasion is of course the standard approach of oligopolists in the private sector, where coercion is (presumably) illegal. For states, persuasion entails trying to sustain demand for a currency by buttressing its reputation, above all by a public commitment to credible policies of "sound" monetary management. The idea is to preserve market confidence in the value and usability of the nation's brand of money—the "confidence game," as Paul Krugman has ironically dubbed it.[8] Coercion—legally, the unique privilege of sovereign governments in a Westphalian world—means applying the formal regulatory powers of the state to avert any significant shift by users to a more popular foreign money. Possible measures range from standard legal-tender laws to limitations on foreign-currency deposits in local banks and even to the extremes of capital controls or exchange restrictions. Both floating and contingent exchange-rate rules are consistent with a strategy of market preservation.

A desire to continue producing a national money is understandable, given the historical advantages of a formal monetary monopoly. But at what price? As currency competition accelerates, tactics of persuasion or coercion become increasingly costly, as we shall see in chapter 4. Growth and employment may have to be sacrificed, more and more, in order to keep playing the confidence game; widening distortions in the allocation of resources may be introduced by controls or restrictions. The rising cost of defending monetary sovereignty is real, especially for the many "junk currencies" near the bottom of the Currency Pyramid. And as the cost continues to rise, the alternative of outsourcing to a more efficient producer becomes increasingly appealing—or, at least, less unappealing.[9] Not surprisingly, therefore, in a growing number of countries, more attention today is being paid to the alternative options offered by the Two S's—the possibilities of either subordinating or sharing monetary sovereignty in some degree, which we shall explore in chapters 5 and 6.

In Latin America, for example, much thought is being given these days to the possibility of replacing national monies altogether with the U.S. dollar—the most radical form of vertical regionalization, which, as noted in chapter 1, has come to be known generically as "full" or "formal" dollarization. The idea of full dollarization has become a topic of hot debate since Argentina's President, Carlos Menem, spoke out in its favor in early 1999. Others in positions of authority in the region had considered the option from time to time,[10] but never before had it been publicly endorsed by the head of one of the Hemisphere's largest states. Weary of the high costs of the confidence game, Menem suggested formal adoption of America's greenback as a way of resolving doubts about his nation's money. "The dollar is the global currency par excellence," wrote one of his key advisers (Castro 1999, 7, 16). Dollarization offers an opportunity "to gain comparative advantage in a global frame characterized by uncertainty and frequent financial turmoil." Though subsequently rejected by Argentine policymakers following the completion of Menem's term of office in late 1999,[11] the option did soon find favor elsewhere—most notably in Ecuador, which formally dollarized in 2000, and El Salvador, which followed a year later. Discussion continues in other Western-Hemisphere countries as well.

Likewise, in East-Central Europe and the Mediterranean, formal adoption of the euro—a European version of dollarization frequently referred to as "euroization"—increasingly is touted as a natural path for countries with close ties to the European Union or with hopes of joining the EU one day. Should more governments around the world decide to go the dollarization route, emulating Ecuador and El Salvador, it is not too difficult to imagine the gradual emergence of two giant monetary blocs, one centered on the United States and one on Europe. (More question exists whether a third bloc would ever coalesce around the Japanese yen.) Such an outcome is frequently predicted.[12] In the words of one observer (Beddoes 1999, 8): "By 2030 the world will have two major currency zones—one European, the other American. The euro will be used from Brest to Bucharest, and the dollar from Alaska to Argentina—perhaps even in Asia. These regional currencies will form the bedrock of the next century's financial stability."

Much will depend, of course, on the policies adopted by the market leaders, which could significantly alter the relative costs and benefits of followership as contrasted with strategies of either market preservation or alliance. But while there is more than enough incentive to motivate leaders to promote use of their currencies by market actors, there is much less reason to expect any of them to go out of their way to induce state actors to join a formal currency bloc, as we shall see in chapter 3.

Alternatively, some governments might prefer to look to the idea of horizontal regionalization in some form. One long-standing monetary alliance, the CFA Franc Zone,[13] already exists in Africa; another, the Eastern Caribbean Currency Union (ECCU), functions smoothly in the Caribbean; and since the Maastricht Treaty in 1992, which formally laid the groundwork for Europe's Economic and Monetary Union (EMU), prospects for more such alliances have been discussed in almost every region of the world.[14] EMU is clearly viewed as a test case for a strategy of pooling rather than surrendering monetary sovereignty. If Europe's experiment comes to be seen as a success, it might have a powerful demonstration effect, encouraging similar initiatives elsewhere. That would seem especially likely for groups of states engaged in a common integration project—South America's Mercosur,[15] for example, or the ten-member Association of Southeast Asian Nations (ASEAN).[16] Alongside two (or three) major currency zones, it is not inconceivable that a variety of new joint currencies could eventually also emerge in addition to the euro.

Scenarios of currency regionalization, therefore, seem not at all implausible—indeed, arguably for a good number of states perhaps the most reasonable outcome to be expected from today's accelerating deterritorialization of money. Why should governments not yield to the market power of more efficient producers, replacing national monies with regional currencies of some kind? Regionalization of the world's monies has happened before, in medieval Europe and again during the nineteenth century, as Eichengreen and Sussman (2000) have reminded us. Obviously, it could happen again.

No wonder, then, that the Contraction Contention is rapidly gaining popularity among specialists. Indeed, for some, the process has an air of historical destiny about it. One example is Ricardo Hausmann, formerly chief economist of the Inter-American Development Bank, who insists that "national currencies are a phenomenon of the twentieth century; supranational currencies are the solution of the future."[17] Another is George von Furstenberg, who speaks of regionalization as "inevitable. . . . the wave of the future."[18] Such categorical formulations may be far too deterministic. Nonetheless, there seems little doubt that alongside national monies some kind of new geography of regional currencies could begin to emerge. The question is: What might that new geography look like? Scholars are only beginning to address this critical question.[19]

Degrees of Regionalization

The new geography will be anything but simple, since for individual countries a wide range of scenarios is possible, depending on the *degree* of regionalization involved. It is important to recognize, in practical terms, that whether a government is considering alliance or followership, considerable leeway exists for variations of design along two key dimensions. These dimensions are institutional provisions for (1) the issuing of currency and (2) the management of decisions. Examples of currency regionalization, both vertical and horizontal, have differed dramatically along each dimension, providing policymakers with a rich menu from which to choose. A guide to this diversity is provided in the appendix to this chapter, which contains a complete listing of all cross-border currency arrangements presently in existence around the world.

Currency Issue

The highest degree of currency regionalization is attained when just a single money is used by all participating countries. That is the way dollarization works in many of the smaller enclaves and microstates around the globe that have eschewed any currency of their own, such as Micronesia and Liechtenstein (table 1).[20] That is also the way it works in a case of a monetary alliance such as the ECCU, which shares the Eastern Caribbean dollar, and the way it now works in Europe since euro notes and coins replaced existing national currencies in 2002. But a single money is by no means universal in regional currency arrangements. Relationships, in practice, may involve not one money but two or more bound together more or less tightly—some form of exchange-rate union.

Though the idea might seem counterintuitive, parallel circulation of two or more monies is in fact fully consistent with formal dollarization. Two currencies, for instance, has long been the case in Panama, even though the economy has been formally dollarized since shortly after the country came into existence in 1903. Although Panama agreed to issue no paper currency of its own under an agreement with the United States signed in

1904, token amounts of locally issued balboa coins circulate freely along-side the greenback at a fixed rate of exchange.[21] Ecuador and El Salvador, too, are expected to maintain limited circulation of their own currencies even with formal dollarization, as do Kiribati and Tuvalu in the Pacific (table 2). Local coins also used to be issued by several independent en-claves in Europe, such as San Marino and Andorra, prior to introduction of the euro. Though all such monies are no more than Pseudo-Currencies, their presence does imply a somewhat lower degree of dollarization. Such cases may be labeled *near-dollarized* countries. The foreign currency domi-nates domestic money supply but falls short of absolute monopoly.

An even lower degree of dollarization is represented by a *currency board*, such as has long existed in Brunei, Djibouti, and Hong Kong. With a currency board, a local money accounts for a large, if not dominant, part of domestic money supply but is firmly tied to the availability of a designated anchor currency. The exchange rate between the two monies is rigidly fixed, ostensibly irrevocably. Most importantly, any increase in the issue of local money must be fully backed by an equivalent increase of reserve holdings of the anchor currency, making the local currency little more than foreign money by another name—in effect, "a proxy for the reserve currency," as one source puts it (Osband and Villaneuva 1993, 215). The anchor currency may or may not enjoy legal-tender status in the dependent country. During the 1990s new currency boards were es-tablished in a number of economies around the world, starting with Ar-gentina in 1991 and later including Bosnia and Herzegovina, Bulgaria, Estonia, and Lithuania (table 3). All these arrangements still continue in operation except for Argentina's, which collapsed in early 2002.[22]

The lowest degree of dollarization is *bimonetarism*, where legal-tender status is extended to one or more foreign monies, which circulate as paral-lel currencies, but without the strict ties characteristic of a currency board. Local money supply is not dependent on the availability of an anchor currency, and the exchange rate is not irrevocably fixed. Bimonetarism is typical of countries with Quasi-Currencies or Permeated Currencies and exists in a diverse range of states, from Bhutan to the Bahamas (table 4).

Parallel circulation of two or more currencies is also consistent with a strategy of monetary alliance, as several present and past examples dem-onstrate (table 5). Closest in spirit to a single money today is the so-called CFA Franc Zone, born out of France's former colonial empire in Africa, which combines two separate regional currencies, each cleverly named to preserve the CFA franc appellation, plus one national currency, the Comorian franc (CF) for the Comoros Islands, located in the Indian Ocean. One of the regional currencies is issued by the eight members of the West African Economic and Monetary Union (WAEMU)[23] and a sec-ond by the six members of the Central African Economic and Monetary

Community (CAEMC).[24] Together these two groups comprise the African Financial Community. Technically each of the two regional currencies is legal tender only within its own region and managed by its own regional central bank. But since the arrangement is very strict, in the sense that it makes no allowance for any change of the exchange rate between the two CFA francs, circulation between the two regions is not at all uncommon.

Essentially similar were two notable exchange-rate unions established in late nineteenth-century Europe—the Latin Monetary Union (LMU), which grouped together Belgium, France, Italy, Switzerland, and Greece; and the Scandinavian Monetary Union (SMU), comprised of Denmark, Norway, and Sweden. The LMU was created in 1865, the SMU eight years later. The purpose of both was to standardize existing gold and silver coinages on the basis of a common monetary unit—in the LMU, the franc, and in the SMU, the krone (crown). Although close in spirit to a single money, national currencies and central banks continued to exist. Within each group, the separate currencies circulated freely at par, and no changes of official rates were even contemplated until the breakdown of the gold standard during World War I, which ultimately led to formal dissolution of both unions in the 1920s.

A less symmetrical, albeit comparably strict, model was provided by the Belgium-Luxembourg Economic Union (BLEU), which lasted nearly eight decades from 1922 until finally absorbed into EMU in 1999. Separate national monies were issued by each government, as in the LMU and SMU; but only one, the Belgian franc, enjoyed full status as legal tender in both states. The Luxembourg franc was limited in supply by a currency board–type arrangement and was legal tender only within Luxembourg itself. The arrangement was quite binding. Only once, in 1935, was there ever a change in the exchange rate between the two francs (subsequently reversed during World War II).

At the opposite extreme is the so-called Common Monetary Area (CMA) combining the Republic of South Africa—a sovereign state for decades—with two former British colonies, Lesotho and Swaziland, and South Africa's own former dependency, Namibia (formerly the United Nations trust territory of South West Africa). The origins of the CMA go back to the 1920s when South Africa's currency, now known as the rand, became the sole legal tender in several of Britain's nearby possessions, including Basutoland (later Lesotho) and Swaziland, as well as in South West Africa, previously a German colony. But following decolonization, an arrangement that began as an early example of dollarization based on the rand has gradually been transformed into a much looser scheme representing a much lower degree of regionalization, as each of South Africa's partners has introduced a distinct currency of its own. Today the CMA encompasses no fewer than four national currencies, only one of which, the rand, is legal tender outside its country of issue. The rand circulates legally in Lesotho and Namibia—both of which can now be described as bimonetary countries—but no longer in Swaziland. The rand serves as anchor for South Africa's three neighbors, but each government formally retains the right to change its exchange rate at will.[25]

Decision Making

Provisions for the delegation of decision-making authority may be equally varied, again whether we are speaking of vertical or horizontal regionalization. The logic of a regional currency, by analogy with national money, would seem to call for a single central agency with strong supranational powers—the highest possible degree of regionalization—and indeed that is the case in several instances. Microstates like Micronesia or Liechtenstein, totally without any money of their own, naturally cede all powers to the central bank of the country whose currency they use. The relationship is strictly *hierarchical*, with no assurance at all that the dependent state's specific needs or views will be taken into account when monetary decisions are made. Likewise, both the ECCU and EMU have created joint institutions—respectively, the Eastern Caribbean Central Bank (ECCB) and the European Central Bank (ECB)—with exclusive authority to act on behalf of the group. Monetary sovereignty is fully *pooled* on a principle of parity, officially a relationship of equal partnership. But these are by no means the only possibilities. Other examples exist to demonstrate how formal powers may be more decentralized, reducing the degree of regionalization involved.

Most unusual is the CFA Franc Zone, with its two subregional central banks—a case of shared or dual supranationality. More common is the persistence of national monetary authorities with more or less symmetrical rights and responsibilities. The greater the degree of symmetry, the weaker is the element of supranationality.

Closest in spirit to a single central authority is the sort of highly asymmetric relationship characteristic of near-dollarized countries like Panama or Ecuador. A national monetary agency exists but without significant powers. Somewhat less demanding is a currency-board relationship, as in Bulgaria today or Luxembourg under BLEU, where local authorities may retain a significant degree of discretion depending on how the rules are written. A currency-board relationship is inherently asymmetrical, plainly favoring the central bank of the dominant partner, but need not be entirely one-sided. And yet less demanding are bimonetary relationships of the sort that exist in the Bahamas and Bhutan. Least demanding is a wholly decentralized model of the sort practiced in the nineteenth century's LMU and SMU, where monetary management remained the exclusive responsibility of the members' separate central banks. Though in each case there was one central bank that could be said to enjoy disproportionate influence (the Banque de France in the LMU, the Swedish Rijksbank in the SMU), powers within each bloc were in principle symmetrical. The element of supranationality was minimal. The same principle of decentralization, implying a minimal degree of regionalization, is also characteristic of the CMA today.

Benefits and Costs

With such a rich menu to choose from, how will governments decide among the three broad options of market preservation, followership, or alliance? That is the core question for analysis. At issue are potential benefits and costs, both economic and political. Rational policymakers must take five key factors into account, corresponding to the five benefits of a territorial currency outlined in chapter 1. All these factors can be expected to vary systematically with the form and degree of currency regionalization under consideration.

Economic Factors

On the economic side three factors stand out, each familiar from the conventional theory of optimum currency areas. These are implications for (1) transactions costs; (2) macroeconomic stabilization; and (3) the distribution of seigniorage. The first of the three factors argues clearly for currency regionalization in some form. The remaining two, both stressed in chapter 1 as benefits of a territorial currency, can be expected to reinforce a preference for market preservation.

TRANSACTIONS COSTS

As compared with a world of separate territorial monies, currency regionalization has one unambiguous benefit: a further reduction of transactions costs. We have already noted how, historically, currency territorialization facilitated the emergence of integrated and coherent national markets. In turn, when diverse local monies are replaced by a single regional currency—whether via monetary union or dollarization—additional savings can be realized since there is no longer a need to incur the expense of currency conversion or hedging in transactions between participating economies. Trade, consequently, could be increased substantially—by as much as a factor of three, according to empirical estimates by Andrew Rose and others[26]—generating considerable efficiency gains. This is the standard economic argument for monetary integration and a key underlying assumption of OCA theory.

Related to this benefit are three other efficiency gains that also enhance the appeal of currency regionalization. First, outsourcing means a reduction of administrative costs, since individual governments will no longer be obliged to incur the expense of maintaining an infrastructure of their own dedicated solely to production and management of a national money. That saving would of course be of most interest to poorer or more diminutive sovereignties because of the diseconomies of small scale involved in monetary governance. Second, as a supposedly irreversible institutional change, currency regionalization could also establish a firm basis for a sounder financial sector—a benefit that would be of particular value to states that previously have not enjoyed much of a reputation for price stability or fiscal responsibility. And finally, with regionalization there could be a substantial reduction of interest rates for local borrowers in countries that have not yet succeeded in establishing a sound credit rating in international financial markets. All of these gains represent additional transactions-costs savings and, as such, carry the same implied preference for the broadest currency regions possible.

Because of the power of economies of scale, savings will be substantial for even a low degree of regionalization. Marginal benefits will diminish with successively higher degrees of regionalization.

MACROECONOMIC STABILIZATION

Counterbalancing regionalization's efficiency gains, however, which are all of a microeconomic nature, is a potentially serious cost at the macroeconomic level: the loss of an autonomous monetary policy to manage the aggregate performance of the economy. This is the standard economic argument *against* monetary integration and another key assumption of conventional OCA theory. Individually, governments give up control of both the money supply and exchange rate as policy instruments to cope with unexpected disturbances. The more shocks there are likely to be and the more they can be expected to be asymmetric between economies, the greater will be the disadvantage of a single regional money. Ceteris paribus, this factor implies a preference for *avoiding* currency regionalization to the extent possible—just the reverse of the transactions-costs factor. As Krugman has written, the challenge "is a matter of trading off macroeconomic flexibility against microeconomic efficiency" (Krugman 1993, 4).[27]

All this assumes, of course, that macroeconomic flexibility matters. In fact, the loss of an autonomous monetary policy may be regarded as costly to a government only if discretionary management of the money supply and exchange rate can be expected to achieve a sustained impact on "real" economic performance—an expectation that, as noted in chapter 1, is unlikely to be fulfilled over the proverbial long term. Over a truly long time-horizon, we know, monetary policy controls little other than the price level. For many economists, therefore, the only legitimate function of monetary policy is to provide a stable nominal framework for market activity—in which case, not much would be sacrificed by a commitment to regionalization in some form.[28] But that hardly reflects the calculus as seen by governments themselves; and even most economists are prepared to concede the practical usefulness of the money supply and exchange rate as policy instruments over the shorter timehorizon of most relevance to public officials. In most countries, monetary policy is still seen as having a critical role to play in macroeconomic management. Its loss, accordingly, would indeed be understood as a potentially serious cost.

On balance, the loss will be considered least onerous in countries that have already experienced substantial erosion of their capacity for independent macroeconomic management owing to the growing deterritorialization of money. The greater the degree of currency substitution that has already occurred, reflecting a local currency's lack of competitiveness, the greater is the degree of constraint already imposed on a government's ability to influence real economic performance. As a recent IMF report (Baliño et al. 1999, 1, 3) concluded: "[Informal] dollarization can complicate . . . monetary policy by introducing a foreign currency component into the money supply. . . . Dollarization may complicate stabilization and cause additional volatility." In effect, with a foreign component freely selected by market actors, the central bank can no longer control the total of money holdings. Aggregate money supply is no longer exogenously determined by public policy but rather becomes endogenous. That is precisely the circumstance that is leading increasing numbers of countries to look for a more efficient producer of money. Indeed the loss of control may even be welcomed, for reasons already suggested in chapter 1, in countries where past abuses of a monetary monopoly have led to persistent instabilities or inflation. By tying the hands of policymakers, currency regionalization in some form might be seen as the only way to restore a reasonable degree of monetary stability. Conversely, the loss of policy flexibility will be felt most acutely in more insular states that still enjoy a significant measure of monetary autonomy.

Comparing degrees of regionalization, it is evident that relatively little autonomy is sacrificed with bimonetarism or in relatively symmetrical alliances like the CMA. Both money supply and the exchange rate can still be changed should circumstances warrant. The impact on policy flexibility, at the margin, will rise significantly with successively higher degrees of regionalization.

THE DISTRIBUTION OF SEIGNIORAGE

A final economic issue involves seigniorage, which in the modern era derives from the difference between the interest-free liabilities of the central bank—cash in circulation—and the interest earned on the central bank's counterpart assets. It is, in effect, a pure profit attributable to the central bank's traditional position as a monopolist. In absolute terms seigniorage may not be very large, amounting to just a small fraction of a percent of gross domestic product (GDP). But as a supplemental source of finance to support government spending, it could be of substantial value—a privilege not to be abandoned lightly.

Ceteris paribus, this factor, too, implies a preference for avoiding currency regionalization to the extent possible—another consideration that has been raised, at times, as an argument against monetary integration.[29] With any form of regionalization, a certain amount of seigniorage profit will by definition be diverted elsewhere, going to either a joint institution or a dominant foreign power. For governments with inefficient or underdeveloped fiscal systems, the loss of access to seigniorage revenue could impose a significant constraint on public finance.

Here, too, however, it is evident that relatively little is sacrificed when the degree of regionalization is low. A bimonetary relationship or even a currency board keeps a national currency in circulation, permitting retention of some measure of seigniorage revenue; the same is also true of a decentralized monetary union. But here, too, the impact, at the margin, will rise significantly with successively higher degrees of regionalization, unless provisions can be agreed upon to compensate governments for interest earnings forgone. One precedent for such compensation is provided by the CMA, where the South African government makes annual payments to Lesotho and Namibia according to an agreed-upon formula for seigniorage-sharing, in order to encourage continued use of the rand. Another is provided by EMU, where any net profits of the ECB are distributed in proportion to the shareholdings of each member central bank.

Political Factors

On the political side, two factors stand out. These involve issues of (1) political symbolism and (2) diplomatic influence. Both were also stressed in chapter 1 as benefits of a territorial currency and, likewise, can also be expected to reinforce a preference for market preservation. In fact, each goes to the heart of the fundamental purpose of the state in world politics: to permit a community to live in peace and to preserve its own social and cultural heritage. Such matters cannot be dismissed lightly as mere "politics as usual."

POLITICAL SYMBOLISM

Money has long been consciously used by state authorities as a symbol to help promote a sense of national identity, as Eric Helleiner (1998b, 2002b) has documented. This powerful symbolic role goes far to explain why so many governments are still determined to stick to monetary strategies of market preservation, keeping their currencies on life support, no matter how uncompetitive they may have become. Such behavior is not at all irrational insofar as value continues to be attached to allegiance to a distinct political community.

The role of national identity is typically discounted in conventional monetary analysis. In reality it is central to how policy is formulated and assessed. As Helleiner (2002a, 323) writes: "The dominant discourse of our age remains a deeply embedded nationalist one, one that evaluates economic ideas primarily according to their impact on the nation." Societies develop collective identities to distinguish themselves from other "imagined communities"; and these identities, in turn, help to define the aims of economic policy.[30] In the words of Rawi Abdelal (2001, 2), "nationalism endows policy with fundamental social purpose, related to protecting and cultivating the nation." Many governments today seek to compensate for the increased permeability of territorial borders in a globalizing world economy by reinforcing the psychological boundaries demarcating their separate peoples (Goff 2000). An exclusive national money can play an especially useful role in highlighting a society's distinctiveness and autonomy in the international system.

Moreover, once in place, a territorial currency can take on a psychological life of its own in defiance of all economic or political logic. Indeed, it is difficult to overestimate the emotional attachment that most societies come to feel for their money—even monies that have clearly failed the test of market competition. Mainstream economists are inclined to dismiss such feelings as technically irrelevant—mere "misplaced pride," to quote one prominent theorist (Alesina 2001, 223)—but the force of their impact on practical policymaking cannot be ignored.

The symbolic role of money would obviously be compromised by regionalization in any form, whether via dollarization or monetary alliance. Ceteris paribus, therefore, this factor, too, would appear to imply a preference for avoiding currency regionalization to the extent possible. Here, too, however, relatively little is sacrificed when the degree of regionalization is low. Even with a currency board or decentralized monetary union, a national money is preserved, thus continuing to provide a basic symbol to help sustain a society's sense of community. It is only at the highest degrees of regionalization—full or near-dollarization or something like EMU or ECCU—that the total impact of this factor will be felt.

DIPLOMATIC INFLUENCE

Money has also long been consciously used by state authorities as an instrument of diplomatic influence. Indeed, as Jonathan Kirshner (1995, 29, 31) has written, "Monetary power is a remarkably efficient component of state power. . . . the most potent instrument of economic coercion available to states in a position to exercise it." Money, after all, is at its most basic simply command over real resources. If a nation can be threatened with a denial of access to the means to acquire vital goods and services, it is clearly vulnerable in geopolitical terms.

This factor, too, implies a preference for avoiding currency regionalization to the extent possible. Monetary sovereignty enables policymakers to avoid dependence on some other source for their purchasing power. In effect, a clear economic boundary is drawn between the state and the rest of the world, promoting political authority. Government is insulated from outside influence or constraint in formulating and implementing policy. Conversely, that measure of insulation will be compromised by any form of dollarization or monetary alliance. Followership necessarily creates a patron-client relationship. Again, the sacrifice is relatively modest when the degree of regionalization is low, since exit costs will be correspondingly small. So long as national currency remains in circulation, with some degree of decentralization of decision making, room exists for a restoration of monetary sovereignty to escape painful diplomatic coercion. But here, too, the impact, at the margin, will rise significantly with successively higher degrees of regionalization.

Maximum Acceptable Regionalization

Taking all five factors into account, two implications become clear. First, it is evident why so many states instinctively prefer to continue producing their own money. A regional currency's saving of transactions costs, on its own, would seem unlikely to outweigh the considerable negatives implied: the losses of macroeconomic flexibility, seigniorage, a political symbol, and diplomatic insulation. In effect market preservation—defense of national monetary sovereignty—is a government's default strategy.

Second, it is evident why there is such wide variation in the design of regional currencies. Lower degrees of regionalization help to alleviate of some of the perceived disadvantages of an upward shift of authority. The considerable leeway for variation of design offers more opportunity to accommodate the interests of individual participants.

Is there, then, some degree of regionalization that will encourage more governments to depart from their default strategy? At the risk of oversimplifying a highly complex decision, the key elements for rational poli-

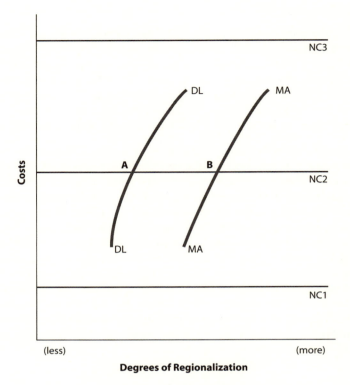

Figure 1. Choice Diagram

cymakers can be reduced to a single two-dimensional diagram comparing the cost of market preservation with the costs of either an alliance strategy or a followership strategy, as in figure 1.

Call this the Choice Diagram. Along the horizontal axis of the Choice Diagram are alternative degrees of regionalization, whether vertical or horizontal, ranging from the lowest forms at the left (e.g., bimonetarism or something like the CMA) to the highest at the right (e.g., full dollarization or something like the EMU). In principle one should distinguish not one but two metrics for regionalization, corresponding to the two separate dimensions involved—institutional provisions for currency issue and decision making. But as a first approximation, it is enough to collapse the two dimensions into a single scale that may be read from left to right as a rough measure of the share of formal authority delegated elsewhere by the individual state.

On the vertical axis are total costs as perceived by a nation's policymakers, ranging upward from low to high. Begin with the cost of maintaining a strictly national currency (NC). NC may be represented by a horizontal line, since the estimated cost of a national currency at any particular moment is given no matter what degree of regionalization might be considered as an alternative. In more technical language, NC is invariant to the degree of regionalization. The height of the line, low or high, will vary considerably from state to state, reflecting cross-country differences in the circumstances that determine the cost of a default strategy of market preservation. The height of the line can also vary over time as the circumstances of an individual country change. Overall, for most countries today, the height of NC is rising pari passu with the growing deterritorialization of money, reflecting the marked redistribution of power in monetary affairs described in chapter 1. As currency competition grows, the net benefits of monetary sovereignty are correspondingly reduced for all but the small handful of states with the most widely accepted monies. Where half a century ago most governments might have faced a line as low as NC1, today many may be confronted with lines as high as NC2 or even NC3.

Curves DL and MA represent the net costs of, respectively, dollarization and monetary alliance. Each is a composite of the five factors just outlined—microeconomic efficiency gains, which decline at the margin with successively higher degrees of regionalization; and the losses of macroeconomic flexibility, seigniorage, a political symbol, and diplomatic insulation, all of which are a rising function of the degree of regionalization. Though it is manifestly difficult, a priori, to assign specific weights to each of these five factors, the overall direction of the relationship is clear. The greater the share of formal authority that is delegated away from the state, either vertically or horizontally, the higher is the estimated net cost as compared with a national currency. For any single country, the maximum acceptable degree of dollarization is represented by point A, where the cost of preserving a national currency equals the cost of the least demanding form of followership strategy. By similar reasoning, the maximum acceptable degree of monetary alliance is point B.

The positions of DL and MA relative to NC will vary considerably from country to country, yielding diverse outcomes. For some, the cost of maintaining a national currency may already have become so elevated that it is now somewhere in the neighborhood of NC3, where there is no point of intersection with either DL or MA. Even the strictest form of vertical or horizontal regionalization would thus be an acceptable option. By contrast, for others the position of NC might still be closer to NC1, below both DL and MA, making neither regionalization option acceptable in even its most diluted form. For some, DL might lie below MA, making some form of dollarization more acceptable (A); for others, MA might lie below DL, resulting in just one point of intersection (B) where monetary alliance is the preferred option; and for yet others, DL and MA could lie close together, making the choice between dollarization and monetary alliance especially difficult.

The key question is: What determines the relative position of the three curves in the Choice Diagram for any given country?

Determining State Preferences

At issue are state preferences. The more we know about what it is that influences policymakers' estimates of prospective benefits and costs, the easier it will be to see through the mist to predict preferences and therefore the delegation of authority that is ultimately likely to emerge in individual countries. There is of course no substitute for detailed analysis, as we shall see in chapters 4 through 6, since policymakers can be expected to vary greatly in the importance they attach to particular gains or losses depending on each country's unique circumstances. Anticipating subsequent discussion, however, a few generalizations do seem warranted.

Study of the empirical record suggests four conditions that appear especially influential in determining strategic choices. These are: (1) country size; (2) economic linkages; (3) political linkages; and (4) domestic politics. The first two conditions figure prominently among the country characteristics stressed in standard OCA theory (though other variables drawn from OCA theory seem less decisive); the latter are familiar from conventional political analysis. As we shall see, much insight will be gained by looking at all these variables together in the context of specific cases.

The Empirical Record

There are limitations to the empirical record, of course. We do have an abundant population of states committed to one form of currency regionalization or another, as the Appendix shows: some eighteen fully dollarized or near-dollarized economies, seven currency boards, seven bimonetary systems, and thirty-seven countries in a total of four different monetary unions, adding up to nearly a third of all sovereign entities in the world. This would certainly seem a large enough sample to look for meaningful patterns of behavior. But it is also evident that relatively few of these arrangements are the product of calculated decisions by fully independent governments. The majority, in fact, grew out of relationships that originated in colonial times or in United Nations trusteeships. These include most of the fully dollarized and near-dollarized economies listed in tables 1 and 2 as well as three of the four monetary unions listed in table 5 (all but EMU). In all such cases it was currency regionalization that was the default position, not some form of exclusive national currency.

Moreover, the empirical record is at best only an *indirect* indicator of preferences, since government choices are rarely unconstrained. In most cases it must be assumed that observed relationships are the outcome of strategic interactions and bargaining rather than of unilateral calculation and decision making.

Nonetheless much can be learned, despite such limitations. Path dependency may be pervasive, but governments were not, after all, *compelled* to preserve inherited arrangements. A decision *not* to abandon a regional currency can tell us as much about preferences as a decision to adopt one.[31] Moreover to this sample we may add other governments that, once given the opportunity, *did* in fact abandon a regional currency. These cases, too, tell us something about government attitudes. One instructive set of precedents is offered by the host of Third World countries that, once decolonization began after World War II, rapidly chose to abandon colonial-era currency boards for their own separate monies. Most notably, these included two sizable monetary unions in Africa that had long been managed by Britain under its East African and West African currency boards, neither of which survived the coming of independence.[32] Other, more recent precedents are provided by the successor states of recently failed federations—the former Soviet Union, Czechoslovakia, and Yugoslavia—nearly all of which chose to establish monies of their own in one form or another as soon as they gained their independence.

Likewise, choices may not be unconstrained, but outcomes may still be interpreted as evidence of revealed preference. The difficulty of inferring preferences from outcomes is a familiar one in social-science methodology but is generally not considered an insuperable barrier to analysis, so long as observations are handled with caution.

So what does the record suggest to us?

Country Size

One thing the record clearly suggests is that country size matters, at least for the world's smallest states. Of all the economies that have been fully or near-dollarized, the largest until recently was Panama, with a population of less than three million. Most have been truly tiny enclaves or microstates—willingly submitting, as economist Willem Buiter (1999a, 199) puts it, to "the monetary equivalent of a marriage between an elephant and a mouse." Small size also dominates among nations that have adopted currency boards or bimonetarism and is an accurate description of the members of both the ECCU and CFA Franc Zone. One safe bet, ceteris paribus, is that the smaller an economy's size—whether measured by population, territory, or GDP—the greater is the probability that it will be prepared to surrender the privilege of producing a money of its own.

The logic is simple. Smaller states are least able to sustain a competitive national currency. For them the NC curve is already greatly elevated. Conversely, these are the economies that stand to gain most from a reduction of transactions costs. Whether in the form of dollarization or monetary alliance, some degree of regionalization offers both enhanced network externalities and lower administrative costs. Moreover, since in most cases these countries are also inherently vulnerable in political terms, less importance is likely to be attached to the risks that go with dependence on some other source for their purchasing power. Indeed, advantage may be seen in the protection that could be offered by association with either a powerful patron or a local partnership. Hence either DL or MA, or both, may fall below NC, encouraging governments to abandon strategies of market preservation.

How small must a state be? Throughout most of the twentieth century, regionalization seemed the preference of only the poorest and most diminutive specks of sovereignty around the globe. The threshold was very high. But as globalization has gradually elevated the NC curve, even bigger nations, as we know, have begun to join in, such as Ecuador and El Salvador. The threshold is clearly shifting downward, increasing the number of potential candidates.

Size, however, by no means explains all. Obviously there are many small states that have elected *not* to go the regionalization route—at least, not yet. These include the many former colonies and trust territories, as well as most of the successor states of recently failed federations, that even today remain intent on preserving, to the extent possible, the privileges of a national monetary monopoly. Small size per se is by no means a sufficient condition to predict the choice of strategy. Conversely, there are also some larger nations that have indeed chosen to delegate monetary authority elsewhere, most notably Bulgaria and Estonia with their currency boards, and the members of EMU. Small size is not a necessary condition, either.

Economic Linkages

Another condition that appears to matter, not surprisingly, is the intensity of economic linkages between nations. Many of the countries that make use of a popular foreign currency have long been closely tied to a market leader economically. This is especially true of the numerous dollarized or bimonetary systems in the Caribbean and Central America, as well as the several dollarized enclaves of Europe and the Pacific. Likewise, we know that nearly half a century of deepening integration preceded the start of EMU. Another safe bet, ceteris paribus, is that closer economic bonds will also increase the probability that a government will be prepared to surrender the privilege of producing its own money.

Here again, the logic is simple. Economies that are already closely linked would, because of the efficiency gains involved, appear to be natural candidates for a regional money of some kind. Linkages might operate through trade, as is evident in the European Union, or through financial relationships developed from formal or informal currency use. The higher the level of interaction, the more we would expect to see both greater savings of transactions costs and closer convergence of economic activity. If relations are mostly concentrated on a market leader, lowering the DL curve, some form of dollarization might prevail. This would especially be the case where currency substitution has now become widespread, as in Latin America or East-Central Europe. Conversely, if links are closer within a group of neighboring states, say as a result of a common integration project like the EU, MA would be lowered, making currency unification more likely.

It is clear, however, that this condition, too, on its own, is neither necessary nor sufficient for predictive purposes. Both Mexico and Canada are more closely tied to the United States than most other Hemispheric economies, yet to date each remains firmly committed to defending its traditional monetary sovereignty. Conversely, both the ECCU and CFA Franc Zone continue to thrive despite an absence of much reciprocal trade among their members, while successor states of recently failed federations have mostly preferred to produce their own national monies in spite of the previously close integration of their economies. Economic linkages alone are rarely decisive. The reason is that they bear on only two of the five factors of interest to rational policymakers: the trade-off between microeconomic efficiency and macroeconomic flexibility. Governments are undoubtedly sensitive to such considerations, but not exclusively.

Political Linkages

A third condition that appears to matter is the intensity of political linkages between nations, whether formal or informal. Ties may take the form of a pre-existing patron-client relationship, perhaps descended from a previous colonial or trusteeship association; or they may be embodied in a network of cooperative diplomatic arrangements, possibly institutionalized in a formal political or military alliance. Whatever the form, the influence of such ties is unmistakable—in currency groupings that have failed as well as those that have survived.

On the negative side, I have already mentioned the several monetary unions that have broken up in recent decades: in British East Africa and West Africa following decolonization, as well as in the former Soviet bloc following the end of the Cold War. We also know that many former dependencies of the old imperial powers, once granted independence, quickly rejected dollarization or colonial-era currency boards in favor of a money of their own. Plainly, in all these cases, governments were motivated by a desire to assert their new found rights and prerogatives as sovereign states; in other words, to *reduce* political linkages. Conversely, in the monetary alliances that survived decolonization (ECCU and CFA Franc Zone), as well as in EMU and CMA, inter-state ties have always been stronger; and the same is true of most of today's dollarized entities as well, which have long been accustomed to a hierarchical relationship with the designated source of their money. These are cases where governments are *least* interested in a reduction of political linkages.

Thus a third safe bet, ceteris paribus, is that closer political bonds, too, will increase the probability that a government will be prepared to surrender the privilege of a national money. The logic is that political linkages reduce two of the key costs associated with regionalization—the loss of a political symbol and the increase of vulnerability to outside influence. For states with already close ties to one of the market leaders, this means a lower DL curve, making some form of followership relatively more attractive. Candidates might include many of the countries of Latin America, ever in the shadow of the United States, or numerous economies of the former Soviet bloc, Mediterranean basin, or sub-Saharan Africa, with their close links to Europe. Likewise, for states already engaged in a common integration project, such as Mercosur in South America or ASEAN in East Asia, political linkages could lower the MA curve, making a strategy of monetary alliance seem an increasingly natural choice.

Here again, however, as with size or economic linkages, the condition is rarely decisive, since it, too, bears directly on only a subset of the factors of interest to policymakers. Djibouti, for example, which is a former French dependency, has a dollar-based currency board despite a paucity of direct ties to the United States. Israel, conversely, has expressly rejected dollarization in spite of its close relationship with Washington (Cohen 1998, 38). Political linkages, too, on their own, are neither necessary nor sufficient for predictive purposes.

Domestic Politics

Finally, we can hardly ignore domestic politics, as already emphasized at the outset of this chapter. Though political scientists have firmly established the importance of distributional considerations in government choices of exchange-rate regimes,[33] remarkably few studies yet exist that directly identify the role of domestic interest groups or institutions in currency regionalization.[34] Strong hints, however, are provided by a related literature that has focused on the wave of financial liberalization that swept emerging-market economies in the 1980s and 1990s.[35] Details differ from country to country, of course, and interests are not always clear-cut. Yet on balance it is evident that certain critical constituencies benefited measurably from the integration of local financial markets into the growing structure of global finance. Principally, these were the sectors most heavily involved in cross-border activity, including especially big tradable-goods producers, banks and other financial-services firms, and large private asset-holders—those that Frieden (1991) refers to as "integrationist" interests. Exporters and importers, as well as domestic banks, gained improved access to loanable funds and lower borrowing costs; the owners and managers of financial wealth were freed to seek out more profitable investments or to develop new strategies for portfolio diversification. Most of these integrationist interests, research reveals, were active in lobbying policymakers to reduce or eliminate past restraints on capital mobility.

Extrapolation from this literature suggests that many of these same powerful constituencies should be expected to favor currency regionalization, as well, since a regional money offers the same basic advantage—namely, financial openness. These are the actors who will benefit most from the anticipated reduction of transactions costs; for them, the DL and MA curves appear lower than they do to others. And they are not the type of actors who are apt to be shy about promoting their own interests. Much rests, therefore, on the degree of political influence exercised by such groups as compared with other domestic constituencies, such as producers of non-tradable goods and services, as well as workers and small farmers, who might oppose abandoning a national currency—"anti-integrationist" forces who feel they would benefit more from preservation of some measure of monetary autonomy to cope with local circumstances.

Integrationists' degree of influence, in turn, will be a function of domestic institutions and political structures. The issue is the extent to which government decision making is insulated from the pressures of such important groups. How much attention is paid to their specific preferences and demands? This is less a matter of formal regime type than of practical access to the corridors of power. The greater the relative influence of integrationist interests, the more probable it is that policymakers will be prepared to delegate monetary authority elsewhere. This seems another safe bet, again ceteris paribus.

Conclusion

Firm predictions, as indicated, are difficult. But four broad generalizations do seem plausible. First, while the deterritorialization of currency is clearly imposing growing constraints on traditional forms of monetary governance, it by no means dictates the choices that governments will eventually make. Confronted with the logic of market competition, a good number of countries will consider some form of regionalization, either dollarization or monetary alliance—but by no means all.

Second, we should expect to see few *pure* cases of either dollarization or monetary alliance. Not many countries are apt to go the way of the Marshall Islands or Monaco, which willingly forgo any claim to a national money of their own. Likewise, even in the small handful of common integration projects now under way in the developing world—most notably, Mercosur and ASEAN—partnerships remain far from the degree of closeness that would be required to establish something as far-reaching as EMU or the ECCU. Regionalization, for many, may seem a logical corollary of currency competition, but it does not follow that sovereign states will spontaneously delegate *all* their authority elsewhere, outsourcing management either vertically to a market leader or horizontally to a joint central bank. Most governments are likely to prefer somewhat more mixed models, involving a more limited compromise of monetary sovereignty.

Third, what those mixed models might look like in practice will vary considerably, depending on *bargaining context*. Practical experience demonstrates that many different degrees of regionalization are possible, both vertical and horizontal, to accommodate the economic and political interests of participating states. No uniform outcome should be expected for either dollarization or monetary alliance. Much will depend on the policies adopted by the market leaders.

Fourth, bargaining context in turn will depend greatly on the key conditions of country size, economic linkages, political linkages, and domestic politics. Higher degrees of regionalization are more likely where states are small, economic and political linkages are strong, and domestic politics is heavily influenced by tradable-goods producers and financial interests. Conversely, lower degrees of regionalization may be expected insofar as countries are larger, economic and political linkages with others are weaker, and the domestic political setting is more pluralistic. In the largest states, with the weakest economic and political linkages and the most pluralistic politics, defense of national monetary sovereignty is most likely to remain the default strategy.

In short, there seems little doubt that a new geography of money is beginning to emerge. But as it evolves, the world's monetary map will in all probability retain all the diversity of the existing Currency Pyramid rather than coalesce into some simple landscape of giant blocs and joint currencies. The essential determinants are clear. What cannot be foretold is how these complex elements will work out in specific bargaining contexts. To get a better view through the mist, more detailed exploration is required.

Appendix

TABLE 1
Fully Dollarized Countries[a]

Country	Currency Used	Since
Andorra	euro (formerly French franc and Spanish peseta, with limited amounts of Andorran diners)	2002
Cyprus, Northern[b]	Turkish lira	1974
East Timor	U.S. dollar	2000
Kosovo[c]	euro (formerly Yugoslav dinar and deutsche mark)	1999
Liechtenstein	Swiss franc	1921
Marshall Islands	U.S. dollar	1944
Micronesia	U.S. dollar	1944
Monaco	euro (formerly French franc, with limited amounts of Monacan francs)	1865
Montenegro[c]	euro (formerly deutsche mark)	1999
Nauru	Australian dollar	1914
Palau	U.S. dollar	1944
San Marino	euro (formerly Italian lira, with limited amounts of San Marino lire)	2002
Vatican City	euro (formerly Italian lira, with limited amounts of Vatican lire)	2002
TOTAL = 13		

Sources: International Monetary Fund, Europa World Year Book, various government sources.

[a] Independent states that extend exclusive legal-tender rights to a single foreign currency.

[b] De facto independent; under the protection of Turkey.

[c] Semi-independent; officially still part of the former federal state of Yugoslavia, renamed Serbia and Montenegro in 2003.

TABLE 2
Near-Dollarized Countries[a]

Country	Currency Used	Since	Local Currency
Ecuador	U.S. dollar	2000	sucre
El Salvador	U.S. dollar	2001	colon
Kiribati	Australian dollar	1943	own coins
Panama	U.S. dollar	1904	balboa
Tuvalu	Australian dollar	1892	Tuvaluan dollar
TOTAL = 5			

[a] Independent states that rely primarily on one or more foreign currencies but also issue a token local currency.

TABLE 3
Currency Boards[a]

Country	Anchor Currency	Since	Local Currency
Bosnia and Herzegovina	euro (formerly deutsche mark)	1998	Bosnian marka
Brunei Darussalam	Singapore dollar	1967	Brunei dollar
Bulgaria	euro (formerly deutsche mark)	1997	lev
Djibouti	U.S. dollar	1949	Djibouti franc
Estonia	euro (formerly deutsche mark)	1992	kroon
Hong Kong[b]	U.S. dollar	1983	Hong Kong dollar
Lithuania	euro (formerly U.S. dollar)	1994	litas
TOTAL = 7			

[a] Countries with a formally irrevocable exchange-rate link to a foreign currency, both of which circulate domestically as legal tender and are fully interchangeable. A currency board also existed in Argentina from 1991 to 2002.

[b] Special Administrative Region of China.

TABLE 4
Bimonetary Countries[a]

Country	Currencies Used	Since
Bahamas	Bahamanian dollar, U.S. dollar	1966
Bhutan	Bhutan ngultrum, Indian rupee	1974
Guatemala	Guatemala quetzal, use of other currencies permitted	2001
Haiti	Haitian gourde, U.S. dollar	n.a.
Liberia[b]	Liberian dollar, U.S. dollar	1982
Palestinian territories[c]	Israeli shekel, Jordanian dinar	1967
Tajikistan	Tajik ruble, use of other currencies permitted	1994
TOTAL = 7		

[a] Countries with one or more foreign currencies in circulation that are recognized legally but are subsidiary to the local currency as legal tender.

[b] Near-dollarized, with only token amounts of Liberian dollars in circulation, from 1944 until 1982.

[c] Occupied by Israel since 1967. The Israeli shekel is the exclusive legal tender in the Gaza Strip; both the shekel and Jordanian dinar are recognized in the West Bank.

TABLE 5
Monetary Unions

Union	Member Countries	Institutional Arrangements	Since
Eastern Caribbean Currency Union	Antigua and Barbuda, Dominica, Grenada, St. Kitts-Nevis, St. Lucia, St. Vincent and the Grenadines[a]	single currency (Eastern Caribbean dollar), single central bank	1965
Economic and Monetary Union (European Union)	Austria, Belgium, Finland, France, Germany, Greece, Ireland, Italy, Luxembourg, Netherlands, Portugal, Spain	single currency (euro), single central bank	1999
CFA Franc Zone	Benin, Burkina Faso, Cameroon, Central African Republic, Chad, Comoros, Congo-Brazzaville, Côte d'Ivoire, Equatorial Guinea, Gabon, Guinea-Bissau, Mali, Niger, Senegal, Togo	two regional currencies (both named CFA franc) and one national currency (Comorian franc); two regional central banks and one national central bank (Comoros)	1962–64
Common Monetary Area	Lesotho, Namibia, South Africa, Swaziland	three currencies pegged to S. African rand, four central banks (South African rand is legal tender in Lesotho and Namibia)	1986
TOTAL = 36			

[a] Also includes as full members two British dependencies, Anguilla and Montserrat (see table 6).

TABLE 6
Dependent Territories

Territory	Administered by	Currencies Used
American Samoa	United States	U.S. dollar
Anguilla	United Kingdom	Eastern Caribbean dollar
Bermuda	United Kingdom	U.S. dollar, Bermuda dollar
Bovet Island	Norway	Norwegian krone
British Indian Ocean Territory	United Kingdom	U.K. pound
British Virgin Islands	United Kingdom	U.S. dollar
Cayman Islands	United Kingdom	U.S. dollar, Cayman dollar
Christmas Island	Australia	Australian dollar
Cocos (Keeling) Islands	Australia	Australian dollar
Cook Islands	New Zealand	New Zealand dollar
Dronning Maud Land	Norway	Norwegian krone
Falkland Islands	United Kingdom	U.K. pound, Falklands pound
Faroe Islands	Denmark	Danish krone, Faroese krone
French Guiana[a]	France	euro (formerly French franc)
French Polynesia	France	CFA franc[b]
Gibraltar	United Kingdom	U.K. pound
Greenland	Denmark	Danish krone
Guadeloupe[a]	France	euro (formerly French franc)
Guam	United States	U.S. dollar
Guernsey	United Kingdom	U.K. pound, Guernsey pound
Heard and McDonald Islands	Australia	Australian dollar
Isle of Man	United Kingdom	U.K. pound, Manx pound
Jersey	United Kingdom	U.K. pound, Jersey pound
Johnston Island	United States	U.S. dollar

[a] Formally, overseas departments of France.
[b] Comptoirs Français du Pacifique franc, a colonial currency linked via a currency board to the euro (formerly the French franc).

TABLE 6 (*cont.*)
Dependent Territories

Territory	Administered by	Currencies Used
Martinique[a]	France	euro (formerly French franc)
Mayotte[a]	France	euro (formerly French franc)
Midway Islands	United States	U.S. dollar
Montserrat	United Kingdom	Eastern Caribbean dollar
New Caledonia	France	CFA franc[b]
Niue	New Zealand	New Zealand dollar
Norfolk Island	Australia	Australian dollar
Northern Mariana Islands	United States	U.S. dollar
Pitcairn Island	United Kingdom	New Zealand and U.S. dollars
Puerto Rico	United States	U.S. dollar
Reunion[a]	France	euro (formerly French franc)
Saint Helena	United Kingdom	U.K. pound
Saint Pierre and Miquelon[a]	France	euro (formerly French franc)
South Georgia and South Sandwich Islands	United Kingdom	U.K. pound
Svalbard	Norway	Norwegian krone
Tokelau	New Zealand	New Zealand dollar
Turks and Caicos Islands	United Kingdom	U.S. dollar
U.S. Virgin Islands	United States	U.S. dollar
Wake Island	United States	U.S. dollar
Wallis and Fortuna Islands	France	CFA franc[b]

[a] Formally, overseas departments of France.
[b] Comptoirs Français du Pacifique franc, a colonial currency linked via a currency board to the euro (formerly the French franc).

Three

Life at the Peak

EXPLORATION can begin at the peak of the Currency Pyramid. As previously suggested, money's future will very much depend on the behavior of the market leaders, since their policies greatly influence the strategic choices available to all other governments. Today's most widely used monies include the dollar, the acknowledged Top Currency, along with two Patrician Currencies, the euro and yen—a trio we can call the Big Three. What can we expect of life at the peak in years to come? Again the same two factors, market competition and state preferences, will be instrumental in determining outcomes.

Market Competition

At the peak of the Currency Pyramid, today's Big Three dominate because they offer all the qualities required for sustained competitive success, as outlined in chapter 1—low inflation and inflation variability, exchange convenience and capital certainty, and broad transactional networks. Consideration of these essential attributes permits two broad inferences. First, among currencies in circulation today, there seems no candidate with even the remotest chance in the foreseeable future of challenging the top rank presently enjoyed by the dollar, euro, and yen. Second, among the Big Three, there seems a very real chance of significant shifts in relative market standing.

No New Challengers

The first inference follows logically from observable fact. We know that there is a great deal of inertia in currency use that can slow down the transition from one equilibrium to another. Recall, for instance, how long it took the dollar to supplant the pound sterling at the top of the Currency Pyramid even after America's emergence a century ago as the world's richest economy. As Paul Krugman (1992, 173) has commented: "The impressive fact here is surely the inertia; sterling remained the first-ranked currency for half a century after Britain had ceased to be the first-ranked economic power." Similar inertias have been evident for millennia in the prolonged use of such international monies as the bezant or the Mexican silver dollar long after the decline of the imperial powers that first coined them. It has also been evident more recently in the continued popularity of America's greenback despite periodic bouts of exchange-rate weakness. For reasons noted in chapter 1, such inertia is very much the rule, not the exception, in currency relations.

Because of this conservative bias in market behavior, no new challenger can ever hope to rise toward the top of the Currency Pyramid unless it is first able to offer a substantial margin of advantage over existing incumbents. The dollar was able to do that, in relation to sterling, once New York overtook London as the world's pre-eminent source of investment capital—though even that displacement, as Krugman notes, took a half-century or more. Today, it is difficult to find any money anywhere with a comparable promise of competitive advantage in relation to the present Big Three.

Some sources suggest a possible future role for China's currency, the yuan (also known as the renminbi), given the enormous size of the Chinese economy—already, by some measures, the second largest in the world—and its growing role in world trade. However broad the yuan's transactional network may eventually become, though, the currency's prospects suffer from the backwardness of China's financial markets and still lingering uncertainties over domestic political stability—to say nothing of the fact that use of the yuan continues to be inhibited by cumbersome exchange restrictions and capital controls. Similar deficiencies also rule out the monies of other large emerging markets, such as those of Brazil or India. Conversely the Elite Currencies of some economically advanced countries, such as Switzerland or Canada, or even Britain, are precluded, despite obvious financial sophistication and political stability, by the relatively small size of the economies involved. (Britain's pound in any event is expected eventually to be absorbed into Europe's monetary union.) Nowhere, in fact, does there seem to be any existing money with a plausible chance of soon overcoming the powerful forces of inertia favoring today's incumbents. For the foreseeable future, the dominance of the Big Three seems secure.

Relative Shifts

Continued collective dominance, however, does not preclude the possibility of significant shifts in relative standing among the Big Three. In today's monetary geography, the dollar reigns supreme—the Top Currency. But might that change? Could the greenback's market leadership be challenged any time soon by either the euro or the yen?

Less probability may be attached to a successful challenge by the yen, despite Japan's evident strengths as the world's top creditor nation and its enviable long-term record of success in controlling inflation and promoting exports. Cross-border use of the yen did accelerate significantly in the 1970s and 1980s, during the heady years of Japanese economic expansion. Internationalization was strongest in bank lending and securities markets, where yen-denominated claims were especially attractive to investors. But the yen never came close to overtaking the popularity of the dollar, or even the DM, and was little used for either trade invoicing or currency substitution. Worse, its upward trajectory was abruptly halted in the 1990s, following the bursting of Japan's "bubble economy," and there seems little prospect of resumption in the near term so long as Japanese domestic stagnation persists.

In fact use of the yen abroad in recent years has, in relative terms, actually decreased rather than increased. In exchange markets, the percentage of transactions in yen has dropped from a high of 27 percent of global turnover in 1989 to under 23 percent in 2001; similarly, in central-bank reserves, the yen's share of the total has shrunk from some 7 percent at the end of the 1980s to under 5 percent a decade later.[1] Overall, the yen's position at the peak of the Currency Pyramid has slipped substantially below both the other market leaders, as informed observers now readily acknowledge.[2]

Largely, the yen's decline in popularity abroad mirrors Japan's economic troubles at home, which include not only a fragile banking system, but also a level of public debt, relative to GDP, that is now the highest of any industrial nation. Japanese government bonds have already been downgraded sharply by rating agencies, discouraging investors. By mid-2002, Japan's credit rating had sunk to the level of the likes of Cyprus, Latvia, Poland, and Mauritius—below even a country as poor as Botswana—severely denting Japanese pride.[3] The decline of foreign use of the yen has been most dramatic in neighboring Asian countries, where bank loans and other Japanese investments have been rolled back dramatically. "The country's financial muscle in Asia is waning," reports the *New York Times* (26 December 1999). "Japanese investment in the region may never be the same."

The biggest problem for the international standing of the yen is Japan's financial system, which, despite recent improvements, has long lagged behind American and even many European markets in terms of openness or efficiency. Indeed, as recently as two decades ago, Japanese financial markets remained the most tightly regulated and protected in the industrial world, preventing wider use of the yen. Strict controls were maintained on both inward and outward movements of capital, securities markets were relatively underdeveloped, and financial institutions were rigidly segmented. Starting in the mid-1970s, a process of liberalization began, prompted partly by a slowing of domestic economic growth and partly by external pressure from the United States. Capital controls were loosened, new instruments and markets were developed, and institutional segmentation was relaxed—all of which did much to enhance the yen's exchange convenience and capital certainty. Most dramatic was a multiyear liberalization program announced in 1996, dubbed the Big Bang in imitation of the swift deregulation of Britain's financial markets a decade earlier.[4] Under the Big Bang all remaining capital controls were quickly eliminated and a variety of other ambitious measures were scheduled, including improvements in the settlement system, reductions of taxes and regulations, and increases in the range of products available to match the cash-flow and risk-management requirements of market actors.

The reform process, however, is still far from complete and could take many years to come even close to approximating market standards in the United States or Europe. One recent study, an exhaustively researched history of Japanese finance, applauds the prospective shakeout of the banking sector but admits that the transition is unlikely to be fully executed for many years to come (Hoshi and Kashyap 2001). Other sources are even less encouraging, questioning whether Japan's public authorities have the political will needed to overcome determined resistance from powerful vested interests.[5] Both Ito and Melvin (2000) and Schaede (2000) emphasize the extent to which success of the Big Bang will depend on completion of complementary reforms in tax codes, regulatory processes, and the institutions of law enforcement and legal recourse—initiatives that would require fundamental changes in the way business is done in Japan. Tokyo's politicians so far have shown little enthusiasm for such radical transformation.

Yet, without further progress, the yen will remain at a competitive disadvantage relative to both the dollar and euro, as even its most ardent champions acknowledge (Kwan 2001, 9). International traders and investors will have little incentive to bear the costs and risks of switching from either of the other leading currencies to the yen. Indeed, if left to market forces alone, the trend is more likely to continue moving the other way, toward gradual erosion of the yen's standing in a manner reminiscent of sterling's long decline in an earlier era.

More probability, by contrast, can be attached to a successful challenge by the euro, which started life in January 1999 with many of the key attributes necessary for competitive success already well in evidence. Together, the twelve present members of EMU—familiarly known as "Euroland"[6]—constitute a market nearly as large as that of the United States, with extensive trade relations, not only in the European region but around the world. The potential for network externalities is considerable. Likewise, Euroland started with both unquestioned political stability and an enviably low rate of inflation, backed by a joint monetary authority, the European Central Bank, that is fully committed to preserving confidence in the euro's future value. Much room exists, therefore, for a quick ascendancy as an international currency, just as many observers have predicted.[7] The euro has already surpassed the past aggregate share of the DM and other EMU "legacy" currencies in foreign trade and investment.[8] The only question is how high the euro will rise and how much business it will take from the dollar.

Two factors, in particular, will determine the answer. At the political level, much will depend on how well the euro is managed in relation to the greenback as well as other currencies in the exchange market. Under the 1992 Maastricht Treaty, considerable ambiguity remains about who is responsible for the critical matter of exchange-rate policy. While the ECB is assigned day-to-day operational responsibility for the euro's external value, authority over the more general orientation of policy is uneasily shared with other EU institutions, including both the Council of Ministers representing national governments and the European Commission, the EU's central administrative body in Brussels. Considerable ambiguity remains as well about who is to speak for Euroland on broader macroeconomic issues such as policy coordination or the management of financial crises. No coherent authority exists to represent the group at the IMF or in other global forums.

Uncertainties like these, which are an understandable byproduct of the negotiating compromises that were needed to get agreement on EMU in the first place, are frequently criticized for their potentially adverse political consequences (Henning 2000; McNamara and Meunier 2002). How can the EU expect to project power in international monetary affairs if it cannot even agree on its own institutional mechanisms for exchange-rate management or external representation? But such uncertainties could also have serious economic consequences if they sow doubts or confusion among the new currency's prospective users. The risk is that fragmented decision making might fail to provide a clear indication of official intentions, acting as a disincentive for market actors. The longer that risk persists, the more it will discourage international acceptance.

At the economic level the answer rests first and foremost, as with the yen, on prospective developments in financial markets. Even with the euro's promise of broad economies of scale and stable purchasing power, the greenback will be favored by the natural advantages of incumbency unless euro transactions costs, which historically have been higher than those on the more widely traded dollar, can be lowered to more competitive levels. The level of euro transactions costs, in turn, will depend directly on what happens to the structure of Europe's financial markets. Without sustained improvements in market efficiency and openness, it will be difficult for the euro to overcome the forces of inertia characteristic of international currency use. Economists Richard Portes and Hélène Rey (1998, 308) put the point most succinctly: "The key determinant of the extent and speed of internationalization of the euro will be transaction costs in foreign exchange and securities markets."

In fact, prospects for the structural efficiency of Europe's financial system seem good. On a purely quantitative basis, introduction of the euro will eventually create the largest single-currency financial market in the world. The aggregate value of Euroland financial claims (fixed-income securities, equities, and bank loans) is already almost as great as that of the United States and will undoubtedly keep growing in the future. Beyond that, there are bound to be major qualitative improvements in market depth and liquidity as previously segmented national markets are gradually knitted together into an integrated whole. The elimination of exchange risk inside EMU has already intensified competition among financial institutions, particularly in such hotly contested activities as bond underwriting and syndicated bank lending, encouraging cost-cutting and innovation. Over the longer term, harmonization of laws and conventions and the development of new cross-border payments systems will enhance the marketability of euro assets of all kinds.

Progress to date has been swiftest in money markets and the corporate bond market, where instruments and procedures are already largely standardized (Santillán, Baylen, and Thygesen 2000). Primary equity markets have also expanded rapidly and become more closely integrated (Fratzscher 2001), in turn spurring efforts to merge national stock exchanges. Although a projected merger of the Frankfurt and London exchanges failed to materialize, a successful partnership has been created by the bourses of Paris, Amsterdam, and Brussels under the label Euronext. Full consolidation of the market for public debt, by contrast, is expected to take longer owing to the persistence of differential credit and liquidity risk premiums among countries as well as variations in legal traditions, issuance procedures and calendars, and primary dealer systems. Market segmentation has been prolonged by intense competition among governments to establish their own issues as Euroland benchmarks (IMF 2001, 99–111).

There is little reason to doubt that improvements in the structural efficiency of Europe's markets will have a substantial effect on international investment practice. To be sure, foreign investors so far have been slower than anticipated to add to their holdings of euro-denominated assets, despite the greater depth and liquidity on offer. In fact, the euro's share of world portfolios has changed little from the previous aggregate of legacy currencies. Most likely, the comparatively low demand can be attributed to uncertainties about the euro's exchange rate, which declined markedly in the currency's first years of existence. But the impact of EMU is already clearly evident on the borrowing side, where nonresidents have been attracted by the opportunity to tap into a much broader pool of savings. In bond and money markets, new foreign issues jumped sharply after the euro's introduction and have remained significantly higher than the share of EMU legacy currencies prior to 1999.[9] Equity issues have also grown substantially, while the euro share of international bank lending has risen by several percentage points. Comprehensive surveys of the euro's early days (Detken and Hartmann 2000, 2002; Danthine, Giavazzi, and von Thadden 2001; ECB 2001) agree that major changes are occurring in the European financial landscape.

Yet the question remains: Will Europe's structural improvements lower euro transactions costs enough to overcome the powerful conservative bias inherent in the dynamics of the marketplace? About that, legitimate doubts remain. Certainly much of the increase of business will come at the expense of the dollar, reducing the greenback's present margin of leadership. But in key respects the dollar's advantages will persist. For example, as Richard Cooper (2000) points out, it will be many years before the EU, with its separate national governments, can develop a universal financial instrument to rival the U.S. Treasury bill for exchange convenience and capital certainty. Likewise, the unique worldwide acceptance of the dollar, which the euro is still far from challenging, continues to make the greenback a far more attractive vehicle for currency trading. As noted in chapter 1, the dollar's role in the global foreign-exchange market remains dominant. Three years after its introduction, there was still no evidence of any significant increase in the euro's role as a vehicle for currency exchange, as compared with the pre-EMU share of the deutsche mark (Detken and Hartmann 2002, 564–66).

On balance, therefore, it seems likely that anticipated efficiency gains in Europe's financial markets, though substantial, will not suffice on their own to displace the greenback from top rank. Neither Detken and Hartmann (2000) nor Danthine, Giavazzi, and von Thadden (2001) found much evidence of reduced transactions costs immediately after the currency's introduction; indeed, for some categories of transactions, bid-ask spreads have actually increased over time relative to the corresponding spreads for the DM prior to EMU (ECB 2001; Goodhart et al. 2002; Hau, Killeen, and Moore 2002a, 2002b). In any event, no one expects that transactions costs for the euro will ever decline to a level significantly below those presently quoted for the dollar. Spontaneous market developments, therefore, will almost surely have to be reinforced by deliberate policy actions for the crown to pass securely to the euro. Again, Portes and Rey (1998, 310, 326) put the point most succinctly: "If they wish to promote the emergence of the euro as an international currency, European authorities must make the domestic euro financial markets more efficient, more integrated and cheaper for participants. . . . In the end, transactions costs on the euro market will depend on policy decisions."[10]

In short, the logic of competition tells us that, in terms of market forces alone, the only serious challenge to the dollar in coming years will be from the euro—in all likelihood not from the yen and most certainly not from any other existing national currency. Even for the euro, however, the outcome will be determined not just by market developments, but also by official policy actions. This brings us to the subject of state preferences. What policies can we anticipate from the Big Three governments at the peak of the Currency Pyramid—the United States, Euroland, and Japan?

State Choices

As indicated in chapter 2, there are good reasons to assume that a unilateralist strategy to maintain or enhance market position will be the preferred choice of the market leaders. Rational policymakers are hardly likely to turn their back on the considerable benefits to be derived from broader circulation of their currency. But a critical distinction must be drawn between two different kinds of leadership: *informal* and *formal*.

Given the stakes involved, there seems little doubt that the Big Three will all do what they can to sustain the underlying competitiveness of their currencies, with the objective of defending or promoting widespread use by *market* actors. Rivalry for market share—what we may call informal leadership—is natural in an oligopoly. It is less evident, however, whether any will be motivated to go a step further, to seek to influence the behavior of *state* actors, lending support to policy strategies of market followership—that is, to sponsor formation of an organized currency bloc, what we may call formal leadership. Will any of the leaders offer direct inducements to governments to encourage some form of dollarization? About this prospect there is more uncertainty, not least because the balance of benefits and costs implied by that extra step is not at all clear.

What is clear is that whatever one of the three rivals does is sure to be closely watched by the other two. Strategic interdependence of decision making is also natural in an oligopoly. Any move to promote formal leadership would transform the low politics of market competition, by definition, into the high politics of diplomatic confrontation. The risk is that policy maneuvering, in turn, could lead to increased tensions among the Big Three, particularly if currency initiatives were perceived to be encroaching on established regional relationships. Precisely for that reason, however, it is more likely that all three, ultimately, will act with restraint to avoid direct confrontations that could jeopardize more vital political and security interests. The safest bet is that currency rivalry will be restricted mainly to the realm of market transactions.

Informal Leadership

In the oligopolistic setting created by deterritorialization, both Euroland and Japan have obvious incentives to promote the competitiveness of their respective currencies—to "sell" their brand of money to as many potential users as possible. On the European side, the successful launch of EMU has created a golden opportunity to move up significantly in the Currency Pyramid. Conversely, on the Japanese side, recent setbacks have increased pressure to take defensive measures to prevent any further slide down in global ranking. The obvious target for both is the dollar, the incumbent Top Currency. Gains by the euro or yen need not necessarily mean losses for the United States in absolute terms; the game need not be strictly zero-sum. But success for either would almost certainly cost the greenback in relative terms, and Washington is unlikely to remain passive in the event of a substantial loss of market share. Overt actions on either side will almost certainly provoke U.S. countermeasures. Rivalry at the market level, therefore, could be intense.

Consider Europe, for example. Officially, European aspirations remain modest. According to authoritative statements by the European Central Bank, the development of the euro as an international currency—to the extent it happens—will mainly be a market-driven process, simply one of many possible byproducts of EMU. Euro internationalization, says the ECB, "is not a policy objective [and] will be neither fostered nor hindered by the Eurosystem. . . . The Eurosystem therefore adopts a neutral stance."[11] But these carefully considered words may be dismissed as little more than diplomatic rhetoric, revealing nothing. Behind the scenes it is known that there is considerable disagreement among European policymakers, with the eventual direction of policy still unsettled. Many in Europe are indeed inclined to leave the future of the euro to the logic of market competition. But many others, aware of the dollar's strong incumbency advantages, favor a more proactive stance to reinforce EMU's potential. Few Europeans are unaware of the many advantages that the United States derives from the greenback's perch atop the Currency Pyramid—what Charles de Gaulle famously denounced as America's "exorbitant privilege." The euro has long been viewed in some circles, particularly in France, as the EU's best chance to challenge the dollar's long-resented dominance.

Much more revealing, therefore, is not what the ECB says but what it does. Especially suggestive is the bank's controversial decision to issue euro notes in denominations as high as 100, 200, and 500 euros—sums far greater than most Europeans are likely to find useful for everyday transactions.[12] Why issue such large notes? Informed sources suggest that the plan may have been decided in order to reassure the German public, fearful of losing their beloved deutsche mark, that notes comparable to existing high-denomination DM bills would be readily available. But that is hardly the whole story. As knowledgeable experts like Kenneth Rogoff (1998) and Charles Wyplosz (1999) have observed, it is also likely that the decision had something to do with the familiar phenomenon of currency substitution: the already widespread circulation of large-denomination dollar notes, especially $100 bills, in various parts of the world. Market-driven dollarization translates conservatively into an interest saving for the U.S. government, a form of seigniorage earnings, of at least $15 billion a year (Blinder 1996)—not a huge profit but nonetheless large enough, apparently, to persuade EMU's authorities to plan on offering a potentially attractive alternative. As Rogoff (1998, 264) has written: "Given the apparently overwhelming preference of foreign and underground users for large-denomination bills, the [ECB's] decision to issue large notes constitutes an aggressive step toward grabbing a large share of developing country demand for safe foreign currencies." Europeans who favor more widespread use of the euro have openly applauded the plan. Writes one: "The United States is able to obtain goods and services by simply giving foreigners pieces of green paper that cost pennies to print. . . . There is no reason why the United States should monopolize these benefits" (Hüfner 2000, 25).

What more could Europe do, apart from issuing high-denomination notes? More international investments in euro bonds and stocks might be encouraged with selected tax incentives, including abolition of any withholding or reporting requirements. Likewise, greater cross-border use of the euro as a vehicle currency could be underwritten with targeted subsidies for European banks, lowering the cost of commercial credit for third-country trade. As indicated, much room remains for policy actions designed to reduce the cost of doing business in euros.

Or consider Japan, which has given every indication that it, too, intends to stay in the race, competing actively to preserve as much as possible of the yen's shrinking international role. Unlike the Europeans, the Japanese have been uncharacteristically frank in declaring their aspirations. Reversal of the currency's slide in standing was made an official policy objective in 1998 (Kwan 1999, 12; Hughes 2000, 249) and was given further impetus the next year by a widely publicized report of a Ministry of Finance advisory group, the Council on Foreign Exchange and Other Transactions (1999). Declared the Council (1999, 1–2): "Internationalization has not necessarily kept pace with what is warranted by the scale of the Japanese economy. . . . Recent economic and financial environments affecting Japan point to the need for the greater internationalization of the yen. . . . The question of what Japan must do to heighten the international role of the yen has re-emerged as a vital issue." Tokyo, like the British government after World War II, seems determined to resist its currency's decline even at the risk of skepticism or even ridicule.

Most emphasis has been placed on continued implementation of the Big Bang reform process, which, it is hoped, will eventually succeed in lowering yen transactions costs to levels more like those for the dollar or euro. Along the same lines, the government has also floated a plan to drop two zeros from the yen (Kwan 2001, 124–25), currently valued at over one hundred yen for either the dollar or the euro. Establishing a rough parity with the U.S. and European monies, Japanese authorities think, might also facilitate wider use of their currency. Simplifying the yen's denomination, said one official when the plan first came to light, "would be good for internationalizing and regaining trust in the yen."[13] Commented a foreign banker in Tokyo: "If there's a liquid market in dollars and a liquid market in euros, there's a risk of Japan becoming a sort of second-string market. . . . They don't want the yen to become the Swiss franc of Asia."[14] It is evident that Tokyo will not allow further erosion of its currency's standing without a fight.

How will Washington react to such competition? Officially, the United States remains unconcerned. Policy statements regarding prospective challenges from the euro or yen have been studiously neutral, avoiding provocation. EMU, for example, is said to be strictly Europe's business, not America's. "The emergence of the euro as an international currency should not be viewed with alarm," cautioned Bill Clinton's Council of Economic Advisers (1999, 297). "It is unlikely that the dollar will be replaced anytime soon" (299). But such words, too, may be dismissed as diplomatic rhetoric, concealing as much as they reveal. As Portes (1999, 34) observes, "It is difficult to believe that the American authorities are indifferent."

In fact, in Washington, too, there is considerable disagreement behind the scenes about what should be the eventual direction of policy. But much sentiment exists to respond in kind to any direct threat to the dollar's Top-Currency status. Introduction of the ECB's large-denomination bills, for example, has already generated a counterproposal to issue a rival $500 Federal Reserve note, designed to preserve America's seigniorage earnings abroad.[15] Japan's efforts to revive the yen are no less likely to arouse opposition and even irritation in Washington. As even a yen enthu-siast like David Hale (1995, 162) acknowledges, there is "a risk that [Jap-anese initiatives] will be interpreted as a threat by some Americans [and] could intensify the economic conflicts that are already straining U.S.-Japan relations." The probability is that aggressive policy measures from either Euroland or Japan will ultimately provoke countermeasures from Washington, with all of the Big Three doing what they can to maximize market use.

Formal Leadership

This does not mean, however, that any of them will necessarily go the next step, to seek to influence *state* behavior, lending direct support to policy strategies of market followership. As compared with the benefits of informal leadership, the additional gains from sponsoring a formal currency bloc could be considerable. But so, too, could be the costs, politi-cal as well as economic, making any prediction chancy. In fact no pre-sumption can be established either way, whether for or against policies to encourage some degree of official dollarization. Rational policymakers could be pulled either way.

Involved here are the same five factors that confront governments with less competitive currencies, as outlined in the previous chapter: transac-tions costs, macroeconomic stabilization, the distribution of seigniorage, political symbolism, and diplomatic influence. Except for the first of these factors, however, which offers an opportunity for mutual gain, the calcu-lus for market leaders is almost exactly the reverse of that for other coun-tries. Essentially, the remaining four factors are all in the nature of a zero-sum game, one side's gain being the other's loss. We know from chapter 1 that in inter-state relations, the market leaders can already be considered winners as a consequence of market-driven deterritorialization. The ques-tion is: How much more can be gained by formalizing the informal?

Some gain, of course, will come in the form of reduced transactions costs, as compared with a geography of separate territorial currencies. The use-fulness of money is enhanced for all its basic functions: medium of exchange, unit of account, and store of value. Opportunities for trade and investment, accordingly, could be enhanced. For market leaders, however, efficiency gains will be marginal at best, since even without a formalized relationship we can assume that in a world of accelerating currency competition much of their business with potential client states is *already* being conducted in their own money. Indeed, that is what deterritorialization means.

In fact, most of the benefit of transactions-cost savings will accrue to the residents of countries that are persuaded to give up attempts to preserve an uncompetitive national currency. For such countries exchange costs, by definition, will be eliminated when doing business with the market leader (or with any other economy using the leader's currency). Costs will also be reduced when doing business with third countries, where at present two transactions are typically required owing to a lack of direct bilateral markets in weaker local monies. First local money must be converted into one of the leading currencies, where large transactional networks make for lower transactions costs; and then the leading currency, in turn, must be converted into a third country's money. The economies of scale involved explain the disproportionately large vehicle role of the Big Three currencies in the global foreign-exchange market. Followership eliminates the need for the first of these two conversions, simplifying trade or investment transactions considerably.

More gain for leaders could come from the remaining four factors, though as also noted in chapter 1 much depends on possible offsetting risks whose probability cannot be easily estimated a priori. For example, we know from chapter 1 that more latitude for macroeconomic management will be provided insofar as formalization of followership adds to the effective range for equilibrating capital flows denominated in a leader's own money. The greater the degree of official dollarization abroad, the greater will be the gain of monetary autonomy at home. But there are also potential disadvantages that can hardly be ignored. Most salient is the possibility that by placing a larger share of a leader's currency in foreign circulation, official dollarization could eventually impose an awkward constraint on monetary policy. If money demand in a currency bloc turns out to be subject to sudden or frequent shifts, net cross-border flows would be generated that might increase the short-term volatility of domestic monetary aggregates. Such liquidity shocks would make it tougher for the leader's central bank to maintain a steady course over time. More remote is the possibility that at some point one or more dollarized states might suddenly decide to reintroduce a money of their own—to *de*-dollarize—precipitating a mass dumping of the leader's currency in global exchange markets. The result could be a serious depreciation, generating increased inflationary pressures.

Similarly, opportunities for seigniorage will be increased for a leader, particularly if foreign states elect to go the route of Ecuador and El Salvador. Near- or full dollarization means that a government must give up interest-bearing dollar reserves in order to acquire the currency notes and coins needed to replace local cash in circulation. The interest payments thus forgone represent a net savings for the market leader—a profit that, as we know, comes at the direct expense of dollarizing countries. On the other hand, we must also take into account the seigniorage that a market leader presumably already gains from the foreign circulation of its currency, owing to past currency substitution. The greater the degree of prior informal dollarization in potential client states, the smaller will be the additional transfer generated by formal dollarization. In addition, account must be taken of the cost of any provision that might be negotiated to compensate governments for their lost seigniorage, following the precedent of the CMA.

Status and prestige, too, will be enhanced if a market leader's money becomes the cornerstone of a formal currency bloc. "Great powers have great currencies," Robert Mundell once wrote (1993, 10). In effect the leader's money becomes a potent symbol of primacy, if not hegemony—an example of what political scientist Joseph Nye (1990) has called "soft power," the ability to exercise influence by shaping beliefs and perceptions. Symbols, however, can prove to be a double-edged sword, depending on circumstances. What in prosperous times may be accepted as benign, even natural, might become a focal point for protest in the event of recession or crisis. The dominant foreign government may be blamed for any failures of economic management at home. It is even possible to imagine local authorities deliberately fomenting popular protests as a way of diverting attention from their own policy errors. Prestige for the leader could come at a high price, creating an easy target for grievances.

Finally, in geopolitical terms, opportunities for direct diplomatic leverage will be amplified. Most forms of dollarization, from a currency board on up, signal a surrender of authority to a foreign central bank, making the dollarized country in effect a monetary client. The relationship is clearly hierarchical—a link of dominance and dependence—and hierarchy unavoidably implies a degree of vulnerability to influence or coercion from the leader. But this, too, is a sword that can cut two ways, since it might also become difficult for the leader to ignore adverse developments in the periphery of its own currency bloc. Even in the absence of any explicit commitments, dollarization may create an implicit expectation of future monetary bailouts—a kind of contingent claim on the leader's resources in the event of financial crisis or instability. Such an expectation is the flip side of the leader's enhanced political authority. With primacy, it may be argued, comes not only greater influence, but also, potentially, greater responsibility. Like it or not, the leader's policymakers could find themselves frequently under pressure to accommodate the specific needs or fragilities of clients. The central bank might be lobbied to take explicit account of the priorities of dollarized economies in setting policy goals—especially in the event of asymmetric payments shocks—or to open its discount window to local financial institutions. In time, dependent governments might even begin to campaign for indirect or even direct representation in the central bank's governing institutions, seeking in effect to convert from vertical regionalization to something more like a monetary alliance.

Generalization, therefore, is difficult. The calculus of benefits and costs for the market leaders is complex and, in most respects, inherently subjective, leaving a wide latitude for policy debate. A closer look at each of the Big Three suggests, however, that in the end the risk of outright conflict at the level of high politics is comparatively low.

The United States

Public debate has proceeded furthest in the United States where, as in Latin America, interest in dollarization has simmered briskly since Carlos Menem first broached the subject in early 1999. With the Argentine president's initiative, an idea that previously had been treated as little more than an intellectual curiosity now suddenly gained real political credence. Congressional hearings were convened, official statements were issued, and a lively debate has been carried on in the pages of the financial press. The central question is whether Washington should encourage or discourage other governments that might be thinking of emulating the examples of Ecuador and El Salvador. The central focus is on the Latin American region, which already exhibits a high degree of followership in its monetary relations with the United States.[16] Latin America is considered the most natural home for a formal dollar zone. Until now, however, U.S. policy has remained cautiously neutral—a strategy of "benign neglect," to borrow a phrase from an earlier era. That policy will most likely continue unless Washington feels seriously challenged by either of the other market leaders, Europe or Japan.

Pros and Cons

The terms of debate in the United States are fairly clear. On the affirmative side, advocates such as Robert Barro (1999) and Judy Shelton (1999) stress the economic advantages of dollarization—in particular, the potential for creating an improved environment for U.S. trade and investment in the Western Hemisphere.[17] This is not only a matter of reduced transactions costs, but also, even more importantly, a promise of increased stability in countries struggling to defend uncompetitive national monies. Latin American central banks, with their histories of high inflation and debauched currencies, do not enjoy a great deal of credibility. Adoption of the dollar, by contrast, would mean that loose monetary policy could no longer threaten renewed financial crisis. In the words of Michael Gavin (2000), a business economist, the monetary regime would now be "accident-proof," ostensibly removing a key impediment to development.

Steadier growth would mean faster growth, and this in turn would mean healthier markets for U.S. exports and direct investments. As Julie Katzman (2000, 208), another enthusiast, comments: "Dollarization would eliminate the cycle of boom and bust, inflation and recession, and overvaluation and devaluation. . . . This would simultaneously create a more secure market for U.S. goods and for U.S. companies who have become substantial players in the domestic economies of Latin America."

But would the monetary regime really be "accident-proof?" Dollarization addresses only one among many of the causes of economic instability in Latin America—ineffective monetary policy—but offers no direct corrective for other critical deficiencies, such as undisciplined budgetary policy, poor banking supervision, or labor-market rigidities. The hope is that with the straitjacketing of monetary policy, additional structural reforms would fall into place. But as economist Walter Molano has warned, that could be "just wishful thinking."[18] Molano continues: "Dollarization is a one-sided look at the problem. . . . Dollarization is not a solution to the institutional flaws that led to the crisis in the first place. It does nothing to shape the political will needed to sustain the exchange rate regime" (2000, 60). In short, too much faith may be invested in a single institutional innovation. Dollarization, summarizes Catherine Mann, "does not produce magic changes" (1999, 56). A case in point was provided by Argentina, where the straitjacket established by the currency board in 1991, limiting monetary policy almost as tightly as formal dollarization might have done, did not prevent the fiscal crisis that eventually caused the Argentine peso to collapse in 2002.

Besides, as many sources have noted (Sachs and Larrain 1999; Fontaine 2000; Rojas-Suarez 2000), Latin America's economies are by no means a natural fit for a monetary union with the United States. In more technical language, the Western Hemisphere is not self-evidently an optimum currency area. Apart from Mexico, few of America's southern neighbors are closely integrated with the U.S. economy or convergent with U.S. macroeconomic performance. All are commodity exporters, subject to wide swings in world demand and prices, whereas the United States is mostly a commodity importer. Moreover, most Latin American economies lack the degree of factor mobility and price flexibility needed to adjust smoothly to terms-of-trade volatility without the "shock absorber" that a flexible exchange rate can provide. Many, therefore, could find themselves experiencing more rather than less variance of real income over time. The market environment for U.S. business might turn out to be considerably less healthy than suggested.

On the negative side, opponents such as Robert Samuelson (1999) and Jane D'Arista (2000) stress the political disadvantages of a formal currency bloc—in particular, the risk of being forced to take responsibility for financial affairs throughout the Hemisphere.[19] Americans have long enjoyed a high degree of insularity in the making of monetary policy and would not welcome any obligation, however limited, to compromise domestic priorities for the sake of undisciplined, perhaps even ungrateful, foreigners. Granted, this course would also mean forgoing potential benefits, economic as well as political. But gains in any event might turn out to be marginal at best—their sacrifice, it is argued, would be a small price to pay to maintain the nation's traditional monetary autonomy. The risks associated with dollarization are said to be simply too great to contemplate. In Samuelson's (1999) words: "We are courting trouble if many countries dollarize. They would blame us for their problems; and they would try to influence U.S. policies. . . . Dollarization is a vast black hole. . . . We should discourage other countries from dragging us over the edge."

Much depends, though, on the counterfactual: What will happen in Latin America if the choice of dollarization is foreclosed? Several scenarios are possible, each corresponding to one of the three basic strategies available to regional governments. Easiest to imagine is a future in which governments seek to continue producing their own independent monies, as they have done in the past (market preservation). In that case, the risks of currency fragility and volatility would remain as salient as ever. Would the United States really be better off if its southern neighbors continue to suffer periodic bouts of financial crisis? Alternatively, some Hemispheric states might consider promoting monetary alliances on their own, on the model of EMU. In such an event, the United States would by definition avoid any responsibility but might also suffer a decline of status and influence in the region, as well as opportunities for seigniorage, as new joint currencies mature. Finally, a third possibility is that some countries, still preferring a strategy of followership, might decide to throw in their lot with Europe, adopting the euro in lieu of the dollar as a replacement for their own national monies. In that case, America's power and prestige would be even more directly challenged, this time by a strengthened European Union.

In the middle are observers such as Fred Bergsten (1999) and William Niskanen (2000), who defend benign neglect as an optimal policy compromise. The risks to monetary autonomy are acknowledged, but so, too, are prospects for considerable benefit. Why sacrifice advantages needlessly, it is asked, so long as no formal commitments are offered. Governments considering dollarization might be given moral support and perhaps some technical assistance, but otherwise could be left more or less on their own. Adoption of the greenback, they would be told, must be entirely unilateral, as has already occurred in Ecuador and El Salvador. By thus leaving the door open, rather than slamming it shut, the United

States can avoid any hint of responsibility for Latin American economies yet still hope to harvest potential gains. Effectively, Washington could have its cake and eat it, too.

But could it? The main drawback of a benign-neglect strategy involves an empirical question: How many states will actually be willing to transform themselves into a monetary client of the United States, with all the disadvantages implied, without some sort of formal quid pro quo? Ecuador, as we shall see in chapter 5, proceeded on its own only because of a massive financial collapse that seemed to leave Quito policymakers no plausible alternative, while El Salvador was simply too small to have much bargaining leverage in Washington. In both cases, the NC curve in the Choice Diagram (see fig. 1) was seen to have risen greatly in relation to DL. But the same may not be true elsewhere in the Hemisphere, other than, perhaps, in some of the smaller economies of Central America, the Caribbean, and the Andes. (I will have more to say on the preferences of potential followers in chapter 5.) The risk, from the U.S. point of view, is that so long as Washington's policy stance remains officially neutral, the number of countries that will ultimately choose some form of dollarization will not be large.

The Outlook

Despite such a risk, the prevailing policy of benign neglect has been forcefully defended by Washington officials. Both Federal Reserve Chairman Alan Greenspan and former Treasury Secretary Lawrence Summers went on record early to underscore their neutrality in the matter. "It is absolutely not our intention to close the door on consideration of this issue," Summers said at congressional hearings in April 1999.[20] But at the same time he and Chairman Greenspan made abundantly clear that nothing would be done to help underwrite dollarization efforts. On the contrary, governments were urged to look first to policy reforms at home. "There just is no substitute for sound policies," Greenspan cautioned (1999, 14). "If you try to create something out of nothing, you will end up not with something, but with nothing." There are few indications in the domestic politics of the United States to suggest the possibility of any significant change of policy in the near term.

Unlike more politicized issues of foreign economic policy, such as trade, dollarization has attracted remarkably little attention from domestic interest groups. Political cleavages on the issue, if they exist at all, remain greatly muted—though all that could of course change if more neighboring states seek to adopt Washington's money as their own. It is clear that a number of sectors can be expected to profit from dollarization, in particular those "integrationist" interests who, because of their heavy involvement in cross-border activity, would benefit from the elimination of exchange-rate risk. These include inter alia U.S. banks and other financial intermediaries, export and import interests, and portfolio investors. Conversely, there could also be some key losers—most prominently, blue-collar workers who might find themselves unemployed if dollarization encourages U.S. corporations to locate more production south of the border. In principle, therefore, we might expect vigorous lobbying efforts to develop on both sides of the issue, pro and con. Yet in practice such activity has been most conspicuous by its absence, suggesting that no group foresees much of a direct impact on its own material interests.

Most positively affected, in all likelihood, would be the financial sector. Earnings could be increased at U.S. banks, which are naturally advantaged relative to their rivals in dollarized countries by their privileged access to the resources of the Federal Reserve. These extra profits have been labeled "denomination rents" by economists, who have long recognized that international use of a currency disproportionately benefits financial intermediaries based in the country of issue (Swoboda 1968). Yet no evidence exists of any systematic campaign, public or private, by either individual institutions or representative associations to shape opinion on dollarization. A few finance professionals have spoken out in a personal capacity, some quite vigorously. But voices have been anything but uniform, with opinions ranging from highly enthusiastic (Gavin 2000; Katzman 2000) to firmly opposed (D'Arista 2000; Molano 2000). Nor has there been any formal response from the side of organized labor, despite the risk of lost jobs. "The AFL-CIO has no official position on dollarization," insists a former high union executive.[21]

Some public debate has occurred, in academic conferences and journals, congressional hearings, and the pages of leading newspapers and magazines. Yet here, too, voices have been anything but uniform, with few readily discernible patterns. Experts of a more conservative hue, who tend to put a high premium on monetary stability, do seem more inclined to favor dollarization (Barro 1999; Shelton 1999)—though for reasons that have more to do with the interests of potential dollarizers than with prospective gains for the United States. Their argument, simply put, is that central banks in Latin America cannot be trusted. Economies will be better off if instead they import their monetary policy from the Federal Reserve. But there are also noted conservatives who oppose dollarization (von Furstenberg 2000a, 2000b), while more liberal elite opinion is all over the map (Bergsten 1999; Frankel 1999; Samuelson 1999). Positions seem determined less by ideology or partisan affiliation than by the sheer subjectivity of personal judgments about prospective gains and losses.

Overall, therefore, the private sector appears unlikely to play much of a role in shaping U.S. policy. Given the lack of strong, coherent lobbies on either side of the issue, the outcome is more likely to be determined by preferences within the public sector than by pressures from outside it. Within the public sector, new initiatives could conceivably come from Congress. But lacking the stimulus of pressure from key constituencies, congressional leaders are more apt to await a signal from the executive branch before taking a stand one way or the other. Within the executive branch, in turn, it is most likely that the inclinations of the Treasury, along with the Federal Reserve, will prove decisive in setting the tone of policy. The Treasury and the Federal Reserve are the government's lead agencies on international monetary questions. Most other agencies defer to these two when it comes to matters of finance, which are seen as essentially technical, if not downright arcane, in nature.

The only exception could be the State Department, which is sure to take heed of the geopolitical advantages of dollarization. Why pass up a chance to help consolidate U.S. leadership in the Hemisphere? Most economists scoff at the relevance of such considerations. The words of former Council of Economic Advisers member Jeffrey Frankel are typical:[22] "I have to say that during my time in the U.S. administration and when subjects related to [dollarization] came up, I never heard anybody say, yeah, let's go for U.S. imperialism: That this would have foreign policy benefits. But I'm sure that there are political science types out there that would talk about that." But this is naïve. One does not have to be a "political science type" to recognize the State Department's bureaucratic interest in exploiting any opportunity for enhancing diplomatic leverage. Obviously no one—certainly no diplomat—is going to speak bluntly in favor of U.S. "imperialism," even in the privacy of policy councils. Foreign-policy specialists simply do not talk in such terms.[23] But neither is the department that is formally charged with responsibility for the nation's external relations apt to ignore any potential new instrument for the exercise of influence abroad. The real question is whether the State Department might actually gain much sway in the final shaping of policy. In fact, that is unlikely. The State Department rarely prevails on matters of international finance. Tradition in Washington has long assigned principal responsibility in this area to the Treasury and Fed.

And what can be expected of these two agencies? The policy priorities of Treasury and Fed are not entirely congruent, of course, owing to their differing institutional responsibilities and interests. But on this issue there appears to be little disagreement. A policy of benign neglect is entirely consistent with the revealed preferences of both agencies. Both are known to be cautious to a fault, loath to take any action that might destabilize financial markets. Fed Chairman Greenspan, as indicated, has already made clear his desire to avoid precipitous behavior. "We have to be very careful," he has said (1999, 16), "to distinguish whether in fact any change in our policy would make any difference at all." Nor have Summers' successors at Treasury shown any sympathy for a bold new initiative on dollarization, pro or con. On the contrary, the Bush administration's preference clearly is to maintain a hands-off policy toward monetary developments in Latin America, as its deliberate silence during the crisis that led to the collapse of Argentina's currency board eloquently testified.[24]

Of course, it is always possible that the Treasury and Fed are dissimulating. In the eyes of many Latin Americans, Washington's underlying ambitions are clear: to dominate the Hemisphere, economically and politically. If Greenspan and other policymakers resist the temptation to encourage neighboring governments publicly to adopt the greenback, it is only in order to avoid provoking anti-American reactions and to elude opprobrium should dollarization experiments go awry. Representative are the words of one Peruvian commentator (Schuldt 2003): "The U.S. government cannot intervene in the initial decision concerning official dollarization. . . . That could lead to a series of demands and accusations against the U.S., which will want to be avoided by all means. . . . However, we all know that . . . from an official American perspective [dollarization] seems to be an effective mechanism to fortify their hemispheric and world hegemony." Little evidence, however, exists to back up suspicions of this sort, which remain largely a matter of conspiratorial conjecture.

Among available strategies, therefore, the most likely outcome would appear to be continuation of the policy of benign neglect that has prevailed until now. Neither the Treasury nor the Fed will see any reason to forgo potential benefits. But neither will they have any appetite to assume undue risk. Prudence will almost certainly dominate decision making for the foreseeable future.

Seigniorage-Sharing

It is possible, of course, to think of circumstances in which U.S. policy might become more proactive. One possibility might be a prolonged downturn in America's domestic economy, which could lead policymakers to promote dollarization as a means of creating more assured markets for U.S. exports and investments. Another might be renewed financial crises in Latin America, which could enhance the attractions of an arrangement that promises greater stability of monetary conditions. Neither contingency, however, can be predicted with any degree of certainty.

Much more likely as a stimulus to new thinking would be an escalation of competition by one (or both) of the other market leaders, Europe or

Japan. Suppose either the Europeans or Japanese were to take overt measures to build a formal currency bloc, going beyond the less provocative low politics of cultivating market demand. If such an escalation were seen as seriously encroaching on any of America's established regional relationships, it would not be at all difficult to imagine a growth of enthusiasm in Washington for a more activist policy, offering specified incentives to encourage some degree of dollarization by potential clients.

What might those incentives be? Economist Guillermo Calvo (2000) has daringly proposed that dollarizing countries be offered seats at the Federal Reserve Board, first perhaps as observers but eventually as full voting members. Others have suggested providing some kind of financial safety net to be available in time of need. Not surprisingly, though, such ideas have won few fans in Washington. Given the importance that Americans traditionally attach to the autonomy of their monetary policy, foreign representation or access at the Fed would undoubtedly be widely resisted if proposed officially. It is difficult to imagine any commitments along these lines any time soon.

Easier to imagine would be some form of seigniorage-sharing, as advocated by voices both inside government (Mack 2000; Schuler and Stein 2000) and outside (Barro 1999; Gavin 2000). From a foreign government's point of view, the loss of seigniorage revenue is by far the most visible cost involved in dollarization. It also seems the least equitable since it reverts directly to the U.S. Treasury as a pure windfall gain. Why, Latin Americans are entitled to ask, should the wealthy United States profit at the expense of poorer neighbors? Should they not be entitled to reclaim at least a part of their forgone earnings as compensation for their surrender of monetary autonomy? Though dismissed by some as a "distant political prospect" (Sachs and Larrain 1999, 87), seigniorage-sharing could well find resonance with many Americans, who like to pride themselves on their sense of fair play. In the eyes of many, it is the sine qua non for a proactive strategy. As one source asserts (Katzman 2000, 213): "The U.S. decision on how to address this issue will give a clear signal of the support it intends to give to dollarization."

Seigniorage-sharing could be most easily accomplished simply by transferring to each dollarizing country all the cash greenbacks needed to replace local currency, as Barro (1999) has suggested. That way, governments could retain their existing dollar reserves. Not only would this enable them to continue to receive interest payments in the future. It would also leave them with resources to cope with possible liquidity or banking crises. Federal Reserve notes might be given as a pure gift—a one-time allotment to get the process started—or, in a close equivalent, could be sold to dollarizing countries at a price covering no more than the cost of printing (Niskanen 2000). But such an approach is opposed by others who fear the possibility, alluded to earlier, of future de-dollarization by one or more countries. Suppose some government were in fact to defect, reintroducing a currency of its own. In that case its entire supply of dollars would become available to be spent in the United States, representing a windfall gift of major proportions. To avoid that risk, notes might instead be offered initially as part of a formal exchange, either for the existing stock of local money in circulation—a straight currency swap (Gavin 2000)—or else for dollar-denominated, non-interest-bearing government bonds. Either way the United States would then hold a claim that could be used to absorb, if needed, a returning flood of greenbacks.

Alternatively, if dollar reserves were to be used initially to retire the local currency, Washington could commit to making regular future transfers to each dollarizing country calculated to replace some or all of the interest earnings forgone, as South Africa does in the CMA. For the United States a key, albeit unspoken, advantage of this approach is political. It provides a convenient instrument for the exercise of diplomatic influence. A suspension of transfers—or even merely a threatened cut-off—could suffice to persuade governments to avoid policies inconsistent with U.S. preferences. The main disadvantage is that it would inject the seigniorage issue squarely into Washington's annual budgetary process, where it might easily become a political football. At a minimum, there could be a potential for misunderstandings and partisan wrangling. At worst, it is possible to imagine a future Congress changing its mind altogether, voting to terminate any further compensation to dollarized economies.

The International Monetary Stability Act

Seigniorage-sharing was central to the failed International Monetary Stability Act—the most prominent legislative initiative yet proposed to support dollarization. The act was submitted in 1999 by Senator Connie Mack of Florida, then chairman of the Joint Economic Committee of the Congress. Informally dubbed the Mack Bill, the act called for annual rebates to dollarizing countries of up to 85 percent of all lost seigniorage (with the remaining 15 percent to finance rebates to countries that are already dollarized, such as Panama and Ecuador, and to help pay related costs of the Federal Reserve and Treasury). Governments would initially have used their own reserves to replace local currency in circulation. Seigniorage was then to be paid in the form of interest on a consol, a perpetual debt instrument, that would be issued as soon as the U.S. Treasury certified that a country's money supply was officially dollarized.[25] The measure's purpose, as Senator Mack emphasized, was quite self-consciously to promote adoption of the greenback. "It is time," he declared, "for the United States to show leadership and encourage dollarization."[26] Though reported out by the Senate Banking Committee on a voice vote in July 2000, the act was never debated by the full Senate and died at the end of the legislative session. A companion House version, sponsored by Representative Paul Ryan of Wisconsin, never made it out of committee; and a successor bill, introduced in the new 107th Congress in 2001, went nowhere.

Was the Mack Bill the best way to encourage dollarization? From a strictly U.S. perspective, there was still a risk that other responsibilities might be thought implicit in the legislation. Explicitly, the act provided that "the United States is not obligated to act as a lender of last resort to officially dollarized countries, consider their economic or financial conditions in setting monetary policy, or supervise their financial institutions." Yet not even such blunt wording might have proved sufficient to relieve pressures on Washington in the event of a crisis. Once having encouraged countries to adopt the greenback, could Washington really be expected to turn its back if any of them got into trouble?

Conversely, from the point of view of potential dollarizers, there seemed reason for concern about the uncompromising unilateralism built into the act. Certification of eligibility for seigniorage rebates was to be at the sole discretion of the U.S. Treasury secretary. Might the process be used to promote narrow U.S. interests? Among the considerations listed by the act was whether a country had opened its banking system to foreign competition. Such a provision clearly would have favored U.S. intermediaries because of their privileged access to the Federal Reserve, reinforcing the benefits they could naturally expect from dollarization. Certification could also have been withdrawn at any time, threatening to make the consols yet one more handy tool for the exercise of U.S. power. As much, ironically, was admitted by two of the act's biggest boosters, congressional staffers Kurt Schuler and Robert Stein, when they wrote that "the latitude that the Secretary has is one factor that should induce countries . . . to cooperate fully with the United States" (Schuler and Stein 2000, 8). In the words of an avowed critic of dollarization (von Furstenberg 2000b, 119):

> The consols to be issued to the dollarizing country may be declared null and void under certain conditions. These conditions are unlikely to remain fixed at the hands of the U.S. Congress and the administration when penalizing or pressuring an officially dollarized country becomes politically attractive for any reason. . . . Interest on the consols may also be attached under what could be a broadening list of conditions.

For many in the Hemisphere, dollarization would be more palatable if accomplished through a negotiated treaty, spelling out mutual rights and obligations, rather than exclusively at the pleasure of the United States.

But for many Americans, any sort of written agreement would only serve to heighten concern about future contingent claims on the U.S. government. A manageable balance between the sensitivities of the two sides would not be easy to find. In the meantime the most likely outcome, barring unforeseen circumstances, is a continuation of Washington's status quo of passive neutrality. Formal adoption of the greenback will not be actively discouraged, but neither is it likely to be aggressively encouraged—at least not in the absence of a serious challenge from Europe or Japan.

Europe

A challenge from Europe is certainly possible—but improbable. The Europeans, as indicated, will no doubt make every effort to promote the use of their new money at the market level. It is also evident that they will not discourage some form of official "euroization" by nearby governments, particularly in East-Central Europe and the Balkans. But none of this will trigger a more proactive policy in Washington unless the EU's aspirations appear to spread beyond its immediate neighborhood to regions more traditionally aligned with the United States, such as Latin America. The chances of a more aggressive scenario along those lines are slim at best.

That is not to say that there are no Europeans with global ambitions for the euro. Quite the contrary. Portes and Rey (1998), for example, plainly favor what they call the "big euro" scenario, where the euro would join the dollar as the peak of the Currency Pyramid. The dollar, they declare, "will have to share the number-one position" (1998, 308).[27] Similar sentiments are expressed by Gerhard Michael Ambrosi, a German economist, who asserts that "the self-interest of the Europeans . . . should work towards an orderly cohabitation of these two currencies" (Ambrosi 2000, 225). Even more explicit is Martin Hüfner, another German, who calls for active encouragement of euroization wherever possible—even as far away as East Timor. "Euroization," Hüfner (2000, 24) writes, "will play an important role in cementing the global importance of Europe's new currency."

These, however, are minority views. Most informed opinion in Europe accepts that there are limits to what might be regarded as the natural home for a formal euro zone.[28] Not even the European Central Bank (2001) expects an EMU bloc to develop beyond what it calls the "euro-time zone."

Some participants are obvious, such as the several currency enclaves that have long existed within the borders of the EU. These include Monaco, which previously used the French franc; San Marino and the Vatican, which previously used the Italian lira; and the unusual case of Andorra, which for centuries had granted legal-tender status to the currencies of both France and Spain (the joint guarantors of Andorran independence). All have already switched over to the euro. Euroization has been of the fullest degree, with token issues of local coins (Monacan francs, San Marino and Vatican lire, and Andorran diners) no longer permitted.[29]

Potential participants of course also include the reluctant trio of Britain, Denmark, and Sweden, all of which are expected one day to join their fellow EU partners in EMU. Informally, the euro has already begun to penetrate their monetary spaces. As one British observer has commented, "There may be those who want to keep Britain out of the euro, but you can't keep the euro out of Britain."[30] More distantly, non-EU neighbors Norway and Switzerland could be drawn in, as well, as circulation of the euro widens. Already, according to the *New York Times* (24 February 1999), Switzerland—completely surrounded as it is by EMU members—is quickly becoming a two-currency nation.

On a broader scale, an EMU bloc would also naturally include most if not all of the countries of East-Central Europe and the Balkans, many of whom have long aspired to membership in the EU itself. One jurisdiction, Montenegro, has already formally adopted the euro as its sole legal tender;[31] several economies are pegged to the euro via currency boards, including Bosnia and Herzegovina, Bulgaria, Estonia, and Lithuania; and most others in the region are more loosely linked. Some maintain basket pegs that give greatest weight to the euro; others have adopted systems of managed floating with the euro unofficially used as an anchor. Empirical studies demonstrate that there is already a high degree of followership in the monetary relationship between EMU and the Eastern European countries.[32] Momentum toward full euroization will only grow as EU enlargement proceeds. As Pier Carlo Padoan (2000, 101) suggests: "The case is easily stated. What matters is not 'if' but 'when.'" One source predicts that EMU will have some 18 members by 2007 and as many as 33 members a decade later (Walter 2002).

Indeed, for the EU, the problem is not whether to speed up euroization in East-Central Europe and the Balkans but rather to slow it down. An additional ten countries are set to join the EU in 2004, after years of arduous negotiations, and still more applicants remain in the queue.[33] Though all new entrants must commit to adopting the euro as a condition of EU membership, full participation in EMU will not occur automatically. Formally, after joining the EU, governments will first be obligated to meet a number of demanding conditions—the same so-called convergence criteria that were demanded of present participants before they, too, could become full partners in EMU. Under the Maastricht Treaty, four convergence criteria were specified, including tough restrictions on inflation, interest rates, fiscal deficits, and public debt. In addition, aspirants must participate successfully for a minimum of two years in a pegging arrangement to the euro known as the Exchange-Rate Mechanism (ERM 2).[34] Several of the candidate countries, however, have spoken openly of the possibility of adopting the euro unilaterally, as Ecuador and El Salvador did with the dollar, without waiting first to meet the Maastricht conditions. Why postpone the advantages of access to one of the Patrician Currencies of the world?

In Bulgaria, for instance, some prominent local economists launched Project Euro 2000, aimed at replacing the country's present currency, the lev, with the euro as quickly as possible (Angarski and Harsev 1999; Nenovski, Hristov, and Petrov, 2000). A popular website was created for the purpose of promoting euroization in Bulgaria.[35] At times, Estonia and Poland, too, have expressed keen interest in early euroization (*The Economist*, 1 June 2002, 69–70). The Slovenian government has argued that candidate countries should be given credit for a record of exchange-rate stability prior to joining the EU—and thus have the right to adopt the euro immediately rather than being forced to wait for two years (*The Economist*, 29 January 2000, 81–82). Similarly, the Polish government has suggested relaxing the Maastricht rules on fiscal deficits in order to ease the path to full EMU participation (*The Economist*, 7 December 2002, 68–69).

EU authorities, however, have been doing all they can to forestall a rush to the euro, mainly on the grounds that participation without adequate preparation could prove unmanageable, straitjacketing governments at just the time when flexibility will be most needed. Strains could arise due to changing economic structures and shifts in monetary demand, as well as sizable and possibly volatile capital flows and differential growth trends in productivity.[36] In the words of the European Commission, "attempts at too early adoption of the euro [could be] highly damaging."[37] A gradual approach has been forcefully advocated by both the Council of Ministers and European Parliament. In November 2001, EU heads of government formally insisted that candidate countries should follow the prescribed path. In public, the European Central Bank is more equivocal, suggesting that candidates could adopt the euro if they wish so long as they understand that the ECB would not be obligated to take them into account when making policy. In private, monetary officials are more adamant, worrying about the impact that unilateral euroizations might have on their control of the supply of euros in circulation. The last thing they want at this stage is to be burdened with responsibility for underwriting still underdeveloped and fragile banking systems.[38]

Whatever the rate of momentum, though, the United States is unlikely to take offense as long as this is as far as European aspirations go. Washington has never questioned the EU's privileged interests in what is universally acknowledged as its own backyard. As Wyplosz (1999, 89) writes, "This is the euro's turf." Indeed, the United States might even be inclined to prod the Europeans along, encouraging more positive support for euroization in candidate countries insofar as it promises to bring greater stability to a potentially volatile region. As Randall Henning (2000, 18) has observed: "The consolidation of the monetary union contributes to economic and political stability in Central and Eastern Europe. . . . If the monetary union were to fail, Central and Eastern Europe would probably be considerably less stable. . . . As a consequence, U.S. manpower and resource commitments would have to be correspondingly greater. This geopolitical consideration is profoundly important for U.S. foreign policy."

Might Europeans aspire to go further? Beyond Europe's backyard, an EMU bloc could conceivably also be extended to include countries of the Mediterranean region and sub-Saharan Africa, most of which have close economic and political linkages with the EU. These are euro–time zone countries, too. Some of their currencies are already pegged to the euro, including most prominently the CFA franc, for which Europe's new money has seamlessly taken over the anchor role previously played by the French franc; and many others, even if not formally linked, show a relatively high degree of covariance with the euro (Bénassy-Quéré and Lahrèche-Révil 1999). Though none of these nations, apart from the special case of Turkey, has any realistic chance of being considered for future EU membership, all could be receptive to some limited degree of euroization, perhaps in the form of a currency board or bimonetarism. (Again, I will have more to say on the preferences of potential followers in chapter 5.) But there has been little public discussion of the subject in Europe, outside the specialized research literature,[39] and no evidence of any serious effort to mobilize opinion to favor offering formal support for strategies of market followership.

Even less does there appear to be any sentiment for looking further afield, outside the euro–time zone, say to Middle Eastern oil exporters, Latin America, or Asia. In fact, European authorities are generally agreed that they already have more than enough on their plate, coping with the EU's impending enlargement. A confrontation with America over formal currency leadership is the last thing they are looking for.

Japan

From Japan, by contrast, the chances of a challenge are higher. The reason is simple: the Japanese have more to lose. The euro, clearly, is a currency on the rise. Even if European authorities do nothing, an EMU bloc will continue to coalesce as a natural result of EU enlargement. The yen, on the contrary, is a money in retreat. If Tokyo does nothing the yen's slide could become irreversible, even in East Asia, a region that the Japanese prefer to think of as their own backyard. It is difficult to imagine that Tokyo will accept such a loss of status without a struggle. But it is also difficult to imagine that any Japanese challenge would be carried to the point of open confrontation with the United States, which has its own established relationships in the Asian region. There are good reasons to believe that tensions between the two governments on currency matters, though almost certainly unavoidable, will not be unmanageable.

Historically, as noted in the previous chapter, Japanese policymakers were long ambivalent about the desirability of a yen bloc, fearing especially the increased constraints that might be imposed on the autonomy of domestic monetary policy. More recently, however, as the yen's international standing has eroded, the weight of opinion has clearly swung toward a more favorable view, stressing advantages rather than disadvantages.[40] The change is fundamental, as I suggested in *The Geography of Money* (1998, 163), part of a broader and more far-reaching transformation that has gradually taken place in public attitudes toward Japan's place in the world—a coming of age, as it were. For a new generation of politicians—best symbolized by the appointment of reformist Junichiro Koizumi as prime minister in 2001—the time has arrived to "normalize" the country's international status by assuming more of the roles of a great power (Green 2001). One of those roles, it is assumed, is leadership of a currency zone. In the words of one informed source (Castellano 1999, 5): "Success at internationalizing the yen would be tantamount to achieving greater political prominence. . . . [It is] a bid to expand Japan's global political influence."

In fact, Japanese officials have made no secret of the fact that their aspirations now extend well beyond mere informal currency leadership. The best defense for a beleaguered yen, they seem to have decided, is a strong offense. Promoting the currency's market competitiveness is of course regarded as an imperative given the yen's dwindling standing, even in Asia where the dollar is still more widely used for most purposes.[41] But greater market appeal only begins to define the Japanese government's ambitions, as a variety of sources attest.[42] Beyond "selling" its brand of money to market users, Tokyo seems intent on "selling" it to neighboring governments, too—in short, to do what it can to build a formal bloc— even though this would unavoidably come at the expense of America's dollar. Few regional governments, as yet, seem prepared to "buy" the yen in the sense of full adoption—"yenization?"—or even in the form of a currency board or bimonetarism. (Again, this is a subject for chapter 5). But in Japanese official circles, it is apparently not regarded as unrealistic to hope that neighbors might be persuaded, at a minimum, to anchor their exchange rates to the yen and to make the yen their principal reserve currency, displacing the greenback. Efforts along these lines have persisted despite the risk of provoking Washington.

In 1996, for example, Japan signed a series of swap agreements with nine Asian governments to lend their central banks yen if needed to help stabilize exchange rates. Though the United States offered no criticism at the time, informed sources had little doubt that these pacts were deliberately designed to increase Japanese influence among members of a putative currency zone. "It's a manifest attempt to take leadership," said one bank economist in Tokyo.[43]

Japan's biggest opportunity came a year later, in mid-1997, when the great Asian financial crisis began, triggered by a collapse of Thailand's currency, the baht. Soon nearly every economy in the region came under pressure from investor panic and capital flight—a contagion of "bahtulism," as some grimly quipped.[44] In September 1997, Tokyo seized the occasion to propose a new $100 billion regional financial facility, quickly dubbed the Asian Monetary Fund (AMF), to help protect local currencies against speculative attack.[45] This time Washington's reaction was much stronger since, by shutting out the United States, the AMF would have gone far to institutionalize Japanese dominance in Asian currency relations. The prospect frankly dismayed U.S. officials. As *The Economist* (27 September 1997, 80) dryly commented, "the Americans were highly dubious of any initiative that did not include them" and fought successfully to get the proposal blocked.

The Japanese denied any ulterior motives. Said one Japanese diplomat, "We don't want to establish a regular organization that will be seen as antagonistic."[46] Indeed, there is indication that the exclusion of the United States was at least partly the result of a misreading of Washington's intentions by Japanese officials.[47] At the outset of the Asian crisis, when the baht first came under attack, the United States was most notable by its absence from the rescue initiative put together by Tokyo and the IMF. The explanation had to do mostly with domestic politics in the United States, where following an earlier rescue of Mexico in 1994 a critical Congress had imposed restraints on U.S. participation in future crisis-management efforts (Henning 1999). From that precedent, Japanese policymakers appear to have concluded that they had little choice but to move ahead on their own without help from Washington.

The American side, however, was not convinced of Tokyo's innocence and regarded all protestations to the contrary as disingenuous. The *New York Times* (28 September 1997) quoted Robert Rubin, then U.S. Treasury secretary, as charging that an "Asia-for-Asians fund" would undermine American interests in the region. Above all, Washington was concerned about a possible challenge to the IMF's central role in monetary affairs. Any threat to the fund was also a threat to the leadership of the United States, as the institution's largest member. Washington has long regarded the IMF, in the words of one Treasury policymaker, as "a convenient conduit for U.S. influence."[48] Officials were determined to avert any weakening of America's local predominance. As Richard Higgott (1998, 346) summarizes: "Viewed through American eyes, a successful AMF was not consistent with overall U.S. interests. It would have reinforced the trend . . . of the Japanese replacement of the U.S.A. as . . . the major force . . . in the region. For many in the U.S. foreign economic policy-making community, the AMF seemed like a potential first step towards a yen zone."[49]

Nonetheless, despite economic troubles at home and the steady repatriation of private investments from abroad, Tokyo has persisted in seeking new ways to promote its regional currency role. In October 1998, then Finance Minister Kiichi Miyazawa offered some $30 billion in fresh financial aid for Asia in a plan soon labeled the New Miyazawa Initiative;[50] and more recently, in May 2000, agreement was reached on a planned new network of swap arrangements with Asian nations, named the Chiang Mai Initiative, after the town in Thailand where negotiations took place.[51] Because both initiatives were confined to the so-called ASEAN + 3 (the ten nations of ASEAN plus China, Japan, and Korea), with no explicit part for the United States, many see them as further affirmation of Tokyo's continued interest in creation of an exclusive yen bloc—subtle attempts to achieve the aims of the AMF by incremental means while avoiding the politically more provocative step of establishing a formal institution.[52] As such initiatives multiply, tensions with Washington seem set to continue, perhaps even to grow.

Tension, however, is not the same as conflict. Tokyo may aspire to assume more of the role of a great power, but almost certainly not at the expense of the broader political and security relationship that it has long enjoyed with the United States. "The bilateral relationship with the United States," writes one expert," is the indispensable core of Japan's position in the world. . . . On issues of fundamental interest to the United States, Japan remains deferential and cautious" (Green 2001, 3–4). In fact, a delicate balancing act is involved, as students of Japanese foreign policy have long understood (Vogel 2002). As another specialist comments, "The underlying Japanese strategy has always been to maintain economic dominance in East Asia, but at the same time it has aimed to keep the USA . . . engaged economically and politically in the region."[53] This delicate balance is well illustrated by the Chiang Mai Initiative, which is directly premised on IMF involvement—and thus indirectly assumes a part for the United States, the fund's most influential member—as a condition for assistance.

Nor can Japan ignore the threat of an emergent China looming on the horizon, which increases even more the value of preserving a special relationship with Washington. China has already gained a good deal of diplomatic clout throughout East Asia as a result of its rapid economic expansion in recent years and shows every sign of intending to challenge Japanese aspirations for regional leadership.[54] "For all the countries in Asia," says one U.S. specialist, "China is such a large force, the only rational response is to figure out how to work with it. It can't be stopped."[55] Resistance to the Chinese juggernaut would be especially difficult without backing from the Americans.

Tokyo, in short, has no interest in alienating its most powerful ally. Nor is Washington eager to jeopardize a decades-old relationship that is still valued highly for the stability it helps bring to a troubled part of the world. Both sides can be expected to continue to maneuver for advantage in Asian finance. But neither is likely to let their monetary rivalry get out of control.

Conclusion

Overall, then, life at the peak of the Currency Pyramid promises to be competitive—but within limits. Rivalry at the level of informal leadership, aiming to influence the preferences of market actors, will be intense. But there is little in the record to suggest that the low politics of market competition is likely, any time soon, to be transformed into the high politics of diplomatic confrontation. For its part, the United States will not abandon the benign neglect of its dollarization policy unless seriously challenged for formal leadership by either Europe or Japan. For their part, neither the Europeans nor the Japanese appear to have any appetite for overt currency conflict with Washington. None of the Big Three, therefore, should be expected to offer direct inducements of any significance to alter the incentive structures facing other governments (with the possible exception of Japan in East Asia). In thinking about the tricky choice they face among the options of monetary preservation, followership, or alliance, most states will find themselves more or less on their own.

Four

The Art of Survival

LEFT TO THEIR own devices, most governments would instinctively prefer to go on producing their own money—the default strategy of market preservation. But that ignores the *cost* of defending a state's monetary sovereignty, which we know is being pushed upward by the pressure of cross-border competition among currencies—especially for countries with monies near the bottom of the Currency Pyramid. In terms of the Choice Diagram (see fig. 1), the key issue is the position of the NC curve. Can the cost of maintaining a national currency be kept from rising significantly relative to either DL or MA? Available options, as indicated in chapter 2, include tactics of either persuasion or coercion. As deterritorialization accelerates, many governments will find it increasingly difficult to practice the demanding art of survival.

Persuasion and Coercion

Tactics of persuasion are natural in an oligopoly, where competition compels suppliers to seek to manage the demand side of the market—to "sell" their product to as many users as possible. In an industrial oligopoly, rival firms may enhance the appeal of their products via price cuts, quality improvements, aggressive advertising, or any number of similar marketing devices. In the global arena, states can try to do the same by investing in their money's reputation, acting to reinforce the attractiveness of a currency for any or all of the usual monetary purposes. The idea is to enhance confidence in the money's continued usefulness and reliability— the "confidence game," to recall Paul Krugman's (1998a) name for it. The label is ironic because, as in any con game, the effort to play may prove an exercise in futility.

Until recently, the element of oligopoly in currency relations was not widely recognized.[1] Today, however, as the deterritorialization of money spreads, the parallel between currencies on the one hand and goods sold under registered trademarks on the other has become unmistakable. As economist Robert Aliber quips (2002, 106), "the dollar and Coca-Cola are both brand names." Dollarization advocate Judy Shelton is no longer a rare exception in remarking on the imperative of producing "better products" in a world of currency competition. "To out-perform rivals," she has written, "a money producer would have to offer the public a better brand of money than the competitors" (Shelton 1994, 231).

The element of brand-name competition in currency relations is by no means exceptional. In fact, in today's rapidly globalizing world economy, state branding is increasingly becoming an imperative of foreign policy. As one source observes (van Ham 2001, 3–4): "Globalization and the media revolution have made each state more aware of itself, its image, its reputation, and its attitude—in short, its brand. . . . Smart states are building their brands around reputations and attitudes in the same way smart companies do." Money is just one of the more visible signals of the rise of the "brand state." As Aliber summarizes (2002, 106, 108): "Each national central bank produces its own brand of money [and] has a marketing strategy to strengthen the demand for its particular brand of money."

Demand may be strengthened in several ways. Most narrowly, as noted in chapter 1, currency policy may be transformed into an exercise in political symbolism. The competitive success of a more attractive foreign money can be treated as the equivalent of a military invasion, calling for allegiance to the local currency as an act of patriotism. This was, for example, one of the tactics adopted by Indonesia when the national currency, the rupiah, came under attack at the outset of the Asian financial crisis in 1997. Public-service advertisements appeared showing a currency trader wearing a terrorist mask made of U.S. $100 bills. "Defend the rupiah," the notices urged. "Defend Indonesia." In the end, however, Jakarta's campaign notably failed, suggesting that such a gambit is unlikely to suffice to restore confidence in a currency in the absence of other more substantive policy actions.[2]

Beyond exhortation, use of a money might be encouraged by special tax advantages, convertibility guarantees, or higher rates of return on selected assets. More broadly, governments can try to promote acceptance by facilitating expansion of a money's transactional network—as, for example, both the Europeans and Japanese are doing by promoting development of asset markets denominated in their own currency to enhance exchange convenience and capital certainty. Most fundamentally, a money's reputation may be buttressed by a credible commitment to "sound" macroeconomic management. "Sound" in this context is generally understood to stand for a strong emphasis on stability, promising the qualities of low inflation and inflation variability that are so prized in the Darwinian struggle among monies. For most governments, playing the confidence game means acquiescing to the redistribution of power in monetary governance, from states to markets, that was described in chapter 1. Highest priority is placed on placating the preferences of societal actors with the capacity and opportunity to choose among alternative currencies.

The advantage of such an approach is that it enables governments to preserve at least some of the advantages of a national monetary monopoly—in particular, the political benefits of symbolism and insulation. The country's currency survives to continue promoting a sense of national identity, and policymakers are still able to hold down exposure to foreign influence or coercion. The economic goal of an integrated and coherent national market is also facilitated. But there are two distinct disadvantages, as well, both essentially economic in nature and each quite serious. One is a limit on a government's access to seigniorage, a constraint on fiscal policy. The other is a limit on a government's flexibility in managing prices and interest rates, a constraint on monetary policy. Both limits are regarded as imperatives of "sound" management—the price to be paid for defending a currency's reputation—and both tend to raise the height of the NC curve.

The constraint on fiscal policy stems from past abuses of a state's "revenue of last resort." Rational market agents are unlikely to be attracted to the currency of a government that cannot seem to resist the temptation to willfully exploit the seigniorage privilege, which so often results in depreciation of a money's value. Not for nothing has the process earned the unflattering sobriquet "inflation tax." If states wish to rely on persuasion to sustain market loyalty, therefore, they must practice a kind of fiscal self-denial—a "patience for revenue," as one economist puts it (Ritter 1995, 134)—voluntarily limiting the amount of public spending that is financed via money creation. Though seigniorage remains available in principle, it must be largely forsworn in practice. But such forbearance will clearly be costly for governments with underdeveloped revenue systems or that may be confronted with frequent unexpected emergencies.

Similarly, the constraint on monetary policy stems from past abuses of a state's capacity to stimulate the overall pace of economic activity. Rational market agents are unlikely as well to be attracted to a currency that appears to be overused for expansionary purposes, a practice that can also result in depreciation of value. States wishing to rely on persuasion must therefore practice a kind of monetary self-denial, too, stressing price stability above all in management of the supply of money and credit. But that, too, will be costly to governments if it results in slower growth or higher unemployment.

Together, these two constraints impose a discipline on policy that, once introduced, will be difficult to remove. Reputation is not something that can be enhanced quickly, and certainly not without substantial, sustained effort. As one source has commented, "Monetary confidence cannot be created overnight [and] is not a free good" (Melvin 1988, 440). Peter Aykens (2002) distinguishes three stages in the difficult process of trust development: (1) "momentary trust," based on calculations of risk resting solely on immediately available information; (2) "reputational trust," derived from growing familiarity and experience; and finally (3) "affective trust," representing stable and unquestioned sets of expectations. Only when the final stage of affective trust is attained—the end-product of a long process of social interaction and learning—can a government feel that it has truly won the confidence game. But getting to that stage, if it is feasible at all, will normally require considerable time as well as, possibly, a good deal of pain.

Reputation is also something that is much easier to destroy than to build, given the market's constant vigilance. Financial markets, says banker Walter Wriston (1998, 340) approvingly, are like "a giant voting machine that records in real time, real world evaluations of . . . currencies." While trust is being built, market actors are understandably sensitive to even the slightest sign of recidivism by governments. A commitment to "sound" management, therefore, once undertaken, cannot be easily relaxed. States cannot let down their guard even for a moment if they are to succeed in establishing a successful brand name for their money.

Monetary discipline is of course by no means undesirable, as any victim of past policy excesses can attest. Cross-country studies clearly indicate, over the long term, a strong negative relationship between inflation and growth, particularly at more elevated inflation rates.[3] High and variable price increases can destroy savings, distort incentives, and depress productive investment. Living standards will surely suffer.

But what about the shorter term, measured in years rather than decades, which is the time-horizon of more relevance to most policymakers? Governments wishing to maintain their money's reputation are usually urged to exercise strict policy discipline. Above all, this is the theme stressed by the International Monetary Fund when approached by countries with troubled currencies. Tight control of monetary and fiscal policy—what Krugman (2001b) calls "root-canal economics"—is central to the adjustment programs demanded by the IMF in return for its financial assistance. But does it necessarily follow that an abrupt shift to "sound" management will soon lead to rising prosperity? Empirical analysis suggests otherwise, indicating that IMF programs actually tend to lower growth rates significantly, even after program participation comes to an end (Przeworski and Vreeland 2000). Even the IMF's own economists acknowledge "it is possible that the process of disinflation may—at least in the short run—depress GDP growth."[4] Disinflation may also lead to greater income inequality and increasing numbers of families below the poverty line (Madrick 2001).

The problem with root-canal economics, recalling the last chapter's discussion of dollarization, lies in the many structural deficiencies that can inhibit an economy's ability to adjust quickly or smoothly to a more con-

THE ART OF SURVIVAL

strained policy environment. Monetary stabilization, to repeat, does not produce magic changes. The main result may well be not faster growth but, rather, the searing pain of recession and perhaps even prolonged stagnation. Journalist Thomas Friedman (1999) calls the market's discipline a "golden straitjacket" because it is expected ultimately to yield a positive payoff. This optimistic view, however, presumes that economies can move swiftly to produce new jobs as disinflation takes hold—an heroic assumption at best. As the noted economist Joseph Stiglitz (yet another Nobel laureate) remarks, "it is easy to destroy jobs" but far more difficult to create them. "Few economists have believed in instantaneous job creation, at least since the Great Depression" (2002, 59). The reality in many countries is that stabilization does little more than impart a persistent deflationary bias to policy. Monetary discipline may be necessary for sustained growth, but it is certainly not sufficient. The golden straitjacket may never yield a payoff.

Indeed, quite the reverse may be true as the deterritorialization of money spreads, offering societal actors an increasingly wide choice among currencies. The easier it is for market agents to move from one money to another, the more pronounced will the deflationary bias of policy have to become in order to remain effective. The Choice Diagram's (see fig. 1) NC curve will be pushed ever higher, particularly for countries whose monies are near the bottom of the Currency Pyramid. Worse, the goal itself may prove illusory, owing to the subjective nature of the very notion of confidence. If, as indicated in chapter 1, the interdependencies of decision making involved in currency choice create the possibility of multiple equilibria, no one can really know what policies will persuade the market. As Dani Rodrik (1999, 118) writes: "If market confidence comes only after sound policies are followed and sound policies are defined as policies that trigger confidence, financial markets . . . can, in principle, converge on any arbitrary set of policies." The game may indeed turn out to be a con.

Credibility, in short, does not come cheap. To be persuasive to market actors, states must literally put their money where their mouth is—and even then, they may not be successful in defending market share. Playing the confidence game is frustrating and can indeed prove futile, The issue is: Is the game worth the candle? As Krugman (1998a) summarizes the dilemma: "The perceived need to play the confidence game supercedes the normal concerns of economic policy. It sounds pretty crazy, and it is. . . . Isn't there a better way?"

If there is a better way, it can only lie in the direction of coercion, the alternative to tactics of persuasion. In principle, monetary sovereignty can also be managed by using the formal powers of the state, the government's legal right to coerce, to limit the degree of competition between home and foreign money. In practice, this means imposing some form of restriction on the ability of market actors to choose between currencies—in short, *capital controls*.[5] Capital controls are highly controversial, advocated by some, abhorred by others.

Do controls offer a better way? In fact, three questions are involved. First, should such interventions be used at all? Second, if they are in fact used, will they be less costly than the confidence game? And third, even if they are less costly, will they be any more successful than the confidence game in keeping the NC curve from rising over time? While the answer to the first question is clearly in the affirmative, the answer to the second is uncertain, and the answer to third, regrettably, is in the negative. Coercion, in some circumstances, *may* offer a better way than persuasion, but over time will be no more effective than the golden straitjacket in holding down the cost of maintaining a national currency.

Legitimacy

First, should capital controls be used at all? In the opinion of many, controls cannot be considered a legitimate policy instrument for purposes of monetary governance because they are seen as violating deeply held political values. Despite such concerns, however, expert opinion today is on balance increasingly receptive to the use of selective restraints in certain circumstances.

Political Values

As instruments of political authority, capital controls are said by many to be intrinsically incompatible with standard norms of democracy. In the words of economist David Hale (1998a, 11), "capital controls represent a form of command economy intervention which could have implications for a country's political freedom, not just its economic freedom." Journalist Samuel Brittan (1998) puts the point even more bluntly: "The most basic argument against exchange control . . . is that it is one of the most potent weapons of tyranny which can be used to imprison citizens in their own country." Controls, in short, destroy liberty.

Underlying this view, which may fairly be described as libertarian, is a basic distrust of government. Libertarians celebrate all limitations on political behavior imposed by the decentralized decision making of the marketplace. For them, the market serves two valuable functions. It disperses power in society and also provides a potent counterweight to the awesome authority of the state. Deterritorialization of money, therefore, is a good thing because it promotes individual choice. Are we not all better off if states are deprived of their monopoly and forced to act as oligopolists, competing keenly with one another for the allegiance of market actors? Moreover, libertarians insist, markets are inherently democratic because they reflect the attitudes and decisions of millions of individual transactors, functioning in effect as a sort of perpetual opinion poll—Wriston's giant voting machine. Conversely, controls are a bad thing because in place of market rationality, we would be subject to the arbitrary actions of public officials. We should all fear a governance structure that takes power from the people.

It is obvious, of course, that the power inherent in capital controls could be abused. Restraints on currency choice are highly attractive to policymakers for self-interested reasons.[6] Controls make it easier to exploit the seigniorage privilege to underwrite public spending. Resources can be willfully extracted from the private sector via inflationary money creation. They also can be used to protect a government's formal revenue base by closing off opportunities for tax avoidance. Nonetheless, the libertarian perspective is seriously deficient in two key respects, as I noted in *The Geography of Money* (1998, 147–49). It neglects issues of both equity and accountability.

First, it is true that cross-border competition among currencies gives many societal actors more power in relation to potentially abusive government: the right to switch monies if they disapprove of official policy. But such votes are distributed not by individuals—the traditional One Person, One Vote—but by wealth. The notion of equality before the law is thus violated if not fatally compromised. In the words of the economist Arthur Okun (1975, 29), writing of the "big trade-off" between the principles of democracy and capitalism, "money transgresses equal political rights." Those with the most money have the most votes. Such a skewed franchise is actually quite inconsistent with standard norms of democracy.

Worse, there is less accountability in a system of governance that gives as much influence to a select set of market agents as it does to elected officials. As an approach to political rule, such a regime may be regarded as regressive or even pernicious, insofar as it subverts the will of the general electorate. Politicians may be ineffectual or unsavory, but in many countries—certainly in representative democracies—they are supposed to govern with the consent of the governed. In other words they can, at least in some degree, be held accountable for their actions. Market agents, by contrast, are neither elected nor politically accountable, and they may not even be citizens. If the will of the majority, however poorly refracted through the lens of representative government, can be thwarted by the economic power of an anonymous minority, democracy itself is threatened.

At the level of principle, therefore, freedom of currency choice enjoys no special advantage in contrast to controls. Indeed, insofar as they are the product of a representative government, controls might arguably be defended as potentially *more* consistent with accepted notions of equity and accountability.

Taken to its logical conclusion, the libertarian perspective denies the very purpose of the state, which in a Westphalian world is uniquely the embodiment of legitimate coercive authority. In fact, governments violate personal liberty all the time in the name of serving a greater good. What libertarians conveniently neglect is that markets are social constructs that can function efficiently only in a context of agreed standards and rules; and these standards and rules, normally, require the enforcement powers of the state. The dichotomy between the market and politics is a false one. State coercion is essential to overcome critical collective-action problems and to provide needed public goods, such as a functioning judiciary to ensure respect for property rights. Freedom is not absolute, and not all state intervention is an arbitrary form of tyranny. Indeed, markets may exercise a form of tyranny of their own, as they surely do for countries choosing to play the confidence game. Controls may thus appeal as a possible corrective to protect the well-being of the national community.

In any event, the right of governments to regulate monetary use is well established in international law and practice. Interventions began in the nineteenth century with such familiar devices as legal-tender laws and public-receivability provisions. The Westphalian model of monetary geography, after all, did not come into existence by persuasion alone. Capital controls, which were first invented during the Great Depression, were a natural extension of that same tradition. In broadest terms, they could be regarded simply as a logical corollary of a currency strategy of market preservation. As one source concludes, summarizing the results of a study by prominent mainstream economists, "Capital controls are not tangential but fundamental elements of economic policy and management" (Ries 1997, 1).

Historical Perspective

In fact, once invented, capital controls soon became quite fashionable despite their heretical violation of traditional free-market principles. Many observers fail to remember that the original design of the International Monetary Fund, negotiated in 1944 at Bretton Woods, New Hampshire, did not actually call for unlimited currency choice. Quite the contrary. Reflecting an abhorrence for the sort of "hot-money" flows that had so destabilized monetary relations in the 1920s and 1930s, the Fund's charter made explicit allowance for the preservation of capital controls.

Virtually everyone involved in the Bretton Woods negotiations agreed with the influential League of Nations study, *International Currency Experience* (Nurkse 1944, 188), that some form of protection was needed against the risk of "mass movements of nervous flight capital." The option of controls, therefore, was explicitly reserved to the discretion of national governments, provided only that restraints might not be intended to restrict international commerce.[7] The idea was to afford governments sufficient policy autonomy to promote stability and prosperity at home without endangering the broader structure of multilateral trade and payments that was being laboriously constructed abroad. It was a deliberate compromise between the imperatives of domestic interventionism and international liberalism—the compromise of "embedded liberalism," as John Ruggie (1983) later called it.[8]

Pivotal in promoting that compromise was none other than John Maynard Keynes, universally respected as the greatest economist of his day and intellectual leader of the British delegation at Bretton Woods. For Keynes, nothing was more damaging than the free movement of speculative capital, which he viewed as "the major cause of instability. . . . [Without] security against a repetition of this . . . . the whereabouts of the better 'ole' will shift with the speed of the magic carpet. Loose funds may sweep round the world disorganising all steady business. Nothing is more certain than that the movement of capital funds must be regulated."[9] Keynes carefully distinguished between genuinely productive investment flows and footloose "floating funds." The former, he concurred, were vital to "developing the world's resources" and should be encouraged. It was only the latter that should be controlled, preferably as a "permanent feature of the post-war system."[10] Following Bretton Woods, Keynes expressed satisfaction that his objectives in this regard had been achieved: "Not merely as a feature of the transition, but as a permanent arrangement, the plan accords to every member Government the explicit right to control all capital movements. What used to be heresy is now endorsed as orthodox."[11]

The achievement, however, did not last. Over the course of the next half-century, as the deterritorialization of currencies gradually accelerated, Keynes's strictures were largely forgotten, and what had been endorsed as orthodox now once again became heresy. Capital controls fell out of favor, reflecting the later emergence of what has come to be known as the "Washington Consensus"—an uncompromising "neoliberal" economics emphasizing the virtues of privatization, deregulation, and liberalization wherever possible.[12] For more than two decades the Washington Consensus has been widely promoted by U.S. government officials together with the IMF and World Bank, both of which happen to be based in Washington. First the more advanced economies of Europe and Japan, then most emerging-market economies in East Asia and Latin America, undertook to dismantle as many of their existing controls as possible.

Though still maintained by many poorer countries,[13] restraints on currency choice eventually came to be frowned upon in leading policy circles as a relic of an older, more *dirigiste* mentality—wrongheaded if not downright anachronistic.

During the 1980s, financial liberalization became the goal of almost every self-respecting industrial or middle-income country. Indeed, by the 1990s, the tide was clearly moving toward the consecration of free capital mobility as a universal norm. Perhaps the high-water mark was reached in early 1997 when a key decision-making body of IMF, the International Monetary and Financial Committee (IMFC), then known as the Interim Committee, approved a plan to begin preparing a new amendment to the Fund's charter to make the elimination of capital controls a specific IMF objective and responsibility.[14]

But then just a few months later came the Asian financial crisis, which forced a fundamental reconsideration of the merits of financial liberalization. What began as a limited case of investor jitters, sparked by concerns about the sustainability of mounting currency and maturity mismatches in local debt, soon deteriorated into a full-scale stampede to ostensibly safer foreign monies. Governments in East Asia, which previously had taken pride in the competitiveness of their currencies, suddenly found themselves unable to preserve user loyalty. Strategies that had once seemed adequate to sustain market share now had to be reevaluated in the light of a massive "flight to quality" by market agents. Inevitably, policymakers were drawn to take a new look at the old case for controls. As one source commented at the time, "capital curbs are an idea whose time, in the minds of many Asian government officials, has come back" (Wade and Veneroso 1998a, 23). Fashion once again began to swing in favor of limitations of some kind.[15]

Perhaps most influential in shifting the terms of discourse was a widely quoted article by the prominent economist Jagdish Bhagwati, which appeared in May 1998.[16] Although other economists had been making the case for controls for some time,[17] Bhagwati's celebrity succeeded in bringing the issue to a new level of public awareness. After Asia's painful experience, Bhagwati asked, could anyone remain persuaded by the "myth" of capital mobility's beneficence? In his words (1998, 8–9):

> It has become apparent that crises attendant on capital mobility cannot be ignored. . . . When a crisis hits, the downside of free capital mobility arises. . . . Thus, any nation contemplating the embrace of free capital mobility must reckon with these costs and also consider the probability of running into a crisis. The gains from economic efficiency that would flow from free capital mobility, in a hypothetical crisis-free world, must be set against this loss if a wise decision is to be made.

In a similar vein, shortly afterward, Krugman decried the failure of more conventional tactics of persuasion, which he labeled "Plan A." "It is time to think seriously about Plan B," he contended, meaning controls. "There is a virtual consensus among economists that exchange controls work badly. But when you face the kind of disaster now occurring in Asia, the question has to be: badly compared to what?"[18] Likewise, within months, the financier George Soros (1998, 192–93) was writing that "some form of capital controls may . . . be preferable to instability even if it would not constitute good policy in an ideal world." By the fall of 1998 the momentum had clearly shifted toward some manner of reappraisal of neoliberal orthodoxy. As Bhagwati (1998, 12) concluded: "Despite the . . . assumption that the ideal world is indeed one of free capital flows . . . the weight of evidence and the force of logic point in the opposite direction, toward restraints on capital flows. It is time to shift the burden of proof from those who oppose to those who favor liberated capital."

Thus an approach only recently dismissed as obsolete—a leftover of a more interventionist era—was now firmly back on the policy agenda. Soon the merits of controls of some kind were being endorsed at the highest levels of the international financial community,[19] and were being actively touted by a growing number of independent specialists.[20] Even the IMF changed its tune, dropping discussion of a new amendment to promote financial liberalization and talking instead of the possible efficacy of at least some types of restraint in specified circumstances[21]—a tentative step back to the future envisaged by Keynes and others when the Fund was first created. In 2001, use of capital controls in crisis situations was given formal support by the Fund's newly appointed deputy managing director, Anne Krueger (2002), as part of a proposed new approach to sovereign debt restructuring.

Though still challenged by many, the legitimacy of financial limitations for the purpose of monetary governance has today come to be widely accepted as a matter of principle. Plainly, for at least some governments, the pressure of events had conspired with a reawakened sense of history to cast the case for capital controls in a new and more respectable light.

Benefits and Costs

With light, however, has also come heat, as specialists hotly debate the practical pros and cons of controls as compared with the more conventional tactics of "sound" monetary management.[22] Critics oppose restraints as inefficient and unworkable. Advocates justify them as a tonic for stricken economies. No one doubts that controls could be costly.

Where opinion differs is whether, for states determined to defend their monetary sovereignty, coercive limitations on currency choice would be *more* costly than the alternative of the confidence game. Evaluation of contending arguments suggests that for some countries, in some circumstances, the price to be paid for using controls may indeed be lower than that demanded by the golden straitjacket.

The traditional case against capital controls is simple. It is of course the case for free markets, based on an analogy with standard theoretical arguments for free trade in goods and services. Trade liberalization is assumed to be a mutual-gain phenomenon in terms of economic welfare, conventionally defined by the availability of goods and services for final use. So why not financial liberalization, too? Like trade based on comparative advantage, capital mobility is assumed to lead to critical efficiency benefits—a more productive employment of investment resources as well as increased opportunities for effective risk management and welfare-improving intertemporal consumption smoothing. We are all presumably better off as a result.[23] In the words of Federal Reserve Chairman Alan Greenspan (1998, 246), an authoritative representative of neoliberal orthodoxy: "The accelerating expansion of global finance . . . . enhances cross-border trade in goods and services, facilitates cross-border portfolio investment strategies, enhances the lower-cost financing of real capital formation on a worldwide basis, and, hence, leads to an expansion of international trade and rising standards of living."

All these cost savings, conversely, would be threatened by controls, which it is assumed would almost certainly create economic distortions and inhibit socially desirable risk taking. Worse, given the inexorable advance of financial technology across the globe, restrictions in the end might not even prove to be effective. Again in Greenspan's (1998, 249) words: "We cannot turn back the clock on technology—and we should not try to do so." Any government that still preferred controls was, in effect, simply living in the past.

Against these arguments, which have long dominated thinking in policy circles, two broad lines of dissent have been proposed. One approach focuses on the assumptions necessary to support the traditional case, which are as demanding for trade in financial assets as they are for trade in goods and services. Strictly speaking, as a matter of theoretical reasoning, we can be confident that free capital flows will maximize economic welfare only in an idealized world of pure competition and perfect foresight. In reality economies are rife with distortions, such as "sticky" prices and wages or asymmetries in the availability of information, which prevent attainment of "first-best" equilibrium. As Richard Cooper (1999b, 105) writes: "It has long been established that capital mobility in the presence of significant distortions . . . will result in a misallocation of the world's capital and, indeed, can even worsen the economic well-being of the capital-importing country."[24] A plausible case for controls, therefore, may be made on standard "second-best" grounds. Judicious introduction of another distortion in the form of capital restrictions could actually turn out to lift rather than lower welfare on a net basis. For every possible form of market failure, there is in principle a corresponding form of optimal intervention.

The logic of this kind of argument is not disputed. An omniscient government dealing with one clear distortion could undoubtedly improve welfare with some form of financial restraint. What is disputed is the value of such logic in the real world of multiple distortions and imperfect policymaking. As Michael Dooley (1996) has noted, the issue is not theoretical but empirical.[25] The assumptions necessary to support an argument based on second-best considerations are no less "heroic" than those underlying the more conventional laissez-faire view.

The second line of dissent, much more relevant to a comparison with the orthodox confidence game, looks not to economic distortions at the microeconomic level but rather to the very nature of financial markets and their impact at the macroeconomic level. Even in the absence of other considerations, markets for monetary claims tend to be prone to frequent crisis and flux, owing to the interdependencies of expectations inherent in the buying and selling of claims. Interdependencies of expectations unavoidably lead to both herd behavior and multiple equilibria. Currency markets are especially vulnerable to self-fulfilling "bubbles" and speculative attacks. They also have a disturbing tendency to react with unpredictable lags to changing fundamentals—and then to overreact, rapidly and often arbitrarily.[26] The resulting flows of funds, which may be massive, can be highly disruptive to national economies owing to their amplified impact on real economic variables. Hence here, too, a logical case may be made for judicious intervention by state authorities, in this case to limit the macroeconomic instabilities and contagion effects endemic to the operation of financial markets. Representative are the words of a former deputy governor of the Bank of Mexico (Buira 1999, 8–10):

> Recent experiences of market instability in the new global, electronically linked markets. . . have made the potential costs of massive speculative flows difficult to ignore or underestimate. . . . The assumed gains from free capital mobility will have to be balanced against the very real risks such mobility poses. Some form of regulation or control. . . seems necessary to protect emerging-market economies from the devastating financial crises caused by massive capital movements.

The value of this sort of argument, too, is open to challenge on empirical grounds, depending on how great the risk of macroeconomic instability may be assumed to be. In fact, the risk is considerable. Recent research demonstrates that financial liberalization clearly increases the probability, sooner or later, of serious systemic crisis (Williamson and Mahar 1998;

Haggard 2000). For governments determined to stick to tactics of persuasion to defend their monetary sovereignty, it is the persistent threat of such crisis that makes a commitment to "sound" management so difficult to relax. In effect, income and employment at the macroeconomic level are sacrificed for the sake of preserving efficiency gains at the microeconomic level. Even if financial markets operated with textbook smoothness, that would seem a questionable, if not perverse, trade-off. Evidence cited by economist Lance Taylor (2000) suggests that more often than not, financial liberalization results in lower, rather than higher, economic growth over time. In turn it is this persistent deflationary bias of macroeconomic policy, resulting from the golden straitjacket, that has been so decisive in shifting the terms of discourse on capital controls.

Increasingly, therefore, the issue is posed in terms of trade-offs. Why should freedom of currency choice be given absolute priority over all other public considerations? Why, in effect, should governments tie one hand behind their back as they seek to promote the well-being of their citizens? Optimal policy design would seem to call for making use of all available instruments of policy—including capital controls—so long as their costs do not exceed their benefits.

The Element of Time

But therein lies the rub. Even if controls can be devised that would be less costly than the confidence game, they are no more likely to be successful at keeping the Choice Diagram's (see fig. 1) NC curve from rising eventually. The element of time here is critical. Restraints may be applied either to outflows of funds (sales of the national currency) or to inflows (purchases). Evidence suggests that either kind of limitation, if properly designed and implemented, can be successful in achieving its objectives in the short term. Benefits, in terms of defense of monetary sovereignty, may be considerable. Over time, however, effectiveness will almost certainly be eroded unless restraints are extended repeatedly, risking greater and greater efficiency losses. The market position of a currency can surely be maintained by controls—but, regrettably, only at the price of an ever higher NC curve. Worse, the poorer the competitiveness of a currency, the more rapidly the NC curve will rise.

Outflows

Limitations on outflows are what most people think of when capital controls are mentioned. Outward restraints may aim either to curb new acquisitions of foreign currency or to reverse currency substitution, compelling repatriation of past acquisitions. Both variants certainly seem consistent with the logic of market preservation. The privileged position of the national currency within a country's borders will obviously be protected if access to more attractive foreign monies can be suppressed, as it still is in many poorer economies around the world, from sub-Saharan Africa to China.

But there is also a downside if such restraints are enforced for any length of time. Because barriers to outflows drastically reduce currency choice, limiting opportunities for escape from inferior domestic money, they sow frustration and create considerable motivation for evasion. In the dry words of the IMF (Ariyoshi et al. 2000, 28), "controls do not provide lasting protection in the face of sufficient incentives for circumvention." The longer curbs remain in force, the more likely it is that they will simply feed the public's appetite for more currency substitution.[27] Restraints ultimately will have to be reinforced and amplified if their impact is not to be gradually eroded.[28] Currency deterritorialization, once begun, is a difficult process to reverse.

In part this is attributable to the well-known inertia of monetary behavior, which provides the motivation for market actors to seek to preserve hard-won access to more competitive foreign monies. And in part it is attributable to institutional factors, which offer the practical opportunity. One of the more pernicious byproducts of financial liberalization in many parts of the world has been the creation of a vast network of private intermediaries, backed by the latest in information technology, that can be used—legally if possible, illegally when deemed necessary—to work around even the most draconian of official restrictions. Given the availability of this support network for market agents, restraints will simply encourage a search for new routes of escape from the government's authority, much as water seeks its own level. Richard Cooper (1998, 17) puts the point well when he writes that "it is probably true that anyone determined to export private capital from a country can find a way, at a price, to do so." The dike will have to be built ever higher and wider to contain turbulent liquidity, at ever increasing cost.

A prime example was provided back during the 1980s when several Latin American countries tried to block capital flight by imposing controls, forcibly converting foreign-currency accounts in domestic banks into local money. These included Bolivia and Mexico in 1982 and Peru in 1985. In all three cases, the response ultimately was a decisive vote of no confidence—a clandestine shift of funds into accounts abroad that undermined, rather than bolstered, the market position of national money.[29] Studies indicate that overall, taking into account deposits held in foreign as well as domestic banks, outflows actually increased rather than decreased after the restrictions were instituted (Savastano 1996). In all three countries, the failed measures were ultimately abandoned.

Experiences like these do not mean that limitations on outflows are inherently unworkable, as critics often charge. But they do suggest that curbs are apt to be most effective if they are temporary, imposed only in moments of crisis, rather than permanent. Economist Sebastian Edwards (1999a) labels these "curative" controls. In the midst of a currency crisis, when confidence in the home money suddenly collapses, the challenge is simple: how to stop the hemorrhaging. The solution seems equally simple: restrict access to competing currencies in any way possible. Then, once the fever of panic subsides, the medicine can be stopped. There seems little question that curative controls, which were what Krugman meant by "Plan B," may well be workable for the limited period in which they are meant to be in force.[30] It is only when restraints remain in place indefinitely that their impact is at risk of erosion.

Moreover, the longer curbs remain in force, the more they tend to invite corruption and cronyism, as market actors seek to attain through bribery or political favors what is no longer available by legal means. Again Richard Cooper (1998, 12) puts the point well when he cites the risk that controls "will favor scofflaws over law-abiding citizens, with corrosive effects on public morality." The implication, once more, is that if restraints are to be used at all, they should be imposed only at times of emergency and even then only as a transitory measure, until more stable conditions return.

A paradox, therefore, is evident. Restraints on outflows work best if they are temporary. But precisely because they are temporary, curative controls do nothing to maintain a currency's market position over time, given the availability of more attractive brands of money elsewhere. Conversions into more competitive currencies can be hampered only by making restraints permanent. Edwards (1999a) labels these "preventive" controls. But precisely because they are permanent, preventive controls are likely to become increasingly costly because of the persistent threats of evasion and corruption. A rise of the NC curve cannot be eluded.

The advantages of curative controls are well illustrated by Malaysia, which alone among East Asian economies chose to limit capital outflows on a comprehensive basis in response to the crisis that began in 1997. The disadvantages of preventive controls are well illustrated by China, which has found it increasingly difficult to keep liquidity dammed up within its own borders.

Malaysia

Malaysia was the only Asian country during the recent crisis to resort to a full set of controls on financial outflows. During the first year following the 1997 crash of the baht, Malaysian policy was strictly orthodox. Interest rates were sharply raised and the government's budget was cut by nearly a fifth. Yet the economy shrank by close to 7 percent, the national currency, the ringgit, by 40 percent, and the Kuala Lumpur stock market by 75 percent. By mid-1998, Malaysia's authoritarian leader, Prime Minister Mahathir Mohamad, was losing patience with the neoliberal policies of his finance minister (and then heir apparent), Anwar Ibrahim, who was fired and later jailed on a variety of charges. Playing by the rules of the confidence game, the suspicious prime minister believed, simply meant collaborating in a Western conspiracy to ruin the Malaysian economy. The time had come, he asserted, to take back control from international "speculators," led by George Soros and "the Jews."

The change came 1 September 1998. Strict limitations were imposed on the convertibility of the ringgit for both trade and investment uses. Ringgit trading was to be carefully controlled, and a moratorium was declared requiring foreign capital, once invested, to remain in the country for at least twelve months before it could be repatriated.[31] The idea was to provide room for more expansionary policies than had otherwise seemed possible within the constraints of the golden straitjacket. Monetary policy was immediately eased, and in October a new budget was brought in combining substantial tax cuts with heavy new public-spending programs. "The plan," Dr. Mahathir told legislators, "aims at freeing Malaysia from the grip of the Asian financial crisis and to place Malaysia's economy on a stronger footing."[32]

That the prime minister's radical new controls would prove controversial was hardly surprising. Though easy to ridicule for his conspiratorial suspicions, Dr. Mahathir nonetheless posed a difficult challenge for conventional views on monetary governance, which took the primacy of unrestricted international investment as a given. For years, emerging nations had been lectured on the virtues of financial liberalization—yet here was a government that was doing just the reverse. Dr. Mahathir's audacity, many thought, could turn out to have a powerful demonstration effect. What if Malaysia should indeed recover more quickly as a result of its freshly installed insulation from investor panic? The experiment was carefully watched.

In fact, the experiment lasted no more than a year. In February 1999, the twelve-month moratorium on repatriation of foreign investments was replaced by a graduated exit tax, with lower rates applying the longer funds remained in the country; and seven months later, exactly one year to the day after the program's start, the graduated levy was, in turn, replaced by a single uniform tax of 10 percent on all repatriated profits. Dr. Mahathir's intention, clearly, was not to abandon the confidence game altogether. His government's rapid return to orthodoxy was widely applauded and was effectively certified by the investment firm Morgan Stanley Capital International, whose influential portfolio indexes are widely used by fund managers and others as a guide to investment in emerging-market economies. After having been removed from the Morgan Stanley indexes when the controls were first imposed, Malaysia was fully reinstated in November 1999. "It's a big booster," said one Malaysian broker when plans for the reinstatement were announced.[33] The last remaining remnant of the experiment, the uniform 10-percent exit tax, was formally dropped in May 2001. By mid-2002 Malaysia's credit rating had risen above that of China.

Was the experiment successful? Certainly the restraints were effective in stemming the flood of money that was then rushing for the exits, as numerous studies confirm.[34] The hemorrhaging ceased and the economy soon rebounded, achieving growth at an annual rate near 10 percent by the end of 1999. As the new millennium dawned, exports were up, the stock market was again on the rise, and foreign capital was returning—all seemingly vindicating Dr. Mahathir's audacious challenge to conventional wisdom. As early as the spring of 1999, the prime minister was already publicly proclaiming victory in his determined war on speculators.[35] His curative controls seemed to have worked.

Not everyone concurs. As many observers have noted,[36] most other crisis-hit countries also recovered during the same period—some even more rapidly than Malaysia—suggesting a less triumphalist interpretation. Typical are the remarks of economist Linda Lim (1999, 39), who has argued that "capital controls in Malaysia were neither necessary nor sufficient for economic recovery. . . . Indeed, given Malaysia's much stronger macroeconomic fundamentals and financial institutions before the crisis, one would have expected its recovery to be faster and stronger than that of other countries. That this has not happened suggests that capital controls . . . may be exerting a drag on recovery." Particular stress is put on Malaysia's delay in imposing controls until a time when the crisis in the region already seemed to be subsiding. As Dornbusch (2001b, 10, 13) wrote, by September 1998 "markets had already settled in Asia, interest rates had been coming off and would soon do so everywhere under the impact of Fed rate cuts and a reduction of jitters. . . . Accordingly, it cannot be argued that a situation that otherwise would have been much worse was contained by the effects of capital controls." The barn door, in short, was being locked after the horse had already bolted.

But these demurrals overlook the fact that the full impact of the crisis came later to Malaysia than to most other countries in the region. In the summer of 1998 Malaysia was in fact significantly more threatened than many of its neighbors, such as South Korea and Thailand, where conditions had already begun to stabilize. Malaysia's response was delayed because, as compared with these other economies, its crisis was delayed.

The horse had not in fact yet bolted. As one source comments (Kaplan and Rodrik 2001, 5–6):

> In early September, 1998, neither Korea nor Thailand faced another imminent crisis. . . . Contrast that with Malaysia's situation [where] existing policies were unsustainable because of intense and continued speculative pressure against the ringgit [which] reached its peak just before the Malaysian authorities decided to implement capital controls. . . . It is hard to believe that Malaysia would have experienced Thailand's or Korea's economic performance in subsequent months while maintaining its existing policy configuration.[37]

In short, it seems reasonable to conclude that in the midst of an emergency, Malaysia's curative controls did indeed prove to be a "better way" than the confidence game. Even IMF officials, once critical of Dr. Mahathir's approach, now concede that he may have been right (*New York Times*, 21 August 2002). Moreover, since the restrictions were removed quickly, they were also able to lance the market's fever at comparatively low cost. As Krugman (1999a, 4) suggests, "Malaysia has proved a point—namely, that controlling capital in a crisis is at least feasible." In the face of panic, a nation's money can be effectively defended.

China

But what if restraints on outflows remain in force indefinitely, as they have in China? The Chinese experience suggests that preventive controls, too, are feasible to defend a money's market position, even in the absence of an immediate emergency. But it is also evident that a successful defense is not without cost; and it would appear that the longer preventive controls remain in force, the higher their price will have to be in order to remain effective.

Ever since the Communist Party came to power in 1949, China has maintained a vast panoply of restrictions to limit the currency choice of its citizens. The national money, the yuan, is formally inconvertible. Anyone wishing to exchange yuan for foreign currency must obtain permission from the central bank, the Bank of China. Conversely, anyone receiving foreign currency is legally obligated to sell it to the central bank for yuan. The aim of the controls has been to limit the country's vulnerability to speculative attacks or financial contagion. Their success in this regard was well demonstrated in 1997–1998, when even as many of its neighbors were suffering massive outflows, China remained crisis-free—an "island of stability," as then U.S. Treasury Secretary Robert Rubin described it.[38] While other Asian economies were being pushed into recession by their commitment to the confidence game, Chinese growth barely faltered; and at a time when other regional currencies were being depreciated in value (from 10 to 20 percent in Taiwan and Singapore to as much as 80 percent in Indonesia), the yuan held rock steady. The explanation, most observers agreed, was plain. In the words of the *New York Times* (25 June 1998), "the primary reason the Chinese yuan hasn't budged is that currency markets lack the mechanism to topple it."

Over time, however, corruption and evasions have grown, requiring the Chinese authorities repeatedly to expand and tighten existing regulations. Leakage became especially evident after the start of the Asian crisis, when, despite huge trade surpluses, the country's foreign-exchange reserves failed to increase. As much as $20 billion may have been illicitly transferred out of the country in 1997 and perhaps another $11 billion during the first half of 1998 (Ariyoshi et al. 2000, 30).[39] In September 1998, Beijing responded with a severe crackdown on what the official press described as "black-market activities." Stricter supervision of foreign-currency transactions was announced, calling for more detailed documentation and verification, and new limits were placed on the issue of foreign debt. And even tighter curbs were imposed in June 1999, restricting most overseas transactions in yuan, after it became apparent that Chinese enterprises were finding ways to acquire yuan cheaply in Hong Kong or elsewhere and then remit them back into China in exchange for foreign currency at more favorable rates.

China's dike, in short, keeps growing higher, and with it the cost to the Chinese economy in terms of distortions and lost growth. Addressing concerns that repeated reinforcements of controls might impact negatively on trade and investment, a government official averred: "It's simply the price we pay in order to combat crimes."[40] Defense of China's monetary sovereignty does not come cheap.

Inflows

As mentioned, restraints may be applied to inflows as well as to outflows of funds. Limitations on inflows obviously do nothing directly to increase demand for a local brand of money, since by definition they are intended to do just the reverse—to suppress demand. But they can be useful *indirectly* insofar as they reduce the potential for future capital flight, enhancing a currency's stability, and hence its appeal, over time. Here, too, though, it is evident that market position can be maintained only at the price of an ever higher NC curve.

When, following the outbreak of the Asian crisis, the IMF and others began to change their tune on controls, the most favorable attention was reserved for restraints on purchases rather than curbs on sales of vulnerable currencies.[41] Analysts generally concurred that a key factor contributing to the distresses of 1997–1998 was the preceding flood of capital that had poured into national financial systems as yet unable to handle so much liquidity effectively.[42] The crisis, it was noted, might have been far less disruptive had there not been such a large pool of foreign investments in domestic currency poised to flee at a moment's notice; and clearly, there would not have been so much footloose foreign capital had there been less financial liberalization in preceding years. On prudential grounds, therefore, it seemed reasonable to think in terms of curbing inflows as a way of reducing the risk of later outflows. Restrictions today could succeed in reducing exposure to a reversal of sentiment tomorrow.

Moreover, precedents exist for this kind of tactic. Early in the last decade, even as financial markets generally were being liberalized, selective restraints on inflows were introduced in a number of emerging-market economies, including those of Brazil (1993–1997), Chile (1991–1998), Colombia (1993–1998), Malaysia (1994), and Thailand (1995–1997). During the 1980s, international flows had dropped sharply owing to the uncertainties generated by Latin America's debt problems. At the time the challenge for middle-income countries was to attract foreign capital, not deter it. But once investments revived at the start of the 1990s, the reverse quickly became true. Governments began to worry about both the magnitude and potential volatility of inflows. Large-scale liquid investments seemed to threaten the autonomy of domestic monetary policy as well as to raise the risk of future crisis. Limitations on inflows, therefore, became increasingly appealing. The goal, in the spirit of the postwar compromise of embedded liberalism, was to limit the scope for massive hot-money movements that might destabilize national economies.

Were they successful? Most controversy has swirled around the program in Chile, which was the first of the new wave of inward restraints in Latin America and lasted the longest.[43] The surge of capital movements into Chile that began as early as 1989 generated a growing conflict between the government's internal and external policy objectives. The immediate imperative was to maintain a tight monetary policy without generating an exchange-rate appreciation that might hinder export competitiveness. The longer-term challenge was to reduce the risk of later massive outflows. The solution, officials decided in 1991, was a program of administrative measures designed to discourage short-term borrowing or portfolio investment from abroad.

Central was the so-called unremunerated reserve requirement (URR) on most forms of external financing.[44] Any investor or lender wishing to enter the Chilean market was required to leave a deposit equal to a specified percentage of the transaction with the government for a period of one year. The percentage was gradually raised to as high as 30 percent and then, in 1998, reduced to 10 percent before finally being phased out. Since no interest was received on the deposit, the requirement acted in effect like a tax on capital inflows. But since the fixed holding period implied that the financial burden diminished with the maturity of investments, an incentive was created to switch toward less liquid, longer-term forms of investment, reducing the risk of volatile movements into and out of the national currency, the Chilean peso.

Chile's measures have been the subject of a substantial number of studies.[45] Overall, the evidence suggests that the program was not particularly successful in terms of its more immediate goals, failing to assure either domestic policy autonomy or a competitive exchange rate. As Edwards (1999a, 82) summarizes: "The controls on inflows had no significant effect on Chile's real exchange rate, and only a very small effect on interest rates."[46] With respect to its longer-term goal, however, of shifting the maturity composition of the country's external debt, the program appears to have been far more effective. Recorded short-term inflows, which had accounted for more than 90 percent of inward capital movements in 1989–1991, dropped to less than 75 percent in 1991 and to below 10 percent in 1995–1997. The change was in sharp contrast to the experience of most other emerging-market economies, where more liquid forms of investment continued to dominate. It began immediately after the URR was instituted in 1991 and persisted for as long as the program remained in operation. Yet even though the total volume of inflows continued to mount until 1997, Chile was spared any serious fallout from the Asian crisis, unlike some of its neighbors like Argentina and Brazil—as Eichengreen (1999, 53) suggests, "a perfectly happy result . . . precisely what [was] intended."

Of course, it is possible that the shift in the maturity composition of Chile's debt was more apparent than real. Chilean data, as in most countries, classifies inflows as short-term or long-term simply on the basis of contracted maturity. But as Edwards (1999a, 1999b) points out, what really matters is not "contractual" maturity, but rather "residual" maturity, as measured by the value of claims due within one year. Looking at foreign bank loans, Edwards finds that when recalculated in terms of residual maturity, the percentage of Chile's debt that was effectively short-term was more like half the total, not under 10 percent. This was not dissimilar to other emerging markets and in fact was higher than in Mexico, a country without inflow restraints. But the calculation is misleading, mainly because it relies on such a narrow measure of external liabilities. As William Cline (1999) has shown, if the analysis is broadened to include nonbank liabilities, as well—a more accurate estimate of the total—the share of debt maturing in less than a year turns out to have been under 20 percent, only slightly higher than in the official statistics. On balance, therefore, there seems little question that Chile's controls were indeed effective in reducing vulnerability to the risk of sudden capital flight. And this conclusion is confirmed by broader comparative studies looking at other countries that have also experimented with inflow controls.[47] Overall, inflow restraints do appear capable of successfully defending a nation's currency against massive outflows.

Again, however, it is evident that, over time, effectiveness will almost certainly be eroded unless the controls are persistently extended. Admittedly, as compared with outward restraints, barriers to inflows may be sustainable for longer periods, since it is obviously easier to keep capital out than in. Whereas restrictions on outflows drastically reduce the choices available to a currency's users, inward curbs limit only one option among many, leaving investors abroad free to continue looking for profit opportunities elsewhere. As John Williamson (2000, 39) writes, "incentives for evasion are typically . . . much greater in the case of outflows." But even on the inflow side it is likely that market actors will eventually learn to exploit potential loopholes, forcing the authorities in turn to build the dike ever higher. This was certainly the case in Chile, where the coverage of the URR had to be repeatedly broadened as the markets kept shifting from targeted categories of transactions to those that were still exempt. What started out as a relatively limited measure, applying mainly to certain types of short-term borrowing, ultimately was extended to virtually all forms of foreign financing other than "nonspeculative" direct investment. And much the same happened elsewhere, as well (Ariyoshi et al. 2000; Kaminsky and Schmukler 2001), contributing to rising distortions over time. Inflow restraints, in the end, are no more likely to be cost-free than outward controls.

Conclusion

The conclusion, then, is clear. Governments determined to go on producing their own money have a legitimate choice between tactics of either persuasion or coercion. In some circumstances, the neoliberal orthodoxy of the confidence game may be preferable; in other conditions, inward or outward capital controls may offer a better way. But neither approach can be counted upon to prevent the NC curve in the Choice Diagram (see fig. 1) from rising over time, more or less rapidly. This does not mean that most states, therefore, will necessarily decide to buy their currency from a more efficient producer, choosing one or the other of the Two S's. That decision will also depend on what is happening to the DL and MA curves, to which we turn in the next two chapters. But it does mean that states cannot evade for long the pressures generated by money's rapidly changing geography, particularly states with the least competitive currencies. Governments must consciously address the tripartite choice among strategies of market preservation, followership, or alliance.

Five

Follow the Leader

Is SOME FORM of dollarization the answer? Given the persistent upward pressure today on the cost of defending uncompetitive national currencies, it is not surprising that some governments might now be prepared to consider the alternative option of following a leader, surrendering part or all of their monetary sovereignty to a dominant foreign power. Referring again to the Choice Diagram (see fig. 1), the issue is the position of the DL curve *relative* to a rising NC curve. Are many states likely to find some degree of subordination more attractive than the difficult art of survival? Is the geography of money, as some predict,[1] really evolving toward two or three giant blocs centered on the dominant monies at the peak of the Currency Pyramid?

At issue, once again, are the five key factors outlined in chapters 2 and 3: transactions costs, macroeconomic stabilization, the distribution of seigniorage, political symbolism, and diplomatic influence. Only the first of these factors, we know, offers an opportunity for mutual gain, benefiting followers as well as leaders. All the remaining four factors are in the nature of a zero-sum game, one side's gain being the other's loss. In the sovereignty bargain that vertical regionalization represents, the cost of a followership strategy rises with the degree of subordination involved— which, of course, is precisely why we observe such wide variation in the design of regional currencies, to accommodate the interests of individual countries. A fair number of governments could be attracted to less demanding forms of followership, depending on bargaining context. But relatively few are apt to be comfortable with the idea of full dollarization, the highest degree of vertical regionalization.

Dollarization

Dollarization, in the strictest sense of the term, means giving up a national currency entirely—*full* dollarization.[2] Nothing but the dominant foreign money is recognized as legal tender within the domestic economy. A close approximation is *near*-dollarization, where a local currency continues to circulate but only in very limited amounts. Because both involve a degree of subordination of monetary sovereignty that is more akin to unconditional surrender, it is evident that neither will be naturally attractive to most sovereign governments. That does not mean that dollarization can be written off as a nonstarter. But it does mean that if more states choose to go this route, emulating the recent examples of Ecuador and El Salvador, it will most likely be because the cost of defending an existing national currency has become intolerably high, not because the cost of such a radical departure is seen to have become temptingly low.

Benefits?

Consider, to begin, full dollarization. Much is to be gained from abandoning a weak national currency, mainly at the microeconomic level, where a switch to a leader's money is bound to reduce transactions costs for all concerned. Moreover, as indicated in chapter 3, a disproportionate share of the mutual saving will accrue to the dollarizing country, whose residents would no longer have to put up with the inconvenience of an uncompetitive local brand of money. About this potential benefit there is little dispute.

More controversial, however, are three other claims that are often offered in support of dollarization. None of the three is certain, and all may prove to have more downside than upside.

First is the argument that as a supposedly irreversible institutional change, adoption of a leader's money will establish a firm basis for a sounder financial sector (Hausmann 1999a; Hausmann et al. 2000). Most developing countries, it is said, suffer from the "original sin" of a weak national currency that cannot be used for borrowing abroad or even for long-term borrowing at home. Domestic borrowers, therefore, must book loans either in foreign currency or at short term, meaning that investments will be at risk in one of two ways: either of a currency mismatch, because projects that generate local currency are financed with foreign-currency loans; or of a maturity mismatch, because longer-term investments are financed with short-term loans. That is a surefire "recipe for financial fragility," as Hausmann (1999a, 67) sadly puts it. But with dollarization, deeper and more resilient markets may be promoted, making it easier for market agents to weather potential shocks. Because borrowers and savers alike will now gain access to financial institutions that have proved their competence internationally, domestic intermediaries will be forced to upgrade the quality of their services and products if they wish to remain competitive. Moreover, institutions lacking liquidity at home will now be able to borrow more easily from markets abroad; and with the risk of runaway inflation constrained by the link to the leader's monetary policy, lending at longer term will be greatly encouraged. Enthusiasts point to the fact that Panama, until recently the only dollarized sovereign economy in the Western Hemisphere, has been able to capitalize on its integration with the U.S. banking system to position itself as a major offshore financial center. It also happens, not coincidentally, to be the only Latin American country with a domestic thirty-year mortgage market.[3]

A sounder financial sector, however, is not guaranteed and may come at a stiff price in terms of greater foreign penetration of the domestic market. We know that banks based in the leader's economy are naturally advantaged relative to local rivals by their privileged access to the resources of the leader's central bank. In turn, as frequently suggested (D'Arista 2000; Vernengo and Rochon 2001), the competitive edge provided by these "denomination rents" could lead to increased foreign control of local financial institutions. Such a development would complicate the task of financial regulation by the national authorities and raise serious questions about the future allocation of credit domestically. As one observer (D'Arista 2000, 4) asks:

> How interested would [foreign banks] be in lending to small businesses, less affluent consumers and homebuyers, farmers, regional governments, municipalities and other borrowers who make up the majority of a "client" country's citizens? Absent a central bank with both monetary authority and regulatory power over the majority of banks in the national market, who can or will take actions to ensure that there is an adequate and balanced flow of credit across the domestic economy?

Second is the claim that interest rates will be lowered significantly. This was clearly in Carlos Menem's thoughts when he first raised the issue of dollarization in 1999.[4] Typically, when borrowing in world financial markets, emerging-market economies like Argentina must pay a considerable premium, conventionally indicated by the spread over equivalent U.S. Treasury securities. This premium, which can amount to hundreds of basis points,[5] reflects two perceived risks for lenders. One is devaluation risk (or currency risk): a fear of depreciation of the local money's exchange rate. The other is default risk (or sovereign risk): a fear of disruption or suspension of a country's payments on foreign debt. Dollarization can do nothing directly to reduce default risk (the "country" premium), which is a reflection of the political reality of national sovereignty. An independent government can always, in extremis, suspend or abrogate its external obligations if faced with, say, a fiscal emergency or political turmoil. But dollarization should largely eliminate devaluation risk (the "currency" premium) since the reform, at least in principle, is supposed to be irrevocable. And it might even indirectly reduce default risk, insofar as some part of default risk reflects the possibility of future currency crises.[6] If so—and barring reintroduction of the local money—exchange-rate disturbances would become a thing of the past, making it easier for a government to meet foreign commitments. With luck, the reduction of interest rates would result in substantially higher levels of domestic investment and future growth.

In practice, however, any reduction of interest rates may be little more than marginal, despite the elimination of devaluation risk. For most potential dollarizers, the really serious problem appears to be not the currency premium but the country premium, reflecting fundamental deficiencies of domestic policies—particularly budgetary policies that persistently add to outstanding government debt—and there is no reason to believe that adopting another nation's money would automatically result in greater fiscal discipline. Quite the contrary, in fact. Analysis by Fatás and Rose (2001) suggests that, on balance, dollarization is associated with less budgetary restraint rather than more. Unceasing deficits are bound to raise legitimate doubts about future debt-service capacity. Default risk could actually be increased rather than decreased.

As much became evident in Argentina during the last years of its currency board. Before the arrangement collapsed in early 2002, it was clear that what worried foreign investors most was not the exchange rate but the possibility of default. Even more apt are the cases of Panama and Ecuador, two fully dollarized countries. Panama, which has never used any currency other than the U.S. dollar, is often cited for the low spreads it enjoys on foreign loans as compared with other Latin American nations.[7] Ostensibly these low spreads are evidence of the benefit of having eliminated devaluation risk. But Panamanian borrowing costs are by no means the lowest in the Hemisphere, remaining significantly higher than Chile's or Costa Rica's, for instance. The difference reflects the parlous state of Panama's public finances, which has forced the Panamanian government into no fewer than seventeen adjustment programs with the IMF in less than thirty years (Edwards 2001; Goldfajn and Olivares 2001). Likewise, little more than two years after adopting America's greenback, Ecuador once again found itself negotiating with the IMF to help cope with a soaring budget deficit (*The Economist*, 13 April 2002, 39). Default risk, plainly, can dilute or even nullify dollarization's hoped-for improvement of interest rates. As one careful study summarizes: "Dollarization can help reduce risk premiums, but only to a limited extent."[8]

Third is the claim that dollarization will yield benefits at the macroeconomic level, especially for countries with a long history of high inflation and debauched currencies. Abandoning a national money, by definition, means forfeiting formal control of monetary policy. But little may be lost, dollarization enthusiasts argue, where performance has been especially poor in the past. Governments known for abuse of their monetary monopolies are most likely to be the target of market-driven currency substitution, which means that their effective policy autonomy has already been significantly compromised. The greater the degree of currency substitution, we know, the weaker will be a central bank's ability to manage local monetary conditions successfully—in other words, the higher will be the cost of continuing to play the confidence game. Conversely, much can be gained by outsourcing monetary policy, adopting a currency whose reputation is already well established and secure. In effect, the brand name of a respected foreign central bank like the Federal Reserve or ECB can be "hired" to create instant credibility—"credibility in a bottle," as Jeffrey Frankel (1999, 2) has quipped.[9] No longer will it be necessary to invest heavily in efforts to build the reputation of the nation's own brand of money in order to ensure some degree of monetary stability.

But here, too, there is a downside. Greater monetary stability may be possible but could also come at a stiff price, this time in terms of diminished future growth. Dollarization, recalling an earlier discussion in chapter 3, does not produce magic changes. If nothing is done to discipline budgetary policy or correct structural rigidities in the local economy, growth on balance might actually be stunted rather than stimulated. Research by Sebastian Edwards and others suggests that when compared to countries elsewhere, dollarized economies may well achieve significantly lower and more stable inflation rates, as enthusiasts suggest.[10] But on average, in real-income terms, these same economies also appear to grow at significantly lower rates over time in contrast to countries with more autonomous monetary policies. Claims for the beneficial macroeconomic effects of dollarization, Edwards (2001, 263) concludes, are "a typical case of misleading advertisement."[11] Credibility cannot be easily bottled.

Costs

On the other side of the ledger, dollarization simultaneously entails distinct *costs*, which are acknowledged even by its supporters. The downside of adopting a leader's currency is far more certain than the upside and could be of considerably greater magnitude.

Four costs, in particular, are threatened. First, and most obvious, is the loss of seigniorage as local money is withdrawn from circulation. Where previously the national central bank could earn a profit from the difference between its cost-free liabilities and the interest earned on its counterpart assets, now reserves must be liquidated in order to acquire the foreign notes and coins needed to replace local cash. The amounts involved could be substantial, as frequently noted.[12]

Economists typically place great stress on the seigniorage issue, perhaps because this is the easiest of all of dollarization's effects to quantify. Following an approach first developed by Stanley Fischer (1982), two alternative measures are distinguished. The loss can be calculated either as a one-time *stock* cost, in terms of the initial amount of new currency that a dollarizing country must acquire, or else, equivalently, as a continuing *flow* cost represented by the future earnings of interest forgone.[13] For potential dollarizers, many of which are comparatively small and poor countries, these costs, however measured, would not be inconsiderable. In Argentina, for instance, where the current discussion of dollarization first started, it was estimated that the stock cost of formally switching to the greenback would have been the redemption of some $15 billion in domestic currency held outside the central bank, about 4 percent of GDP; in flow terms, the annual cost would have amounted to about $700 million, roughly 0.2 percent of GDP.[14] Elsewhere in Latin America, potential flow costs have been estimated to range from 0.8 percent of GDP in Mexico to as high as 2.5 percent in Peru (Bogetić 2000a, 2000b)—all a "very high financial tribute," in the words of a noted critic of dollarization (von Furstenberg 2000b, 109), to be transferred directly to the market leader.[15]

Champions of dollarization demur. The revenue loss is real, they admit, but offsetting it should be a fiscal gain from the anticipated reduction of risk premiums, which would lower the cost of servicing public debt.[16] As already indicated, however, any easing of interest rates is likely to be rather more limited than hoped for. On the other hand, the financial tribute to the market leader could ultimately turn out to be even higher than standard calculations suggest. By focusing just on the stock of reserve assets that will be initially converted into cash or the flow of interest earnings to be forgone on that stock, conventional estimates fail to take account of the potential for *future* growth of the demand for money. Implicit is the assumption that the domestic monetary base will remain constant over time, which, of course, is unrealistic. In actuality, both inflation and real growth can be expected to expand monetary demand in the future. Taking these two sources of money growth into account, which would otherwise add to a central bank's profits, one source (Schmitt-Grohé and Uribe 1999) contends that the transfer of seigniorage might actually be as much as five times as great as commonly estimated. Unless provisions can be negotiated with the market leader for some form of compensation, as was proposed for the United States in the now-defunct Mack Bill, the prospective revenue loss could prove to be a severe deterrent for many governments.

A second potential cost, related to the role of a monetary monopoly in managing macroeconomic performance, is the loss of a lender of last resort (LOLR) for the domestic banking system. In adopting a foreign currency a country also gives up a central bank capable of discounting freely in times of financial crisis. Local banks, therefore, may be more exposed to liquidity risks, threatening economic turmoil.

Admittedly, in practical terms, this disadvantage may be less serious than it appears, since the government is not without other options, as dollarization advocates remind us (Calvo 1999). The LOLR function is conventionally associated with the ability of a central bank, in its capacity as monopoly supplier, literally to create money out of thin air. But there are also other ways to provide bank liquidity—out of a central bank's international reserves, for instance. Dollarization reduces the overall supply of reserves, because of the obligation to liquidate exchange assets to acquire the requisite foreign notes and coins. But dollarization also reduces the overall need for reserves, since a share of external transactions that previously required foreign currency can now be treated as the equivalent of internal transactions. As indicated in chapter 3, the central bank's remaining exchange assets would thus be available to cope with possible liquidity or banking crises. Alternatively a contingency fund could be built up over time from tax revenues, or flexible credit lines with foreign banks or monetary authorities could be negotiated using reserves or future tax revenues as collateral. A model for a foreign credit line was developed in Argentina where, in support of its now-defunct currency board, the government established a Contingent Repurchase Facility allowing it to sell dollar-denominated bonds to selected international banks when needed in exchange for cash dollars.

None of these precautions, however, are as convenient as the historical ability of a central bank simply to issue money on demand. All require negotiation or institutional innovation and all involve some measure of real burden in terms of public or private expenditures forgone. As Morris Goldstein (2002, 30) writes, "self-insurance mechanisms carry a cost."

Third is the loss of a vital symbol of national identity, a cost that is not easily calculated but can scarcely be ignored. In the popular mind, a strong bond still exists between money and nation. How else can we explain the reasoning of the former Archbishop of Canterbury, a determined foe of British membership in Europe's EMU? The clergyman insists that "I want the Queen's head on the banknotes. . . . The point about national identity is a very important one. For me, being British is deeply important. I don't want to become French or German."[17] Or how else can we explain the paradoxical results of an opinion poll in Mexico, querying public attitudes on currency choice? When asked whether they would like to see America's greenback used freely throughout the economy, some 86 percent answered in the affirmative. Yet when asked if Mexico should dollarize formally, eliminating the peso, an overwhelming majority declared opposition.[18] In most parts of the world abandonment of a national money, no matter how uncompetitive, would be widely seen as something akin to a military defeat—a severe blow to national self-esteem. No government can disregard the risk that a change of monetary allegiance might weaken the emotional attachment that citizens feel to their country. In

Latin America, even dollarization enthusiasts acknowledge the resentment that could greet adoption of a currency featuring Founding Fathers
and past presidents of the great colossus to the north. Perhaps the dollar
bill might be redesigned, one source suggests, to feature Christopher Co-
lumbus as a more acceptable symbol for the Hemisphere's money.[19]

Finally, there is the loss of a degree of insulation from external influence, owing to the element of dependency inherent in the arrangement.
Full dollarization, in effect, formalizes in its most extreme form the hierarchy implicit in the Currency Pyramid. The relationship is one of powerful
patron and vulnerable client—"reinventing colonialism," in the words of
one critic (D'Arista 2000, 2). The risk that currency dependency might
actually be exploited for coercive ends may be low, but it is real.

For a case in point consider again Panama, which learned in the late
1980s just how exposed to external coercion a dollarized economy can
be. The story began with accusations of corruption and drug-smuggling
against General Manuel Noriega, commander of the Panamanian armed
forces and the country's de facto leader. In March 1998, the Reagan administration finally lost patience with Noriega. Panamanian assets in U.S.
banks were frozen and all payments or other dollar transfers to Panama
were prohibited as part of a determined campaign to force the general
from power—in effect, an exercise of expulsion. The impact was swift.
Most local banks were compelled to close, and the economy was squeezed
by a severe liquidity shortage. The effect was devastating despite rushed
efforts by the Panamanian authorities to create a substitute currency,
mainly by issuing checks in standardized denominations that they hoped
recipients would then treat as cash. The country was effectively demone-
tized. In the words of a former U.S. ambassador to Panama, Washington's
coercive actions had done the most damage "to the Panamanian economy
since Henry Morgan, the pirate, sacked Panama City in 1671."[20] Over
the course of the year domestic output fell by nearly one-fifth.

The sanctions, as it happens, were not enough to dislodge Noriega on
their own. Ultimately, in late 1989, Washington felt it necessary to mount
a military invasion and temporarily occupied the country until a new,
friendlier government could be installed. But there can be no doubt that
the liquidity squeeze was painful and contributed greatly to Noriega's
downfall. Dollarization clearly makes a country more vulnerable to external pressure. The lesson is obvious, as economist Lawrence Klein (1993,
112–13) has prudently suggested: "Panama . . . uses U.S. dollars for its
monetary units. As long as relations remain cordial, this is not a bad
arrangement. . . . But for Panama the risk price is very high for having
the convenience of U.S. dollars. The small country would be in a better
and more independent position if it had not let some of its monetary
actions be governed by foreigners."

Near-Dollarization

Given all these costs, as well as the uncertainty of potential benefits, it is hardly surprising that the number of states choosing to dollarize *in full* has so far remained small. All fully dollarized economies, as indicated in chapter 2 (see table 1), are tiny microstates like the Marshall Islands and Liechtenstein. Other states that have gone the dollarization route prefer to retain at least a token amount of notes or coins of their own—*near*-dollarization (see table 2). Most near-dollarized countries also tend to be quite small, though we do find among them as well the long-standing case of Panama and now Ecuador and El Salvador. Included too, until the advent of the euro, were the minute European enclaves of Andorra, Monaco, San Marino, and the Vatican.

Near-dollarization has one main disadvantage as compared with full dollarization—namely, the risk of higher transactions costs resulting from the parallel circulation of two separate monies. But the efficiency loss is not apt to be great so long as the quantity of the local money remains limited and the exchange-rate link to the anchor currency remains firm. Moreover, from the dependent state's point of view, any such disadvantage will be more than compensated for by possible benefits. Near-dollarization's main advantages, as compared with full dollarization, are that with even a token amount of local money in circulation the government preserves both a possible source of seigniorage and a visible symbol of the nation. Most importantly, the presence of a local money, even if only a Pseudo-Currency, reduces potential exit costs should a country ever decide to reduce its monetary dependence by de-dollarizing. It is obviously easier to add to the circulation of a money already in existence than it would be to create one from scratch.

The possibility of de-dollarization cannot be dismissed lightly. Consider the case of Liberia, which for many years used the U.S. dollar for most monetary purposes. Liberia, as is well known, owes its very existence to initiatives originating in the United States; and from its birth in 1847 has always maintained a special relationship with Washington, which during the colonial era persistently supported the country's efforts to preserve its independence in the face of French and British encroachments. In 1944, as the U.S. built up its wartime presence in Liberia, Monrovia agreed to make the greenback the country's sole legal tender, replacing the British West African colonial coinage that had previously dominated the local money supply (Bixler 1957). Over the next half century, however, the trend in Liberia has moved very much the other way, toward something that today looks much more like bimonetarism.

First, beginning in the 1960s, greenback circulation in the country was supplemented by a limited issue of small-denomination Liberian coins, also named the dollar—a shift from full to near-dollarization. In 1974, the National Bank of Liberia was opened. And then in the 1980s, following a coup d'état under the leadership of Army Sergeant Samuel Doe, came severe political turmoil and fiscal deficits, leading to the issue of much larger amounts of higher-denomination coins as well as notes. Five-dollar coins, which quickly came to be known as Doe dollars, were introduced in 1982, with five-dollar notes following in 1989—a classic example of a struggling government resorting to seigniorage as a revenue of last resort. Also true to form, Gresham's Law quickly went to work, making a mockery of the official one-for-one exchange rate between the U.S. and Liberian dollars. By the start of the 1990s the greenback had almost completely disappeared from circulation, even though the monetary agreement with Washington remains nominally in effect. Formally, America's dollar is still the principal currency of Liberia, though it no longer actively circulates much as a medium of exchange and is convertible into the Liberian dollar only at a fluctuating rate of exchange. In practice, the country is now effectively de-dollarized.

In broader perspective, it is clear that the Liberian case was something of an aberration—by no means the product of a considered decision but rather part of the fallout from violent revolution and a near total breakdown of civic order. Liberia by the end of the 1980s was a "failed state," unable to implement even the most rudimentary elements of governance within its own borders. Indeed, for a period during the 1990s two different versions of the Liberian dollar, representing rival political factions, circulated in direct competition with one another, each legal tender in a different part of the country (Ellis 1999, 97). Happily, not many other states find themselves in the same dysfunctional condition; and certainly none of those that are at present formally dollarized.[21] Nonetheless, the precedent is of importance to governments that might otherwise hesitate to commit themselves formally to reliance on another country's currency. Sovereign authorities do not like to leave themselves without a viable exit option of some kind.

Recent Experience

Even with an exit option, however, dollarization will lack natural appeal to most governments owing to the high costs involved. If the approach today is attracting growing interest, it appears to be more because of the increasing disadvantages of defending uncompetitive national currencies (a rising NC curve in the Choice Diagram [see fig. 1]) than because of a new appreciation of the advantages of adopting a foreign currency (a declining DL curve). Recent experience suggests that most states are likely to remain resistant to an outright surrender of monetary sovereignty to one of the market leaders.

True, two countries have in fact chosen to go the dollarization route—namely, Ecuador and El Salvador. But in neither case can it be said that the decision reflected a sudden love affair with the *Yanqui* dollar. Both were really much more in the nature of a reluctant capitulation to forces, economic or political, beyond the government's control.

This was especially evident in the case of Ecuador, where the dollarization decision was taken in the midst of an acute national emergency. Troubles began with the Asian financial crisis of 1997–1998, which by 1999 had spread to much of Latin America. Following devaluation of the Brazilian real in February 1999, Ecuador's currency, the sucre, came under intense pressure, declining by more than two-thirds in value before the end of the year despite frantic efforts by the government in Quito to play the confidence game. While inflation soared to more than 60 percent, GDP shrank by more than 7 percent, Ecuador's worst recession since the 1930s. By January 2000 it was clear that the economy was near collapse. Despairingly, on January 9, President Jamil Mahuad proposed abandoning the sucre for America's greenback, which by this time had already come to account for two-thirds of all banking deposits in the country.[22] In effect, formal responsibility for monetary policy was to be handed over to the Federal Reserve—"the last-ditch move of a desperate politician," in the words of *The Economist* (15 January 2000, 21). Said a prominent local economist: "This is an act of desperation in the face of a crisis that is spinning out of control. . . . It is the unconditional surrender of a country that recognizes its own inability to conduct a monetary policy of its own."[23]

Mahuad's proposal was by no means a popular one. The president of the central bank, together with two top deputies, resigned in protest, and violent riots broke out in the streets. Some of the reaction reflected concern that dollarization would lead to even steeper inflation, hurting the urban poor and farmers in particular—"the dollarization of poverty," according to one labor-union leader.[24] Other protests were motivated more by fear of becoming just another client of the United States, in the manner of Panama. "More than a dollarization of the economy," charged one legislator, "this measure can be considered the Panamaization of the economy."[25] Opinion polls showed as much as three-quarters of the population opposed to the move.[26] In the context of Ecuador's shaky political system, however, what mattered more was the response of private-sector business groups, all of which lined up solidly in support of the plan.[27] With their backing the proposal was quickly approved by parliament, despite the overthrow of President Mahuad himself, and fully implemented within months. The stock cost to the country amounted to some $450 million required to redeem the bulk of existing sucre notes in circulation.

Today , despite lingering misgivings, dollarization in Ecuador is generally regarded a fait accompli.[28] As much was conceded even by the country's current president, Lucio Gutierrez, following his election in late 2002. Despite campaign promises to seek an alternative currency arrangement, once elected he pledged to preserve and strengthen dollarization in hopes of improving Ecuador's access to international capital markets (*The Economist*, 30 November 2002, 32).

In El Salvador, there was no sudden emergency, but the forces at work were much the same as in Ecuador—specifically the rapidly rising cost of defending the national currency, the colon. During the 1990s, conservative governments did everything they could to develop a reputation for "sound" monetary management. Yet foreign borrowing costs remained stubbornly high, while growth sagged to less than half that of neighboring countries like Costa Rica and Nicaragua. As early as 1995, discouraged officials floated a plan to formally replace the colon with the greenback in hopes of stimulating lower interest rates and faster growth. Though soon dropped, owing to opposition to the loss of a national symbol, the idea was not forgotten and received fresh impetus from Carlos Menem's remarks in 1999 and Ecuador's reluctant precedent in 2000. Relatively little organized opposition was evident, therefore, when the plan was officially revived in November 2000 and implemented two months later. In El Salvador, too, dollarization is now seen as a fait accompli.[29]

Elsewhere, however, dollarization continues to be resisted on grounds that its cost, on balance, would still be higher than that of the status quo. In terms of the Choice Diagram (see fig. 1), the DL curve is still widely seen as higher than the NC curve. An early case in point was provided by Israel more than two decades ago, when in the midst of raging hyperinflation the incumbent finance minister, Yoram Aridor, suggested replacing Israel's own money, the shekel, with the more solid dollar. The public was outraged, mainly for nationalistic reasons. As Lawrence Klein (1993, 113) later wrote: "When [Aridor] suggested . . . that Israel 'dollarize' in order to cope with uncontrolled inflation and other economic ills, [he] had to leave the government. It was unthinkable that a proud independent nation could be without its own currency." Another source (Glasner 1989, 31–32) reports the suggestion of one Israeli politician, not at all unusual at the time, that if the idea were to be implemented Israel might as well start flying the American flag and singing the "Star Spangled Banner"!

Perhaps an even more apt example was provided by Argentina, the country most responsible for reviving today's interest in dollarization. Despite former President Menem's eagerness before he left office to replace Argentina's dollar-based currency board, the idea was never implemented by his government and, as indicated in chapter 2, was ultimately rejected by his successors. In many respects, Argentina seemed an ideal candidate for dollarization. The country had strong economic linkages with the United States through currency substitution and its dollar-based currency board. At end-1999, the greenback accounted for some 56 percent of total bank deposits,[30] as well as an unknown—but undoubtedly large—share of paper currency in circulation. Buenos Aires had also grown close to the United States politically and was long accustomed to Washington's leadership role in the Western Hemisphere.

But Argentina was also Latin America's third largest economy, a middle-income emerging market with a fair amount of industry—far different from Ecuador and El Salvador, both much smaller and relatively poor. Moreover, the country's politics, from the late 1980s at least, were also more open and pluralistic than in Ecuador or El Salvador, where interest groups favorable to financial openness are more likely to predominate. Particularly in Ecuador, with crisis conditions prevailing, few opportunities existed for opposition to mobilize effectively against the government's dollarization strategy. "Integrationist" forces were able to dominate decision making. In Argentina, by contrast, "anti-integrationist" forces—particularly, labor unions—are much better organized and represented politically, creating a more level playing field. Indeed, even while Menem was still in office, parties opposed to dollarization controlled the lower house of Argentina's parliament. The country's bargaining context, therefore, was really quite different from that facing either the Ecuadorians or the Salvadorians. Buenos Aires was both pushed by its size and pulled by its domestic politics to hold out for a better deal, preferably in the form of a bilateral treaty of monetary association with Washington.[31]

At a minimum, Buenos Aires wished to recover some of its prospective seigniorage loss, which as indicated was expected to amount to at least $700 million a year. Other goals were reported to include LOLR access for Argentine banks at the Federal Reserve and cooperation regarding bank supervision.[32] Most importantly, if the nation was to surrender what remained of its historical monetary sovereignty, proud Argentines wanted to be seen as partners of the United States, not mere dependents. When Washington politely declined all such concessions, maintaining its stance of benign neglect, Buenos Aires elected instead to try to remain with its less demanding currency board.

Future Prospects

So which countries are more indicative of future prospects: Ecuador and El Salvador, which have embraced dollarization; or Israel and Argentina, which resisted it? Barring a major global crisis, which could drive many governments to seek the shelter of one of the Big Three currencies, the answer would appear to be inclined much more toward the latter. Numerous states are considered candidates for dollarization, but relatively few are likely to rush to imitate Ecuador and El Salvador.

Not everyone agrees. In the Western Hemisphere, for example, some sources take for granted that dollarization is the wave of the future. Predicts one specialist flatly (Schuldt 2003): "The complete official dollarization of most of our subcontinental economies will become a reality in the present decade." Adoption of the dollar across the region has been vigorously promoted by internationally prominent economists such as Ricardo Hausmann (1999a) and has been favorably commented upon by a wide variety of influential Latin Americans, from the president of the central bank of Costa Rica (Joint Economic Committee 2000a) to the heads of some of the biggest private corporations in Mexico (O'Grady 1999). Yet resistance throughout the Hemisphere remains strong, for reasons relating to all of the prospective costs involved. The rejection of dollarization by Carlos Menem's successors in Argentina has been widely echoed. Not even Mexico, with its proximity and close economic ties to the United States, shows any sign of eagerness for what many ordinary Mexicans would regard as a demeaning new form of dependency (Starr 2002). When Vicente Fox, for instance, was asked shortly after his election as president if he would consider dollarizing the Mexican economy, his firm reply was, "Not in the six years I will be in power."[33] In fact, there is little evidence in Latin America of any significant momentum in the greenback's direction. It is simply not true, as Robert Barro (2000) has claimed, that many regional governments are "keen" to join the dollar club.

The dollar club may yet grow, of course, as the costs of defending uncompetitive national currencies continue to mount. Even if lacking in enthusiasm, some countries could yet find it expedient to throw in the towel, just as the Ecuadorians and Salvadorians did. As one source (Fernández-Arias and Hausmann 2000, 179) writes, "The willingness to abandon current monetary arrangements will be related to the degree of frustration they generate." Suggestive is the decision by Guatemala in late 2000 to legalize the use of foreign currencies for certain transactions. The country's own money, the quetzal, is among the most threatened in Latin America by competition from the greenback, which already circulates widely throughout the local economy. In Guatemala, where many families depend on remittances from relatives working in the United States, "foreign currencies" means the dollar. The government's initiative effectively establishes a bimonetary system, which could turn out to be a precursor to eventual dollarization. And similar scenarios are possible elsewhere in the Hemisphere, as well.

Interest, however, is more resigned than keen. Lacking any significant concessions from Washington, such as the kind of seigniorage-sharing envisaged in the failed Mack Bill, membership in the club is apt to be pursued less as a privilege than as refuge.[34] Most likely are scenarios like Ecuador's—an acute national emergency of some kind that appears to leave policymakers with no viable alternative. Indeed, as political scientist Pamela Starr (2001) has argued, a "shared national trauma" may be the only way to overcome domestic resistance to such a radical reform.[35] Willem Buiter puts the point bluntly. Dollarization, he suggests (2000, 52), "should be of interest only to a chronically mismanaged economic basket case, whose only hope of achieving monetary stability is to unilaterally surrender monetary sovereignty." One is reminded of Groucho Marx's remark that he would never want to join a club that would have him as a member.

The most likely candidates are the smaller economies of Central America, the Caribbean, and the Andes, for whom the cost of a strategy of market preservation tends to be especially high—countries with Permeated Currencies or Quasi-Currencies whose domains have already been deeply penetrated by the dollar's more competitive brand of money. Most knowledgeable observers agree.[36] Two IMF economists (Berg and Borensztein 2000a, 41) put the point most simply: "The more the U.S. dollar is already used in their domestic goods and financial markets, the smaller the advantage of keeping their national currencies." The list of potential entrants would include, inter alia, Bolivia, Costa Rica, Nicaragua, and Peru, all among the Hemisphere's economies with the highest rates of informal dollarization according to recent estimates.[37] Timing, as in Ecuador, is most likely to be determined by the impact of local economic or political shocks that reduce resistance, at least temporarily, to an unconditional surrender of monetary sovereignty.

Similarly, in East Asia, no governments appear to be in a rush to "yenize," despite Tokyo's ardent efforts to build the foundations of a formal currency bloc. The reasons are both economic and political. In economic terms, "yenization" is obviously unattractive so long as Japan's economy remains stagnant and the international standing of the yen continues to decline. In political terms, a commitment to follow Japan is problematic so long as local governments seek to maintain cordial relations with other aspirants for regional leadership, most notably China. Typical is the recent remark of Malaysia's Mahathir Mohamad, who ruefully conceded that "we need to live with the fact that there is a China there and it is going to be a very prosperous, very big and economically powerful China."[38] In any event, East Asians find it quite difficult to get over their historical suspicions of Japanese motivations and interests. As one analyst (Castellano 2000, 8) suggests: "Much of East Asia remains wary of any form of Japanese leadership. China is deeply suspicious of Japan and would never allow it to establish a de facto economic hegemony. South

Korea harbors similar sentiments and likely would resist any plan to adopt the yen as a regional currency."

Significantly, the one economy in the region to go the dollarization route in recent years was East Timor—and that choice was not voluntary but rather was imposed initially by the outsiders who, in the name of the United Nations, took over management of the territory after it broke off from Indonesia in 1999. Moreover, when it came time to decide what currency to use in East Timor, the yen was not even considered. The main candidates were the euro, reflecting the territory's historical colonial links to Portugal (a member of EMU), together with the U.S. and Australian dollars and the Indonesian rupiah. America's greenback ultimately was chosen, even though it entailed the inconvenience of importing large shipments of U.S. coins to accommodate the low denomination of most local transactions.[39] Use of the dollar was retained after East Timor attained full independence in 2002.

A similar story also unfolded in Afghanistan following the fall of the notorious Taliban regime in late 2001. Here, too, some form of dollarization was actively considered once a new government was put in place in Kabul.[40] At the time, as many as seven rival versions of the national currency, the afghani, could be found in circulation—one issued by the Taliban itself, another by its victorious opponents in the so-called Northern Alliance, and yet others by local warlords such as General Abdurrashid Dostum, based in the city of Mazar-i-Sharif.[41] Temporary adoption of a strong foreign currency was seen as the easiest way out of the prevailing monetary chaos. But here again it was clear that the option, if chosen, would be something less than voluntary; and here again it was clear that the yen was never even a contender. The only foreign currencies seriously considered were the dollar and the euro.[42]

In fact, there would appear to be just one part of the world today where the prospect of adopting a dominant foreign money is viewed with anything like enthusiasm. That of course is among the EU's incoming members in East-Central Europe and the Balkans, where, as noted in chapter 3, there is much sentiment in favor of "euroizing" as quickly as possible. Immediate adoption of the euro, it is argued, would bring to the candidate countries the usual economic benefits, including lower transactions costs and interest rates and a chance to upgrade their financial markets and institutions. In the unique circumstances of transition to full EU partnership, it would also ensure a valuable degree of monetary stability, promote macroeconomic convergence with other Euroland economies, and help attract inward investment. In the words of Robert Mundell (2000c, 165), an outspoken champion of euroization: "Suddenly they will have a first-class currency. They give up currencies that are useless . . . they are getting something that will give them capital markets and an efficient monetary and financial system."[43] Perhaps most importantly, euroization would be seen as certification of their success in "rejoining Europe." But few of the applicants are likely to act rashly against the wishes of EMU's present members, whose good will remains vital to them in the admission process. The euro will most certainly come to the candidate countries, but not prematurely.[44]

Less likely is full or near-euroization in any of the other states of the euro–time zone, such as those in the Mediterranean region or sub-Saharan Africa. Some more limited degree of linkage with the euro will undoubtedly be of interest to many governments to Europe's south, given the depth of existing ties, both economic and political. But all are countries that have gained their independence only in recent decades. Dependency is something they have been trying to reduce, not increase. The last thing they want to do is reinvent colonialism in a blatant new monetary form.

Currency Boards

Like it or not, though, a choice must be made. Given the relentless pressures of currency competition, increasing numbers of states are certain to find themselves caught uncomfortably on the horns of a dilemma—between the persistently rising cost of defending a national currency and the still limited appeal of the dollarization alternative. Some governments, of course, might seek a way out of the dilemma by way of an alliance strategy in some form. But prospects for a multiplication of monetary unions are also dim, as we shall see in chapter 6. For many, the more appealing option could turn out to be one of compromise between preservation and followership—a more diluted form of vertical regionalization that, in principle, might ease the disadvantages of holding onto an uncompetitive national currency while retaining more of the advantages of monetary sovereignty. In practical terms, this would mean some variant on the theme of a *currency board*.[45]

Pros and Cons

The essence of the currency board, in its purest form, is a clear and publicly observable monetary rule, typically backed by formal legislative mandate. As indicated previously, the rule normally combines three key features: a fixed-price relationship with a dominant foreign money, unrestricted convertibility into the anchor currency, and foreign-currency backing for new issues of domestic money. Together, these three features effectively subordinate monetary sovereignty to the competitive power of a market leader. The approach has long been favored by partisans of greater central-bank discipline. The best known advocate is economist Steve Hanke, who with a varying cast of colleagues—labeled "monetary evangelicals" by John Williamson (1995, 1)—has for years campaigned tirelessly for adoption of currency boards in virtually every part of the world.[46]

The disadvantages of a currency board are the same as with dollarization. In principle, local monetary authority is minimized. A pure currency board can neither create money nor devalue at will. No new money can be generated, as central banks customarily are able to do by purchasing domestic assets in exchange for their own freshly created liabilities. Nor is any exchange-rate adjustment possible in the event of a capital outflow or trade deficit. Instead, the board is expected to act in a wholly passive manner to accommodate any variation in the supply of or demand for foreign currency—essentially a modern version of the old nineteenth-century gold standard where market-driven movements of gold were expected to dictate domestic monetary conditions, making money supply wholly endogenous. The country can neither manage its own macroeconomic affairs nor provide as cheaply for a lender of last resort. It will also find itself less effectively insulated from external political influence. The significance of the erosion of state authority is minimized by currency-board advocates such as the late Rudi Dornbusch, who wrote that in this context "sovereignty cannot be taken seriously."[47] But that was the economist talking. No student of politics would ever assume that governments are, or should be, indifferent about their practical capabilities.

As compared with dollarization, however, a currency board also offers two distinct advantages. First, the domestic money remains a prominent part of the money supply, circulating not in mere token amounts but as a full-bodied alternative to the anchor currency. Psychologically, this is bound to enhance the money's symbolic value as a catalyst for national identity.[48] Financially, broad circulation of domestic money preserves the flow of seigniorage that can be earned by the government, a point frequently stressed by critics of dollarization.[49] Instead of liquidating foreign assets to replace domestic notes and coins, the authorities can continue to receive interest earnings from reserves of the anchor currency held as backing for the local currency. Politically, retention of a domestic money reduces potential exit costs, since less foreign money would have to be replaced if the followership strategy were ever to be reversed.[50]

Second, a currency board offers an opportunity for more policy flexibility as compared with dollarization. When a leader's money is formally adopted as the follower's main currency, little leeway remains for the local government to influence monetary conditions or evade diplomatic coercion. A currency board, by contrast, allows for more "wriggle room" if needed, depending on how the monetary rule is written. While in principle a currency board is supposed to have no discretionary powers at all, in practice a fair amount of policy autonomy may be preserved to respond to contingencies or resist foreign pressures. Even during the colonial era, rules were frequently eased to accommodate local conditions.[51] The key to a currency board's flexibility lies in four interconnected issues of design. Two relate to the foreign-currency backing of domestic money—first, what is to be backed; and second, how much backing is to be required. The third relates to the price relationship with the anchor currency and the fourth to the possibility of an exit option. Much variation is possible along all four dimensions.[52]

First, what is to be backed? Monetary aggregates, as we know, can be calculated in a number of ways, from the core measure, M0, comprising notes and coins in circulation and the cash reserves of commercial banks—what economists call "base money" or "central-bank currency"—to M1, which adds conventional checking accounts (demand deposits), to even broader measures including other "reservable" deposits (M2) and progressively less liquid classes of financial claims (M3, M4). At its most demanding, a currency board would be required to provide backing for *all* liquid monetary assets in the economy, meaning at a minimum M2, otherwise known as broad money supply. But, in practice, coverage may be—and typically is—drawn much more narrowly, to apply only to some portion of base money, the only part of the money supply that comes directly from the state (in the form of liabilities of the central bank). Among currency boards in operation today, mandated coverage ranges from 70 percent of the central bank's current liabilities in Brunei to 105 percent of cash in circulation in Hong Kong.[53]

Theoretically even such a narrowly drawn mandate, limited only to central-bank currency, should ensure that monetary conditions respond passively to variations in the supply of, or demand for, foreign currency, the gold-standard model. That is because in a fractional-reserve banking system, variations in base money are expected to have a systematic, multiple effect on the level of bank deposits—explaining why base money is also known as "high-powered money." Much depends, however, on applicable reserve requirements for banks, which remain under the government's control. The ability to vary bank reserve requirements preserves another element of discretion for policymakers.

Second, how much backing is to be required? At its most demanding, a currency board would be required to provide *full* backing for domestic money—nothing less than 100-percent coverage in the anchor currency. But again, in practice, an element of discretion may be preserved if some part of the backing is allowed to take the form of domestic assets, such as government securities, that can be bought and sold on the open market.

One example was provided by Argentina, where, under its now-defunct currency board, the central bank was permitted to hold up to one-third of the backing for its currency in Argentine public debt.[54] Another example is Hong Kong, where since 1988 the currency board, known formally as the Exchange Fund, has been legally authorized to conduct open-market operations at its own discretion.[55] Central banks conventionally rely on open-market operations in domestic assets as a major instrument of monetary policy.

Third is the price relationship with the anchor currency. How solid is the rate of exchange between the two monies? Is it formally irrevocable, a hard peg firmly defined by law? Or is it established administratively and subject to possible alteration? Here, too, an element of discretion may be preserved insofar as the price relationship falls short of absolute rigidity.

Finally, there is the issue of exit. Is the arrangement permanent, ostensibly locking in a country's monetary regime for all time? Or is there a possibility that at some point the government's commitments on backing or the exchange rate might be relaxed, either to cope with unanticipated shocks or to pave the way back to a full-service central bank? For some analysts, currency boards are best seen just as a transitional device, to be replaced once the competitiveness of national money is firmly re-established. As one source puts it (Kopcke 1999, 22, 36), currency boards "represent a beginning rather than an end in the evolution of monetary regimes . . . a temporary shield for cultivating reputable central banks and financial institutions." The ideal for any self-respecting sovereign state, according to this view, is still One Nation/One Money. Hence a well-defined exit strategy is needed as a matter of prudent planning. For others an exit strategy is more a matter of insurance against risk, making sure that a government will be able to cope with unanticipated economic or political disturbances. Even an ostensibly permanent arrangement could use some sort of escape valve to prevent possible explosions (Baliño and Enoch 1997, 24–25). Either way, the result will be yet another element of discretion for policymakers.

Flexibility brings its own trade-offs, of course. The greater the wriggle room that is built into the arrangement, the more the country will risk losing the main benefits of a followership strategy, as purists like Hanke and his monetary evangelicals never cease to emphasize. Any departure from the rigors of an "orthodox" currency board, they argue, is "internally contradictory" and hence bound to compromise the credibility that is supposed to be gained by hiring the policies of a respected foreign central bank.[56] Lithuania's government discovered that danger, to its regret, in late 1994, six months after first introducing its currency board. Attempts by officials to use the board indirectly to augment fiscal revenues led to a nearly disastrous capital flight, which ended only when the authorities renewed pledges to accept the constraints of the system. As one source has commented (Camard 1996, 2, 19), "The experience of Lithuania . . . . illustrates the danger of pursuing flexibility too far."

Even more spectacularly, Argentina discovered the danger in the last years of its currency board, when the government began to lose the confidence of foreign investors. The two cases demonstrate that if market actors suspect that the commitment to the discipline of a currency board is less than absolute, pressures on the national money may remain strong. The currency premium on foreign borrowing will remain high, and the authorities will still be forced to play the confidence game at substantial cost to the local economy. Ultimately, as occurred in Argentina, the result might even be a total collapse of the arrangement, an outcome persistently predicted by currency-board critics like Nouriel Roubini (1998).

Nonetheless the option can be appealing to governments, precisely because so much latitude is available to tailor arrangements to specific national circumstances. Effectively, the authorities must choose between two different kinds of discipline—the discipline of the market versus the discipline of a dominant foreign power. The more a government is willing to follow the lead of one of the states at the peak of the Currency Pyramid, the tighter the arrangement can be in terms of rules for backing, the exchange rate, and exit. In practice, the outcome might fall not much short of near-dollarization. Conversely, the more policymakers value their own authority, resisting its formal delegation elsewhere, the looser ties can be. Though it sounds like an oxymoron, a currency board may in fact be proactive rather than passive. Indeed, flexibility could be pushed to the point where a regime becomes virtually indistinguishable from bimonetarism, the lowest degree of vertical regionalization, where only the loosest linkage remains between the national money and its foreign counterpart. In practical terms, the options here are many. Currency boards are remarkably plastic.

Recent Experience

Flexibility, of course, was the furthest thought from anyone's mind when currency boards were first developed by the British government, starting in the nineteenth century. The aim then was not to encourage local autonomy but rather to help stabilize London's financial relations with its overseas dependencies. Adaptations came only much later.

Like the empire itself, Britain's currency boards were a product not of deliberate design but rather of haphazard experimentation. Although a prototype was set up on island of Mauritius in the Indian Ocean as early as 1849, the definitive form was attained only in 1912 with establishment of the West African Currency Board for the Gambia, Gold Coast (now Ghana), Nigeria, and Sierra Leone. The West African scheme subsequently served as a model for London's other overseas possessions. By guaranteeing convertibility of local currency into the pound sterling on demand at a fixed rate, currency boards eliminated all foreign-exchange risk in trade with the mother country and effectively integrated colonial financial institutions into Britain's domestic banking system. British banks could operate as if foreign dependencies were nothing more than localities of the United Kingdom. This model was subsequently emulated by other colonial powers as well as by some nominally sovereign states, among them the free city of Danzig in 1923–24 and Ireland from 1928 until 1943.[57]

But such passivity was soon renounced once the great epoch of decolonization began after World War II. Currency boards may have assured colonies a degree of monetary stability, but they were also widely resented as symbols of imperial oppression. The absence of a central bank with discretionary powers served, it was thought, merely to perpetuate dependency and stifle development. The requirement that all currency-board assets be held in a foreign money seemed to mean fewer resources for domestic investment; similarly, a fixed conversion rate into the anchor currency precluded active management of local conditions. So why not seize control of the creation of money, just as the colonial powers had done for themselves in the nineteenth century? As the noted monetary historian Anna Schwartz (1993, 170) has written: "It became an article of faith that independence would enable former colonies, once freed from imperial control, to utilize their resources more productively and thereby achieve faster economic development. . . . Currency boards did not fit this vision."

In any event, as a matter of principle, continued monetary dependence seemed wholly inconsistent with newly won political independence. As noted in chapter 1, the Westphalian Model now reigned supreme, and every state's sovereign right to its own exclusive currency had become a universal norm. Very quickly, therefore, currency boards were abandoned in favor of more indigenous arrangements, most often based on a principle of strict territoriality. The only exceptions of any note were to be found in East Asia, where both Singapore and Brunei chose initially to preserve a form of currency board after attaining independence; and in Djibouti, a former colony of France in East Africa, where a currency board has existed since 1949 (though, as noted in chapter 2, linked to the U.S. dollar rather than to the French franc). Except for a brief interlude in the 1970s, a currency board has also been maintained in the former crown colony of Hong Kong, even after its return to Chinese sovereignty as a "special administrative region" in 1997. Elsewhere, the approach was rejected as an outmoded relic of a bygone era, including in Singapore where the currency board was ultimately abandoned in 1973.[58]

More recently, though, currency boards have made something of a comeback. The first new such arrangement in decades, as indicated in chapter 2, was adopted by Argentina in 1991 as part of a stabilization program dubbed the Convertibility Plan. The scheme was intended to reverse a pattern of persistent price increases that had reached hyperinflationary proportions in 1989–1990. Although the country's central bank was retained, its discretionary powers were severely curtailed by a law stipulating full convertibility of a "new" peso (Argentina's fourth currency in six years) into the U.S. dollar at a fixed one-for-one parity.[59] Later, formal currency boards were also established by two successor states of the former Soviet Union, Estonia in 1992 and Lithuania in 1994;[60] in war-torn Bosnia and Herzegovina under the Dayton peace accord signed in December 1995;[61] in Bulgaria in 1997;[62] and were also being actively discussed in many other parts of the world. Indeed, by the end of the decade, their comeback seemed assured. "Currency boards," one knowledgeable source asserted (Ghosh, Guide, and Wolf, 2000, 271), "are back in fashion."

Future Prospects

Fashion trends, however, can be exaggerated. Currency boards are not, in fact, about to appear by the dozens. For states that feel most pressured by the declining competitiveness of their own brand of money (a rising NC curve in the Choice Diagram [see fig. 1]), the approach will undoubtedly look more acceptable than the more radical dollarization alternative. With their notable plasticity, currency boards demand a lower degree of subordination and offer a wider range of options along the length of the DL curve. But this does not mean that the approach will be embraced with any greater enthusiasm by a large number of countries. It just means that if and when governments do decide to follow a leader, accepting that they can no longer defend their traditional monetary sovereignty, some form of currency board is the more likely path to be chosen.

Certainly there was no spontaneous groundswell of support motivating the comeback of currency boards in the 1990s. Logically, the case for currency boards rests on their attractiveness as a compromise between strategies of market preservation and followership. In only two instances, however—Argentina and Bulgaria—could the choice be regarded as having been the direct outcome of the Darwinian struggle among currencies; and even in these two countries, as in Ecuador and El Salvador, the initial decision was mostly in the nature of a reluctant capitulation to adverse circumstances. In each case, years of inflation had largely destroyed the appeal of the nation's own money. A currency board seemed a promising way to forestall a further loss of market share. Elsewhere, special circumstances prevailed. In Estonia and Lithuania, the problem was inexperience and a lack of credibility for newly created currencies, respectively the kroon and the litas. Both Baltic states had only recently returned to the family of sovereign nations. Their hope was to borrow from the reputation of a market leader to accelerate acceptance of their own new monies pending entry into the EU and EMU. In Bosnia and Herzegovina the problem was to restore order after a period of horrific conflict. The stability of a currency board seemed essential to the process of postwar reconstruction.

Furthermore, experience to date has not been kind to the reputation of currency boards. Certainly some arrangements have worked well, quietly achieving their objectives. That is especially so in Estonia and Lithuania, where the kroon and litas have indeed gained general acceptability; and in Bosnia and Herzegovina, where control of money has been successfully removed as a possible point of contention among the rival Croat, Serb, and Muslim communities. The long-standing arrangements in Brunei and Djibouti also continue to function effectively, attracting little attention. Overall, studies demonstrate, the approach tends to produce lower inflation rates than either floating exchange rates or soft pegs.[63] As a group, however, currency-board countries also appear to experience growth rates that are both lower on average (Levy-Yeyati and Sturzenegger 2001) and more volatile over time (Ghosh, Gulden, and Wolf, 2000). Moreover, within the group, there have been some prominent disappointments that have only served to reinforce doubts about even this limited form of followership.

Instructive for many was the near-foundering of the Hong Kong currency board in 1997–1998, in the midst of East Asia's financial crisis. As neighboring currencies depreciated sharply in value, Hong Kong's dollar appeared to become significantly overvalued; and not even the territory's respected currency-board arrangement, with its supposedly irrevocable commitment to a fixed parity, proved sufficient to avert fears that an exchange-rate adjustment was imminent. Upward pressure on interest rates, generated by panicky capital flight, imperiled local asset values and threatened to destabilize financial markets. Finally, in mid-1998, the authorities felt forced to intervene. The stock market was stabilized with massive purchases of equities amounting to as much as U.S. $15 billion, making the government the territory's largest shareholder. In addition, a number of new regulatory measures were introduced to reduce the risk of speculative manipulation of the exchange market, in effect an indirect form of capital controls. Hong Kong's efforts have been hailed by some as a successful recalibration of the tensions inherent in a currency-board arrangement. As Ghosh, Gulde, and Wolf (2000, 304) write approvingly: "The most recent measures aimed at increasing credibility . . . while at the same time enhancing flexibility. By managing to bridge these apparently opposing needs, Hong Kong appears to have improved the basis for the long-term sustainability of the system." But skeptics cannot not be blamed for questioning the appeal of a regime which, even after more than two decades of seemingly flawless operation, could suddenly become the target of near-crippling speculation.

Even more spectacular was the sad case of Argentina, where both the advantages and the disadvantages of a currency board were vividly on display before the arrangement's collapse in early 2002.[64] On the positive side, the 1991 Convertibility Plan clearly did stop hyperinflation in its tracks, achieving the government's main objective. Within two years, price increases dropped from a high above 5000 percent a year to single digits. Peso interest rates, correspondingly, fell from over 12 percent per month to under 2 percent, and by 1994 the economy was expanding at an annual rate near 10 percent, up from negative growth at the start of the decade. Moreover, with its currency board securely in place, Buenos Aires was better placed to cope with a devastating outflow of capital that was triggered in late 1994 by the financial crisis in Mexico—a contagion effect in financial markets that was quickly dubbed the "tequila effect." As Steve Hanke commented shortly afterwards: "As the Duke of Wellington often observed, victory is the avoidance of being crushed by an onslaught, and Argentina's currency board–like system has certainly kept Argentina from being crushed by the tequila effect."[65] After a brief recession in 1995, economic growth resumed in 1996–1998.

But then in early 1999, after months of financial pressure on Brazil, came the devaluation of the Brazilian real, highlighting the negative side of a currency board. Brazil is Argentina's main trading partner. Brazilian devaluation thus meant an immediate loss of competitiveness for Argentine exports and import-competing production, throwing the country once more into recession. Yet Buenos Aires could neither adjust its own exchange rate nor ease monetary policy in response. Only an activist fiscal policy might have been used to prevent a downward spiral. But that route was ruled out by the high level of public debt, much of it in the hands of foreign creditors who already harbored doubts about the government's debt-service capacity. Even with a currency board, therefore, Argentina was forced to go back to playing the confidence game, with all its attendant costs in terms of unemployment and soaring interest rates. Frustration with this turn of events explains why Carlos Menem soon turned to the more radical idea of dollarization, in hopes of bringing interest rates back down again. But when that initiative foundered, officials found themselves with few remaining options. Said *The Economist* (21 July

2001, 30) after two years of crisis: "The choices are austerity or bust," meaning default and an end to the currency board.

Interestingly, for many Argentines, the preferred choice was austerity, if only for symbolic reasons. Repeal of the Convertibility Plan was regarded as unthinkable, something that would be tantamount to confessing that the country could not be taken seriously. In *The Economist*'s words (3 November 2001, 44): "Most Argentines still cling to the currency board, as if it expressed their lingering self-image of being a far-flung corner of Europe." So policymakers resorted instead to increasingly questionable gimmicks to loosen the Convertibility Plan's straitjacket without formally discarding it. In moves intended to provide the equivalent of a disguised devaluation, tax and trade policies were modified in early 2001 to encourage exports and discourage imports, and legislation was passed to replace the currency board's original one-for-one peg to the dollar with a basket made up in equal parts of dollars and euros.[66] Subsequently provinces and the central government began to introduce large amounts of emergency currency—in actuality, low-denomination bonds of questionable value—in order to pay their bills.[67] The government even flirted briefly with the idea of issuing a wholly new money alongside the peso, to be called the argentino, to help finance public spending. By the end of the year, however, it was clear that the unthinkable could no longer be averted. After a brief period of political chaos over the New-Year's period following the resignation of President Fernando de la Rúa, Carlos Menem's successor, the currency board was terminated by the country's new leader, Eduardo Duhalde (ironically, the man whom de la Rúa had defeated by a wide margin two years earlier). In little more than a decade Argentina had gone, as one source (Pastor and Wise 2001) put it, "from poster child to basket case."

A similar pattern has also been evident in Bulgaria, where initial success in attaining monetary stabilization has been followed more recently by a striking failure to sustain growth or employment. So much, critics conclude, for the attempted compromise between market preservation and followership.

Disappointments like these do not mean that the currency-board approach is necessarily flawed. But they do suggest that, on their own, such arrangements are no more likely than dollarization to produce magic changes. Doubts are warranted. As one source (Gulde, Kähkönen, and Keller 2000, 6) puts it: "Currency boards are neither a quick fix nor a panacea." In the case of Argentina, for example, it is tempting to blame the Convertibility Plan for all the economy's recent ills, as Krugman (2001a) did before the currency board was terminated. "Why is Argentina's economy depressed?," he asked. "Basically, it comes down to the currency board." But Dornbusch (2001a, 6) was undoubtedly right in countering that it was "a grave mistake to read the Argentine experience with a currency board in this fashion. . . . The adoption of the currency board did not change three fundamental facts. First, Argentina has high debt levels . . . [second] Argentina has invested little over the past 50 years. . . . Third, Argentina has a legacy of unconstructive labor relations."[68] A more accurate reading would be that, like all policy compromises, currency boards offer no universal solutions and will not work effectively in all countries in every circumstance. The approach will appeal, at most, to just a limited subset of nations.

Which nations might these be? The most obvious candidates, plainly, will be found in the same two regions as potential dollarizers—in the Western Hemisphere, widely acknowledged as the natural home of a greenback zone, and in the EU's backyard in the euro–time zone, from East-Central Europe and the Balkans to the Mediterranean and sub-Saharan Africa. We know that many countries in these regions are burdened by the increasingly prohibitive cost of defending an uncompetitive national money. Yet powerful resistance remains to the idea of full or near-dollarization. In these challenging circumstances, the currency-board approach offers a more acceptable degree of regionalization.

In the Western Hemisphere, resistance to dollarization comes from potential followers. Many regional governments are simply unwilling to surrender their monetary sovereignty unconditionally. But they also understand that the reality of the *Yanqui* dollar's popularity cannot be evaded. So why not consider instead a more limited followership strategy? Where currency substitution is already so widespread, some form of currency board would not in fact be a radical departure. That was Dornbusch's position. "It is obvious," he firmly declared (2000a, 153), "that a currency board model suits Latin America, using the dollar." Mexico in particular, he argued (2001a, 8), was "an obvious candidate for a currency board arrangement." But there are also many in the Hemisphere who disagree, stressing not the benefits but the risks involved in giving up control of monetary policy. A currency board, warn two Mexican economists, "would culminate in a costly and failed experiment. . . . It is illusory to think that the Federal Reserve would modify its practices to give precedence to Mexico's specific problems."[69]

Of course, even more flexible arrangements are possible. The process could be started gradually, by declaring the dollar legal tender for some or all domestic purposes, as Guatemala has done (and as has long prevailed in the Bahamas and Haiti). From bimonetarism it would then be but a short step eventually to institutionalize links to the greenback in more formal terms while at the same time leaving policymakers room for maneuver, depending on how the rules are written. The approach might be particularly attractive to the smaller economies of Central America, the Caribbean, and the Andes, where trade ties with the United States dominate and where a patron-client relationship with Washington would hardly be a novelty. Some observers (e.g., Whalen 2001) suggest that bimonetarism might also appeal to Mexico—"so far from God, so close to the United States," as the former dictator Porfirio Díaz wryly said. For these countries the Choice Diagram's (see fig. 1) DL curve will be lower than for a larger and more distant economy like Brazil, which trades as much with Europe as with the United States and which has leadership pretensions of its own in South America.

In the EU's backyard, the resistance comes not from potential followers but from the leader—the European Union itself, which, as we know, has done everything it can to discourage early "euorization" by prospective entrants. Applicants in East-Central Europe and the Balkans have been warned not to straitjacket themselves prematurely, before necessary structural adjustments, which will undoubtedly be quite extensive, can be made in their domestic economies. Rather, for the time being at least, they are urged to accept the much more modest constraints of the ERM 2, which effectively is no more than a soft peg. Given the enthusiasm of many of the candidate countries for "euroizing," however, some form of currency board might seem more appealing as a way to demonstrate their monetary credentials quickly without defying the will of present members. Research suggests that a currency-board arrangement, while demanding, would by no means be inconsistent with the requirements leading up to eventual adoption of the euro,[70] and both the European Commission and the ECB have given indication that currency boards would be deemed compatible with the ERM 2 (Szapáry 2000, 6–7; ECB 2002, 59–60). A currency board or bimonetarism might also be of interest to other states in the European orbit, around the Mediterranean or in sub-Saharan Africa, where links to the euro are still strong. A more limited degree of followership would enable them to avoid the sense that they are reinventing colonialism while still maximizing the advantages of their already close relations with Europe.

In East Asia, by contrast, there seems no more prospect for currency boards than for "yenization"—and for much the same reasons (Nicolas 2000). With their diversified economic and political relations, few regional governments see any significant advantage in tying themselves exclusively to a currency whose best days seem behind it. The only exceptions might be Cambodia and Laos, where the possibility of institutionalizing some kind of currency-board arrangement has come up for discussion.[71] But in these cases the anchor currency would be not the yen but the dollar, which already accounts for the bulk of broad money supply in both countries.

Elsewhere currency boards are less likely and will most probably emerge, as have the majority of recent arrangements, only as a result of special circumstances. Estonia and Lithuania, for example, have demonstrated the usefulness of the approach in supporting the creation of credible currencies in newly independent states. Their experience provides a precedent for other aspiring entrants into the family of sovereign nations, such as Palestine if and when peace ever comes to the Middle East. Other possible candidates could include the many restless—and potentially secessionist—provinces to be found in fractured and fractious states around the world, from West Irian in Indonesia to the Western Sahara in Morocco. Likewise, the experience of Bosnia and Herzegovina suggests that a currency board can be highly useful in facilitating the restoration of order following war or civil insurrection.

Finally, currency boards could emerge on a more localized basis, reflecting unique regional connections. In the South Pacific, for instance, Australia already enjoys a modest leadership role in monetary affairs by virtue of past or present colonial relationships. Its own brand of dollar is the principal money in three nearby states—Kiribati, Nauru, and Tuvalu—as well as in several island dependencies (see table 6); and suggestions are frequently made to extend use to more neighbors, as well, including East Timor (McLeod 2000; de Brouwer 2001), Papua New Guinea (Xu 1999; Duncan and Xu 2000), and most other Pacific island nations (de Brouwer 2000b). These tiny microstates would appear to be prime candidates for full or near-dollarization yet may be disinclined to surrender their monetary sovereignty completely. A currency-board arrangement based on Australia's dollar might thus seem an appealing compromise. Similarly, in South Asia, where the Indian rupee is already legal tender in Bhutan (alongside the country's own currency, the ngultrum), it is not difficult to imagine the relationship one day being institutionalized in the form of a currency board. America and Euroland are not the only monetary leaders who might attract a followership.

Conclusion

In general, therefore, it seems evident that some number of countries could well choose to substitute a degree of subordination for strategies of market preservation. But predictions that, as a result, the geography of money is evolving toward a simple structure of two or three giant blocs seem seriously misleading. Despite relentless upward pressure on the Choice Diagram's (see fig. 1) NC curve, not many governments will opt outright for the currency of another country. Apart from the special case of states aspiring to membership in the European Union, there will be few more Ecuadors and El Salvadors. Much more likely are decisions to opt for a less demanding degree of vertical regionalization, in the form of a currency board or bimonetarism. The monetary world will include a growing number of followers, but most will resist surrendering their formal authority unconditionally to a market leader.

Six

Hanging Together

WHAT, THEN, of the third option—a monetary alliance of some kind? If vertical regionalization seems too demanding for many states, despite the rising cost of defending uncompetitive national currencies, perhaps some degree of horizontal regionalization might appeal instead. Benjamin Franklin famously said, on the eve of the American revolution, "We must indeed all hang together or, most assuredly, we shall all hang separately." The logic applies equally to the geography of money, where governments today might find it easier to promote the market share of a single joint currency rather than seek to preserve separate and diverse national brands. In terms of the Choice Diagram (see fig. 1), the MA curve might well be seen as lower not only relative to the rising NC curve, but also relative to the DL curve, as well. Monetary unions, merging uncompetitive local currencies, have been advocated or predicted in virtually every corner of the world. Is hanging together likely to prove a more popular strategy than following a leader?

The main advantage of hanging together is that, in contrast to any form of dollarization, monetary sovereignty is *pooled* rather than subordinated or surrendered. With this type of sovereignty bargain, a share can be retained in all the benefits of regionalization—not just the saving of transactions costs, which is by its nature a mutual gain, but also all other benefits, as well, which with a followership strategy tend to go mainly to the leader. Therein, however, also lies the main disadvantage, since pooling necessarily implies some measure of *collective* action in the production and management of money. Horizontal regionalization in fact is no less demanding than vertical regionalization, and possibly even more so. An alliance requires allies—other states with similar preferences and a disposition to act cooperatively. In practice, willing partners among sovereign states are just not all that plentiful. As with dollarization, a fair number of governments could be attracted to less demanding forms of an alliance strategy, depending on bargaining context. But prospects for many full new monetary unions do not appear bright.

Monetary Union

Monetary union, in the strictest sense of the term, means the same as full dollarization—complete abandonment of a separate national currency. Only a newly created joint money is recognized as legal tender for a designated group of countries, and all decision making is lodged in a single central agency with strong supranational powers. As compared with dollarization, a full monetary union offers distinct advantages to participants, both economic and political. But there are also potential disadvantages that create serious obstacles to a successful sovereignty bargain. The conditions needed to facilitate the requisite degree of cooperation are demanding and exist only rarely in practice.

Effects

Analytically, the effects of a monetary union, as compared with the default strategy of market preservation, are similar to those of dollarization. On the one hand, the individual state can anticipate a reduction of transactions costs. The network externalities may be smaller than with dollarization, since the saving will be in transactions with just one's partners rather than with a market leader (together with all those who use the leader's currency). The transactional domain of a leader's money will almost certainly be larger than that of any newly merged currency, at least initially. Nonetheless, the gain could be considerable and will grow exponentially with the number of countries involved.

On the other hand, the individual state will also suffer losses in terms of all the other key factors at issue: macroeconomic stabilization, the distribution of seigniorage, political symbolism, and diplomatic influence. For each government separately, a monetary union necessarily implies an erosion of sovereign power and privilege. No longer can the exclusivity of a territorial currency be unilaterally exploited to help manage domestic economic performance or raise revenue for the government. Nor can a distinct state-sponsored money now be relied upon to enhance the nation's sense of identity or insulate it from outside influence. The benefits that derive from a strictly national monetary monopoly are obviously compromised.

The main difference from dollarization has to do with the *distribution* of losses. Who is the counterpart gainer? With dollarization, clearly, the gainer is the market leader. Apart from the shared reduction of transactions costs, benefits go directly to the dominant foreign power pari passu with the transfer of authority over money. With a monetary union, by contrast, authority is not surrendered but pooled—delegated not to the market leader but to the joint institutions of the currency partnership, to be shared, and in some manner collectively managed, by all the countries involved. Each partner's loss, therefore, is simultaneously also every other partner's gain. Authority may be diluted at the national level but is reconstituted at the group level. The individual state may no longer have much latitude to act unilaterally, but each government retains a voice in decision making for the group as a whole. They are all, in this sense, gainers.

Net effects for participants, therefore, could turn out to be rather more favorable than they might be with dollarization. Like any cartel, a monetary union aims to improve the market position of its members—to create a single joint currency that, as compared with weakly competitive national monies, will have more appeal to market agents. The greater the appeal of the new currency, the more the benefits of monopoly, eroded at the national level, will be replicated at the group level; the more governments will be able to resurrect the privileges once enjoyed before the advent of deterritorialization, albeit now collectively rather than separately. By hanging together, policymakers will be more strongly positioned to resist market pressures—in effect, to tilt the balance of power back from societal actors to states. They will thus be better able to guide macroeconomic performance, generate seigniorage revenue, promote a sense of community, and avoid external dependence. On all these scores the group could gain substantially as compared with what each government might achieve on its own. Joint gains could exceed the sum of individual losses by a sizable margin.

Obstacles

Why, then, do we not see more monetary unions sprouting up around the globe? Despite the similarity of effects of the two approaches to regionalization, a monetary union would seem to offer significant advantages over dollarization, as numerous commentators have suggested. For George von Furstenberg the critical issue is seigniorage.[1] Vertical regionalization is a distinctly second-best solution to the problem of uncompetitive national currencies, he argues, because it means that all the revenue from the production of money will go as a windfall profit to a market leader like the United States. By contrast, with horizontal regionalization—what von Furstenberg calls the "multilateral sharing model of monetary union"—seigniorage stays with the members, to be divided up in some agreed-upon fashion. "Multilateral union is much kinder to small countries," he suggests (2000b, 115, 117). "Why pay royalties to the U.S. dollar forever?" A first-best solution would be "co-ownership and co-management of [a joint currency] in multilateral monetary union with like-minded countries" (2000b, 109). As he summarizes, not without a touch of sarcasm (2000c, 311): "The model of shared control and ownership . . . is more sustainable as it contributes to the wealth of a plurality of nations and does not just make the monetary wealth flow from the periphery to the center, or e pluribus ad unum."

For others, the advantages of a monetary union are more political. Participating states would be less exposed to the risk, noted in the previous chapter, of market penetration by banks based in a market leader's economy (D'Arista 2000; Vernengo and Rochon 2001). Interest rates and exchange-rate policy would be decided jointly rather than ceded passively to a market leader (Salvatore 2001), and members would be less vulnerable to coercive pressure from a powerful foreign patron (Dellas and Tavlas 2001). Participants thus avoid reinventing colonialism in the form of a new monetary dependency.

Yet despite all such advantages, the number of monetary unions presently in existence around the globe remains tantalizingly small. In addition to two arrangements left over from the era of colonialism (CFA Franc Zone and ECCU), only one new union, EMU, has come on the scene in recent years—in sharp contrast to the two cases of voluntary dollarization (Ecuador, El Salvador) and five currency boards that were created just since the start of the 1990s.[2] Clearly, obstacles lie in the path of a "multilateral sharing model"—most notably, in the very fact that the model must be *shared*. If a government wishes to adopt another country's currency or to cement a link via a hard peg, it can freely do so at its own initiative, as all recent cases demonstrate. Vertical regionalization is a strategy that can be designed and implemented unilaterally. Horizontal regionalization, on the other hand, is by definition mutual, an exercise in collective action. An alliance requires allies, as previously noted, and it must be negotiated. Willing partners in a sovereignty bargain like monetary union are difficult to find and may be even more difficult to negotiate with. Bargaining context matters.

Can the obstacles be overcome? Put differently, can conditions be identified that will facilitate the requisite degree of cooperation? Regrettably the contemporary empirical record, with only one new monetary union—Europe's EMU—to date, offers few direct clues. Indirectly, though, as I have suggested elsewhere (Cohen 2001a), much can be learned from analysis of the conditions that have determined the *sustainability* of monetary unions over time: that is, the factors that appear to influence whether such arrangements, once established, are fated to live or die. As noted in chapter 2, the historical sample of currency unions, including all those that have eventually failed as well as those that still survive, is quite large—certainly large enough to make clear just why an alliance strategy can be so challenging. The same factors that *sustain* monetary unions can be assumed to be instrumental in promoting their *creation*, as well.

Economic linkages, on their own, are clearly not enough to sustain the necessary cooperation. In assessing prospects for monetary unions, economists generally rely on the standard theory of optimum currency areas, highlighting the diverse variables that might affect the cost of commitment to an alliance strategy. But as often noted, the explanatory power of OCA theory appears limited at best. For every one of the characteristics stressed by theorists, there are contradictory historical examples—cases that conform to expectations suggested by the theory and others that do not (Cohen 2001a). Moreover, for any one country it is rare that all the factors cited point in the same direction, adding to the difficulties of forecasting; nor are all the variables necessarily mutually independent or easy to measure or compare for relative importance. In practice, none appears sufficient to explain observed outcomes. As one astute observer concludes: "The evidence . . . suggests that the theory of optimum currency areas has relatively little predictive value."[3]

Nor is much help offered by the details of institutional design—that is, the agreed-upon legal provisions to govern the issuing of currency and the management of decisions. Such organizational formalities, as we know, have differed sharply in various cases. In principle, such differences might be thought to matter insofar as they affect the net costs of cooperation by individual states. Recent theoretical literature on transactions costs emphasizes the key role that institutional design can play in promoting credible commitments, by structuring arrangements to match anticipated incentive problems (Martin and Simmons 1999). The higher the exit costs involved, the greater the disincentive for any government to defect. In looking at historical experience, therefore, we might reasonably expect to see a direct correlation between the degree of centralization of a monetary union and its sustainability over time. In practice, however, no such relationship can be found.

Most decisive are *political* linkages, which may take either of two forms. One, suggested by traditional realist approaches to international-relations theory, is the presence or absence of a powerful state committed to using its influence to keep a monetary union functioning effectively on terms agreeable to all. The other, suggested by more institutional approaches to world politics, is the presence or absence of a broad constellation of related ties and commitments sufficient to make the sacrifice of monetary sovereignty, whatever the costs, basically acceptable to each partner. Judging from the historical record, it seems clear that one or the other of these two types of linkage is necessary to sustain the requisite degree of cooperation among independent states. Where both types have been present, they have been a sufficient condition for success. Where neither was present, unions have tended to erode or fail.[4]

The first type of linkage, which implies a degree of subordination as well as a sharing of monetary sovereignty, calls for a locally dominant country—a leader or "hegemon"—and is a direct reflection of the distribution of inter-state power. Scholars have long recognized the critical role that the leadership of a powerful state can play in maintaining the stability of a monetary regime. At issue, as David Lake (1993) has emphasized, is the provision of a type of public good—an essential "infrastructure" that will support both short-term stabilization and longer-term growth. The leader must be not only able but willing to use its power, via side-payments or sanctions, to lower the costs or raise the benefits of cooperation for its partners.

The second type of linkage calls for a well-developed set of institutional connections and reflects, more amorphously, the degree to which a genuine sense of solidarity—of *community*—exists among the countries involved.[5] Scholars have also long recognized the demanding psychological dimension of bargains to pool sovereignty. Participating states, at a quite fundamental level, must come to accept that individual interests can best be realized through joint commitments—through what Keohane and Hoffmann (1991, 13) call a "network" form of organization "in which individual units are defined not by themselves but in relation to other units." Without such a sense of solidarity, governments will be more preoccupied with the costs of cooperation than with the benefits.

The underlying logic of these linkages is clear. Sovereign governments need strong incentives to stick to bargains that might, at some point, turn out to be inconvenient. In practice, such incentives may derive either from the encouragement or discipline supplied by a single powerful state or else from the opportunities and constraints posed by a network of institutional linkages. Economic ties may be weak or strong; likewise, organizational details may differ. But such factors appear to be of secondary importance at best. What matters most is a convergence of state preferences, supported either by a committed local hegemon or by a common project of integration. Von Furstenberg's (2000b) reference to "like-minded countries" is apt.

In turn, this logic suggests why a full monetary union may be so challenging to implement in the first place. In how many places can a suitably committed hegemon or necessary sense of community be said to exist? Where in the quarrelsome family of nations can the requisite like-mindedness be found? The obstacles to finding willing partners are formidable and, in most instances, likely to turn out to be insurmountable.

Europe

As a case in point consider Europe, home to the one new monetary union to be successfully negotiated in recent decades. For EMU, willing partners were in fact found—twelve in all by the time euro notes and coins made their appearance in 2002—with, as we know, even more countries throughout East-Central Europe and the Balkans clamoring to join. At first glance, the successful launch of the euro would seem to suggest that the obstacles to a full currency merger are not so formidable after all. But upon reflection it is clear that just the opposite conclusion is warranted, given the considerable time and effort Europeans had to put into getting the enterprise to this point. In many ways a unique undertaking, EMU is best understood not as evidence for enthusiasts but as the exception that proves the rule.

That EMU is exceptional is unquestioned. Never before, in modern history, has a group of fully independent states voluntarily agreed to replace existing national currencies with one newly created money. Even while retaining political sovereignty, member governments have formally delegated all monetary sovereignty to a common authority, the ECB. These are not former overseas dependencies like the members of ECCU or the CFA Franc Zone, inheriting arrangements that had originated in colonial times; nor are they small, fragile economies like those of Ecuador or El Salvador, surrendering to an already proven and popular currency like the dollar. Rather, these are established states of long standing and include some of the biggest national economies in the world, engaged in a gigantic experiment of unprecedented proportions. It is not without reason that, as I indicated in chapter 2, EMU is being closely watched around the globe as a test case for an alliance strategy.

But what does EMU prove? Obviously, the Europeans have demonstrated that the obstacles involved are not insurmountable. Participating governments did indeed find it possible to commit to the necessary degree of cooperation, despite the hardship of meeting all of the tough conditions laid down in the Maastricht Treaty. By the time the euro came into existence in 1999, most EU members were judged to have met the treaty's convergence criteria or at least to have made substantial progress toward achieving them. The one exception, Greece, was allowed to join the club two years later.

But it is also obvious that the path to EMU was not easy, requiring more than four decades of determined effort despite unusually favorable circumstances. The European Union was in fact a near ideal setting for implementation of an alliance strategy. On the one hand, members were already intimately connected to one another through a dense network of institutional linkages, which greatly eased the practical task of organizing a joint central bank and currency. The EU's sovereignty bargain has only continued to spread and deepen over time. Indeed, growing like-mindedness is implicit in their common integration project. At the same time there was also a powerful local hegemon, Germany, with a strong policy commitment to monetary integration. As noted in chapter 2, successive governments of the Federal Republic had found it useful to confirm their European credentials in this way even at the cost of sacrificing the country's own monetary independence. Yet two generations had to pass before EMU could be realized. If it took so long to get a currency union started in Europe, why should we expect it to be any easier elsewhere?

Admittedly, monetary union was not on the agenda of the EU when it first came into existence in 1958. Originally called the European Economic Community or Common Market, later simply the European Community (EC), the EU began as a pure customs union, freeing trade in manufactures among its six founding partners (France, Germany, Italy, and the three Benelux countries) and unifying their commercial policies vis-à-vis outsiders. Indeed in its founding document, the Rome Treaty of 1957, there was no mention of a common currency at all. But it did not take long for serious consideration to be given to the possibility of supplementing the customs union with a monetary alliance, beginning in 1962 with a proposal from the European Commission, the EC's executive body. Over the years, even as EU membership grew from a half dozen to fifteen, repeated efforts were made to promote a currency merger among the governments involved. These included the "snake in the tunnel" initiative in the early 1970s, the European Monetary System in 1979, and ultimately the Maastricht Treaty in 1992, which also rechristened the group, from EC to European Union. It was not until 1999, however, that the goal of a common currency was finally achieved.[6]

Moreover, even after four decades of effort it proved impossible to persuade all fifteen of the EU's members to join the project. Britain, Denmark, and Sweden, as indicated, all still prefer to stay outside Euroland, despite their full participation in other parts of Europe's common project, with little prospect of a change of mind any time soon. Even less enthusiasm, despite the euro's widening circulation, is manifested by close neighbors Switzerland and Norway. And even in Euroland itself, popular support long remained lukewarm at best. According to an opinion poll taken in the spring of 2001, only 53 percent of Germans favored introduction of the euro and even fewer in several other EU countries.[7] Only after euro notes and coins finally came on the scene at the start of 2002 did public antipathy begin to fade.

Reasons for the long resistance to monetary union in Europe are not difficult to find. The problem has never been the prospective loss of the seigniorage privilege, to which little attention is paid. Unlike in many developing nations, governments in Europe have long ceased to rely regularly on money creation to finance public deficits, and most have developed ample alternatives to augment spending when needed. But many Europeans do worry about removing yet another layer of national insulation against outside influence, to be wielded in this instance by a supranational ECB. Many worry as well about each government's diminished capacity to manage its own economy in the event of unanticipated shocks.

With activist fiscal policy severely constrained by the Maastricht Treaty's restrictions on budget deficits, what would compensate for the loss of both the money supply and exchange rate as instruments of macroeconomic policy? And in at least some member countries, there was also a deep reluctance to sacrifice what many regarded as a vital symbol of national identity. Again, as I argued in chapter 2, this is more than just a matter of "misplaced pride." Politicians concerned about remaining in office could hardly afford to ignore such strongly held sentiments.

In Germany, for instance, it was long clear that the public's coolness toward the euro was mostly psychological in origin. From the date of the deutsche mark's creation in 1948, replacing the older reichsmark inherited from Hitler's Nazi regime, the DM was revered as the most visible symbol of the new respectable Germany that was born out of the ashes of World War II—"an indispensable talisman of the 'good' Germany," as one observer put it (Shlaes 1997, 188). In the words of a former president of the Bundesbank: "The German people have a broken—an interrupted—relationship with their own history. They can't parade like others. They can't salute their flag with the same enthusiasm as others. Their only safe symbol is the mark."[8] Echoed another former Bundesbank president: "The D-mark has always been more than just a currency. It was an emotional thing, a symbol of renewal after the destruction of World War II. To the man in the street, it was a symbol of German power."[9] Could all this really be dismissed as mere "misplaced pride?"[10]

In Britain antipathy toward the euro persists even today, reflecting the still profound bond that many Britons feel between money and nation. Polls consistently show that as much as two-thirds of the public remains opposed to joining EMU. The former archbishop of Canterbury's concern about national identity was quoted in the last chapter. Along similar lines, a prominent Conservative politician hails resistance to EMU as "an opportunity to halt the demise of our country and register our belief that Britain is worth keeping," while a Labor counterpart declares that a decision on the euro will be about "whether or not to close the book on Great Britain itself." Asserts a former Labor foreign minister, now in the House of Lords, Britons resist giving up the pound because they fear that it will mean forgoing some of the "essential sinews of nationhood."[11]

What EMU proves, therefore, is that even in the most favorable circumstances, monetary union is difficult if not impossible to achieve. An alliance strategy is bound to encounter stiff resistance, for reasons both rational and emotional. In Europe, opposition has stemmed from worries about outside control, macroeconomic stabilization, and political symbolism. Elsewhere, potential seigniorage losses could also be a legitimate issue of concern. The obstacles to monetary union can surely be surmounted, given appropriate leadership and political linkages. But even when willing partners can be found, the process is unlikely to be consummated swiftly or easily. The burden of proof, in terms of the Choice Diagram (see fig. 1), will always be on those who wish to argue that the MA curve has declined sufficiently relative to a rising NC curve.

Unwilling Hegemons

In this light, the outlook for many new monetary unions around the globe seems dim at best. As indicated in chapter 2, prospects for horizontal regionalization have been debated in almost every region of the world, from East Asia to West Africa and from South America to Canada. In some cases, the idea has been to marry a smaller state in bilateral union with a larger neighbor. Examples include Canada, New Zealand, and Belarus. In each of these countries there has been lively discussion of the possibility of a currency merger with a larger power next door—respectively, the United States, Australia, and Russia. In other cases, the idea has been to build on regional integration projects comparable, in some degree, to the successful model of the European Union—including, most notably, groupings in Southeast Asia, South America, the Caribbean, West Africa, and the Persian Gulf.

Talk, however, is cheap. The real question is whether the necessary political linkages exist or can be promoted. In practice, the obstacles remain overwhelming. Smaller countries considering a bilateral union have not found a suitably committed hegemon; likewise, in existing regional projects, the necessary sense of community has been most notable for its absence. A *tour d'horizon* of today's monetary geography confirms the difficulty of cultivating the requisite like-mindedness among potential partners.

Canada–United States

We can begin with the three bilateral cases. Consider, first, Canada, where the possibility of a monetary union with the United States has been actively debated in recent years.[12] The two neighbors are already closely linked economically through the North American Free Trade Agreement (NAFTA), which came into operation in 1993,[13] as well as through a variety of other political and military arrangements and through closely related cultures and social histories. Though by no means a single community, the two certainly do not lack for a significant sense of solidarity. If in similar circumstances Europeans could agree to complement their free-trade zone with a common currency, many Canadians ask, why cannot North Americans do the same?[14] A name has even been invented for a future joint money—the *amero* (Grubel 1999), in flattering emulation of the euro.[15] Unfortunately for its advocates, however, the idea of the amero has elicited no interest whatsoever south of the longest unguarded border in the world.

Most prominent among advocates of a North American Monetary Union (NAMU) are economists Thomas Courchene and Herbert Grubel,[16] who naturally tend to focus on the standard economic benefits and costs of currency regionalization. Efficiency gains, in particular, are stressed. Canada, it is argued, is becoming an increasingly open economy, in terms of both trade and investment. With up to 85 percent of Canadian exports now going to the United States, accounting for upwards of 40 percent of GDP, transactions costs would be significantly reduced by a merger of currencies. The result could be a substantial further growth of trade and income. At the same time, potential costs are discounted. Little, allegedly, would be sacrificed in terms of macroeconomic stabilization, since Canadian inflation and employment rates are already so sensitive to developments below the border. Owing to the overwhelming dominance of America's economy, which is twenty times larger than Canada's, business cycles in the two countries have long been highly synchronized. Nor would the government be forced to forgo any of the seigniorage that it currently earns from printing money, estimated at some C $ 2–2 1/2 billion a year (Grubel 1999, 16; Robson and Laidler 2002, 12), since NAMU would presumably include provisions for seigniorage-sharing. On balance, Canada would come out a winner. The Choice Diagram's (see fig. 1) MA curve, for Canadians, is relatively low.

Not everyone agrees, of course. NAMU also has its opponents, who raise two principal types of objection. The first, essentially economic in nature, concerns exchange rates.[17] Canada's dollar—familiarly known as the "loonie" after the loon, a native bird, depicted on dollar coins—is presently allowed to float freely vis-à-vis all other currencies, including its U.S. counterpart. The advantage, in principle, is that a floating rate can function as a shock absorber to help cushion producers of primary goods from external disturbances. Commodity prices, as we know, tend to be relatively volatile, and among advanced economies Canada remains disproportionately dependent on its farming and extractive sectors, which still account for as much as a third of all exports. Independent analysis confirms that exchange-rate flexibility plays a useful role in buffering the Canadian economy against asymmetric shocks (Arora and Jeanne 2001; Carr and Floyd 2002). By contrast, the currency cushion would be lost in the event of a monetary union with the United States. For all the synchronization of business cycles, the structures of the two economies remain strikingly divergent, with their terms of trade tending to move in opposite directions in response to fluctuations of commodity prices. The pair can hardly be described as an optimum currency area.

There are some grains of truth here, reply NAMU proponents. The exchange-rate cushion does help buffer the domestic economy—but at what price? In fact, they contend, the costs of preserving a separate Canadian dollar with a floating rate are considerable. The Choice Diagram's NC curve is high and rising. In the short term, the argument goes, Canada's flexible rate tends to be volatile and subject to a good deal of "noise," sending confusing signals to the domestic economy. Over the longer term, floating is said to contribute to poor economic performance by delaying adjustments by both business and government to a secular decline in global natural-resource prices.[18] Overall, NAMU proponents conclude, Canadians have suffered a marked loss of real income relative to their American neighbors, reflected in the sustained drop in the value of the loonie from near parity with the greenback as recently as the mid-1970s to not much more than sixty U.S. cents at end-2001—the currency's lowest level in over a century. NAMU, by contrast, would supposedly send clearer price signals and encourage a quicker shift of resources from commodity production to more profitable sectors such as technology and services, accelerating growth of productivity and living standards.

The second type of objection encompasses familiar concerns about sovereignty and symbolism.[19] Are Canadians really prepared to give up their embattled loonie and all it represents about the distinctiveness of Canada's culture and society? As Eric Helleiner (2003b) writes, "the political battle over NAMU is inevitably a debate over Canada's national identity." More tangibly, are Canadians really willing to become junior partners of the Americans, as they inevitably would in any joint institution created to manage the amero? With less than one-tenth of America's population, Canada could hardly expect to receive equal representation in decision making. At best, the country might hope to become something equivalent to a thirteenth district of a widened Federal Reserve System, with correspondingly little influence. Summarizes Willem Buiter, a noted skeptic (1999b, 298, 302): "The nation state is weakened by this surrender of monetary sovereignty . . . complicated by the strong symbolic significance often attached to the national currency. . . . The political arguments against it appear to be overwhelming."

Again some grains of truth, reply NAMU proponents—but overwhelming? Critics are cautioned against exaggeration. Many of the same arguments were made against NAFTA before its ratification and ultimately proved far from the mark. In fact, giving up a national currency by no means implies surrender of cultural autonomy or political independence. In all respects other than money, the nation would remain as sovereign as ever. As Grubel (1999, 19–20), a former member of Parliament, concludes: "The basic fact is that the introduction of the amero does nothing to the existing national border and the ability of Canadian governments to pursue policies that get them re-elected. Nationalists do not have a good case to oppose the amero except on the grounds that it results in the loss of national monetary sovereignty. But [even] this loss is incurred in the expectation of large economic gains."

Though neither side in the debate lands a knockout blow, it is clear that the case for the amero cannot be dismissed out of hand. In fact, NAMU has roused widespread interest among Canadians and has even been the subject of parliamentary hearings in the nation's capital, Ottawa. Popular support is substantial, including key elements of the business community. At the end of 2001, according to a major opinion survey (Centre for Research and Information on Canada 2002), some 55 percent of Canadians favored a monetary union of some kind with the United States. Typical are the remarks of one prominent business economist, once an opponent of a currency merger who has now come around to champion it. "Let's face it," she says, "our currency does not float, it sinks. . . . Let's [negotiate a currency union] and get it over with. . . . I do believe it's inevitable."[20]

Inevitable or not, though, Canada faces a serious problem. Even if approval among Canadians were to become universal, a towering impediment remains—namely, a total lack of interest on the part of the United States. As the much larger of the two countries, the United States is clearly in a position to play the role of supportive hegemon. But as even the most enthusiastic of NAMU proponents acknowledge, currency union holds little appeal below the border and has attracted even less attention.

What accounts for the lack of interest among Americans? One reason could be a suspicion that NAMU might dilute the brand-name appeal of the dollar, reducing the benefits of international currency use presently enjoyed by the United States. Would demand for an unfamiliar amero be as great as for the comfortable old greenback?

Even more to the point is the matter of national monetary sovereignty. Americans, as noted in chapter 3, have had trouble enough working up any kind of enthusiasm for dollarization on the model of Ecuador or El Salvador, which involves no direct infringement at all on U.S. monetary sovereignty. They appear even less enthralled with the idea of a currency merger that would, by definition, require their monetary sovereignty to be shared. In a 2002 survey of U.S. public opinion, an overwhelming 84 percent of respondents rejected the notion of a new common currency for North America (Robson and Laidler 2002, 25). The point is well put by Canadian economist John McCallum (2000, 2), who observes that "the European Union model, in which independent states share decision-making and sovereignty, is alien to American thinking and American history. . . . If the United States will not contemplate changing the orientation of its monetary policy to suit a dollarizing country, it is obviously light years away from according such a country any formal role in the setting of United States policy, let alone contemplating a move to a supranational, euro-style currency." Grubel regretfully concurs. "The biggest obstacle," he concedes (1999, 39), "will be indifference in the United States."

In short, Canada lacks a willing partner; and without a willing partner, no collective action will be possible.

New Zealand-Australia

A similar problem looms in the South Pacific, where the possibility of a monetary union between Australia and New Zealand has also been actively debated. Like the United States and Canada, the two antipodean neighbors are already closely linked through a free-trade accord, the Closer Economic Relations (CER) Agreement dating from 1983, as well as through other political and military arrangements and closely related cultures and social histories. And as in North America, interest has been piqued by the precedent of the euro. Here, too, a name has even been invented for the future money to replace the present Australian and New Zealand dollars. It would be called the ANZAC dollar—"Zac," for short.[21] The problem is that here too the debate so far has been largely confined to the smaller of the two neighbors, New Zealand.

Interest at the eastern end of the Tasman Sea is evident. Acutely aware of their country's tiny size and geographic isolation, many New Zealanders feel that close integration with Australia, a market seven times larger, is imperative to ensure their future economic security. CER is viewed as just the beginning, with monetary union a natural corollary— simply, as one source puts it (A. Grimes 2000, 14), "the next logical step in the CER process." Discussion received a particularly strong impetus from the appearance in 2000 of a public manifesto for monetary union authored by two locally prominent economists, Arthur Grimes and Frank Holmes.[22]

Direct savings on transactions costs, advocates admit, would not be especially large, since only about a fifth of New Zealand's trade is with Australia, accounting for less than 5 percent of GDP. At most, according to a study at the country's central bank (Hargreaves and McDermott 1999, 23), savings might amount to a minuscule 0.13 percent of GDP. But New Zealanders could gain substantially from lower and more stable interest rates, which by promoting economic growth might in turn generate further expansion of trade and investment. One informed source (Coleman 2001, 182) suggests that "a doubling of trade is not out of the question."

Furthermore, advocates argue, New Zealand would have relatively little to lose in terms of macroeconomic stabilization, since the two economies are essentially alike both structurally and cyclically. Because each exports mainly primary commodities, terms-of-trade movements in the two countries are highly correlated, and business cycles tend to be synchronized. Hence New Zealand should have less need of a flexible exchange rate to buffer itself against adverse developments originating from its larger partner. Indeed, empirical evidence is cited to suggest that a joint money with Australia might actually provide a more effective shock absorber than the New Zealand dollar can on its own (A. Grimes 2000, 12). Likewise, as in Canada, there would presumably be little, if any, revenue loss for the government, since an arrangement for revenue-sharing could be anticipated.

In fact, the evidence on the cushioning role of New Zealand's floating exchange rate is mixed, as numerous studies demonstrate.[23] While the correlation of shocks is high, it is far from perfect, owing to the differing composition of commodity exports from the two countries. Whereas Australia relies more on minerals, New Zealand ships more dairy and forestry products. Simulation exercises suggest that if New Zealand were to lose its ability to set monetary policy independently, the variability of both inflation and output could increase, rather than decrease, over the course of a typical business cycle (Drew et al. 2001). Concludes one analysis (Crosby and Otto 2002, 329), the results "do not present a uniform picture of business cycle synchronization."

Nonetheless, support for an ANZAC dollar is widespread among New Zealanders. In a survey of some four hundred local business firms, Grimes and Holmes (2000) found nearly 60 percent—three of five—in favor of a monetary union with Australia, with only 14 percent against. Opinion polls show a majority of the general public also backing an alliance strategy.[24] Even the prime minister, Helen Clark, has reversed her long-standing opposition. "If the largest countries in Europe see benefit in a currency merger," she said in late 2000, "what is so sacrosanct about the currency of a country with 3.8 million people? It might be one of those things that becomes inevitable as we have closer economic integration with Australia."[25]

But would Australians agree? The problem for New Zealand, as it is for Canada, is that the potential partner is just not interested. Like the United States, Australia clearly is in a position to play the role of supportive hegemon. But the issue is hardly debated at all by Australians, largely because direct benefits of a merger with their smaller neighbor would appear to be negligible at best. As noted in the previous chapter, Australia's currency already enjoys a modest leadership role in the South Pacific and might even acquire additional followers. If New Zealand is so eager for a monetary alliance, Australians suggest, they should simply adopt Australia's dollar as their own, just as have some other nearby island-states (de Brouwer 2000a). "Australians laugh at the prospect of replacing their dollar," claims *The Economist* (14 October 2000, 93). When asked by a reporter what he thought of Helen Clark's remarks, Australian finance minister Peter Costello flatly declared: "We're not interested in any new currency, any third currency. We are happy with our monetary arrangements and we intend to keep them. . . . It's open to other countries to say we would like to adopt your currency. . . . We are not proposing to change the Australian dollar nor are we proposing to go into some new currency."[26]

Unless New Zealanders can find some way to change Australian minds, the whole notion of an ANZAC dollar must be regarded as a nonstarter.

Belarus-Russia

A third example is provided by Belarus, formerly a republic of the Soviet Union, which in Czarist times was known as White Russia or Little Russia. With only eleven million people, an economy overwhelmingly dependent on Russian oil, and an uncertain sense of its own nationhood, Belarus has attached little importance to preservation of any significant degree of monetary sovereignty for itself. On the contrary, its own currency, the Belarusian rubel—derisively known as the "bunny" (*zaichyk*) after the rabbit that appears on the face of bank notes—was adopted only reluctantly, when the old Soviet ruble zone broke up in 1992–1993. Repeatedly, agreements have been signed with Russia calling for renewed monetary union between the two countries, most recently in 2000.[27] Negotiations have been driven by the country's autocratic ruler, Aleksandr Lukashenko, whose fondest dream has been to engineer a political reunification with Russia. Moscow, however, is at best a grudging partner, wary of taking responsibility for Belarus's feeble economy. The Russians have been prepared to sign one document after another to appease a strategically placed segment of their "near-abroad." But they have clearly been averse to going any further, toward any kind of practical implementation. Each accord, Russia's foreign minister has said pointedly, is "a declaration, not a treaty."[28] The latest agreement, in 2000, conveniently set a deadline for merger far enough into the future (2008) to assure that no immediate action would be required. Belarus may be eager for monetary union, but like Canada and New Zealand it lacks a willing partner.

Insufficient Community

Elsewhere, as indicated, monetary unions have been expected to build on regional integration projects already in existence. But nowhere does the local sense of solidarity seem sufficient to sustain the requisite degree of cooperation.

East Asia

One region where monetary union has come up for a good deal of discussion is East Asia. Particularly since the financial crisis that hit the area in 1997–1998, the idea has been widely mooted as a safeguard against future disruptions. The crisis seemed to suggest that the cost of defending diverse national currencies was, for most regional governments, becoming too high to bear. The Choice Diagram's (see fig. 1) NC curve was rising rapidly. Perhaps a single regional currency could better serve their interests.

Typical were the remarks of the head of Hong Kong's monetary authority in early 1999, calling for an Asian monetary union to make the region less vulnerable to speculative attacks. "The time may come," he averred, "when we may want to consider the possibility of our own Asian currency."[29] The goal of a joint money has been promoted by Mahathir Mohamad of Malaysia,[30] and has been formally endorsed as a "distinct possibility" by the heads of government of ASEAN.[31] Numerous private specialists have also spoken in favor, including most notably Robert Mundell.[32] Most experts emphasize the potential saving of transactions costs involved, as well as the prospect for greater insulation against future crises. A common currency would reduce the risk of incompatible exchange-rate movements or other negative regional spillovers of the sort observed after the Thai baht's crash in 1997. One economist with expertise in the region flatly predicts an Asian Monetary Union (AMU) by 2010 (Walter 1998).

But there are problems—not least, the challenge of identifying just which countries might become involved. As one source, otherwise an enthusiast of monetary alliances, ruefully observes: "Asia does not fit obviously into any currency zone" (Beddoes 1999, 13). ASEAN would seem to be the most natural focus. Its ten members are in the process of building a free-trade area, first agreed to in 1992. An AMU, like an ANZAC dollar or NAMU, would seem a logical next step. But not even ASEAN's most ardent admirers think it likely that a monetary merger can be negotiated any time soon.[33] When asked about prospects for a common currency, ASEAN's secretary general typically looks around the room for the youngest person present and responds, "Perhaps in her lifetime."[34] Noting how long it took Europe to conceive the euro, the Philippines finance minister has grimly commented that "perhaps it will also take us that time."[35]

The reasons for such doubts are evident. In the first place the ASEAN partners are an obviously diverse lot in terms of economic structure and development, ranging from modern high-tech Singapore and emerging manufacturing centers like Malaysia and Thailand to rural and still primarily agrarian economies such as Cambodia, Laos, and Myanmar. Trade relations tend to be highly diversified geographically, with relatively little intragroup trade, and there is no evidence of significant convergence in terms of either economic shocks or macroeconomic performance. Econometric studies confirm that the group remains far from anything that might be described as an optimum currency area.[36]

Even more critically, ASEAN is still at an early stage of evolution as a political community. For all their protestations of amity, member governments remain noticeably distrustful of one another and place a high premium on preservation of as much national sovereignty as possible. In fact, the group is rife with historical antagonisms, ethnic and cultural conflicts, and border disputes. Unlike Europeans, East Asians are as yet unwilling to pay even lip service to the notion of "an ever closer union" among their peoples.[37] Most, having only recently emerged from colonial status, are more intent on individual state-building than on promoting regional solidarity. Few demonstrate much inclination to define themselves in relation to one another rather than in their own terms.

Efforts to promote regional solidarity have not been absent, of course. On the contrary, ASEAN governments have invested considerable effort in building a variety of linkages across their borders, including not only their free-trade accord, but also agreements to integrate key infrastructure elements like railways, highways, and electrical grids. In monetary matters, central banks have cultivated closer ties through annual meetings of governors and enhanced cooperation on training and technical matters, and member states have several times pledged to institute a system of mutual surveillance of economic policies.[38] For the most part, however, ASEAN governments continue to rely primarily on informal arrangements and market processes rather than on formal institutions to pursue their objectives. ASEAN, they insist, is a voluntary association of independent states, not an EU in the making. Representative are the admonitory words of the managing director of Singapore's monetary authority: "Eventually some form of cooperation will emerge as market forces bring about economic integration. I would caution against forcing the process."[39]

But if not ASEAN, then which might be the countries to catalyze the creation of AMU? Conceivably, as some analysts suggest,[40] one or more subgroups of ASEAN could take the lead—say, an initiative combining the more advanced "tiger" economies of Malaysia, Singapore, and Thailand. Structural differences among the three tigers are smaller than within the group as a whole, and evidence suggests that they come closer to meeting the criteria of an optimum currency area (Eichengreen and Bayoumi 1999). But even these three remain far apart in political terms; and in any event it is difficult to imagine that they might undertake any joint project—particularly in a matter as vital as money—that would leave the rest of their ASEAN partners behind.

Alternatively, it might be possible to build on the ASEAN + 3 formula established by the Chiang Mai Initiative, as some have suggested.[41] The advantage is that the broader group would include two countries, China and Japan, who separately or together could play the role of supportive hegemon. The disadvantage is that neither Beijing nor Tokyo has the slightest interest in sharing its monetary sovereignty with the other, let alone with a diverse collection of smaller Asian neighbors. Japan, we know, would prefer to create an exclusive bloc based on the yen, while China, with its own great-power aspirations, can be expected to resist any bid by Tokyo for monetary leadership. Moreover, suspicions of both powers remain widespread throughout the region. Wariness about the Japanese, noted in the previous chapter, goes back to Japan's attempts during the interwar period to create a Greater East Asia Co-Prosperity Sphere, which most Asians remember as an exploitative and demeaning relationship. Fears of future domination by a giant, rapidly growing China are equally strong.

Whatever the combination of countries, therefore, it would appear that the requisite like-mindedness is just not there. However rapid the rise of the NC curve may be, willing partners for a monetary union in East Asia are in remarkably scarce supply.

Mercosur

The story is much the same in the four-member Mercosur,[42] in the southern cone of South America, where there has also been discussion of a possible monetary union. These countries, too, have had their share of currency crises, including Brazil's devaluation in 1999 and the collapse of Argentina's currency board in 2002, all suggesting a rapidly rising NC curve in the Choice Diagram (see fig. 1). These, too, however, are a diverse lot in terms of economic structure and development and are still at an early stage of evolution as a political community. Willing partners for a monetary merger are in scarce supply in Mercosur, as well.

Recent discussion was kicked off, as was Latin America's dollarization debate, by Carlos Menem, who raised the possibility of a common currency for Mercosur as early as April 1997 (Giambiagi 1999, 61). Part of Menem's motivation was to find a way to prevent Argentina's peso—tied as it was by its currency board to the strong U.S. dollar—from appreciating relative to the Brazilian real. Argentina needed to maintain price competitiveness in relation to its biggest trading partner. But he was also driven by a genuine commitment to Mercosur as an integration project. It was only when his proposal received a frosty reception from the Brazilian government, then headed by President Fernando Cardoso, that he chose to switch the spotlight to dollarization instead.

Officially, despite Menem's switch of focus, a common currency has now become part of Mercosur's agenda. Brazil's initial response was motivated mainly by a visceral distaste for any sharing of monetary sovereignty. But as a proud nation with leadership aspirations in South America, Brazil liked the idea of dollarization even less, with its implication of reinvented colonialism. "Dollarization is not a valid option for the joint region," declared President Cardoso's finance minister. "Dollarization is not a panacea. A single non-dollar currency for [Mercosur] is within our dreams."[43] By the end of 1999, President Cardoso had publicly warmed to the idea, saying that "it takes some time to realize just how . . . important it is";[44] and Cardoso's newfound enthusiasm was echoed in turn by his successor, Luiz Inácio Lula da Silva, following presidential elections in late 2002 (*New York Times*, 3 December 2002). At the end of 2000, a timetable was agreed for a "mini-Maastricht"—a set of macroeconomic convergence targets similar to those specified by the EU's Maastricht Treaty—that sought to establish the preconditions for an eventual monetary union. The long-term goal of a joint currency is now regularly endorsed at Mercosur meetings.

In practice, however, no one expects to see a monetary merger any time soon. The idea does have its fans.[45] But as one informed observer suggests (Wheatley 2001): "The idea of creating a common currency à la the euro remains a distant dream." One reason is that, like ASEAN, Mercosur is still far from anything that might be described as an optimum currency area, as numerous studies attest.[46] Price trends and cyclical developments in the participating economies remain highly divergent. Mercosur is still not even a true common market, despite the pledges that were made to remove all mutual trade barriers when the group was started back in 1988. In fact, there was some regression after the start of 1999, when Brazil's devaluation led to new import restraints in Argentina and tit-for-tat retaliation by the Brazilians. Intra-Mercosur trade dropped from a high of 25 percent of member exports in 1998 to under 18 percent three years later. Some hope for greater macroeconomic convergence was raised after Argentina abandoned its currency board in late 2001, but little progress seemed likely in the short term.

Even more critically, the four participants are also still far apart politically, all protestations to the contrary notwithstanding. This is especially true of the group's two dominant members, Argentina and Brazil, traditional rivals for South American leadership. Despite their historic reconciliation in the late 1980s, which made Mercosur possible, the Argentines and Brazilians remain wary of each other and fundamentally resistant to any initiative that might make one subject to the dominance of the other.[47] On both sides, political elites have shown great reluctance to cede any significant amount of policy autonomy to joint institutions (Kaltenthaler and Mora 2002). Real progress toward a Mercosur common currency will be impossible without a much higher level of mutual trust between these two uneasy neighbors.

The Caribbean

Monetary union has also come up for discussion in the Caribbean, building on the already established Eastern Caribbean Currency Union. The six sovereign members of the ECCU, embedded in a network of related agreements including the Eastern Caribbean Common Market and the Organization of Eastern Caribbean States, are in turn partnered with eight neighboring states in a broader regional grouping known as the Caribbean Community and Common Market (CARICOM).[48] In 1992, the governors of CARICOM central banks put forward a detailed proposal to launch a Caribbean Monetary Union (CMU) to include all members of CARICOM by the year 2000.[49] The plan was quickly accepted in principle by CARICOM heads of government and officially remains a key objective of the organization.

In practice, however, CMU remains a distant dream. The 2000 deadline has long since passed, and few in the region expect to see the birth of a new joint money any time soon. Typical are the words of the prime minister of Barbados, speaking in 1999: "The ideal is to achieve the common currency. . . . We know it can work. But it took the Europeans forty years to do it. . . . This will take some time."[50] Little has been done to formally implement the 1992 plan, which many informed observers regard as unrealistic for such a diverse set of economies.[51] Though all are relatively small and open, they differ greatly in level of development and export structure. Some, like the ECCU states as well as Bahamas and Barbados, rely mainly on tourism and services, while others depend more on mining (Guyana, Suriname), oil and petrochemicals (Trinidad and Tobago), or light manufacturing (Haiti, Jamaica). CMU has been justified, first and foremost, as a way of imposing discipline on the more inflationary members of CARICOM. (The worst offenders have been Jamaica and Suriname.) But despite the existence of multiple economic and political linkages, the notion has been resisted by some non-ECCU countries, fearful of any compromise of their traditional monetary sovereignty. Most of the non-ECCU countries prefer to continue producing and managing their own separate currencies, however low these monies may rank in the Currency Pyramid.

West Africa

A detailed plan to launch a new monetary union has also been agreed to by six countries of West Africa—Gambia, Ghana, Guinea, Liberia, Nigeria, and Sierra Leone. All are members of the Economic Community of West African States (ECOWAS) together with the eight members of the West African Economic and Monetary Union,[52] which, in turn and as indicated in chapter 2, is part of the CFA Franc Zone. In April 2000, the leaders of the six non-CFA members of ECOWAS declared their intention to complete a "second" monetary union among themselves by January 2003, as a first step toward a wider merger to include all the ECOWAS states by 2004. Initially, the six agreed to create a Convergence Council, to help coordinate monetary policies, as well as a West African Monetary Institute to begin setting up a central bank. Eventually, the new monetary authority would be consolidated with the already existing central bank of WAEMU, the Banque Central des Etats de l'Afrique de l'Ouest (BCEAO).[53]

The West African plan is ambitious and, if it were ultimately to combine with all of the CFA Franc Zone, could encompass nearly half the states of sub-Saharan Africa. Proponents stress the usual efficiency gains of a common currency and discount any costs that might be involved. In the words of a member of the ECOWAS Secretariat,[54] "Given the propensity over the years for monetary mismanagement in West Africa, the costs associated with the loss of national monetary instruments would not really amount to much." Much emphasis is also placed on the psychological importance of monetary union as a high-profile symbol of regional integration. Officials acknowledge that their inspiration comes directly from the euro and its role in the promotion of European unity.[55]

Others, however, question whether the project is realistic. At a technical level, the challenges are considerable. On the model of the EU's Maastricht Treaty, the plan calls for each country to meet a number of macroeconomic convergence criteria no later than 2003, requiring inter alia steep reductions in inflation rates and budget deficits. Given past policy performance in the region, many wonder whether all this could really be accomplished in two years—or even in ten or twenty. As one analysis dryly comments (Masson and Pattillo 2001a, 7), "it is not clear how the list of planned policy measures can be reconciled with the timetable." Likewise, does it really make sense to create an entirely new monetary authority for the six, only to merge it with the BCEAO a year later? Once established, would the new central bank truly be prepared to give up its institutional independence? The practical obstacles to implementation seem imposing.

Even more formidable are challenges at the political level. Apart from their common membership in ECOWAS, the six states have few direct linkages and are not even all geographically contiguous. Even a minimal sense of community is missing. Mutual trade is small, at a little over 10 percent of the average of exports and imports, while historical antagonisms in some instances remain deep and persistent. Moreover, most of these countries have only recently emerged from extended civil strife, making implementation of such demanding new commitments highly problematic. As one outside observer warns:[56] "There is a possibility that ECOWAS won't make enough progress in the other areas of regional integration to make it in the interests of each of the countries involved in monetary union to honor its commitments. The danger is that the monetary union might not last if it is not supported by other policies and institutional arrangements and by a feeling of solidarity among the participants."

The project's best hope is that Nigeria, by far the biggest state in the region, might play the role of supportive hegemon. The political will appears to be there. Indeed, it was as a direct result of Nigeria's leadership, together with that of Ghana, that the six countries were able to reach agreement in the first place. But even if the Nigerians are willing to lead, will others be prepared to follow? It could be difficult enough to persuade other former British colonies in the region, each determined to assert its own distinct nationality, to cede pride of place to Nigeria. It would undoubtedly be even more distasteful to the francophone states of the CFA Franc Zone, with their quite different cultural and political orientations.

In fact, prospects for full implementation of the West African plan are limited at best. Nor, despite much talk, does there seem any likelihood of new currency mergers elsewhere on the African continent, according to recent studies (Guillaume and Stasavage 2000; Honohan and Lane 2001). Even less credibility is attached to the stated intention of the new African Union, which in 2001 replaced the old Organization of African Unity, to establish a common currency one day for the continent as a whole.[57] In Africa, as in the Caribbean, there is still much resistance to any significant compromise of monetary sovereignty.

The Persian Gulf

Finally, there is the strategic Persian Gulf, where since 1981 the six Arab monarchies of Bahrain, Kuwait, Oman, Qatar, Saudi Arabia, and the United Arab Emirates have been grouped together in a loose association known as the Gulf Cooperation Council (GCC). The GCC was initially established as a security alliance, to help safeguard members against possible fallout from the 1979 revolution in Iran and the Iran-Iraq War that began in 1980. As one expert has written (Twinham 1992, 13), "security was what the Gulf Council was all about." To say that the Gulf region was—and, for that matter, still is—unstable would be an understatement. Six countries that otherwise had never felt much solidarity with one another were drawn together in hope of better protecting themselves against threats of external aggression or internal unrest.[58]

Interpreting security broadly, the GCC soon added an economic dimension with a Unified Economic Agreement in 1982, inter alia calling on the six partners to "seek to coordinate their financial, monetary and banking policies and enhance cooperation between monetary agencies and central banks, including an endeavor to establish a common currency."[59] In matters of trade the Unified Economic Agreement has been relatively successful, leading to the elimination of all customs duties among the members and a broad harmonization of external tariff rates. But in matters of money little has been done, in practical terms, to translate rhetoric into accomplishment, despite repeated reaffirmations of monetary union as a goal. The closest members have come to serious action was in 1987, when they agreed in principle to coordinate their exchange rates. But the effort was soon abandoned when governments could not concur on a common anchor (Peterson 1988, 169–170). Little evidence exists of any degree of macroeconomic convergence (Zaidi 1990).

More recently, at a summit meeting in January 2002, GCC leaders renewed their call for a common currency as part of a broad plan for deepening their economic integration. But the deadline for the projected monetary merger was set for as late as 2010—again, as in the Belarus-Russia agreement, far enough into the future that, conveniently, no immediate action would be required. Few observers expect to see significant progress any time soon.

Lesser Alliances

Of course, full monetary union is not the only possible choice. We know that less demanding forms of an alliance strategy are also possible, requiring something short of a complete pooling of monetary sovereignty. As indicated in chapter 2, horizontal regionalization offers at least as much flexibility as does a followership strategy to accommodate the interests of individual countries. In particular, much room exists for variation in the degree of formal authority to be delegated to joint institutions. Monetary powers need not be as centralized as they are in the ECCU and EMU. They may also be more decentralized, with separate currencies remaining in circulation, as in today's CFA Franc Zone and CMA or in the nineteenth century's Latin and Scandinavian Monetary Unions. Like currency boards, monetary alliances, too, can be remarkably plastic.

The merit of a more decentralized alliance is that, like more diluted forms of vertical regionalization, it offers a possible compromise between the rising cost of defending uncompetitive national currencies and the lack of willing partners for a full monetary union. Policies can be decided jointly, including especially goals for monetary growth and interest rates, but implemented individually in accordance with local circumstances. Likewise, the degree of fixity of exchange rates can be made a matter of negotiation. Currencies can be tightly locked together in a hard exchange-rate union or may be allowed some amount of flexibility along lines similar to the EU's early "snake" arrangement or later EMS. The idea would be to enhance the market appeal of participating currencies while retaining at least some of the historical advantages of monetary sovereignty. Might some governments elect to go this route in preference to strategies of either preservation or followership?

In some cases, the answer is almost certainly negative. Smaller countries like Canada, New Zealand, and Belarus, seeking an alliance with a much larger neighbor, might see virtue in the option. They would gain a voice in joint decision making yet not lose their own national currency. But they would face the same problem as with a full monetary union—namely, lack of a willing partner. For the United States, Australia, or Russia, there would be little direct benefit in sharing even a limited amount of their monetary authority with a smaller neighbor. Under less pressure from a rising NC curve, the bigger countries would see more virtue in hanging separately rather than together. Their interests would be better served if their smaller neighbor simply follows their lead, adopting some form of dollarization or currency board, as the Australians suggest to the New Zealanders. In cases such as these, regionalization is more likely to be vertical than horizontal.

Elsewhere, where monetary union is discussed in the context of a broader integration project, the probability of some lesser form of monetary alliance is greater. In some instances, a foundation is already laid— in Mercosur, for instance, with its intended "mini-Maastricht," or in West Africa with its Convergence Council and Monetary Institute. In others, the task will be to build on related institutional links and commitments.

Chances that governments will elect to go this route are lowest in places like the Caribbean or Africa, where ties to one of the Big Three are also strong. In these regions, as suggested in the previous chapter, many countries might be attracted more to some limited form of followership, such as bimonetarism or a currency board, anchored on either the dollar (in the Caribbean) or the euro (in Africa). Chances would be higher in regions where there is no obvious choice for vertical regionalization, as in ASEAN, Mercosur, or the Gulf. In these groups, there will be much incentive for monetary cooperation. At a minimum, a limited partnership might enhance the market appeal of their individual currencies. At a maximum, it could eventually generate the kind of like-mindedness that is needed to realize the still distant goal of a common currency.

Conclusion

The conclusion here is thus much the same as that in chapter 5. There is reason to believe that some groups of countries will move to pool a degree of their monetary sovereignty. But predictions of many full new monetary unions around the globe, on the model of Europe's EMU, appear premature at best, despite the attractions of currency merger. In terms of the Choice Diagram (see fig. 1), the NC curve may be rising, but for most governments the MA curve continues to look even higher still. Few countries share enough group loyalty to make the requisite sacrifice of monetary sovereignty seem acceptable; and even for those that might be prepared to make the commitment, willing partners are hard to find. Though Benjamin Franklin's logic remains impeccable, hanging together will not in fact prove any more popular as a monetary strategy than the option of following a leader. The geography of money will include a growing number of limited alliances but few, if any, new joint monies like the euro.

Seven _____

New Frontiers

CONTRARY TO THE Contraction Contention, therefore, the number of national currencies around the world does not appear set to shrink dramatically. Exploration of the four directions available to governments suggests that there will be much resistance to an outsourcing of monetary policy. However much the cost of a market preservation strategy may be rising, few governments seem prepared to delegate all their formal authority elsewhere. Monetary geography will not be greatly simplified by the power of economies of scale.

Indeed, quite the reverse seems likely, once we also take account of other influences on the supply side of the market. Beyond the misty landscape defined by government preferences lie new frontiers, populated by an increasing variety of currencies emanating from sources other than the sovereign state. National governments have never been the sole suppliers of money. Even during the heyday of the Westphalian Model, when the dominance of state-sanctioned currencies was most complete, numerous nonstate monies could be found in circulation. Prior to the nineteenth century, the role of the private sector as a major producer of money was taken for granted. Today, as demand-driven competition among currencies is once more becoming the norm, there is every reason to expect the role of the private sector to be affirmed again and even reinforced. In a world increasingly accustomed to choice among currencies, there seems little that is anomalous in adding new and potentially attractive nonstate monies to the menu. In this respect, too, monetary geography is moving "back to the future."

Although nonstate monies come in many shapes and sizes, two main species may be distinguished—*local* money and *electronic* money. Both types may be counted on to grow substantially in number, making the future of money even more complex. Controversially, this chapter argues that the growing proliferation of private monies represents a direct threat to the traditional authority of states. Most governments have already lost their traditional territorial monopolies in the geography of money owing to the widening of choice on the demand side of the market. Now, contrary to the view of many respected economists, I contend that states risk losing dominance of the supply side, as well—a development that will intensify still further the contest for market share.

Local Money

Local money is a form of liquid claim deliberately created by nonstate sources to serve the standard functions of medium of exchange, store of value, and unit of account.[1] Its distinguishing characteristic is that it is, by definition, *local*—intended for use only in a restricted transactional network, usually specified in terms of a single community or subnational region. Alternatively labeled "private currencies" or "complementary currencies,"[2] local monies already exist in abundance. In early 2000, as many as 2,500 local currency systems were thought to be in operation in more than a dozen countries, up from an estimated 300 worldwide in 1993 and fewer than 100 in the 1980s.[3] Many more are expected to emerge in years to come, enabling selected groups of actors to claim an increasing share in the overall governance of money.

Approaches

Local currency systems can be created in one of two ways. One approach offers a specialized medium of exchange, generically labeled "scrip," as a means to underwrite purchases of goods and services, often at a discount. The other, typically referred to as barter-based money, is explicitly based on an updated multilateralized form of the primitive bilateral transaction that preceded the invention of money.[4] Both approaches are becoming increasingly popular across the United States and elsewhere.

Scrip-based systems have a long history, having appeared at many different times and in a variety of places. In colonial America and again in the frontier West, where banks were not yet established, many municipalities took it upon themselves to compensate for the dearth of currency in circulation by issuing scrip, typically in paper form or as metallic tokens. Likewise, in isolated communities connected to mining or the lumbering industry, big mining or timber companies frequently used scrip as a way to extend credit to their employees and to direct purchases to their own general stores or commissaries. And during the Great Depression of the 1930s, literally hundreds of temporary scrip issues were put into circulation by a variety of public and private agencies, including state and local governments, school districts, manufacturers, merchants, chambers of commerce, and cooperatives. Common types included certificates of indebtedness, tax-anticipation notes, payroll warrants, clearing-house certificates, credit vouchers, moratorium certificates, and merchandise bonds. According to one early study (Weishaar and Parrish 1933), at least one million U.S. citizens were involved in local scrip networks in the early

1930s. Scrip issues were also widespread during the Depression in Canada, Mexico, China, and many countries of Europe.[5]

More recently, interest in scrip-based systems has revived, particularly among businesses eager to attract or retain customers in a competitive marketplace. Discount coupons are issued, either by a single enterprise or by a business association, that are redeemable in future merchandise. A prototype in the United States, called Deli-Dollars, was established more than a decade ago by a delicatessen proprietor in Great Barrington, Massachusetts, named Frank Tortoriello, who happened to be in need of cash to move to a new location. Denied credit by his bank, Tortoriello instead sold discount notes to customers redeemable after six months for sandwiches or other foodstuffs. Deli-Dollars proved so popular that they have remained in circulation ever since, with subsequent issues used for improvements at the restaurant's new location and for other expansion plans. The scheme has also spawned a variety of local imitators such as the Berk-Shares program, a collective program started by a group of Tortoriello's neighboring businesses in Great Barrington. Local retailers give away one Berk-Share, valued at one dollar for every ten dollars spent. Berk-Shares can then be used for purchases in any participating store during a festive redemption period (L. Solomon 1996, 53–65). In Canada, a similar system has been created by the giant retailer Canadian Tire Stores, which issues specialized discount coupons in the form of so-called Canadian Tire money, humorously designed to resemble the government's own bank notes. Today discount coupons are sold or awarded in return for purchases by a wide variety of retail vendors, from supermarkets to hardware stores.

Scrip systems are popular because they serve the interests of both their suppliers, who can employ such schemes to promote customer loyalty, and their users, who are able to realize savings on purchases. Like state-sanctioned currencies, scrip can be held for shorter or longer periods as a store of value and then eventually be employed as a medium of exchange. All that distinguishes scrip from more traditional money is its limited circulation, which of course is part of its purpose.

Barter-based systems, by contrast, are of more recent origin, beginning with the Local-Exchange Trading System (LETS) invented by a Canadian, Michael Linton, on Vancouver Island, British Columbia, in 1983. In response to a rise of unemployment when a nearby air base closed down, Linton incorporated a nonprofit membership organization to promote a form of multilateral barter among local residents. The idea quickly caught on elsewhere and has since become by far the most common form of local currency system. According to one source, there are now some 30 LETS programs in Canada, as many as 450 in Britain, and over 200 in Australia

(Lietaer 2001, 161–66). Another observer counted over one thousand worldwide in the late 1990s (Douthwaite 1999, 39).

Though much diversity exists in individual systems, the common feature of every LETS program is that its members engage in trade with each other using a monetary unit of their own devising—many of these monies having exotic, not to say eccentric, names such as bats, beaks, bobbins, cockles, hags, and kreds. The LETS organization acts merely as a clearinghouse and information service. Members sign up, paying a small initiation fee to establish an account, and describe the goods and services they are offering or seeking, with all offers and requests published periodically in a print list distributed to participants. The key difference from more primitive barter is that individuals are not forced to find a direct match for the items they desire. Members can trade among themselves without the need for a double coincidence of wants. Items can simply be bought or sold at a mutually acceptable price denominated in the common monetary unit, with all transactions reported to a central bookkeeper who debits the buyer's account and credits the seller's account. Debits and credits are then expected to be unwound in future transactions. Typically, no physical money actually changes hands, though in a few places fixed-value tokens (a form of scrip) are available for small-denomination exchanges. The use of tokens is reported to be especially common among LETS systems in Argentina (Douthwaite 1999, 40).

The greatest advantage of a LETS program is that there is no limit to the volume of transactions that may take place. The most notable disadvantage is that some participants might abuse the system by accumulating "excessive" debit accounts—a risk that is likely to grow as membership expands. LETS programs usually originate with a small group of likeminded and fairly principled individuals. But as numbers increase, making dealings more impersonal, less scrupulous participants may be attracted who, by buying much more than they ever intend to sell, could in effect bankrupt the system. Central to all such operations is the mutual trust that each member will eventually repay all debits. A massive amount of negative balances, which would have to be absorbed by others, could erode confidence to the point that the system might simply collapse. A second disadvantage is the sheer volume of bookkeeping required as numbers increase. To minimize both problems, most LETS programs have remained relatively small, with memberships that rarely rise above 200 at most.

Alternatively, the two problems can be avoided by following a substitute model pioneered by Paul Glover, a community activist in Ithaca, New York. In 1991, Glover created a more flexible form of barter-based system by introducing a paper currency (again, a form of scrip) that he called "Ithaca Hours." Notes, inscribed with the motto "In Ithaca We Trust" in pointed rebuke to the more theistic wording found on Federal Reserve notes, are issued in five denominations from one-eighth of an hour to two hours. Each Ithaca Hour is nominally valued at $10, considered in 1991 to be roughly the equivalent of one hour's wage in Tompkins County where the town of Ithaca is located. As in a LETS program, participants can trade among themselves without the need for a double coincidence of wants. But in lieu of bookkeeping entries, transactions result simply in the transfer of an appropriate amount of Glover's paper currency. To control the per capita supply of Ithaca Hours, notes are normally issued only when a new individual signs up for membership or periodically thereafter in return for continuing participation. Smaller amounts are also created for the benefit of nonprofit community organizations and to cover the system's own expenses. Once in circulation Ithaca Hours may be used by anyone within a radius of twenty miles of the town, whether a signed-up member or not.[6]

In the years since its introduction, Glover's model has attracted more than a thousand participants and cumulatively has generated an estimated volume of transactions in excess of two million dollars (Wallace 2001, 54). It has also spawned dozens of imitators across the country, among them Green Mountain Hours, in Vermont,[7] as well as Santa Barbara Hours and Isla Vista Community Currency that circulate in the neighborhood of the University of California at Santa Barbara.[8] Already by the mid-1990s as many as eighty-five Hours systems were reported to be in existence in the United States (Frick 1996, 34). Similar programs have also emerged elsewhere, especially in Canada and other English-speaking countries. Local versions can be found as far afield as Japan, where a Healthcare Currency has been developed to reward individuals who volunteer to help older or handicapped persons (Lietaer 2001, 201–2), and even in a tiny hill-top village in Italy, where a time-based currency was recently created by a retired law professor.[9] Essentially similar are the many so-called "barter clubs" or "barter fairs" that have recently sprung up in the southern cone of South America, which also make use of paper currency to create more flexible forms of exchange.[10]

In contrast to LETS programs, Hours-type systems offer two distinct advantages. They do away with the need to keep track of individual transactions, thus eliminating cumbersome bookkeeping, and they avoid the risk of excessive debit accounts since all purchases must be fully paid up with currency. But there are also several disadvantages. One is the possibility that some participants may accumulate more currency than they can spend, draining liquidity from the system. Another is the risk that once in circulation—and therefore tradable—the money could become the object of destabilizing speculation. And finally there is the tricky job of piloting the growth of supply over time to avoid either overissue or underissue of currency. Though none of these challenges is unmanageable, each is unavoidable and is indeed intrinsic to any regime of monetary governance.

Motivations

The motivations for local currency systems are clear. Most fundamentally, local money is intended to promote the cohesion and self-reliance of communities. In Glover's (1995) words: "We're making a community while making a living." Local currency systems are self-consciously designed to serve as an instrument of economic empowerment.

In an insightful analysis, Eric Helleiner (2000) identifies three strands in the logic of local money. Advocates, he suggests, hope to pursue a trio of objectives: (1) a more localized sense of economic space; (2) an improved capacity to manage money actively to serve political and social objectives; and (3) a more communitarian sense of identity. All three goals may be understood jointly as a reaction against the increasingly impersonal pressures of the global marketplace, which are thought to be directly responsible for community decay around the world. In the words of one local-money enthusiast: "Whenever [state-sanctioned] money gets involved, community breaks down. . . . [Local] currencies can have exactly the opposite effect [in] building community" (Lietaer 2001, 187).

There is no doubt that modern market mechanisms tend to promote an expanded scale of economic life. Indeed, that is precisely what is intended by the neoliberal agenda described in chapter 4—a dissolution of the barriers separating national economies. One symptom is the increasing cross-border competition among currencies. Against this "globalizing" trend, which integrates markets to the extent possible, advocates of local money laud the virtues of localized, small-scale economies more in tune with the needs and tastes of individual communities. Local currency systems help cultivate a more decentralized sense of economic space by privileging purchases from nearby suppliers. In effect, as Helleiner (2000, 38) notes, they act as a kind of grass-roots protectionism by obliging participants to seek out local goods or services to make use of outstanding balances. Once more in Glover's (1995) words: "As we discover new ways to provide for each other, we replace dependence on imports."

There is also no doubt that modern market mechanisms encourage a "depoliticization" of the economy and its management. Absolute priority is placed on the maximization of economic welfare, a purely materialistic standard. Little consideration is given to alternative desiderata of public policy, such as full employment, alleviation of poverty, or a healthy environment. Local currency systems, by contrast, can be designed to support values other than the purely commercial, fostering an "alternative morality" of money, as Thrift and Leyshon (1999) put it. The supply of local money can be managed in a discretionary way to help promote any number of shared social principles—for instance, to create jobs,[11] extend cheap credit to the poor, or underwrite more ecologically friendly methods of production. It is not without reason that local money is often called "social money" or "green money." A local currency system can also provide something of a buffer against outside shocks or crises. "Just as a breakwater protects a harbor from the open sea," writes one enthusiast (Greco 1995, 36), "a local currency protects the local economy from the effects of the global market."

Finally modern market mechanisms, with their emphasis on the virtues of competition, clearly do discount any spirit of altruism, fostering instead a kind of radical individualism. Indeed, how could reliance on Adam Smith's "invisible hand" not engender a self-interested sense of identity? Advocates of local money, by contrast, are guided by a more communitarian worldview that sees men and women not in isolation but as part of a community. Individuals, they argue, can only realize their full potential in the context of collective social values and experiences. Toward this end local currency systems can play a valuable role by bringing people together through trade, helping to build lasting interactions and networks. Money has always been invested with social meaning, in primitive and modern societies alike.[12] In place of the destructive dog-eat-dog mentality of the marketplace, local currency systems may cultivate a more constructive mindset of fellowship and shared identity.

Consequences

Admittedly, all three motivations smack of a degree of idealism that may be difficult to sustain in practice. The issue, however, is not that local currency systems will necessarily succeed in all their objectives but rather that they afford an opportunity to try. Local money means that selected groups can reach out for a share of the power of monetary governance that central banks long sought to monopolize after the rise of the modern state. The impact at the community level, in terms of economic empowerment, may be considerable.

For central banks, by contrast, the impact until now has been little more than marginal, owing to the still limited number of local monies in existence, as well as the self-imposed restraints on their circulation. Indeed, in some cases central banks have even encouraged the development of local currency systems as a means to provide social support selectively to individual communities without compromising the overall orientation of monetary policy (Lietaer 2001, 226–27). There is no reason, however, why the challenge of these developments might not grow significantly over time.

Though few, if any, are ever likely to trade across national frontiers, local monies by their very existence mean additional competition for state-sanctioned currencies beyond the rivalries already introduced by contemporary deterritorialization. In the geography of money, local currency systems appears as a spreading archipelago within the functional domains of individual national monies. As their population continues to swell, the Darwinian struggle will grow ever more intense, further diminishing the role of the state in the management of monetary affairs. In time, the traditional powers of central banks will almost certainly suffer even greater erosion as compared with the heyday of the Westphalian Model.

Electronic Money

Moreover, that is just one of the challenges that central banks are fated to meet from the private sector. Along a different dimension another new frontier, possibly even more threatening, is opening up in the form of *electronic money*—various innovative payments media and mechanisms, based on digital data, that are emerging in the expanding world of electronic commerce. Around the globe, entrepreneurs and institutions are racing to develop effective means of exchange for transactions across the Internet and World Wide Web. Their aim is to create units of purchasing power that are fully usable and transferable electronically: "virtual" money that can be employed as easily as conventional currencies to acquire real goods and services. The era of electronic money will soon be upon us.[13]

As a practical matter, the line between local money and electronic money is not entirely clear, since some local currency systems (in particular, some LETS programs) do make use of new information technologies to aid with their bookkeeping, and both may be the product of private enterprise. The key difference between the two species of money lies in their respective spatial configurations. Whereas local currency systems, by definition, are typically meant to remain rooted in a single community or subnational region, electronic money's horizons are in principle limitless, potentially encompassing the whole universe of cyberspace. Once electronic monies become firmly established, therefore, their impact on the worldwide competition among currencies will be especially profound.

Approaches

Like local money, electronic money (e-money, also variously labeled digital money or computer money) comes in two basic forms, *smart cards* and *network money*.[14] Both are based on encrypted strings of digits—

information coded into series of zeros and ones—that can be transmitted and processed electronically. Smart cards, a technological descendant of the ubiquitous credit card, have an embedded microprocessor (a chip) that is loaded with a monetary value. Versions of the smart card (or "electronic purse") range from simple debit cards, which are typically usable only for a single purpose and may require online authorization for value transfer, to more sophisticated stored-value devices that are reloadable, can be used for multiple purposes, and are offline capable. Network money stores value in computer hard drives and consists of diverse software products that allow the transfer of purchasing power across electronic networks.[15]

Both forms of e-money are still in their infancy. Earliest versions, going back a decade or more, aimed simply to facilitate the settlement of payments electronically. These initiatives, which *The Economist* (2000) has wryly labeled "e-cash version1.0," have included diverse card-based systems with names like Mondex, Visa Cash, and Visa Buxx, as well as such network-based systems as DigiCash (later eCash), CyberCoin, and Net-Cash. Operating on the principle of full prepayment by users, each has functioned as not much more than a convenient proxy for conventional money—in effect, something akin to a glorified traveler's check. Few have caught on with the general public, and many have already passed into history.[16] A notable exception is PayPal, an online service in the United States that expedites cash transfers between e-mail accounts. In early 2002, PayPal was reported to have over 13 million users with annual revenues in excess of $100 million.[17] In late 2002, PayPal was acquired by the successful auction site eBay for a price of $1.5 billion.

More recent versions, mostly network-based, have been more ambitious, aspiring to produce genuine substitutes for conventional money. Labeled by *The Economist* (2000) "e-cash version 2.0," most until now have been offered as a reward for buying products or services from designated vendors—constituting, in effect, updated electronic forms of scrip. Vendor-specific media are clearly not a direct substitute for general currency, as specialists frequently remind us (Spencer 2001). But for the designated networks for which they are intended, modernized electronic scrip serves all the usual functions of money, just as do local currency systems in their respective communities or regions.

Recent examples of e-cash version 2.0 in the United States have included Flooz (using the comedienne Whoopi Goldberg as a spokesperson) and Beenz, neither of which survived the global economic slowdown that set in during 2001.[18] More successful have been programs that, as it happens, actually started out with other motivations in mind, such as the frequent-flyer miles of today's airline industry.[19] Originally intended, like most scrip programs, to cultivate customer loyalty, frequent-flyer miles have in reality become a widely used new form of money—"currencies in the making for the international traveling elite," as one source describes them (Lietaer 2001, 5). Miles are customarily employed as a unit of account for pricing different types of flights available through airlines award programs; moreover, once awarded, miles can be held more or less indefinitely as a store of value and then eventually employed as a medium of exchange to purchase tickets. Increasingly, miles can be used for other purposes as well—for example, to pay for telephone bills, hotels and other travelers' services, rental cars, and even books and compact discs.[20]

The difference between the e-cash versions 1.0 and 2.0 is vital. Earlier experiments like Mondex or DigiCash, merely added to the velocity of circulation—the flow of transactions using the existing stock of national money. Liquidity was enhanced, but payments still required settlement through the commercial banking system, debiting or crediting third-party accounts. Hence no fundamental threat was posed to the authority of central banks, which retained ultimate control of the clearing mechanism. The same is also true of PayPal today. With later ventures like Flooz or Beenz, by contrast, a potential exists for the creation of entirely new clearing mechanisms, quite independent from the existing money stock. Though Flooz and Beenz themselves failed, other forms of electronic scrip—frequent-flyer miles and the like—still survive, offering new circuits of spending that make no use at all of state-sanctioned bank notes or checking accounts as a means of payment. And of course there is always the possibility of yet more innovative versions emerging, as experimentation with new information technologies persists. As *The Economist* (2000, 68) suggests: "Even if e-cash version 2.0 fails, there will almost certainly be a version 3.0—not least because technology is making it increasingly easy to come up with new schemes."

In time, therefore, it is possible to imagine multiple versions of electronic money emerging to bypass customary settlement systems—"rootless [currencies] circling in cyberspace indefinitely," in the words of one expert.[21] Certainly the incentive is there. Electronic commerce is growing by leaps and bounds, offering both rising transactional volume and a fertile field for experimentation. "The cybersphere," writes another specialist (Lietaer 2001, 68), "is the ideal new money frontier, the ideal space with ample opportunity for creativity around money to emerge." The stimulus for innovation lies not just in the hope of reducing transactions costs but, even more critically, in the alluring promise of seigniorage: the profit that can be gained from the difference between the cost of creating money and the value of what that money can buy. To coin a phrase: Money can be made by making money. That motive alone should ensure that all types of enterprises and institutions—nonbanks as well as banks— will do everything they can to promote new forms of e-currency wherever and whenever they can. In the words of a noted historian of money

(Weatherford 1997, 245–46): "The companies that control this process will have the opportunity to make money through seigniorage, the traditional profit governments derived from minting money. Electronic seigniorage will be a key to accumulating wealth and power in the twenty-first century."

Central to the accumulation of electronic seigniorage will be the ability of these companies to find attractive and, more importantly, credible ways to offer smart cards or network money on *credit*, denominated in newly coined digital units, in the same way that commercial banks have long created money by making loans denominated in state-sanctioned units of account. The opportunity for virtual lending lies in the issuers' float: the volume of unclaimed e-money liabilities. Insofar as claimants choose to hold their e-money balances for some time as a store of value, rather than cash them in immediately, resources will become available for generating income through credit creation.[22] All that income will of course go to the issuers themselves, except for any costs associated with promotion of their new units of purchasing power.

Critical Issues

The process will not happen overnight, of course. Quite the opposite, the emergence of electronic money as a genuine rival to conventional currencies actually is apt to be rather slow and could take decades to be completed. The challenge is to create transactional networks of sufficient size to overcome the incumbency advantages of existing money. Unlike local currency systems, which typically come with networks that are in a sense "ready-made," electronic monies must undertake to build a cadre of loyal users from scratch—a task that is by no means easy.

To begin, a number of tricky technical issues have to be addressed, including inter alia adequate provisions for security (protection against theft or fraud), reliability (low probability of failure), confidentiality (assurance of privacy), and portability (independence of physical location). None of these challenges is apt to be resolved swiftly or painlessly.[23]

Even more critical is the issue of *trust*: how to command confidence in any new form of money. What is required is a degree of confidence akin to Peter Aykens's (2002) concept of affective trust—stable and unquestioning acceptability. Many believe that trust at this level can derive only from the sovereign power of the state, as the German economist George Knapp contended nearly a century ago (Knapp [1905] 1924). According to Knapp's "state theory of money," all money is a product of law and dependent for its validity on formal ordinances, such as legal-tender laws and public-receivability provisions. Trust is a function of political jurisdiction. Would America's green pieces of paper be so widely accepted around the globe, it is asked, if they were not backed by the "full faith and credit" of the United States?

But what, then, of all the private monies that have flourished throughout history? In fact, the historical record is replete with examples of what economist Richard Timberlake (1987) calls *common* tender, in contrast to state-sanctioned legal tender—payments media that have been commonly accepted without coercion through legal means. These range from the playing-card currency that circulated in France's North American colonies in the seventeenth and eighteenth centuries to the cigarettes and chewing gum that served as popular transactions media in post–World War II Germany (Weatherford 1997). All demonstrate that state power is by no means the only source of trust in a money. Past experiences of free banking across a broad span of countries, from Scotland to Australia, also give ample evidence of the capacity of private issuers to promote acceptability for their product (Glasner 1989; Dowd 1992). Likewise, the bursts of scrip-based systems in earlier times, as well as the re-emergence of local currency systems in the present era, testify eloquently to the limitations of the state theory of money.

The reality is that monetary usage can derive from a wide range of influences, private as well as public, and is ultimately social in origin. At its most fundamental, money is a social institution, resting on the reciprocal faith of a critical mass of transactors, as sociologists have stressed (Dodd 1994; Zelizer 1994). Confidence ultimately is socially constructed, based implicitly or explicitly on an intersubjective understanding about an instrument's future usability and purchasing power, and may well reflect nothing more than a transactional network's shared values or the gradual accumulation of competitive market practice. Money is whatever people come to believe will be accepted by others, for whatever reason.

Of course, that does not mean that promoting trust in newly created electronic monies will be easy, given the inertias that generally typify currency use. Monetary history, as earlier chapters have emphasized, also demonstrates that there tends to be a good deal of market resistance to rapid adoption of any new money, however attractive it may appear to be. Indeed, so far, the conservative bias of the marketplace has proved a serious obstacle to the successful introduction of electronic money.

Inertia is by no means an insuperable barrier, however. Quite the contrary, in fact. As the volume of electronic commerce continues to grow, it seems almost inevitable that so, too, will recognition and trust of cyberspace's diverse new means of payment. Something else we learn from monetary history is that even if adoption of a new money begins slowly, once a critical mass is attained widespread acceptance will follow. Confidence in new e-currencies can be enhanced through effective marketing programs or with clever advertising techniques. Most of all, success will depend on the inventiveness of issuing companies in designing features to encourage use. These bells and whistles might include favorable rates of exchange when amounts of electronic money are initially acquired; attractive rates of interest on unused balances; assured access to a broad network of other transactors and vendors; and discounts or bonuses when the electronic money, rather than more traditional currency, is used for purchases or investments. Sooner or later, at least some of these efforts to whet user appetite can be expected to pay off.

Most critical of all is the question of *value*: how to safely preserve the purchasing power of e-money balances over time. Initially at least, this is likely to require a promise of full and unrestricted convertibility into more conventional legal tender—just as early paper monies first gained wide acceptance by a promise of convertibility into precious metal. But just as paper monies eventually took on a life of their own, delinked from a specie base, so, too, might electronic money one day be able to dispense with all such formal guarantees as a result of growing use and familiarity. That day will not come soon, but it does seem the most plausible scenario of the more distant future given present trends. Over the longer term, as *The Economist* (1994, 23) speculated a few years back, "it is possible to imagine the development of e-cash reaching [a] final evolutionary stage . . . in which convertibility into legal tender ceases to be a condition for electronic money; and electronic money will thereby become indistinguishable from—because it will be the same as—other, more traditional sorts of money." Once that stage is reached, perhaps one or two generations from now, we could find all sorts of new currencies competing for acceptance in the marketplace. For banker Walter Wriston (1998, 340), the future has already arrived: "The Information Standard has replaced the gold-exchange standard. . . . As in ancient times, anyone can announce the issuance of his or her brand of private cash and then try to convince people that it has value. There is no lack of entrants to operate these new private mints ranging from Microsoft to Mondex, and more enter every day."

How many electronic currencies might eventually emerge? Almost certainly it will not be the "thousands of forms of currency" predicted by monetary historian Jack Weatherford (1998, 100), who suggests that "in the future, everyone will be issuing currency—banks, corporations, credit card companies, finance companies, local communities, computer companies, Net browsers, and even individuals. We might have Warren Buffet or William Gates money." Colorful though Weatherford's prediction may be, it neglects the power of economies of scale in monetary use, which dictates a preference for fewer rather than more currencies in circulation. Networks must be large to make new monies attractive, but large networks will be impossible unless the number of e-currencies is relatively small.

That said, however, for all the reasons cited in chapter 1, neither is it likely that competition will drive the number down toward the "odd figure less than three" favored by Robert Mundell. Here, too, ultimately, we would expect to see a smallish population of currencies rather than just one universal money.

Consequences for Monetary Policy

The overriding question is: What will be the consequences of electronic money for monetary policy? Remarkably, this momentous issue until recently received relatively little attention in the formal literature,[24] though casual commentary has abounded. Preliminary positions were staked out early. At one pole could be found Stephen Kobrin (1997), a professor of international management, who saw a new day dawning in the governance of money. As he put it (1997, 71): "Private e-currencies will make it difficult for central bankers to control—or even measure or define—monetary aggregates. . . . At the extreme. . . currencies issued by central banks may no longer matter." At the opposite pole was Helleiner (1998a), who perceived not a new day but a false dawn. Fears for the future of monetary policy were overstated, he contended, if not totally misleading. To the contrary, "new forms of electronic money are unlikely to pose a significant threat to the power of the sovereign state" (1998a, 399–400).

These alternative perspectives could hardly be more divergent. More recent years have seen a significant increase in the number of formal studies of e-money's implications, mostly by economists. Yet opinions remain divided along much the same lines. Kobrin's view, for instance, has received implicit endorsement from the noted Harvard economist Benjamin Friedman (1999), who argues that with the development of e-money, monetary policy is at risk of becoming little more than a device to signal the authorities' preferences. The central bank, in Benjamin Friedman's words, is becoming no more than "an army with only a signal corps."[25] Helleiner's view, conversely, has been implicitly endorsed by other prominent economists, including Charles Freedman (2000), Charles Goodhart (2000), and Michael Woodford (2000).[26] In Woodford's words (2000, 233), concerns "for the role of central banks are exaggerated. . . . Even such radical changes as might someday develop are unlikely to interfere with the conduct of monetary policy."

Who is right? The main goal of monetary policy, we know, is to keep the level of aggregate expenditure in an economy broadly consistent with production capacity; in other words, to guide the ship of state between the Scylla of rampant inflation and the Charybdis of prolonged recession.

If electronic money can be expected to have any impact at all on the tradi-tional authority of central banks, it will be through its influence on the linkages between policymakers' decisions and private-market spending. Analysis suggests that eventual outcomes will be closer to the spirit of the predictions by Kobrin and Benjamin Friedman than to the sanguine view expressed by Helleiner and others. It also suggests that the answer will differ significantly depending on what countries we are talking about.

How Monetary Policy Works

To begin, consider how monetary policy works with a traditional territo-rial currency. The goal of monetary policy, to repeat, is to keep aggregate spending generally in line with production capacity. Since the level of ex-penditures (nominal demand) cannot be controlled directly, the trick is to find some way to accomplish the same objective indirectly. Central banks seek to do this by targeting either the overall stock of money or the nomi-nal price of credit (interest rates).

A major problem, of course, is the fact that neither the money stock nor interest rates can be directly controlled, either. Consider the money supply. Chapter 5 noted the many ways in which monetary aggregates can be calculated, from the core measure M0—comprising notes and coins in circulation and bank reserves, otherwise known as base money or central-bank currency—to the successively broader measures M1, M2, et cetera, adding checking accounts, other "reservable" deposits, and progressively less liquid classes of financial claims. Only notes and coins come straight from state authorities. That aggregate, however, is far too narrow a mea-sure for the purposes of monetary policy and in any event is greatly over-shadowed by the mass of deposits in most economies. Yet deposits—oth-erwise known as "bank money"—are created by commercial banks, through their business of retail lending, not by the central bank. Likewise, it is the banks themselves that set the interest rates to be paid by borrow-ers, not the monetary authorities. The challenge for central banks, there-fore, is to develop instruments that can effectively guide the ongoing pro-cess of deposit creation.

Typically, these instruments aim to exercise influence over bank re-serves, on the assumption that the availability and price of reserves will in turn condition bank lending and thus the public's overall access to credit. Again, that is precisely why reserves are also known as "high-powered money." Variations in the availability and price of reserves can, in a fractional-reserve banking system, be expected to result in much larger changes in the volume and price of bank money. The most popular tools of monetary policy are open-market operations, which control the overall quantity of reserves, and discount-rate policy, which controls the price at which reserves are traded among banks or between banks and the central bank. Open-market operations involve purchases and sales of widely traded financial claims, usually government securities, by the central bank with the market in general. Discount-rate policy involves the interest charged by the central bank for providing reserves directly to the banking system, either through lending at a "discount window" or through rediscounting or purchasing assets held by banks. The effectiveness of both tools is a direct function of the size of the central bank's balance sheet (base money).

In fact, therefore, the series of links in monetary policy—what economists call the transmission mechanism of monetary policy—is fairly lengthy, running from (1) open-market operations and the discount rate to (2) bank reserves to (3) deposit creation to (4) aggregate expenditures. Two key implications follow. First, since none of the links in the transmission mechanism is purely mechanical, there is ample room for slippage between central-bank decisions and the actual behavior of spending. Monetary policy is hardly a matter of merely turning a tap on or off. And second, since none of the links can be bypassed, there is ample room for long lags, as well, in the ultimate impact of central-bank decisions. As a vehicle for the implementation of public priorities, monetary policy is hardly swift, either.

Still, so long as the state's own currency is the only money available, ensuring a continuing demand for base money, the central bank has adequate reason to believe that its decisions can be broadly effective in steering macroeconomic performance. Influence over bank reserves may be neither precise nor immediate. But in the absence of any attractive substitutes for the national currency, nominal demand has little option but to adjust, more or less in proportion, to variations of available supply and interest rates. The connection will be looser, admittedly, in the event of an expansionary monetary policy; central banks, it is said, find it difficult to "push with a string." But the connection will most certainly be tight with contractionary movements. The key is the central bank's presumed monopoly over the high-powered reserves that back bank money. By empowering the central bank to manage the money stock and interest rates exogenously, a territorial currency maximizes the practical impact of monetary policy (especially restrictive policy).

Implications of Deterritorialization

Now consider the implications of today's deterritorialization of national monies. Quite obviously, once market agents gain a choice among currencies, the direct connection between nominal demand and national money is broken. The central bank may still be able to exercise a degree of influence over the stock of its own currency, however measured, or the level of interest rates. But to the extent that transactors and investors have access to alternative currencies, reducing demand for the central bank's base money, money supply and interest rates become endogenous rather than exogenous, as noted in chapter 2. Hence variations in the quantity or price of reserves now will have correspondingly less effect on the overall level of spending. The practical impact of monetary policy becomes attenuated, and the economy becomes more vulnerable to frequent bouts of inflation or recession (or perhaps both—stagflation).

It is important to stress where the root of the challenge lies. Analytically, we may distinguish between two key questions—what we may refer to as the separate issues of *control* and *autonomy*. Control refers to the central bank's technical capacity to manage the process of deposit creation. Can officials generate increases or decreases in bank money at will? Autonomy, by contrast, refers to the central bank's policy capacity to manage demand. Can officials generate increases or decreases in aggregate expenditures at will? Clearly, the challenge of deterritorialization is to central-bank autonomy rather than control.

Deterritorialization compromises neither the link running from the instruments of monetary policy (open-market operations and discount rate) to bank reserves, nor the link from bank reserves to deposit creation. The central bank's ability to influence lending denominated in the nation's own monetary unit, therefore, is not directly affected. In that respect, the central bank remains as much a monopolist as ever. Rather, it is the link with expenditures that is infringed upon—the autonomy of monetary policy—owing to the competitive threat posed by the availability of other monetary units within the country. Herein lies the real meaning of the transformation of the state from monopolist to oligopolist in the management of monetary affairs. Substitute currencies mean alternative circuits of spending, affecting prices and employment, and alternative settlement systems that are not directly affected by the traditional instruments of policy. As Benjamin Friedman puts the point (1999, 335), "currency substitution opens the way for what amounts to competition among national clearing mechanisms, even if each is maintained by a different country's central bank in its own currency." The greater the intensity of competition from monies originating abroad, the weaker is the effectiveness of conventional monetary policy at home. Central banks must now make an effort to maintain market loyalty to their own sanctioned currency.

The challenge, of course is universal. As deterritorialization accelerates, no central bank can fully escape the oligopolistic struggle, no matter how competitive or uncompetitive its particular brand of money may be. Rivalry is not limited merely to the most popular global currencies, as is sometimes suggested (De Boissieu 1988). That would be so only if cross-border competition were restricted to international use, alone: the dollar, euro, and yen at the peak of the Currency Pyramid, along with a few lesser rivals like the Swiss franc and pound sterling, vying for shares of private investment portfolios or for use in trade invoicing. But deterritorialization, we know, extends to foreign-domestic use, as well, and thus involves all currencies, to some degree, in direct competition with one another—the weak as well as the strong, those formally protected by controls as well as those that are legally convertible. Money's oligopoly is truly global. The challenge of deterritorialization is faced by every government.

But that does not mean that the challenge is the *same* for every government. Universal does not mean uniform. In reality, the problems facing the favored few producers whose currencies actually do the competing across national borders—most notably, the market leaders: the United States, Europe, and Japan—are in a class apart from those many other countries whose monetary spaces have by now become highly penetrated. The challenge is clearly greater for economies like those in Latin America, the Middle East, or the former Soviet bloc, where currency substitution is already a familiar and accepted fact of life. The implications of electronic money can thus be expected to be comparably differentiated.

E-Money and Less Competitive Currencies

What does electronic money add to the problems facing countries with less competitive currencies? E-money's main impact here, while not insignificant, will be more a change of degree than of kind. The effect will be to *expand the population* of currencies circulating within each country, further eroding an already increasingly tenuous connection between nominal demand and national money. As more substitute currencies become available, variations in the availability and price of bank reserves denominated in the nation's own monetary unit will have even less influence on overall spending. Policy will become even more attenuated.

The key point is that for central banks in these countries, the challenge to monetary autonomy is already difficult enough even without electronic money. As compared with the halcyon era of territorial currency, when central banks could assume a reasonably tight connection between their own decisions and spending behavior, deterritorialization poses a tricky dilemma: how to guide overall expenditures when some part of the money supply available to residents is comprised of currencies other than the state's own monetary unit. The authorities can still use open-market operations and discount-rate policy to guide bank lending in national money. But insofar as the public has access to other monies, too, additional room for slippage or unpredictable lags is created in the transmission mechanism running from policy implementation to bank reserves to deposit creation.

Further refinements of policy are thus required to ensure that overall goals are met. Key questions include: How large is the supply of alternative currencies in circulation? How much spending can these alternative currencies support? And how easy is it for residents to switch back and forth between the national money and others in response to central-bank actions? (Technically, how great is the cross-elasticity of substitution between currencies?) In effect the supply of national money must now be treated as a *residual*, managed so as to complement expected developments in the non-national component of the total money stock in circulation. Once due account is taken of the availability of substitute currencies, parameters can be established for open-market operations and discount-rate policy that will, with luck, still exercise something like the desired influence on macroeconomic performance.

Though tricky, therefore, the dilemma is potentially manageable—but only so long as the residual represented by the supply of national money does not become too small. And there, of course, lies the rub. In reality, in a growing number of countries, the local currency's share of monetary aggregates is already dwindling rapidly as a result of deterritorialization, as the data cited in chapter 1 clearly demonstrate. In many economies, the supply of national money is indeed fast becoming a residual too small to have much direct effect on aggregate expenditure.

In this context, electronic money will add *quantitatively* to a central bank's problems but not, in any meaningful sense, *qualitatively*. For these countries the real discontinuity has already arrived—with deterritorialization, which broke the direct link between national money and nominal demand. Their monetary space has already been penetrated; their central banks are already being forced to fight for market share; their sovereign power, accordingly, has already begun to wane. The advent of electronic money will simply hasten the ebbing of the tide by contributing still more currencies to the competitive fray—some of which could turn out to have wider appeal than the government's own brand of money. As one commentator has suggested (Negroponte 1996): "Most of us would trust GM, IBM, or AT&T currency more readily than that of many developing nations. . . . After all, a guarantee is only as good as the guarantor." The battle facing these central banks will not be new, just more intense.

E-Money and the Market Leaders

What, then, of the market leaders, whose currencies are doing the penetrating? Until now, these economies have enjoyed something of a free ride—all the benefits of competitive success abroad without the corresponding disadvantages of a threat to monetary monopoly at home. For them there has not yet been any real discontinuity breaking the link between national money and nominal demand. For them, therefore, the advent of electronic money truly will be a reversal—a distinct change of kind, not just degree—insofar as one or more e-monies begin to gain widespread acceptance. When that happens the market leaders too, for the first time, will face genuine currency competition on their own turf.

Indeed, if anything, the challenge is likely to be felt by the market leaders *first*, even before any impacts spread onward to countries with less competitive currencies. The reason is evident. It is the market leaders that are most wired—the most plugged in to the new realm of electronic commerce. Online access is far greater in the United States, Europe, and Japan than elsewhere. Hence if electronic money is to gain widespread acceptance anywhere, it will most probably happen initially in these same areas. It is no accident that Flooz, Beenz, and most other experiments to date have all originated in the world's most advanced economies, which are both financially sophisticated and computer-literate. It is precisely these economies that are likely to be the most receptive to innovative new means of payment that can be used and transferred electronically.

Once some of these experiments begin to bear fruit, a new day will indeed have dawned, just as Kobrin (1997) and Benjamin Friedman (1999) assert. As in countries with less competitive currencies, which already face penetration of their monetary space, the population of monies will be expanded, breaking the link between national money and nominal demand. Now, for the first time, the leading central banks, too—the Federal Reserve, European Central Bank, and Bank of Japan—will be faced with the tricky dilemma of guiding expenditures when a significant fraction of the available money stock is comprised of currencies other than the state-sanctioned monetary unit (the dollar, euro, or yen).

Again, however, it is important to note where the root of the challenge lies. Kobrin (1997), for instance, is right to be worried about the potentially profound impact of electronic money on monetary management. But he is right for the wrong reason, insofar as he stresses the *control* aspect of monetary policy rather than its *autonomy*. The problem is not, as Kobrin suggests, that the advent of e-money will make it difficult for central bankers to control monetary aggregates. In the market leaders, as in those countries that have already experienced currency deterritorialization, the central bank's capacity to manage lending denominated in the nation's own unit will not be directly affected. Bank reserves can still be adjusted to guide the growth of local bank money. The challenge, rather, as Benjamin Friedman (1999, 2000) correctly argues, will be to the autonomy of central-bank policy—the capacity to manage demand—owing to the increasing availability of attractive alternatives to state-sanctioned currency. Alan Greenspan and his counterparts in Europe and Japan will now be compelled to refine policy, too, just as less fortunate central bankers elsewhere have already been forced to do; that is, to treat the supply of national money more as a residual, taking due account of the availability of substitute currencies in circulation.

The problem, as elsewhere, lies in the relative size of the residual. Could the local money's share of the total monetary stock become too small to be effective in steering aggregate expenditure? The question has been posed most starkly by a central banker, the ECB's Otmar Issing (2000). In a world of electronic money, Issing asks (2000, 30) "would the familiar existing units of account such as the euro, the U.S. dollar and the pound sterling, continue to mean anything?"

The Empire Strikes Back?

Is the threat real? Helleiner (1998a) and others, as indicated, contend that the challenge is unlikely to be serious. Three broad lines of argument are offered, none entirely persuasive.

First, the very possibility of new privately issued electronic monies is discounted. Both Helleiner (1998a) and Goodhart (2000) argue that the scenario is unlikely because of the inherent advantages of incumbency already enjoyed by existing national currencies. In Goodhart's words (2000, 200–201), conventional money "has first-mover advantages; it is already there. . . . The demise of [conventional money] at the hands of [e-money] will not happen." But that skeptical view ignores the powerful forces gathering to overcome the conservative bias of the marketplace: the immense new opportunities created by the expanding world of electronic commerce; and, above all, the potent allure of seigniorage. As already acknowledged, there is little reason to expect new "rootless" monies to gain acceptance overnight. But there are good reasons to assume that given enough time, the necessary transactional networks can be created. The issue is not the "demise" of conventional money but rather the emergence of nonconventional rivals. Even Goodhart concedes (2000, 200–201) that "over time it is possible that some brand (or brands) of [e-money] may become increasingly widely accepted [and] may indeed substitute for currency in a wider range of possible uses." The more widely accepted these substitutes become, shrinking the demand for base money, the greater will be the reduction in the size of a central bank's balance sheet, which is essential to the effective implementation of monetary policy.

Goodhart also stresses the difficulty, with today's technology, of providing complete confidentiality for transactions in electronic money. "How can the payer/payee be confident," he asks (2000, 192–93), "that the other counter party will not be recording the transaction in a manner that will leave an audit trail that can subsequently be followed?" The question is not unreasonable. Clearly, the technology does not exist to make e-money as anonymous as paper currency—at least, not yet. The trickiness of the challenge of providing adequate assurance of privacy has also been acknowledged. But it is reasonable to note as well that banknotes account for a decreasing share of overall transactions in most economies. The same threat to anonymity exists with checking accounts or with electronic payments systems using conventional currency. Electronic money, in fact, is at no special disadvantage in this regard.

What then of the inherent advantages that central banks enjoy in providing a payments system? This point has been emphasized by Freedman (2000), in effect harking back to Knapp's state theory of money. The fact that the central bank is a governmental institution, Freedman contends, backed by the full power of the state, makes its own settlement mechanism virtually riskless as compared with that of any private money issuer. Hence it is "very unlikely that other mechanisms, including variants of electronic money, will supplant the current types of arrangements for the foreseeable future" (Freedman 2000, 212).[27] Once again, however, this takes an unduly restrictive view of how trust in a money is constructed. Certainly the backing of the state gives conventional currency an extra margin of competitiveness. But for reasons already indicated, even that advantage need not prove an insuperable barrier to the successful introduction of new forms of money.

A second line of argument points to the fact that central banks themselves have professed to be unconcerned about the challenge of electronic money. Helleiner (1998a), for instance, cites a spate of official studies that have generally reached sanguine conclusions. Typical was a 1996 report by the Bank for International Settlements averring that as far as monetary policy is concerned, "it is highly unlikely that operating techniques will need to be adjusted significantly."[28] So if policymakers are not worried by the prospect, Helleiner asks, why should anyone else be? In fact, however, such commentaries tend to date back to the first generation of electronic money (e-cash version 1.0) and address only early prepaid products like Mondex and Digicash. Central bankers have much less reason to be indifferent to more recent versions of electronic money, which offer the possibility of entirely new clearing mechanisms rather than merely another form of liquidity. As Germany's Bundesbank conceded in 1999, "one cannot rule out the possibility of network money circulation becoming independent of monetary policy" (Bundesbank 1999, 51). Most pointed have been the anxious comments of Mervyn King, governor of the Bank of England. Once new electronic currencies make it possible for transactors to bypass state-sanctioned money, King suggests (1999, 411), "central banks would lose their ability to implement monetary policy. The successors to Bill Gates [could] put the successors to Alan Greenspan out of business." Remarks like these seem anything but unconcerned.

A third line of argument, taking the possibility of electronic money more seriously, acknowledges possible risks to monetary policy but nonetheless expresses confidence in the ability of central banks to sustain their traditional influence over nominal demand. The empire has the weapons to strike back, if need be. For Helleiner (1998a), the political scientist, this means using the coercive power of the state. Central bankers, he suggests, are unlikely to remain wholly passive if their traditional prerogatives seem truly in jeopardy. More likely, they will seek to extend their regulatory authority to newly emergent e-monies, imposing on issuers the same reserve requirements as traditionally applied to commercial banks and managing the reserves of issuers via the traditional tools of monetary policy in roughly parallel fashion. As he puts it, "state authorities [could] impose a regulatory structure on stored value devices similar to that which they impose on other forms of money" (Helleiner 1998a, 407). In extremis, they might even try to outlaw new e-monies altogether.

But could central banks do all this? One of the principal characteristics of cyberspace is its divorce from national territory. Producers of electronic currency could conceivably evade control or prohibition by shifting operations to another jurisdiction, just as banks have long since avoided taxation or various restrictions by booking transactions through offshore centers in the Caribbean or elsewhere. I have already alluded in chapter 4 to the vast network of financial intermediaries now in existence around the world that can be used to circumvent even the most draconian of official restraints. Attempts to extend the central bank's regulatory authority to e-money might, in practice, also prove to be an exercise in futility.

For others, such as the economists Freedman (2000), Goodhart (2000), and Woodford (2000), the power to strike back lies not in the central bank's regulatory authority but in its continuing ability to influence interest rates.[29] In Freedman's words (2000, 226): "Even in the extremely unlikely case . . . that the development of network money permitted alternative settlement services to be offered that effectively competed with central bank services, central banks would very likely be able to continue to influence the policy rate." Central banks, it is said, could retain influence over interest rates simply by conducting open-market or discount-rate operations in electronic monies as well as in their own state-sanctioned currency. But how easy might that be for policymakers, requiring transactions in currencies that they themselves do not create? Central banks would have no choice but to build up a war chest of e-currencies in the same way that they now hold foreign-exchange reserves. But that is still not the same as their traditional power to create national money at will. Interest rates might be influenced, but imperfectly at best.

The threat, in short, is indeed real. The risk is not that the power of the sovereign state will disappear—at least not in the sense of the state's ability to control the availability of its own money. Rather it is that as the population of monies grows, the power of the state will simply become more and more irrelevant, as Issing and King fear. The autonomy of monetary policy, gradually, will just fade away. That is—or should be—as much a worry for the market leaders as it already is for others. Arguments to the contrary notwithstanding, the dawn appears to be anything but false.

Conclusion

As the future unfolds, therefore, the worldwide competition among currencies appears destined to grow more intense, not less. Central banks must confront not just one another in an oligopolistic struggle for market share. Increasingly, they will have to cope with challenges from the private sector, too, in a manner not seen since before the era of territorial currency. New frontiers are opening up in the geography of money. Within national borders, state authority is being eroded by the spread of local currency systems, each determined to devolve a share of the power of monetary governance back down to the community or subnational region. Across national borders, state-sanctioned monies face the prospect of multiple versions of electronic currency, each capable of diffusing authority outward to the emerging universe of cyberspace. No longer can governments hope to dominate the supply side of the market as they have done in the past. Public policy will be forced to adjust accordingly.

Eight

Governing the New Geography

HOW WILL THE new geography of money be governed? *Can* it be governed? In the complex mosaic of currencies that is being re-created by the pressures of market competition, authority is coming to be exercised by more, not fewer, agents—not just by states, as in the traditional Westphalian Model, but also by an increasing number of nonstate actors, both as users and suppliers (local currencies and e-money). Power, in short, is increasingly decentralized rather than centralized. The advantage of this transformation is that monetary management in individual countries will be less subject to the exploitative abuses of monopoly privilege. The disadvantage is that the many hands on the tiller could result in instability and even conflict, eroding the usefulness of money in all its traditional functions. The challenge for the future will be to find some way to steer effectively through the hazards of this newly emerging landscape—to minimize the risks of currency competition while preserving its acknowledged benefits.

That brings us back to public policy. A role for the state in the governance of money remains unavoidable, as I argued in *The Geography of Money* (1998, ch. 8). Tempting though it might be to contemplate new nonstate forms of governing institutions, we must be realistic. National sovereignty remains the central organizing principle of world politics; society still looks to the state first for some kind of solution for its problems. Hence it is to established governments that we, too, must look for constructive responses to potential perils. The challenge needs to be met at two levels—at the domestic level, where the management of economic affairs is now increasingly problematic; and at the international level where the defense of monetary sovereignty is becoming more and more difficult. At the domestic level, the imperative is to find some new way to satisfactorily manage macroeconomic performance. At the international level, it is to successfully contain the centrifugal forces let loose by currency competition. At both levels, the core issue is the same: How can state preferences be reconciled with the influence of market forces? At each level, effective governance mechanisms are possible if governments are prepared to seize the opportunity.

CHAPTER EIGHT

The Domestic Level

At the domestic level, the diffusion of power in today's monetary geography represents a fundamental transformation in the manner in which money is governed. No longer is the public sector privileged in relation to societal actors. In a growing number of countries, governance now is uneasily shared between the public and private sectors, greatly weakening the state's ability to manage economic performance through monetary policy. Market agents have gained increased leverage both as users and producers of money. Hence if government is to continue to be held responsible for the broad prosperity of the nation, new means must be found to stabilize activity and promote growth. In practice, this will require a resurrection of fiscal policy as a core tool of macroeconomic management.

The Usurping of Monetary Policy

Recall the discussion in earlier chapters. As compared with a pre-Westphalian world of multiple and overlapping currency domains, an exclusive national money endowed governments with a potentially powerful instrument to influence output and prices. Nominal demand could be expected, to a greater or lesser extent, to be directly responsive to variations in monetary aggregates and interest rates. With the emergence of rival currencies, however, domestic as well as foreign, the efficacy of monetary policy is now seriously compromised, since selected sets of societal actors have more choice and money supply is increasingly endogenized. Market agents can elect to make use of alternative monies; some may even be able to *create* substitute currencies. Spending decisions, therefore, need no longer be tailored to the availability of state-sanctioned money. Quite the opposite, in fact. Now the availability of state-sanctioned money may have to be tailored more to spending decisions, giving the private sector a degree of leverage over public policy that is unprecedented in modern times. In political terms, this amounts to a usurping of the traditional dominion of monetary policy. Some part of the state's governing authority is effectively transferred to the social institution we call "the market."

Is this good or bad? As in the discussion of capital controls in chapter 4, the question here involves deeply held political values. On the one side are libertarians and others, ever distrustful of government authority, who conveniently neglect the constructive role of the state in providing public goods and enforcing the standards and rules that markets need in order to be able to function efficiently. For libertarians, the decentralized decision making of the marketplace is always preferable to the potentially arbitrary acts of public officials. On the other side are those, like myself, who worry more about the issues of equity and accountability that arise when we rely too much on the market's perpetual opinion poll to shape public policy.

The libertarian view clearly has some merit. We know that the monopoly power that states historically sought to establish for themselves has often been abused, usually to the detriment of their own citizens. Macroeconomic management has frequently been misguided, even counterproductive; worse, many governments have habitually become overly dependent on seigniorage to finance public spending, generating inflationary excesses. Monetary choice, by contrast, provides a refuge for a harried public—as suggested earlier, a form of inoculation against the crippling disease of the "inflation tax." But we also know that the cure may well turn out to be worse than the disease, if the price of restoring and sustaining a healthy currency is to get caught up in the endless demands of the confidence game. The more governments are compelled to placate the preferences of influential market actors, the tighter will be the constraints of the golden straitjacket, which can be even more detrimental to public welfare. Root-canal economics can be highly costly in terms of lost growth over time.

Ultimately, much depends on the political regime prevailing in each country—most importantly, the extent to which the government itself can be held accountable to a democratic electorate. The libertarian view is most apt for nations that still lack representative political institutions. For the unfortunate populations of failed or autocratic states, the market may indeed be the only way to express a view on official policy—in effect, to vote with money. Though the franchise may be a skewed one, favoring those with the most wealth or the best connections, it is still better than no franchise at all. But reliance on unelected and unaccountable market agents seems far less justified in the context of representative democracies, where standard political processes enjoy greater legitimacy. Where policymakers govern, at least in principle, with the consent of the governed, the weakening of the state's ability to manage macroeconomic performance must be counted as a real problem. As George Soros (2002) has written, "if international financial markets take precedence over the democratic process, there is something wrong with the system."

Can anything be done to fix the system—to rectify the loss of governing authority? Among monetary specialists three potential solutions are mooted, none very promising.

One possibility, most popular among critics of the neoliberal Washington Consensus, looks to capital controls for relief.[1] The logic of this *dirigiste* approach derives from the Unholy Trinity. Why continue to tolerate capital mobility if it is incompatible with national monetary autonomy? Instead, why not use the state's legitimate powers of coercion to sustain a currency's market share? So long as the right of a government to regulate money is recognized in international law, it is argued, states can trump the market by restricting choice, limiting either outward or inward flows of funds.

But at what cost? As suggested in chapter 4, there is no doubt that capital controls, if properly designed and implemented, can be made to work successfully for a time. But there is also no doubt that over time their effectiveness will almost certainly be eroded unless restraints are extended repeatedly, risking greater and greater efficiency losses. Effectiveness would be especially difficult to sustain in economies where currency substitution is already widespread. Capital controls, in short, are by no means an all-purpose panacea. How many governments will be prepared to pay the increasingly higher material price that would be demanded by this type of defense for an unpopular currency?

A second possibility, going back to the bipolar view of currency regimes that has become so fashionable among mainstream economists, looks to floating exchange rates for relief.[2] Here, too, the logic derives from the Unholy Trinity. If, in a world of capital mobility, monetary autonomy is incompatible with any kind of pegged rate—hard or soft—perhaps policy effectiveness might be restored by adopting flexible rates instead. Many governments have tried going this route in recent years. By the end of the 1990s, nearly half of all IMF member-countries had formally declared some manner of float for their currency, in contrast to just one in four at the start of the decade and less than one in ten in 1980 (Fischer 2001). Their aim has been to create for themselves more room for maneuver by eliminating official exchange-rate targets.

Floating, however, is no panacea either, as many observers are now beginning to acknowledge.[3] In economies where financial markets are still relatively thin, even small movements into or out of a money can spell massive exchange-rate volatility; and this volatility, in turn, can impose its own firm constraint on monetary policy, despite the logic of the Unholy Trinity. Few governments are prepared to live for long with persistent or arbitrary currency swings, which can have a significant dampening effect on investment.[4] In practice, many governments actively intervene to moderate movements of their exchange rate, formal commitments to floating notwithstanding—demonstrating a "fear of floating," in the celebrated phrase of Calvo and Reinhart (2002). The growing disparity between official regimes, as declared by states themselves, and actual practice is by now amply documented in empirical studies,[5] and has even prompted a formal revision in the way the IMF classifies currency arrangements.[6] Not infrequently, intervention to limit volatility occurs directly in the exchange market via purchases or sales of the national currency. More often it occurs indirectly via variations of money supply or interest rates, in effect sacrificing domestic policy goals for the sake of external stabilization. Policymakers still find themselves desperately playing the confidence game. In the words of one acute observer (Fratzscher 2002, 25): "In an increasingly interdependent world we are moving from an 'Impossible Trinity' to an 'Impossible Duality,' i.e., even under flexible exchange rate arrangements it becomes ever more difficult for countries to exert independent and autonomous monetary policy."

A final possibility is that governments might look to institutional reform for relief, in the form of independence for their central banks. This approach has long been favored by many economists.[7] Independence means that, within limits established by statute, a central bank can operate with full autonomy. Though ultimately accountable to elected policymakers, monetary officials are free of political interference on a day-to-day basis and, under normal circumstances, are under no obligation to help underwrite public-sector expenditures. Control over money is formally "depoliticized," promising adherence to strict discipline. The logic here derives from the role that persuasion, rather than coercion, can play as a tactic to sustain market share. If the reputation of a money can be buttressed by a credible commitment to "sound" management, what better way is there to assure trust than by delegating monetary authority to a group of disinterested professionals? Politicians, it is assumed, will be persistently tempted to manipulate the money supply to gain short-term advantage. Central bankers, by contrast, so long as they are insulated from direct political influence, can be expected to take a longer view and to maintain a greater consistency of policy. As one source summarizes (McNamara 2002, 48, 52), "delegation has important legitimizing and symbolic properties. . . . [It] is seen as the key way to enhance commitment."

That route, too, has been tried by many governments in recent years, particularly since the 1980s. Where once the number of independent central banks around the world could be counted on the fingers of one hand, now there are several dozen.[8] Today, monetary policy is managed by independent institutions in all in the advanced economies of Western Europe, North America, and Japan, as well as in many of the emerging-market economies of Latin America, East Asia, and East-Central Europe. Here also the aim is to create more room for policy maneuver, in this instance by easing doubts about the underlying motivations of policymakers.

But central-bank independence is no more a panacea than either of the other two possibilities, even if it does succeed in insulating monetary policy from the hurly burly of politics. The point, after all, is not who is in charge but, rather, of what they are in charge. Even under new management, the national money is now, increasingly, only one among many; and as new rival currencies continue to emerge, intensifying competition, the central bank's ability to attain its ultimate objective—control over aggregate expenditures—can only grow weaker. Depoliticization may slow down the loss of market share, but it cannot restore the state's monopoly privilege; and as suggested in the previous chapter, without that monopoly privilege, the central bank's authority—no matter how "soundly" exercised—risks becoming, simply, more and more irrelevant. Currency competition is like the iceberg that sank the Titanic. The ship will not be saved merely by rearranging the chairs on the upper deck.

The Resurrection of Fiscal Policy

Not all is lost, however. It may no longer be possible to prevent the usurping of monetary policy, whether by capital controls, floating, or central-bank independence. But that does not mean that states are thus left, increasingly, with no choice at all but to yield to the dictates of the market. A degree of governing authority can still be preserved, but only if governments are prepared to resurrect the other traditional instrument of macroeconomic policy—*fiscal* policy, the government's own revenue and spending programs. Appropriately implemented, budgetary policy offers a promising means to promote national prosperity despite the loss of the monopoly privilege of a territorial currency.

Presently, we know, activist fiscal policy is out of favor with most mainstream economists, largely because public budgetary decisions are so often held hostage to the fortunes of electoral or partisan politics. Few knowledgeable observers doubt that if fiscal policy could be managed as flexibly as monetary policy, governments would be much better positioned to help stabilize activity and promote growth. Evidence for the potential effectiveness of contracyclical fiscal policy is strong, particularly if initiatives are targeted directly at disposable personal income.[9] Because many households do not have the means to "smooth" consumption when paychecks rise or fall, well-designed variations of cash transfers or tax rates (e.g., withholding rates or sales taxes) can have an immediate and powerful effect on nominal demand. Broad revenue measures can be much more equitable in their distributional impact than standard monetary policy, the effects of which tend to be highly concentrated in interest-sensitive sectors such as durable-goods manufacturing and real estate.

Even fewer observers, however, expect the requisite policy flexibility to be feasible so long as all budgetary initiatives must go through the legislative meat grinder. The charge, as *The Economist* (2002) writes, is that because of "endless squabbling" by politicians, "governments are incapable of designing the right measures or enacting them at the right time." An apt illustration was provided by the U.S. government following the notorious terrorist attacks of 11 September 2001. Despite the severity of that horrendous shock, which came at a time when the U.S. economy was already in recession, it took the Congress a full six months to agree on the terms of a modest stimulus bill—by which time, ironically, production and employment were already beginning to turn up on their own.

But what if fiscal policy, in some degree, were to be as "depoliticized" as monetary policy is today in so many countries? By analogy with central-bank independence, depoliticization would mean delegating a defined range of fiscal powers to an autonomous public agency, free to respond actively to sustained fluctuations of overall output and prices. Like an independent central bank, the agency would be staffed by disinterested professionals insulated from direct political influence. Also like an independent central bank, the agency would operate within limits established by statute and ultimately be fully accountable to elected officials. Under such an institutional reform, selected budgetary decisions, too, could reflect a longer view and maintain a greater consistency, restoring to the state a measure of influence over macroeconomic performance.

Partial depoliticization of fiscal policy is by no means impractical, despite the acute sensitivities and interests involved. Proposals along these lines have come from several quarters recently, most notably from economist Alan Blinder, formerly vice-chair of the Federal Reserve Board of Governors.[10] It is understood, of course, that because so much of the expenditure side of the budget is central to the basic functions of government, little room exists for delegation of authority over the appropriation and allocation of funds for spending. Besides, most public expenditure programs are relatively "sticky," difficult to start or stop on short notice. Arguably, however, much more room exists on the revenue side, the realm of taxes and transfers, to empower an autonomous fiscal agency in a politically acceptable manner. With proper safeguards, the idea should not be considered fanciful.

The aim would be to make it as easy to vary tax rates and transfer payments at the margin, when needed, as it is for a central banks to vary interest rates and bank reserves. In creating such an agency, the political authorities would set basic goals and parameters; additionally, elected officials would exercise active oversight on a continuing basis, to ensure responsible behavior. But within its statutory limits, the agency would be authorized to implement timely adjustments to the government's revenues in response to changing economic conditions. The scope of potential adjustments could be agreed to in advance as part of the annual budget process, leaving to the agency sole authority to determine the magnitude and timing of specific changes. Or the agency could be granted greater latitude to make such decisions on its own, subject perhaps to some form of legislative ratification or veto. For example, all agency decisions might be made subject to a single up-or-down vote by the legislature within a specified period of time. Alternatively, agency decisions might take effect automatically within a specified time unless legislators vote to override. There are many ways to reconcile democratic accountability with depoliticized policymaking.

Objections could be raised, of course, just as they are against independent central banks. Representative are the remarks of political scientists Sheri Berman and Kathleen McNamara (1999), two critics of central-bank independence, who express understandable apprehension about concentrating so much power in the hands of small groups of unelected individuals. Depoliticization of policy, they argue, "comes at a price. . . . countries surrender much control over their economic fates. . . . Democratic control sometimes produces mistakes and embarrassment, but on balance they also produce moderation, success, and—most important— legitimacy."[11] But as Blinder (1997) counters, there is nothing unusual in the idea of representative governments assigning certain areas of policy to appointed professionals. In public policy, there is always a trade-off between the rough virtues of political struggle and the possible abuses of technocratic expertise. Different nations draw the line differently between political and technocratic decisions; and no one doubts the legitimacy of the many independent bodies that already exist in the United States and elsewhere to insulate specific areas of decision making from political influence—agencies like the Securities and Exchange Commission or the Food and Drug Administration. As Blinder writes (1997, 125), such bodies "are not perfect, but they work." There is no reason why an autonomous fiscal agency could not work, too, so long as its mandate is carefully circumscribed and its operations closely monitored.

In any event, consider the alternative. Without a resurrection of fiscal policy in some form, governments may be left with no means at all to manage macroeconomic performance. Accelerating currency competition is already rapidly depriving many states of the tool of monetary policy. Yet representative governments are still held responsible for the broad prosperity of the nation. Increasingly, therefore, the only choice remaining is a stark one—between some manner of control through a more flexible fiscal mechanism, or no control at all. An autonomous fiscal agency would at least offer some residual role for elected officials. Can we really expect states meekly to cede all power to the market?

The International Level

The challenge is even more daunting at the international level, where yet more actors are involved in the struggle for governing authority. Worldwide, governments face competition not only from the market, but also from one another, each state responding in its own way to deterritorialization's growing threat to monetary sovereignty. The decision-making process summarized in the Choice Diagram (see fig. 1) is an entirely decentralized one. Without some effective coordinating mechanism, there is no guarantee that the strategies selected by individual governments—no matter how rational in terms of a country's unique circumstances—will turn out to be mutually compatible on a global scale. At issue is a classic collective-action dilemma. How can the preferences of multiple states be managed to minimize the risks of currency instability or conflict?

In principle, three broad solutions might be considered possible, depending on who is assigned the role of coordinator—a world central bank, the market leaders at the peak of the Currency Pyramid, or a mediating agency such as the International Monetary Fund. In practice, only some combination of the second and third options would seem to offer real promise in today's monetary environment.

A World Central Bank?

Why not simply create a world central bank, authorized to issue and manage a single money for all humanity? That would certainly be the most direct route to solving the collective-action dilemma. In place of today's crowded population of diverse currencies, there would be just one universal money, available on equal terms everywhere to perform the roles of exchange medium, store of value, and unit of account. Instead of the Darwinian struggle of today's Currency Pyramid, with producers all competing vigorously to promote market share, there would be just one central agency with supranational powers to assure monetary stability. Much as the Federal Reserve, for example, presently functions to coordinate the monetary needs of America's fifty states on a national scale, a world central bank would serve to coordinate monetary needs on a global scale. As a response to the challenge of money's new geography, the approach has the merit of being parsimonious and even elegant. Regrettably, it is also flawed and hopelessly unrealistic.

The idea of a world central bank has long fascinated monetary analysts, going back to the dawn of territorial money in the nineteenth century. Typical was the view of the liberal economist John Stuart Mill (1871, 514–15), who declared the persistence of separate national currencies to be a "barbarism" that would surely be replaced one day by a universal money as a result of "the progress of political improvement." At the International Monetary Conference of 1867, which was held in conjunction with the Universal Exposition in Paris, delegates debated at length whether all national currency systems should be replaced with a single world coinage system.[12] Though ultimately rejected by the conference as utopian, the dream lived on; and in more recent years, with the growing deterritorialization of currencies, it has once again begun to emerge into public discussion. As early as 1970 a retired chairman of the Federal Reserve, William McChesney Martin, was arguing that "in the world of today, a strong world central bank is becoming more and more essential" (1970, 13). And his sentiments are increasingly echoed by others, such as the noted economists Richard Cooper (1974, 1995, 1999a) and Paul Streeten (1991). Writes Streeten (1991, 128): "If we wish to move in the direction of a pluralistic, democratic world order, a world currency will have to be an important part of it."[13] In the last few years, the idea has been espoused by the influential journal *The Economist* (1998) and has been given respectful hearings at meetings of the International Monetary Fund (IMF 2000a) and American Economics Association (Rogoff 2001).

The logic of the idea is plain. It is the logic of scale economies and network externalities—the natural-monopoly argument that, as noted in chapter 1, has led so many informed observers to favor the Contraction Contention, predicting the demise of most of today's "junk currencies." If the efficiency of money production is inversely related to the size of transactional networks, what could be more efficient than a single producer for the whole world? A global central bank would represent an extreme form of sovereignty bargain—the ultimate in the outsourcing of monetary policy.

But the disadvantages of the idea are equally plain. First is the obvious fact that the world as a whole is anything but an optimum currency area. Against the anticipated saving of transactions costs must be balanced potential losses at the macroeconomic level, caused by the suppression of local monetary or exchange-rate policies that might otherwise be capable of easing adjustments to asymmetric shocks. Business cycles around the globe can hardly be described as synchronous; worse, few economies exhibit the high degree of market flexibility that would be needed to make requisite adaptations quickly. Hence instabilities that are currently manifest in variations of interest rates or currency rates might emerge instead as pronounced variations of aggregate production and employment, more than offsetting efficiency gains.

Second, and even more critical, is the disadvantage of monopoly, a concentration of power that could easily be abused. A global central bank also represents the ultimate in supranational governance. States would be expected to delegate upward all their formal authority in monetary affairs—to surrender, voluntarily, all claim to any remaining benefits of national monetary sovereignty, however eroded by currency competition. But without the parallel power of a world government, as Kenneth Rogoff (2001) points out, it would be difficult to establish an adequate system of oversight and accountability to assure maximum responsibility. We have already seen in chapter 5 how resistant most national governments are to the costs of a followership strategy. If even the least demanding forms of subordination are unable to generate much enthusiasm, can we really believe that policymakers might countenance such a radical degree of centralization? In practical terms, a pooling of monetary sovereignty at the global level would require a measure of mutual trust—a harmony among nations—far greater than anything that exists at present or in the foreseeable future. The idea is no less utopian now than it was 1867.[14] As Paul Volcker, another former chairman of the Federal Reserve, has declared (Volcker and Gyohten 1992, 295): "The idea of sovereign governments delegating so much authority to a supranational world central bank . . . simply does not provide . . . a realistic base for planning, however intellectually attractive the idea may seem."

Can the idea be made less utopian? Conceivably, governments might be less resistant if existing national currencies would be allowed to survive even after the creation of a new universal money. A world money may be useful as a coordinating device, but it need not be the only game in town. A universal money could be created for use in international transactions and could, like the ghost monies of more ancient times, serve globally as a common unit of account. At the same time, national currencies might still circulate domestically and thus continue to provide valuable benefits for governments, including most prominently seigniorage revenue, when needed, and a still useful symbol of national identity. Here, too, as in the various forms of currency regionalization, a lower degree of centralization might be feasible as a means to encourage greater acceptability.

Such an approach has long been promoted by Robert Mundell as a practical compromise between the competing imperatives of state preferences and market forces—"one world, one currency area," as he describes it (in IMF 2000a), rather than one world, one currency.[15] Emphasizing efficiency considerations above all, Mundell would favor as much monetary consolidation as possible. He is after all the man who, as noted in chapter 1, has jokingly suggested that the optimum number of currencies, like the optimum number of gods, is an odd number less than three. For the pioneer of OCA theory, potential losses at the macroeconomic level are of secondary importance as compared with anticipated savings on transactions costs. But Mundell is also sensitive to the politics involved, which makes governments highly reluctant to formally surrender all vestiges of their traditional monetary sovereignty. His solution, therefore, is to create a world money—but not a *single* world money. In his words:

Just as it is good to have a world language in which everyone can converse, so it is useful to have a world currency for international transactions. But I would never propose abolishing all national languages in favor of esperanto or

English, not would I propose scrapping all national currencies in favor of the dollar or world currency.

My ideal and equilibrium solution would be a world currency (but not a single world currency) in which each country would produce its own unit.[16]

The key to such an approach, clearly, lies in the relationship that would be established between the world currency and national monies. In Mundell's vision, the linkage would be tight, with each national money firmly fixed to the world currency—which he would call the *intor*—via a currency-board arrangement of some kind.[17] Only a fairly high degree of subordination at the national level would ensure stability of monetary relations worldwide.

But is that idea really any less utopian than one universal money? I have argued in chapter 5 that currency boards can be expected to appeal to only a limited subset of nations, owing mainly to the element of dependency involved. Mostly these would be smaller or poorer economies at the bottom of the Currency Pyramid, where policymakers have little choice. Conceivably, some middle-ranking countries might also be willing to go this route so long as followership were to mean subordination to an international agency rather than to a foreign government. With ties to a world central bank rather than to one of the market leaders, there would be less connotation of a reinvented colonialism. But the higher we go in the Currency Pyramid, the lower will be the disposition to surrender the discretionary powers traditionally associated with a national currency—and least of all at the topmost ranks of the Pyramid, which benefit disproportionately from today's monetary competition. Mundell's vision may appeal to some states, but not to those that matter most.

Conversely, the relationship to be established with a world currency might be left more fluid, to be determined at the discretion of individual governments. But then it is not clear just what would be gained from the whole exercise. A world currency that neither replaces nor disciplines national monies appears to offer little in the way of coordination. Indeed its main consequence, ironically, might simply be to add one more competitor to the Darwinian struggle, exacerbating the collective-action dilemma generated by deterritorialization.

The Market Leaders?

That leaves just two alternatives for the role of coordinator—the market leaders or a mediating agency. In fact, both can play an important role. Though neither option is without practical difficulties, the two in combination offer a real opportunity for some measure of coordination of state preferences.

Begin with the market leaders—the United States, Europe, and Japan. At the peak of the Currency Pyramid, the Big Three are in a position to provide an effective coordinating mechanism by acting jointly in cartel-like fashion as a quasi-substitute for a world central bank. Oligopolistic competition of the sort that has come to exist among national monies need not be chaotic, so long as decisive leadership is provided by the biggest players in the game. The key characteristic of oligopoly, to repeat, is *uncertainty*, bred by actor interdependence and a typically high degree of mutuality in decision making. But much of that uncertainty can be dispelled by strong and consistent signals from acknowledged leaders concerning essential elements of policy. The more that the Big Three work together to provide a clear focal point for expectations, helping to coordinate the decisions of individual governments, the lower would be the risk of serious instability or conflict throughout the system. If relations among the dollar, euro, and yen can be successfully stabilized, the effect might be expected to generalize to all other currencies that are linked to them in one way or another. Coordination at the peak would radiate downward to encompass lower ranks of the Currency Pyramid.

The logic of this idea, too, is plain. As monetary specialists have long recognized, international cooperation can be easily justified as a general principle on straightforward efficiency grounds.[18] Key is the fact that in currency relations, actions of any one government may generate a variety of "spillover" effects—external repercussions and feedbacks—that can significantly influence its own ability, as well as the ability of others, to achieve preferred objectives. Such "externalities" imply that policies chosen unilaterally, even if seemingly optimal from the individual country's point of view, will almost certainly prove suboptimal in a broader regional or global context. The basic rationale for collaboration among any group of related economies is that it can *internalize* these externalities, thus enhancing economic welfare. By giving each government partial control over the actions of others, coordinated decision making relieves the shortage of instruments that prevents each one separately from reaching its own chosen goals. Externalities will be positive rather than negative.

The specific case for cooperation among the Big Three today simply takes this logic one step forward, since it is evident that positive externalities will be greater the more widely used are the currencies involved. Specialists have also long recognized that the exchange rates of the major currencies have something of the character of a public good.[19] Persistent misalignments or volatility in dollar-euro or dollar-yen cross-rates are costly not just for the leaders themselves but for many other economies, as well. Conversely, many other countries, and not just the market leaders, would benefit from stable relations among the Big Three. The case has only been reinforced by the growth of cross-border competition in recent years, which has bolstered even more the widespread influence of the peak currencies.

The fastest route to enhanced cooperation among the Big Three would be via some form of exchange-rate targeting, as advocated most notably by economists at the Institute for International Economics, a prominent think-tank based in Washington.[20] Exchange-rate targets provide an unmistakable focal point for policy management at the domestic level. Stable and consistent relations among the Big Three, in turn, would provide the clear signal needed to coordinate behavior elsewhere, as well. Alternatively, cooperation could target the leaders' domestic policies directly, as long urged by Ronald McKinnon (1984, 1997). Monetary growth and fiscal policy in the United States, Europe, and Japan would aim for a common inflation target, again assuring a clear signal for others. Either way, the hoped-for result would be fewer monetary shocks or misalignments. In the past, proponents of joint targeting focused mostly on benefits of cooperation for the Big Three themselves. But as the use of the dominant currencies has continued to spread around the globe, more and more emphasis is being placed on broader systemic gains, as well.[21]

The approach is not without shortcomings, of course. As with the idea of a world central bank, two main problems stand out. Fortunately, neither represents a fatal flaw.

First, there is the problem of the market leaders. Can the Big Three be persuaded to lead? The practical impediments to monetary cooperation are well known and hardly inconsequential (Cohen 1993). Most salient is the so-called time-inconsistency dilemma: the chance that agreements, once negotiated, might later be violated because of changing circumstances. The underlying assumption of the case for cooperation is that the Big Three will all be prepared to subordinate their individual interests to collective concerns—in effect, to accept that a burden of governance responsibility necessarily goes with the privilege of market leadership. But without some form of enforceable compliance mechanism, is this solution really any less utopian than a world central bank? In practice, it is difficult to see how any of the three could be dissuaded from undertaking unilateral action when they wish. Precisely because they are indeed the market leaders, the Big Three still enjoy more freedom than other governments to shape strategy mainly on the basis of domestic considerations. Moreover, precisely because they remain so well insulated from outside influence, policy autonomy remains prized as something closer to a necessity than a luxury. None shows the slightest inclination to reverse the priority they have long been permitted to accord strictly national objectives. As Max Corden, widely regarded as one of the world's leading experts on such matters, sadly concludes: "This is not likely to change."[22]

Indeed, if anything, the prospect may be for greater variability of exchange rates among the Big Three, rather than less. As large and relatively closed economies, the United States and Japan have never attached much importance to currency stability as a policy target; and now with EMU, the same attitude can be expected of Euroland, as well, which is not only bigger, but also much less open than any of its individual members. Europeans, too, are likely to pay less rather than more attention to exchange-rate management at the global level. A more likely outcome, one source suggests, is a kind of "reciprocal benign neglect" among the Big Three that could result in even greater volatility over time.[23]

But that does not mean that cooperation is impossible under any circumstances. As Peter Kenen (1988) has pointed out, it is important to distinguish between two different kinds of coordination, which make very different demands on national priorities. Regular mutual adjustments of policies to internalize externalities—what Kenen calls the *policy-optimizing* approach to cooperation—do indeed call for more self-restraint than seems consistent with contemporary political realities. But that is less true of what Kenen calls *regime-preserving* cooperation—collective actions taken, when necessary, to defend existing arrangements or institutions against the threat of economic or political shocks. Sudden crises of the sort that hit East Asia in 1997–1998, which appear systemic in nature, can have the effect of altering perceptions of interest enough, at least for a time, to overcome resistance to policy compromise. Cooperation among the Big Three in crisis management is not at all difficult to imagine;[24] nor should its value to the broader stability of currency relations be discounted, even if it falls short of providing the clear and consistent focal point for expectations that would help to prevent the eruption of crises in the first place. Better some coordination, even if only sporadic and reactive, than none at all.

Second, there is the problem of the putative followers: Can other nations be persuaded to follow? Even if the Big Three were indeed to accept the burden of joint governance, the question remains whether—or to what extent—governments elsewhere will be prepared to follow their lead.

The logic of the case for cooperation among the Big Three assumes that most if not all lower-ranked currencies will be linked to their own monies in some way—a limited prospect at best, as we know from chapter 5. Strategies of market followership are by no means universally appealing to governments, despite the rising cost of defending uncompetitive national monies. In reality, no more than a minority of sovereign states are likely to become willing subordinates in the broad currency blocs so frequently predicted by monetary specialists.[25] More governments will undoubtedly stick to strategies of market preservation or might perhaps be attracted to the alternative of monetary alliance in some form. Try as they might, therefore, the market leaders can hardly be expected to provide an effective coordinating mechanism for the world as a whole. Even the strongest signals from the peak of the Currency Pyramid will have little stabilizing effect on states that persist in going their own way.

But again, better some coordination than none at all—at least for those states that do not elect to go their own way. Strategies of market follower-ship may not be universally appealing, but from chapter 5 we know also that there will indeed be governments attracted to some version of vertical regionalization—most notably in East-Central Europe and the Balkans, where enthusiasm for euroization is rife; and possibly also in parts of the Western Hemisphere where, as noted, membership in the dollar club could yet expand to include a number of the region's smaller economies. For countries such as these, firm leadership from the peak would undoubt-edly be of value in lowering the risk of monetary instability or conflict. To that extent, cooperation among the Big Three could indeed make a significant contribution, even if many other states continue to prefer alter-native strategies.

The International Monetary Fund?

For those other states, there remains just one last possibility—mediation by a designated global agency, which in this case would almost certainly have to be the International Monetary Fund. The IMF could counsel such governments on the development and implementation of their individual currency strategies. States resistant to strategies of market followership would remain free to make their own decisions in line with the impera-tives of the Choice Diagram (see fig. 1). For them, the process would remain as decentralized as ever. But the resulting decision making need not be chaotic, despite the persistence of oligopolistic competition, if the IMF formally assumes responsibility to help coordinate diverse prefer-ences. Where signals from the market leaders cannot be relied upon to dispel oligopoly's characteristic uncertainty, cues from the IMF can.

A reconsideration of the IMF's role along these lines would certainly be timely, given recent discussions. Especially since the Asian financial crisis, the traditional practices of the IMF have come under severe scru-tiny, most notably in a highly critical report from a congressional commis-sion headed by conservative economist Allen Meltzer (International Fi-nancial Institution Advisory Commission 2000). For many, the Fund has taken on far too many responsibilities and should scale back its ambitions significantly (Feldstein 1998; Kapur 1998). For others, the issue is not the long reach of IMF operations but rather how they are framed and implemented (Fischer 1998; Hale 1998b). Yet for all the debate, few observers doubt that at a fundamental level the IMF still has an important contribution to make to world monetary governance.

In the context of today's changing monetary geography, where governing authority has become more diffuse than ever, there seems no better job for the IMF than as a coordinator among competing currencies—including even the currencies of the market leaders. IMF mediation would certainly be of value to the many governments that, while wary of a followership strategy, are unsure where their own interests may ultimately lie. It could also play a useful role in helping to promote cooperation among the Big Three, which in turn would benefit those governments that do choose willingly to subordinate their monetary sovereignty to a leading currency. Overall, the positive impact could be considerable.

Assigning a mediation role to the IMF would require no redefinition of the organization's basic purposes, which as stated in its charter are inter alia "to promote international monetary cooperation [and] to maintain orderly exchange arrangements among members."[26] It would, however, demand a material reordering of institutional priorities, which presently fail to take full account of the challenges posed by the changing monetary landscape. Reflecting the macroeconomics perspective favored by most economists, the IMF has always focused first and foremost on exchange rates. "In order to fulfill its functions," the charter goes on to say, "the Fund shall exercise firm surveillance over the *exchange rate policies* of its members."[27] But as I argued in chapter 2, such an approach only begins to scratch the surface of today's policy issues. With the growing deterritorialization of money, much more is involved than a simple choice of exchange-rate regime. Governments must face truly fundamental decisions about the future of their monetary sovereignty. Should they continue to produce their own money and fight for market share? Or should they agree to outsource their monetary policy, in whole or in part? If the IMF is to fulfill its assigned responsibilities in the context of today's Darwinian struggle, this is where its focus should now be turned. Surveillance would be exercised over the choice of *currency* regime, not just the choice of *exchange-rate* regime.

Specifically, this would mean advising governments in detail on the full range of alternatives available to them within the constraints of the Choice Diagram (see fig. 1). A strategy of market preservation intended to defend an uncompetitive national currency, regardless of cost, should not be the sole option considered. Governments should be accurately apprised of all other options, as well, including some degree of vertical or horizontal regionalization. As a disinterested intermediary, the IMF would be ideally placed to offer a dispassionate evaluation of the potential benefits and costs of each possible choice. Given its unique access to information on a global basis, it would also be in an excellent position to anticipate repercussions or feedbacks and hence to internalize any externalities that might result from individual decisions. Where necessary, IMF officials could also help bring together "like-minded countries" in order to surmount some of the obstacles to alliance strategies that were discussed in chapter 6.

The practical advantage of using the IMF as a mediator in this way is that it represents, at worst, a relatively narrow threat to the traditional prerogatives of national sovereignty. Unlike a world central bank, the IMF as presently constituted has only limited supranational powers—mainly authority governing access to credit and the policy conditions to be attached to its loans. Admittedly, to governments in desperate need of financial assistance, these powers may loom large. But no government, no matter how desperate, can be compelled, ultimately, to act against its own will. The IMF has neither the legal standing nor the political leverage to dictate to sovereign entities, *de haut en bas*. Its legitimacy derives not from a surrender but rather from a pooling of formal authority by governments—a sovereignty bargain based on mutual compromise for the sake of collective management, which makes the organization a particularly suitable vehicle to mediate among multiple state preferences.

Likewise, unlike the Big Three, the IMF represents no threat of a reinvented colonialism, pace the views of radical analysts such as Cheryl Payer (1974) who hold that the fund is little more than a crude instrument for advancing the interests of its most powerful members. Such conspiratorial charges are an exaggeration at best and a caricature at worst.

It is undeniable, of course, that the largest countries exercise a disproportionate influence within the IMF's decision-making apparatus. This is particularly true of the United States, as already noted in chapter 3. In reality, the disproportion is intentional, reflecting the preferences of the two principal parties to the negotiations at Bretton Woods in 1944, America and Britain. Relative dominance is built into the design of the IMF by an allocation of voting rights that is heavily weighted toward the wealthiest nations. But it hardly follows that the IMF secretariat, with its cadres of trained professionals from around the world, simply acts as a front for a new form of imperialism. To a remarkable degree the IMF has been able to sustain an effective role for itself as an honest broker among the contending demands of its members.

If there is any truth to radical accusations concerning the IMF's alleged partiality, the effect operates at a more subtle level through the ideas and values that permeate the organization's policies. Louis Pauly (1997, 1999) undoubtedly gets it right when he suggests that the IMF is best understood as a promoter of behavioral norms reflecting a consensus of views among its stronger participating governments—aptly illustrated by the secretariat's unquestioning support in recent decades of the Washington Consensus, embodying the neoliberal economics favored by a succession of U.S. governments. To critics of the IMF such as Joseph Stiglitz, former chief economist at the World Bank, the staff's intellectual biases represent a fundamental flaw because they lead to warped judgments and a rigid close-mindedness. Decisions are made, Stiglitz charges (2002, xiii–xiv), on the basis of "a curious blend of ideology and bad economics. . . . Alternative opinions [are] not sought." But to IMF insiders like Barry Eichengreen (2002a) or Kenneth Rogoff (2002b), the reproach seems both mistaken and unfair.[28] In fact, experiences cited by the two economists demonstrate that minds in the secretariat tend to be anything but closed. "The IMF is not immune to self-criticism," summarizes Eichengreen (2002a, 162), and "has learned from its failures." Fund officials are of course only human beings who cannot be expected to be godlike in their objectivity. But within those natural limits, they do appear to take their responsibilities seriously as neutral arbiters of policy. As an institution, the IMF's integrity is unimpeachable.

The practical advantage of using the IMF as a mediator is of course also its principal disadvantage. Precisely because it cannot dictate to governments in the manner of a world central bank, there is no assurance that its advice will actually be followed. Mediators, by definition, lack the coercive authority of a judge or arbitrator; their impact on behavior, such as it may be, must rely mainly on their powers of persuasion. But this does not mean that any effort to cultivate a role for the IMF along these lines would be meaningless, any more than would an effort to cultivate cooperation among the Big Three. Though the merits of IMF mediation should not be oversold, neither should its value be discounted. A role for the IMF is critical, even if its contribution, like that of the market leaders, will necessarily be constrained by the realities of state sovereignty. In combination, IMF mediation and Big Three leadership might just manage to provide the authority needed to contain the centrifugal forces of currency competition.

Conclusion

In the end, then, effective governance of the new geography of money appears difficult—but not impossible. Overall, there seems little barrier to the growing decentralization of power in monetary affairs. Yet means do exist to cope with the world's increasingly complex currency environment, if governments are prepared to make use of them. At the domestic level, the erosion of monetary policy can be largely offset if states resurrect fiscal policy as a core tool to manage macroeconomic performance. At the international level, the risks of currency instability or conflict can be much reduced by a combination of cooperation among the market leaders and mediation by the International Monetary Fund. The future of money is already upon us, but it is not unmanageable.

Notes

Notes to Chapter 1
The Changing Geography of Money

1. As quoted in *The Economist*, 22 December 2001, 87.

2. The emergence of territorial money is well documented in Helleiner 2003a.

3. The term dollarization of course derives from the U.S. dollar, which, as noted below, is by far the most widely used currency in the world today. But America's greenback is by no means the only money that has ever been or could be adopted by another country. Dollarization as a popular expression has come to mean any money that replaces another national currency.

4. Kobrin 1998 has used the same allusion in a related context.

5. In technical discussions, the term vehicle currency is typically understood to refer mainly to a currency's use in executing transactions in the foreign-exchange market. Here the term is employed in a broader sense to refer to all international uses of a national money.

6. Because each foreign-exchange transaction involves two currencies, the total of shares sums to 200 percent rather than 100 percent.

7. Porter and Judson 1996; U.S. Treasury 2000; Judson and Porter 2001. But see also Feige 1996 and 1997, who suggests a lower figure of about 40 percent.

8. The estimate, based on Seitz 1995, appears to be conservative. According to Doyle 2000, a more accurate figure for the mid-1990s could have been as high as 69 percent. See also Feige and Dean 2002. On the other hand, there is some evidence to suggest that after 1999, when Europe's monetary union first got under way, foreign holdings of German currency declined somewhat owing to uncertainties about the conversion of DM notes into euro notes that was scheduled for January 2002. See Sinn and Westermann 2001a, 2001b; Stix 2001.

9. Hale 1995. Rogoff 1998, inferring from indirect evidence, suggests a higher figure of 25 percent. Publically, the Bank of Japan is unwilling to offer any kind of official estimate. See, e.g., Bank of Japan 1994.

10. See, e.g., Doyle 2000; Stix 2001.

11. Broad money supply, otherwise known as M2, includes all checking accounts (demand deposits) and other "reservable" bank deposits as well as coins and notes (cash) in circulation.

12. See, e.g., de Zamaróczy and Sa 2002, 14.

13. The term Top Currency is of course borrowed from Susan Strange's (1971a, 1971b) classic typology of international currencies.

14. As quoted in Cohen 1971, xi.

15. The number of state-sanctioned currencies was actually as high as 169 prior to the elimination of 12 European currencies by the euro in early 2002, which reduced the total to 158.

16. This was not always the case. In the theory's earliest incarnation, following Mundell's lead, most contributors concentrated on a search for the most appro-

priate domain of a currency irrespective of existing national frontiers. The central issue was simply to find the best criterion for the organization of monetary space. But as the practical limitations of the so-called "criteria approach" (Tavlas 1994, 213) became clear, attention shifted instead to a comparison of costs and benefits of alternative currency domains for individual countries, taking existing frontiers as given—in political terms, a far less naïve approach. Useful recent surveys of OCA theory are provided by Masson and Taylor 1993; Tavlas 1993, 1994; De Grauwe 2000. I will have more to say about OCA theory in chapter 2.

17. As quoted in *IMF Survey*, 22 January 2001, 27.

18. See, e.g., Dornbusch, Sturzenegger, and Wolf *et al.* 1990; Guidotti and Rodriguez 1992.

19. The first edition of *Denationalisation of Money* was published in 1976, six months after *Choice in Currency*, and the second in 1978.

20. Hayek's pro-market views have been especially influential among economists of a more conservative or libertarian persuasion and have been echoed by a number of monetary specialists in both Europe and the United States. See especially Glasner 1989, White 1989, Dowd 1992; Gelfond 2001. For the intellectual origins of Hayek's ideas on money, see Ebenstein 2001, especially ch. 35.

21. See, e.g., Krugman 1992; Matsuyama, Kiyotaki, and Matsui. 1993; Trejos and Wright 1996; Hartmann 1998.

22. See, e.g., Fischer 2001; Rogoff 2001; Alesina and Barro 2001a, 2001b. Most insistent has been Fordham professor George von Furstenberg, who has lost no opportunity to make a strong case for currency consolidation. See, e.g., von Furstenberg 2000a, 2000c, 2001a, 2001b, 2002a, 2002b.

Notes to Chapter 2
Four Directions

1. See, e.g., Mussa, Masson et al. 2000; Fischer 2001; Corden 2002; Glick 2002. For an historical perspective on the evolution of these debates, see Williamson 2002.

2. See also Lamfalussy 2000; Williamson 2000; Kenen 2001; Bénassy-Quéré and Coeuré 2002b; Bird 2002; Willett 2003.

3. The careful reader will note that the number of strategies outlined here is one less than the five listed in *The Geography of Money* (1998, 140). Upon reflection, I have come to realize that two of the strategies listed in my earlier work, identified separately as market preservation and market neutrality, were really variations on the same theme and are best combined.

4. For some discussion, see Moravcsik 1998, ch. 6; Loedel 1999; Garrett 2001.

5. See, e.g., Portes and Rey 1998, 308–10.

6. See also Mattli 2000.

7. The distinction between pooling and surrender of sovereignty, which is generic to the question of how to organize political authority, is of course a familiar one in political science and is used in a variety of contexts—in analyzing differences between confederal states and empires, for instance.

8. Krugman 1998a. Though originally intended by Krugman to refer to the specific challenge of dealing with panicky investors in the midst of a financial

crisis, the term "confidence game" is equally applicable to the more general challenge of sustaining demand for a national currency by tactics of persuasion alone.

9. In a complementary analysis Helleiner 2002b and 2003a stresses the declining benefits of monetary sovereignty rather than, as here, the rising costs.

10. In the late 1970s, for example, according to one knowledgeable source (Díaz-Alejandro 1988, 371), some economic officials in Chile "dreamed of doing away with the national currency altogether" but were deterred by potential opposition from the military. Similarly, in El Salvador, the idea of dollarization was first raised by policymakers as early as 1995, six years before the local currency was finally replaced by the greenback. For more on El Salvador, see chapter 5.

11. Dollarization, according to Menem's immediate successor as president, Fernando de la Rúa, was "not very serious." As quoted in the *New York Times*, 24 January 1999.

12. See, e.g., Eichengreen 1994; Hausmann 1999a, 1999b; LeBaron and McCulloch 2000; Mundell 2000a, 2000d; Mussa, Masson et al. 2000; Rogoff 2002a.

13. CFA stands for *Communauté Financière Africaine*, or African Financial Community.

14. For more detail on the CFA Franc Zone, see Boughton 1993; Clément et al. 1996. For more on the ECCU, see van Beek et al. 2000. A full listing of the memberships of each can be found in table 5. For more on the other regions where prospects for monetary union have been discussed, see chapter 6.

15. Mercosur is an acronym for *Mercado Común del Sur*—the Common Market of the South, whose members are Argentina, Brazil, Paraguay, and Uruguay. For more on Mercosur, see chapter 6.

16. The ten members of ASEAN are Brunei, Cambodia, Indonesia, Laos, Malaysia, Myanmar, the Philippines, Singapore, Thailand, and Vietnam. For more on ASEAN, see chapters 3 and 6.

17. Hausmann 1999b, 96. See also Hausmann 1999a; Hausmann et al. 2000.

18. Von Furstenberg 2000a, 199–200. See especially von Furstenberg 2000c, as well as 2001a, 2001b, 2002a, 2002b.

19. See, e.g., Alesina and Barro 2002; Alesina, Barro, and Tenreyro 2002.

20. I include here only politically sovereign entities, excluding all monetary arrangements involving scattered dependent territories left over from the era of colonialism. In most cases, dependent territories make exclusive use of the currency of the "mother" country. These include the external dependencies of Australia, Denmark, France, New Zealand, Norway, the United Kingdom, and the United States. Exceptions include inter alia Bermuda, the British Virgin Islands, and the Turks and Caicos Islands, all of which use the U.S. dollar though they are territories of the United Kingdom. For a comprehensive list of such arrangements, see table 6.

21. Balboa notes have been issued just once, during the brief presidency of nationalist Arnulfo Arias Madrid in 1941, and were quickly withdrawn from circulation following his overthrow (engineered, it is generally believed, with aid from Washington). For more detail, see Johnson 1973, 223–28.; Collyns 1983, ch. 6; Zimbalist and Weeks 1991.

22. For more on Argentina's brief and ultimately unhappy experience with its currency board, see chapter 5.

23. Benin, Burkina Faso, Côte d'Ivoire, Guinea-Bissau (a former Portuguese colony), Mali, Niger, Senegal, and Togo. WAEMU's franc is designated *le franc de la Communauté Financière de l'Afrique*.

24. Cameroon, Central African Republic, Chad, Republic of Congo, Equatorial Guinea (a former Spanish colony), and Gabon. CAEMC's franc is designated *le franc de la Coopération Financière Africaine*.

25. For more detail on the CMA and other past and present monetary alliances mentioned in the text, see Cohen 2001a.

26. Rose 2000, 2001; Rose and van Wincoop 2001; Frankel and Rose 2002; Glick and Rose 2002; Rose and Engel 2002. Though frequently challenged, the general thrust of Rose's results has been consistently confirmed by other studies, as Rose 2002 demonstrates in a comprehensive analysis.

27. Readers will recognize a more-than-passing familiarity of this trade-off to the central tension identified by Charles Tiebout (1956) and others interested in the optimal level of governance in world affairs—a tension between scale economies and externalities, on the one hand, which argue for larger units and greater centralization of authority, and, on the other, heterogeneity of preferences, which argues for the reverse. Scale economies and externalities are at the heart of the efficiency gains offered by currency regionalization, while macroeconomic flexibility is valued precisely because of the persistence of national differences. But that is not the only trade-off implicated in currency regionalization, as the discussion here will make clear, and may not even be the most salient. Tiebout-type models, while demonstrating the analytical virtues of parsimony, provide too narrow a focus for the purposes of this book.

28. This is the central insight of what Tavlas (1993) labels the "new" theory of optimum currency areas, in contrast to the critical role assigned to monetary-policy autonomy in more traditional OCA theory.

29. For some discussion and citations, see Cohen 1998, 82–83.

30. See, e.g., Tsygankov 2000, 2001; Abdelal 2001.

31. This point is stressed in particular by S. Cooper 1999.

32. For detail, see Helleiner 2003a, ch. 9.

33. Most analyses, working a vein pioneered by Frieden 1994, focus on interest-group preferences and pressures on policymakers. See, e.g., Hefeker 1997; Oatley 1997. For a critique of the sectoral-preferences approach, see McNamara 1998, 32–41.

34. For a few rare exceptions, see Starr 1997; Lopez 2002; Frieden 2003.

35. Notable examples include Pauly 1988; Maxfield 1990; Haggard Lee, and Maxfield 1993; Haggard and Maxfield 1996; Loriaux et al. 1997; Auerbach 2001. I will have more to say on the financial liberalization of emerging-market economies in chapter 4.

Notes to Chapter 3
Life at the Peak

1. The yen's retreat since the start of the 1990s is well documented by Castellano 1999; Katada 2002.

2. See, e.g., Bergsten, Ito, and Noland 2001, who write that "the yen is now a distant third among global currencies, far behind the new euro as well as the dollar" (234).

3. Noting that the Japanese economy is nearly one thousand times as large as Botswana's, Prime Minister Junichiro Koizumi (as quoted in the *New York Times*, 6 July 2002) complained that "it is nonsense to say that Japan's national strength is lower than African countries to which Japan is providing assistance." In 2001, Japan extended $12 million in grants to Botswana and $106 million in loans. But for the rating agencies Botswana, with a debt standing at less than 10 percent of GDP, is simply a better credit risk than Japan, with a debt ratio nearing 150 percent—three times as great as in the United States and higher even than in Italy, previously regarded as the most profligate among industrial nations.

4. For more detail on Japan's Big Bang, see Ministry of Finance 2000; Hoshi and Kashyap 2001.

5. See especially Mulgan 2000; W. Grimes 2001b; Posen 2001. But for a contrary, much more optimistic prognosis stressing the innovative creativity of Japan's private sector, see Helweg 2000.

6. Though following the euro's launch "Euroland" quickly gained popularity across Europe as the preferred label for the new EMU group, the term was not without its detractors—particularly in France, where it was seen as a bit too Germanic. The French Academy even went so far as to issue an official communiqué decreeing that in France the proper expression should be "euro zone." "The Academy advises against the use of 'Euroland,' " the "Immortals" insisted (*New York Times*, 8 January 1999). The European Central Bank has opted for the neutral term "Eurosystem."

7. See, e.g., Bergsten 1997; Alogoskoufis and Portes 1997; Hartmann 1998; Portes and Rey 1998; Mundell 2000a, 2000b; Walter 2000; Frenkel and Søndergaard 2001. But for contrary views, see McCauley 1997; Prati and Schinasi 1997; R. Cooper 2000; Frankel 2000; Rosecrance 2000.

8. The term "legacy" currency, to refer to the separate national monies replaced by the euro, was suggested by Detken and Hartmann 2002.

9. Indeed, in 1999 euro-denominated international bonds and notes issuance briefly exceeded dollar issuance for the first time, before leveling off at an average share of some 29 percent in subsequent years (as compared with a dollar share of some 43 percent). The average share of the euro's predecessor currencies in global issuance in the five years prior to 1999 was 19 percent. See ECB 2001, 7–8; Detken and Hartmann 2002, 566–67.

10. Pier Carlo Padoan (2000, 69) makes the same point, in more theoretical terms, when he suggests that "to shift from one equilibrium to the other, a currency must surpass a minimum critical mass in international use that will allow agglomeration factors, network externalities, to operate. . . . Whether the euro will shift from one equilibrium to another will depend largely on EMU policies."

11. ECB 1999, 31, 45. This position was reiterated, with almost identical wording, in ECB 2001.

12. In most euro-zone countries, the highest value euro bank notes (500 euros) are far larger than the biggest domestic notes previously in circulation—in Greece, for instance, as much as seventeen times the highest note denominated in the old national currency, the drachma. See the *New York Times*, 15 August 2001.

13. As quoted in *The Economist*, 30 October 1999, 85.

14. As quoted in the *New York Times*, 19 November 1999.

15. Makinen 2000, 5. Issues of Federal Reserve notes in denominations greater than $100 were terminated in 1946. Previously, notes were available in denominations of $500, $1,000, $5,000, and $10,000.

16. Monetary followership is evident across the region in a high degree of covariance with the United States along several critical dimensions—including exchange rates, interest rates, and domestic prices—as demonstrated by numerous empirical studies. See, e.g., Frankel and Wei 1998; Alesina, Barro, and Tenreyro 2002; Fratzscher 2002.

17. Others who have argued in favor of dollarization, from a variety of perspectives, include Calvo 1999, 2000; Forbes 1999; Hausmann 1999a; Schuler 1999; Gavin 2000; Katzman 2000; Mack 2000.

18. Molano 2000, 52. See also Eichengreen 2001 and 2002b, who finds little empirical evidence to support the proposition that dollarization will accelerate the pace of structural reform.

19. Others who have argued against dollarization for various reasons include Mann 1999; Sachs and Larrain 1999; Alexander and von Furstenberg 2000; Molano 2000; von Furstenberg 2000a, 2000b, 2000c; Larrain and Velasco 2001; Willett 2001.

20. Summers 1999b, 8. See also Summers 1999a, 16.

21. Personal communication.

22. As quoted in IMF 1999b, 6.

23. I am reminded of the remarks made by William Diebold some years ago when he retired as senior economist at the Council on Foreign Relations in New York. Speaking of the U.S. officials who negotiated the terms of post–World War II reconstruction, which many have since characterized as an exercise of U.S. hegemony, Diebold noted that "I have never seen a memoir published with the title 'My Days as a Happy Hegemon.' "

24. See, e.g., the *New York Times*, 5 January 2002. Subsequently, the administration's hard line was softened somewhat as the ripple effects of Argentina's financial collapse gradually spread to neighboring countries. See, e.g., the *New York Times*, 5 August 2002; 6 August 2002.

25. For additional detail, see Joint Economic Committee 2000b; Schuler and Stein 2000.

26. Joint Economic Committee press release, 8 November 1999.

27. Portes is an American long resident in London. Rey is Belgian.

28. See, e.g., McCauley 1997, 24–32; Padoan 2000, 100–108.

29. See, e.g., *New York Times*, 23 December 1998; *The Economist*, 9 January 1999, 48.

30. Simon Buckby, a pro-euro advocate, as quoted in the *New York Times*, 9 December 2001.

31. Although nominally, together with its larger neighbor Serbia, part of what is left of the former federal state of Yugoslavia, Montenegro chose in 1999 to highlight its de facto autonomy by declaring the deutsche mark to be its national currency, replacing the Yugoslav dinar. From the start of 2002, in turn, the DM was replaced by the euro once euro notes and coins entered circulation. For some

detail, see Bogetić 2002. The euro has also become the sole currency of Kosovo since that Serbian province came under international administration in 1999.

32. See, e.g., Bénassy-Quéré 1996b; Bénassy-Quéré and Lahrèche-Révil 1998, 2000; Bénassy-Quéré, Mojon, and Schor 1998; Frankel and Wei 1998; Alesina, Barro, and Tenreyro 2002; Fratzscher 2002.

33. The ten new members are the Czech Republic, Estonia, Hungary, Latvia, Lithuania, Poland, Slovakia, and Slovenia, together with the Mediterranean island-states of Cyprus and Malta. Active negotiations continue with Bulgaria and Romania. Turkey, which has long sought membership in the EU, is also formally designated as a candidate for entry, but no negotiations are anticipated in the near term.

34. ERM 2 is the successor to the exchange-rate mechanism (ERM 1) that was at the heart of the European Monetary System (EMS), the predecessor to EMU that existed from 1979 to 1999. ERM 2 requires a bilateral parity against the euro within a relatively wide fluctuation margin of 15 percent up or down (i.e., a total band width of 30 percent). For more detail on the terms of EMU participation for candidate countries, see ECB 2000a; IMF 2000b, ch. 4.

35. The address is *http://www.geocities.com/euroize*.

36. See, e.g., Masson 1999; Szapáry 2001. Of particular concern is the so-called Balassa-Samuelson effect, which arises because of the general tendency for productivity growth to differ among sectors while wages tend to be less differentiated. With the transition to EU membership, market competition will undoubtedly accelerate productivity growth in the traded-goods sector, pushing up wages in all sectors and therefore the prices of nontraded goods relative to those of traded goods. The resulting inflationary pressures will be difficult to suppress without some flexibility of exchange rates. See IMF 2000b, 168–69.

37. As quoted in *The Economist*, 6 November 1999, 79. See also "The European Central Bank," *The Economist*, 6 January 2001, 63–65.

38. See, e.g., *Financial Times*, 25 March 2002, 4.

39. See, e.g., Berrigan and Carré 1997; Chauffour and Stemitsiotis 1998; Bénassy-Quéré and Lahrèche-Révil 1999; Honohan and Lane 1999.

40. On the evolution of Japanese thinking on yen internationalization, see Castellano 1999; W. Grimes 2000, 2001a; Kwan 2001, ch. 6; Laurence 2002.

41. Empirical studies show little evidence of anything like a yen bloc emerging at present, even among Japan's immediate neighbors. See, e.g., Bénassy-Quéré 1996a, 1996b, 1999a, 1999b; Frankel and Wei 1998; Kwan 1998; Alesina, Barro, and Tenreyro 2002; Fratzscher 2002. But for partial qualifications, see Aggarwal and Mougoue 1996; Takagi 1999.

42. See, e.g., Hughes 2000; W. Grimes 2000, 2001a; Katada 2001a, 2001b, 2002; Kwan 2001.

43. As quoted in the *New York Times*, 27 April 1996.

44. For more on the Asian financial crisis, see Radelet and Sachs 1998, 2000; Pempel 1999; Haggard 2000; Noble and Ravenhill 2000; Woo, Sachs, and Scwhab 2000.

45. For detail, see Altbach 1997; Rowley 1997; Hamada 1999b; Katada 2001b.

46. Hiroshi Hashimoto, Japan's ambassador to Singapore, as quoted in the *New York Times*, 26 December 1999.

47. See, e.g., Higgott 1998, 343; Katada 2002.

48. As quoted in Cohen 1986, 229. Empirical studies strongly suggest that a country's political relationship with Washington is frequently decisive in determining both the volume and terms of access to IMF credit. See, e.g., Thacker 1999; Stone 2002.

49. Despite Washington's opposition, the AMF proposal continues to attract favorable interest from private commentators, e.g., Bergsten 1998; Wade and Veneroso 1998b; Kiuchi 2000.

50. The adjective "new" was used to distinguish the initiative from an earlier plan that Miyazawa had proposed in 1988, when he had previously been finance minister, to help resolve the Latin American debt crisis. For more detail on the New Miyazawa Initiative, see Hamada 1999b; Katada 2001a, ch. 8.

51. For more detail on the Chiang Mai Initiative, see Henning 2002; Wang 2003. By end-2002, eleven swap arrangements had already been completed and three more were under negotiation.

52. See, e.g., Bergsten, Ito, and Noland 2001, 202–3, 257; W. Grimes 2001a; Bowles 2002.

53. Hughes 2000, 221. See also Katada 2001b, 2002.

54. China, for example, fully backed the United States in opposing the AMF when it was proposed in 1997, fearing what a Japanese-led institution might mean for Beijing's own geopolitical position. See, e.g., Bergsten, Ito, and Noland 2001; Bowles 2002.

55. Nicholas R. Lardy, an economist at the Brookings Institution, as quoted in the *New York Times*, 28 June 2002.

Notes to Chapter 4
The Art of Survival

1. A notable exception was Benjamin Klein (1974), who as much as a third of a century ago spoke of the role that "brand-name capital" played in influencing market assessments of a money's value and reliability. See also Klein and Melvin 1982; Melvin 1988.

2. As part of the same campaign, stickers appeared declaring "I love the rupiah." Responded one citizen: "Never mind the rupiah, I love money" (as quoted in *The Economist*, 24 January 1998, 38).

3. See, e.g., Fischer 1993; Barro 1995; Bruno and Easterly 1996; Corbo and Rojas 1997.

4. Ghosh and Phillips 1998, 674. See also Ul Haque and Khan 1998.

5. The term "capital control" is used here to refer to any form of direct government intervention to regulate currency choice, ranging from narrow, selective restraints on individual categories of transactions to the broadest possible limits on currency convertibility (technically, exchange restriction).

6. See, e.g., Alesina, Grilli, and Milesi-Ferretti. 1994; Schulze 2000.

7. Article VI, sections 1 and 3 of the Articles of Agreement of the International Monetary Fund. In some cases, use of controls could even be made mandatory. In the event of a severe payments crisis, the IMF was authorized to request that a

government impose capital restraints and could even bar access to IMF resources unless the government complied.

8. For more detail, see Helleiner 1994, ch. 2. Ironically, as Helleiner points out, contemporary opponents challenged capital controls on precisely the same libertarian grounds as do opponents today. Controls were viewed as incompatible with a democratic form of government—"coercive" and even reminiscent of Hitler's monetary system (Helleiner 1994, 41).

9. "Post-War Currency Policy," a British Treasury memorandum dated September 1941, reprinted in Moggridge 1980a, 31. For 'ole,' read hole—a handy place to hide one's money.

10. "Plan for an International Currency (or Clearing) Union," January 1942, reprinted in Moggridge 1980a, 129–30.

11. As reprinted in Moggridge 1980b, 17. For more on Keynes's views and how they relate to the contemporary scene, see Cassidy 1998; Kirshner 1999.

12. The term "Washington Consensus" was first coined by economist John Williamson (1990).

13. In fact, as of 1998, 129 of the IMF's 184 members still maintained some form of restrictions on capital-account transactions. See Johnston et al. 1999.

14. Interim Committee Communiqué, 28 April 1997, para. 7. Under the plan, two Articles were to be amended—Article I, where "orderly liberalization of capital" would have been added to the list of the IMF's formal purposes; and Article VIII, which would have given the fund the same jurisdiction over the capital account of its members as it already enjoys over the current account. The language would also have *required* countries to commit themselves to financial liberalization as a goal.

15. The earliest example I can find of this change of tone was a column by *Financial Times* commentator Martin Wolf in early March 1998. Ordinarily a firm champion of free markets, Wolf reluctantly concluded: "After the crisis, the question can no longer be whether these flows should be regulated in some way. It can only be how" (Wolf 1998). Ten months later, at the annual World Economic Forum in Davos, Switzerland—always a useful means for tracking authoritative public- and private-sector opinion—it was clear from most remarks that absolutely unrestricted capital mobility was no longer much in favor. See, e.g., *New York Times*, 29 January 1999. The change of tone was not unanimous, of course. For Dornbusch (2000b, 79), capital controls were still "an idea whose time has gone."

16. Bhagwati 1998. The original article, which was published in *Foreign Affairs*, is reprinted in Bhagwati 2000 along with some subsequent papers expanding on his basic argument.

17. See, e.g., Grabel 1996a, 1996b.

18. Krugman 1998b. See also Krugman 1999c, ch. 9.

19. See, e.g., Little and Olivei 1999, which records the proceedings of a high-level international conference sponsored by the Federal Reserve Bank of Boston.

20. See, e.g., Eichengreen 1999; Wade 1998–1999; Wade and Veneroso 1998a; Vernengo and Rochon 2000; Williamson 2000; Cohen 2000f, 2002a, 2003a.

21. See, e.g., Adams et al. 1998; Eichengreen et al. 1998; Adams, Mathieson, and Schinasi 1999; International Monetary Fund 1999c; Ariyoshi et al. 2000; Mussa, Masson et al. 2000; Edison et al. 2002.

22. For useful reviews of key elements of the debate, see Neely 1999; Evenett 2000.

23. See, e.g., Obstfeld and Rogoff 1996, who provide elegant theoretical arguments to demonstrate the potential for gains from intertemporal trade through a free international market for securities.

24. See also Eichengreen et al. 1998; López-Mejía 1999.

25. On this point, see also Eichengreen 2003, ch. 3.

26. Thomas Willett (2000), an astute observer, calls this the "too much, too late hypothesis." "The markets have frequently failed," he writes, "to provide early warnings. . . . When market discipline finally kicks in, moreover, the markets often overreact" (2000, 2).

27. The point is demonstrated theoretically in Mourmouras and Russell 2000. For a primer on the practical techniques of evasion, see Dunn 2002.

28. For a statement of the same point, see Cohen 1965. In my bolder and more dogmatic youth, I was even willing to raise this observation to the status of an economic law—what I ambitiously labeled the Iron Law of Economic Controls. To wit, "to be effective, controls must reproduce at a rate faster than that at which means are found for avoiding them" (Cohen 1965, 174). Today I find myself less inclined to be quite so categorical.

29. Indeed, in two of the cases, Mexico and Peru, subsequent outflows were so pronounced that policymakers ultimately felt obliged to resort to bank nationalization in an attempt to close off conduits for capital flight. For some discussion, see Maxfield 1992.

30. See, e.g., Ariyoshi et al. 2000, 18–28. But for a more skeptical view, see Edwards 1999a, 69–70.

31. For detail, see Ariyoshi et al. 2000, appendix 3; Haggard 2000; Kaplan and Rodrik 2001.

32. As quoted in the *New York Times*, 24 October 1998.

33. As quoted in the *New York Times*, 14 August 1999.

34. See, e.g., Adams, Mathieson, and Schinasi 1999, 97–101; Ariyoshi et al. 2000, 53–55; Athukorala 2001; Edison and Reinhart 2001; Kaminsky and Schmukler 2001. For a particularly spirited defense of Malaysia's strategy, see Stiglitz 2002, 122–25.

35. *The Economist*, 1 May 1999, 73.

36. See, e.g., Haggard 2000; Dornbusch 2001b; Jomo 2001, ch. 7.

37. See also Adams, Mathieson, and Schinasi 1999, 99; Athukorala 2001.

38. As quoted in the *New York Times*, 25 June 1998.

39. *The Economist*, 26 September 1998, 79.

40. Wu Xiaoling, director general of the State Administration of Foreign Exchange, as quoted in the *New York Times*, 30 September 1998.

41. See especially Eichengreen 1999; Mussa, Masson et al. 2000; Mussa, Swoboda et al. 2000; Williamson 2000.

42. See, e.g., Goldstein 1998; Radelet and Sachs 1998; Wade 1998–1999.

43. Chile had also briefly imposed restraints on inflows in 1978–1982, prior to the start of the debt crisis of the 1980s. See Edwards 1999a, 71.

44. In Spanish, the URR was known as the *encaje*. For detail on Chile's program, see Ariyoshi et al. 2000, appendix 1.

45. For useful summaries of this literature, see Edwards 1999a; Eichengreen 1999, 51–55; Nadal-De Simone and Sorsa 1999; Williamson 2000, 37–45; Ulan 2002.

46. See also Edwards 1999b, 2000. But for a dissenting view, see Williamson 2000, 37–45.

47. See, e.g., Reinhart and Reinhart 1998; Montiel and Reinhart 1999; De Gregorio, Edwards, and Valdés 2000; Mussa, Masson et al. 2000.

Notes to Chapter 5
Follow the Leader

1. See, e.g., Eichengreen 1994; Beddoes 1999; Hausmann 1999a, 1999b; LeBaron and McCulloch 2000; Mundell 2000a, 2000d; Mussa, Masson et al. 2000; Rogoff 2002a.

2. Recent years have seen the development of an extensive literature debating the pros and cons of dollarization. For comprehensive discussions, see Joint Economic Committee 2000a; Berg and Borensztein 2000a, 2000b; Bogetić 2000a, 2000b. Special issues on dollarization have been published by the *Journal of Policy Modeling* 23:3 (April 2001) and the *Journal of Money, Credit and Banking* 33:2 (May 2001). Partisans for or against dollarization (or euroization) are cited in chapter 3.

3. The case of Panama has been much examined recently. Key sources include Moreno-Villalaz 1999; Bogetić 2000a, 2000b; Goldfajn and Olivares 2001.

4. According to Miguel Kiguel, at the time chief of President Menem's cabinet of advisors, a reduction of at least 1.5–2 percentage points was anticipated (as quoted in IMF 1999b, 14).

5. One percentage point of interest—the difference, say, between a 3 percent rate of interest and 4 percent—equals 100 basis points.

6. This issue has been addressed analytically, albeit with inconclusive results, by Frankel 1999; Berg and Borensztein 2000a, 2000b; Powell and Sturzenegger 2002.

7. See, e.g., Moreno-Villalaz 1999; Bogetić 2000a, 2000b.

8. Berg and Borensztein 2000a, 39. See also Berg and Borensztein 2000b; Rojas-Suarez 2000.

9. For a formal model addressing this point, see Chang and Velasco 2003. Dollarization, they argue, "buys credibility at the expense of a suboptimal response to shocks" (54). The greater the past abuse of policy, the more likely it is that macroeconomic performance will be improved rather than suffer from abandonment of a national money.

10. Edwards 2001; Edwards and Magendzo 2001; Levy-Yeyati and Sturzenegger 2001; Begg 2002.

11. Goldfajn and Olivares 2001 draw the same conclusion from a richly detailed case study of Panama.

12. See, e.g., Bogetić 2000a, 2000b; von Furstenberg 2000b; Alexander and von Furstenberg 2000.

13. For additional detail on these alternative methods of calculation, see Joint Economic Committee 2000a, 13–14.

14. See, e.g., Berg and Borensztein 2000a, 2000b; Velde and Veracierto 2000.

15. Roughly similar orders of magnitude in Latin America have been suggested by Williamson 1995; Larrain and Velasco 2001. For a comparable estimate for Cambodia, where the greenback is also widely used, see de Zamaróczy and Sa 2002.

16. See, e.g., Katzman 2000, 212; Dornbusch 2001a, 2.

17. As quoted by Goodhart 1995, 455.

18. *New York Times*, 16 May 1999.

19. Hausmann et al. 2000, 159. See also Hausmann 1999a.

20. Ambler H. Moss, Jr., in testimony before the U.S. Congress in 1989, as quoted in Kirshner 1995, 162. For further discussion and detail, see Kirshner 1995, 159–66; Hufbauer, Schott, and Elliott 1990, 249–67.

21. Most lists of failed states over the years have been limited to such unfortunate countries as Afghanistan, Cambodia, Congo (formerly Zaire), Sierra Leone, Somalia, and Sudan. Some of these countries, too, have suffered through periods of monetary fragmentation. One example is Cambodia, where for many years after the overthrow of the infamous Khmers Rouges regime in 1979, Khmers Rouges holdouts in the western border areas of the country issued their own Khmer riel in direct competition with the central government's official riel (de Zamaróczy and Sa 2002, 4). Another example is Sudan, where separate currencies have been issued by the recognized government in the north and by the rebel Sudan People's Liberation Movement in the south (*The Economist*, 14 December 2002, 68). In Congo monetary fragmentation was caused in part by the government itself, which for a time actually counterfeited its own currency, printing two or more copies for each serial number with duplicates going to cronies of the political leadership (*The Economist*, 14 September 2002, 73). The most notable case of monetary fragmentation in recent years was in Afghanistan, as noted later in this chapter.

22. Confidential source.

23. Alberto Acosta, as quoted in the *New York Times*, 11 January 2000.

24. As quoted in *Financial Times*, 11 January 2000.

25. Léon Roldós, a socialist member of parliament and rector of the University of Guayaquil, as quoted in the *New York Times*, 16 January 2000.

26. *The Economist*, 19 February 2000, 39.

27. *The Economist*, 29 January 2000, 35.

28. As late as end-2001, opinion polls still showed roughly half the population opposed to dollarization—a decline from previous levels, but still high. See *The Economist*, 26 January 2002, 35; Lopez 2002.

29. See, e.g., *The Economist*, 28 September 2002, 34–35.

30. Confidential source.

31. Castro 1999; Guidotti and Powell 2001.

32. The report is from former Council of Economic Advisers member Jeffrey Frankel, as quoted at an International Monetary Fund forum in mid-1999 (IMF 1999b, 6). See also Frankel 1999, 20. Frankel's list of Argentina's negotiating goals was effectively confirmed at the same forum by Menem advisor Miguel Kiguel (IMF 1999b, 15) but was contradicted by Pedro Pou, then president of Argentina's central bank, in a contemporaneous conference convened by the Federal

Reserve Bank of Boston. According to Pou, "we are asking for neither U.S. supervision of Argentine banks, nor the U.S. lender of last resort facilities for our financial system. What we are asking for is basically very simple—a fiscally neutral agreement on seigniorage for both countries" [i.e., full return of lost seigniorage] (Pou 1999, 249). The confidentiality that cloaked the discussions between the two governments makes the full extent of Argentina's goals difficult to verify.

33. As quoted in Whalen 2001, 49.

34. As much is admitted even by such an ardent enthusiast as Michael Gavin (2000, 49), who concedes that "if the United States does not decide to share seigniorage, the odds of official dollarization are very low."

35. See also Jameson 2001.

36. See, e.g., Salvatore 2001; Berg, Borensztein, and Mauro 2002; Hochreiter, Schmidt-Hebbel, and Winckler. 2002; Frieden 2003.

37. Dean 2001. Dean's calculations are notable because they include estimates of U.S. bank notes in local circulation as well as more easily identifiable dollar-denominated bank deposits. Other Latin economies with high levels of informal dollarization according to his figures are, not surprisingly, Argentina (with, until 2002, its dollar-based currency board) and Mexico (with its close trading relationship with the United States).

38. As quoted in the *New York Times*, 28 June 2002.

39. *The Economist*, 2 September 2000, 71.

40. See, e.g., *New York Times*, 31 January 2002.

41. See, e.g., *The Economist*, 6 October 2001, 66–67; *Washington Post*, 29 January 2002; *New York Times*, 2 May 2002.

42. In the end, the decision was made to preserve rather than replace the afghani. Starting in late 2002, a new afghani was issued by the resuscitated central bank to replace all versions previously in circulation (at a rate of one new afghani for up to a thousand of the old, depending on the version exchanged). See, e.g., *New York Times*, 7 October 2002; *The Economist*, 14 December 2002, 37.

43. Others who have argued in favor of immediate euroization include Angarski and Harsev 1999; Nenovski, Hristov, and Petrov 2000; Bratkowski and Rostowski 2001a, 2001b; Coricelli 2001; Dean and Kasa 2001. Opposing arguments are presented by Nuti 2000; Wójcik 2000; Dietz 2001; Gabrisch 2001. The papers by Bratkowski and Rostowski (2001a), Coricelli, Dietz, and Gabrisch are all available on the website of "Countdown," an online workshop for the presentation and discussion of research related to the EU's eastern enlargement (*www.eu-enlargement.org*). Countdown is cofinanced by the City of Vienna and the Federal Chancellery of Austria and is run by the Vienna Institute for International Economic Studies (WIIW). The Nuti and Wójcik papers were also initially contributed to the Countdown project.

44. Ironically, the only exceptions in the region are not among the current applicants for membership and are not even (yet?) formal sovereign states. These are Montenegro and Kosovo, which as noted in chapter 3 (note 31) are now fully euroized.

45. As with the topic of dollarization, an extensive literature has developed in recent years debating the pros and cons of currency boards. For comprehensive discussions, see Williamson 1995; Baliño and Enoch 1997; Kopcke 1999; Ghosh, Gulde, and Wolf 2000. For earlier sources, see Cohen 1998, 52–55.

46. For an up-to-date statement and citations, see Hanke 2002.

47. Dornbusch 2001a, 2.

48. Dornbusch dismissed this issue, as well, writing that "when it comes to national pride it should not come up in most countries" (2001a, 2). But that, too, was the economist talking. As Helleiner (1999, 152) has pointed out, practical politicians have long understood the role that a currency board can play in establishing or promoting trust in a suspect currency.

49. See, e.g., Kopcke 1999, 30; Alexander and von Furstenberg 2000, 216.

50. Berg and Borensztein (2000b, 18) put the same point the other way round when they write that "full dollarization is much like a currency-board with no exit option."

51. See, e.g., Helleiner 2003a, ch. 8.

52. This appears to be the reason why some sources, including especially the IMF, prefer the term "currency-board arrangements" rather than currency board. For further discussion of issues of design and implementation, see Baliño and Enoch 1997; Enoch and Gulde 1997; Santiprabhob 1997; Ghosh, Gulde, and Wolf 2000.

53. For further detail on currency boards in operation today, see Baliño and Enoch 1997; Santiprabhob 1997; Kopcke 1999; Ghosh, Gulde, and Wolf 2000.

54. Originally set at 20 percent when the Convertibility Plan was enacted in 1991, the allowable maximum was raised to one-third of total backing in 1995 when the peso came under pressure following a currency crisis in Mexico. For more detail, see below.

55. Williamson 1995, 8. It might be noted, however, Hong Kong's Exchange Fund has typically used its discretionary authority to *reinforce* the automatic working of the currency-board, unlike the Argentine central bank, which tended instead to use its element of discretion to cushion bank liquidity *against* the working of the currency board—a difference of practice that may help to account for the contrasting outcomes of the two arrangements.

56. See, e.g., Hanke and Schuler 2002.

57. In fact, Ireland's exit from its sterling-based currency board took more than a third of a century to be fully realized. While a central bank was created in 1943, its operations continued to be based on a reserve backing rule that was only gradually eased starting in 1961. Exit was completed in 1979 when the fixed exchange-rate link to the pound was finally dropped. See Baliño and Enoch 1997, 27.

58. Brunei, by contrast, still pegs its currency, the Brunei dollar, to the Singapore dollar in a currency-board arrangement. Both countries had previously participated in Britain's Malayan Currency Board, which also included the Malay States, Sarawak, and North Borneo (Sabah). The latter three entities are now combined in the sovereign state of Malaysia. The Malayan Currency Board was terminated in 1973 when Singapore and Malaysia separately adopted floating exchange-rate regimes.

59. In 1985, the old peso had been replaced by the "austral," which in turn was succeeded by the "new" austral before the new peso was introduced.

60. The Estonian kroon was pegged directly to the deutsche mark (now succeeded by the euro); the Lithuanian litas to the dollar, before switching to the euro in 2002. For more detail, see Camard 1996; Korhonen and Sutela 2000; Sörg and Vensel 2000; Alonso-Gamo et al. 2002; Knöbl Sutt, and Zavoico 2002.

61. During the years of conflict leading up to the Dayton peace accord, several currencies circulated in various parts of Bosnia and Herzegovina, including the Yugoslav dinar in Serb-controlled areas and the Croatian kuna in Croat-populated regions, as well as a Bosnia and Herzegovina dinar that was introduced in October 1994. Under the Dayton agreement, the Yugoslav and Croatian monies were withdrawn from circulation and a new central bank was to be set up to act as a de facto currency board for a minimum of six years, with a new Bosnian marka pegged firmly to the deutsche mark (later the euro).

62. Gulde 1999; Zloch-Christy 2000.

63. See, e.g., Ghosh, Gulden, and Wolf. 2000; Levy-Yeyati and Sturzenegger 2001.

64. For summary and analysis of the Argentine experience, see Pastor and Wise 2001; Mussa 2002.

65. Hanke 1996, 71. Mussa (2002, 21) suggests that good luck may also have had something to do with it, as the economy's external competitiveness was fortuitously aided at the time by a sharp depreciation of the dollar.

66. In fact, the new currency-board peg never took effect, since the legislation specified that it could not be implemented until the euro reached par with the dollar—which Europe's money never did before Argentina's currency board was terminated.

67. The innovation, echoing limited experiments by several provinces during the hyperinflationary 1980s, was pioneered by Buenos Aires province, home to a third of Argentina's population. As early as August 2001, the provincial government introduced its *patacón* (plural: *patacónes*). Though formally labeled a "treasury letter in cancellation of obligations"—a low-denomination bond redeemable in one year—the paper was clearly intended to circulate as a usable medium of exchange. With tax receipts plunging after four years of recession, most other provincial governments soon followed suit, issuing emergency currencies of their own under such colorful labels as *quebrachos*, *bocades*, and *huarpes*. And by the end of the year the central government too, had gotten into the act, printing large amounts of so-called *lecops*. In the early months of 2002 more than a dozen of these Quasi-Currencies could be found in circulation alongside pesos and dollars. For more detail, see *Financial Times*, 11 April 2002, 4.

68. See also Carrera 2002; Mussa 2002.

69. Ibarra and Moreno-Brid 2001, 11, 14. See also Larrain and Velasco 2001, 14–15.

70. See, e.g., Corker et al. 2000; Gulde, Kähkönen, and Keller 2000.

71. See, e.g., de Zamaróczy and Sa 2002; IMF 2002a.

Notes to Chapter 6
Hanging Together

This chapter is adapted from an article, "Are Monetary Unions Inevitable?", to be published in *International Studies Perspectives*, 4:3 (August 2003), and appears here with the kind permission of Blackwell Publishers.

1. See, e.g., von Furstenberg 2000b, 2000c; Alexander and von Furstenberg 2000.

2. One of these five, of course—Argentina's—only survived a decade, as previously noted.

3. Goodhart 1995, 452. See also McCallum 1999b.

4. This interpretation of the historical record, first articulated in 1994 (Cohen 1994), has been explicitly endorsed by most subsequent discussions. See, e.g., Goodhart 1998; Bordo and Jonung 1999. The dominance of politics in this context, though not spelled out in detail, is also stressed by Hamada and Porteous 1992; Capie 1999; Hamada 1999a. Objections to my analysis have been raised by only one source, Andrews and Willett 1997, who contend that a combination of economic and organizational factors perform as well as the political considerations I identify as decisive—despite the fact that, as Andrews and Willett themselves admit, half the cases examined fail to confirm their alternative view.

5. This type of linkage, highlighting the salience of social interaction and learning, has also been stressed by others. Kathleen McNamara (1998), for example, emphasizes the role that shared ideas and values played in leading to a convergence of preferences for monetary union in Europe. Similarly, Scott Cooper (1999), in a comparative political analysis, argues that regional monetary cooperation is facilitated by a high level of intraregional trust, which may be understood as synonymous with what I call a sense of solidarity or community and with what Peter Aykens (2002) calls "affective trust."

6. Numerous histories have been written of Europe's long march to monetary union. Among the most informative are Kenen 1995; Overturf 1997; Ungerer 1997.

7. *The Economist*, 1 September 2001, 62.

8. Hans Tietmeyer, as quoted in Shlaes 1997, 190.

9. Karl Otto Pöhl, as quoted in the *New York Times*, 30 August 2001.

10. Not all Europeans have felt the same way, of course. Many Italians, for instance, were reported to be ecstatic at getting rid of a currency that was widely seen as a symbol of weakness, not strength; while most French citizens seem to take more pride in their art and culture than they ever did in their money. For detail, see the *New York Times*, 27 December 2001 and 29 December 2001. But six months after euro notes and coins were introduced, half the Germans questioned in a European Commission poll said they still wanted the mark back (*New York Times*, 2 July 2002).

11. Respectively John Redwood, Frank Field, and Lord Owen (formerly David Owen), as quoted in *The Economist*, "Undoing Britain? A Survey of Britain," 6 November 1999, 14, 18.

12. Though of recent origin, the current debate in Canada actually has roots going back to the first days of Canada's national currency in the nineteenth century, as Eric Helleiner 2003b has ably demonstrated.

13. NAFTA, in turn, replaced an earlier Canada-U.S. Free Trade Agreement, dating from 1989. The third member of NAFTA is Mexico.

14. Many Mexicans ask the same question, but with little hope that the United States would agree to a new joint Mexican-American currency. For Mexico, the

only realistic choice appears to be dollarization—formal adoption of America's greenback as a replacement for the peso.

15. An earlier proposal to call the future money the "North American dollar" (von Furstenberg and Fratianni 1996) attracted little favor.

16. See, e.g., Courchene 1999; Courchene and Harris 2000a, 2000b; Grubel 1999, 2000.

17. See, e.g., Laidler 1999; McCallum 1999a, 2000; Murray 2000; Robson and Laidler 2002.

18. The alleged impacts on business and government adjustments are known, respectively, as the "lazy managers" and "bad policymaker" hypotheses. See Robson and Laidler 2002.

19. See, e.g., Laidler 1999; Robson 2001; Robson and Laidler 2002.

20. Sherry Cooper, chief economist at BMO Nesbitt Burns, Inc., a well-known Toronto financial firm, as quoted in the *Globe and Mail*, 9 November 2001. Separately, a national poll of 4000 Canadian business executives in mid-2001 found some 45 percent in favor of NAMU, with 42 percent opposed (*National Post*, 16 July 2001).

21. A. Grimes 2000; Grimes and Holmes 2000. ANZAC derives from the initials of the Australian and New Zealand Army Corps created in World War I.

22. Grimes and Holmes 2000. For other presentations of the case for monetary union, see A. Grimes 2000; Coleman 2001. For opposing views, see Brash 2000; Hartley 2001. A balanced review of both sides of the debate in New Zealand is provided by Bjorksten 2001.

23. See, e.g., Hargreaves and McDermott 1999; McCaw and McDermott 2000; Haug 2001; Crosby and Otto 2002; Scrimgeour 2002.

24. As reported in the *Dominion* (Wellington), 20 September 2000.

25. As quoted in the *International Herald Tribune*, 19 September 2000.

26. Press conference, 13 September 2000 (available at *http://www.treasurer.gov.au*).

27. Previous bilateral agreements were signed in 1993, 1996, 1997, and 1999. For discussion, see Abdelal 2001; Tsygankov 2001; International Monetary Fund 2002b.

28. Igor Ivanov, as quoted in the *New York Times*, 26 December 1998.

29. Joseph Yam, as quoted in the *Financial Times*, 6 January 1999.

30. See, e.g., *The Economist*, 19 December 1999, 47.

31. Final communiqué of a meeting of ASEAN heads of government, Manila, Philippines, 28 November 1999.

32. As reported in *IMF Survey*, 8 October 2001, 318–19.

33. See, e.g., Eichengreen and Bayoumi 1999; Bird and Rajan 2002; Laurence 2002.

34. Rodolfo Severino, as quoted in *The Economist*, 12 February 2000.

35. Edgardo Espiritu, as quoted in *The Economist*, 12 February 2000.

36. See, e.g., Bayoumi and Mauro 1999; Eichengreen and Bayoumi 1999; Nicolas 1999; Glick 2002.

37. From the Rome Treaty onward through all subsequent accords, including the Maastricht Treaty establishing EMU, EU members have repeatedly stressed their goal of creating "an ever closer union among the peoples of Europe."

38. For some discussion, see Chang and Rajan 2001; Rajan 2001; Henning 2002.

39. Tharman Shanmugaratnam, as quoted in the *Financial Times*, 5 June 2001.

40. See, e.g., Yuen 2000.

41. See, e.g., Letiche 2000; Park and Wang 2000; Chang and Rajan 2001; Rajan 2001; Bowles 2002.

42. In addition to full members Argentina, Brazil, Paraguay, and Uruguay, Mercosur has two associate members, Bolivia and Chile.

43. Pedro Malan, as quoted by Reuters, 9 May 2000. Echoed Arminio Fraga, president of Brazil's central bank: "Not dollarizing keeps the possibility of a common currency alive" *(New York Times*, 10 January 2002). In fact, Brazilian officials are said to have warned Argentina that they would regard Mercosur as finished had Buenos Aires adopted the dollar. See *The Economist*, 5 January 2002, 31.

44. As quoted in the *Financial Times*, 10 November 1999.

45. See, e.g., Edwards 1998; Giambiagi 1999; Jones 2000; O'Keefe 2000.

46. See, e.g., Eichengreen 1998; Carrera and Sturzenegger 2000; Levy-Yeyati and Sturzenegger 2000b.

47. Brazilians, for example, reacted with contempt when Carlos Menem once suggested that all Mercosur members might adopt Argentina's peso as a single currency *(New York Times*, 6 July 1999). Argentines, conversely, could be expected to be equally leery about common adoption of Brazil's real, an idea proposed by Fratianni and Hauskrecht 2002.

48. The six sovereign members of the ECCU, as indicated in table 5, are Antigua and Barbuda, Dominica, Grenada, St. Kitts and Nevis, St. Lucia, and St. Vincent and the Grenadines (along with two British dependencies, Anguilla and Montserrat). The eight neighboring states that are their partners in CARICOM are Bahamas, Barbados, Belize, Guyana, Haiti, Jamaica, Suriname, and Trinidad and Tobago. CARICOM first came into existence with the Treaty of Chaguaramas, signed in 1973.

49. The plan built on the work of the West Indian Commission, a group of experts set up by CARICOM heads of state in 1989 with a mandate to formulate proposals for advancing the process of Caribbean economic integration. The commission's final report (West Indian Commission 1992) called directly for creation of a common currency. For discussion, see Nicholls et al. 2000; Itam et al. 2000.

50. Owen Arthur, as quoted in *Journal of Commerce*, 7 December 1999, 17.

51. See, e.g., Worrell 1995; Anthony and Hughes Hallett 2000.

52. In addition to these fourteen states, ECOWAS has one additional member—Cape Verde, which continues to maintain its own separate currency. Mauritania was a founding member of ECOWAS but later withdrew.

53. For more detail, see Masson and Pattillo 2001a, 2001b.

54. R. D. Asante, head of the Money and Payments Division of the ECOWAS Secretariat, as quoted in Irving 2001, 26.

55. See, e.g., Irving 1999, 28. The role of EMS as a model for the West Africans can be seen in the Maastricht-like emphasis on convergence criteria and even in the name of the West African Monetary Institute, which echoes that of the ECB's precursor, the European Monetary Institute. Indirectly, some inspiration also may

have come from the common historical experience of four of the six West African states—Gambia, Ghana, Nigeria, and Sierra Leone. As noted in chapter 5, the four former British colonies once shared a joint currency issued by the British-run West African Currency Board. For detail, see Helleiner 2003a, ch. 8.

56. IMF economist Paul Masson, as quoted in Irving 2001, 26.

57. A natural name for such a currency, wags have suggested, would of course be the *afro*.

58. For more detail on the GCC, see Twinham 1992; Peterson 1988. The GCC in turn inspired two similar groupings of Arab states—the Arab Cooperation Council, comprised of Egypt, Iraq, Jordan, and Yemen; and the Arab Maghreb Union, combining Algeria, Libya, Mauritania, Morocco, and Tunisia—both formed in 1989. Neither of these other associations has stood the test of time, however. Iraq's invasion of Kuwait in 1990 effectively destroyed the Arab Cooperation Council, and political differences in North Africa have consistently prevented any effective action by the Arab Maghreb Union.

59. GCC Unified Economic Agreement, 8 June 1982, Article 22. Here, too, as in West Africa (see note 55, pp. 240 and 241), some inspiration may have come from a common historical experience as British dependencies. Prior to independence, the smaller Gulf states were all part of a de facto monetary union based on their shared use of the Indian rupee. Again for detail see Helleiner 2003a, 208–9.

Notes to Chapter 7
New Frontiers

1. A fairly extensive literature exists on the subject of local money, although most contributions have come from enthusiasts seeking to attract support for their cause. Among the most informative sources are L. Solomon 1996; Lietaer 2001. Additional citations are provided by Helleiner 2000, 36–37.

2. The adjective "complementary" (Lietaer 2001) is used to signify that local monies are intended not to replace but to supplement the roles traditionally played by conventional state-sanctioned currencies. Others speak of "multicurrency systems" (Douthwaite 1999) or "multilevel currency systems" (Robertson 1990).

3. The estimates for 2000 and the 1980s are from Lietaer 2001, 5, 159. The estimate for 1993 is from *The Economist*, 24 April 1993, 60.

4. Though, as indicated in chapter 1, *all* money may be understood to multilateralize barter, only certain forms of local money are *explicitly* designed with that purpose in mind—hence the conventional practice of limiting the label "barter-based" to just this class of currency system.

5. For more detail on scrip money, see, e.g., Timberlake 1987, 1992; Lietaer 2001, 148–58.

6. For more detail on Ithaca Hours, see L. Solomon 1996, 43–52; Frick 1996. Paul Glover maintains a website at *http://www.publiccom.com/web/ithacahour* and for a small charge will send a Hometown Money Starter Kit to anyone interested in emulating his model.

7. See *The Economist* 28 June 1997, 29.

8. See the *Santa Barbara News Press*, 9 February 1999, B1, and the university's student newspaper, *Daily Nexus*, 23 October 2000.

9. As reported in the *New York Times*, 30 January 2001.

10. See the *Los Angeles Times*, 6 May 2002. In Valparaiso, Chile, the paper currency of the local barter club is called the *talento*; its counterpart across the border in the Argentine town of Rio Colorado is known as the *credito*. Regrettably, following the collapse of Argentina's currency board in early 2002, the country's economic crisis led in some cases to overissue as well as counterfeiting of barter currencies, devaluing their purchasing power (*The Economist*, 24 August 2002, 29).

11. Lietaer refers to local money as "work-enabling currencies" (2001, 125).

12. In primitive societies such as those still found in the South Pacific, sub-Saharan Africa, and elsewhere, anthropologists have long noted the key role that indigenous monies tend to play in perpetuating basic social structures and relationships. For some discussion, see, e.g., Akin and Robbins 1999. Likewise, sociologists stress how, even in more modern settings, money remains embedded in diverse cultural and social structures. See, e.g., Dodd 1994; Zelizer 1994.

13. Useful introductions to the subject of electronic money include Furche and Wrightson 1996; Lynch and Lundquist 1996; E. Solomon 1997; Lietaer 2001, ch. 3; Spencer 2001.

14. The European Central Bank 2000b prefers the terms "hardware-based products" and "software-based products."

15. E. Solomon 1997 prefers the term "cybermoney."

16. The Bank for International Settlements 2000 provides a detailed survey of prepaid electronic money products. For further detail, see Singleton 1995; Furch and Wrightson 1996, ch. 5; Stewart 1997; ECB 2000b.

17. *New York Times*, 6 February 2002. See also *The Economist*, 5 May 2001, 65–66. PayPal's web address is *http://www.paypal.com*.

18. *New York Times*, 27 August 2001.

19. Other examples include Cybergold and Greenpoints in the United States and iPoints and Tesco Clubcard in Britain.

20. By 2002, such purchases were estimated to account for some 3 percent of mileage redemptions worldwide. See *The Economist*, 4 May 2002, 62.

21. E. Solomon 1997, 75. In the rather drier language of the European Central Bank (2000b, 55), "There is a risk that electronic money might lead to the emergence of multiple units of account."

22. The amounts involved are anything but trivial. For instance, unused balances in frequent-flyer programs, which airlines can sell to nonairline firms in exchange for goods and services, were estimated at end-2001 to sum worldwide to nearly eight trillion miles (*The Economist*, 4 May 2002, 62). With miles typically traded at between one cent and three cents (U.S.) per miles, this total represented a value of between $80 billion and $240 billion that could potentially be put to use to augment revenues (assuming, of course, a sufficient network of vendors prepared to accept miles in payment).

23. For more on these challenges, see Spencer 2001; Tumin 2002.

24. For a rare early exception, see Berentsen 1998.

25. B. Friedman 1999, 321. Others who have since argued along similar lines include Costa and De Grauwe 2001; Cronin and Dowd 2001.

26. Explicitly, the papers by Freedman, Goodhart, and Woodford are framed as direct responses to Benjamin Friedman's 1999 article. B. Friedman 2000, in turn, is a rejoinder to the other three. It is not clear that any of the four was even aware of the earlier contributions by Kobrin and Helleiner. At the time they wrote, Freedman was deputy governor of the Bank of Canada, while Goodhart and Woodford were academics at, respectively, the London School of Economics and Princeton University.

27. For similar views, see Aglietta (2002); Ingham (2002). In Aglietta's words (2002, 66): "This sort of science fiction vision of the future has no chance of coming true."

28. Bank for International Settlements 1996, 7. For other citations, see Helleiner 1998a, 29.

29. See also Henckel, Ize, and Kovanen et al. 1999.

Notes to Chapter 8
Governing the New Geography

1. For citations, see chapter 4.

2. See, e.g., Sachs and Larrain 1999; Mussa, Masson et al. 2000; Larrain and Velasco 2001; Goldstein 2002.

3. See, e.g., R. Cooper 1999a; Hausmann et al. 2000; Calvo and Reinhart 2001; Fratzscher 2002.

4. For some evidence on the negative impact of currency volatility on investment, see Huizinga 1994; Corbo and Rojas 1997.

5. See, e.g., Bénassy-Quéré and Coeuré 2000, 2002a; Levy-Yeyati and Sturzenegger 2000a, 2001; Hausmann, Panizza and Stein 2001; Hernández and Montiel 2001; Reinhart and Rogoff 2002. Edwards 2002 puts a more positive spin on observed interventions, calling them "optimal flotation" rather than fear of floating.

6. See Johnston et al. 1999; Bubula and Ötker-Robe 2002.

7. For discussion and citations, see Cukierman 1992, 1998; Eijffinger and De Haan 1996.

8. See, e.g., Eijffinger and De Haan 1996; Maxfield 1997. Until the late 1980s, the only independent central banks of any importance were the Federal Reserve, Germany's Bundesbank, and the National Bank of Switzerland. The more recent trend began in 1989, in Chile and New Zealand, and quickly spread elsewhere over the course of the 1990s. In the European Union, the Maastricht Treaty of 1992 required all member-governments to grant independence to their central banks before the euro could come into existence. These central banks now are all part of the European System of Central Banks headed by the ECB.

9. See, e.g., Mankiw 2000; Seidman 2001.

10. Blinder 1997. See also *The Economist* 1999, 2002; Seidman 2001.

11. Berman and McNamara 1999, 5, 8. See also Stiglitz 1998.

12. For detail, see Reti 1998. Numerous proposals were in circulation even before the Paris conference. Mundell (1968) cites the Italian Gaspara Scaruffi,

who as early as 1582 published a polemic calling for a uniform currency throughout Europe to be called the *alitononfo*, a Greek word meaning "true light." Half a century after the 1867 Conference, at the Second Pan-American Scientific Conference in 1915, an essentially similar idea for the Western Hemisphere was put forward by the famous "money doctor" Edwin Kemmerer (1916), calling for a common monetary unit for all the countries of the Americas to be called the *oro* from the Latin root for "gold."

13. For a similar argument, see also Frankman 2002.

14. Indeed, for some, the idea would be quite literally *dystopian*—most notably, among the legions of the Christian right in the United States, where the devil's work is seen in any hint of world government. The Christian right's intense distaste for the idea is well expressed in a popular series of millenarian novels, known as the "Left Behind" series, which chronicle the end of days as suggested by the Biblical book, Revelation. Early in the series the Antichrist becomes secretary-general of the United Nations and, in one of his first acts of office, institutes a world currency—fulfilling the prediction that the kings of the earth "shall give their power and strength unto the beast" (Revelation 17:13). By mid-2002, nine installments of the series had sold a total of more than 40 million copies (*The Economist*, 24 August 2002, 27).

15. See, e.g., Mundell 1968.

16. Mundell, in Friedman and Mundell 2001, 29. See also Mundell 2000a. When asked at a meeting in April 2002 how he reconciled this with his optimum number of gods and currencies, Mundell laughingly replied that what he had in mind was not a single god but rather one god and a lot of saints.

17. The name *intor*, combining a contraction of "international" and the Latin root for gold, can be understood as a kind of homage to John Maynard Keynes, who coined the term *bancor* for the global currency that he hoped would be created by the negotiations at Bretton Woods in 1944. Pierre Werner, once prime minister of Luxembourg and, like Mundell, widely remembered as one of the fathers of the euro, also hoped eventually to see the birth of a global currency but preferred the name *mondo*, from the Latin for "world" (*The Economist*, 6 July 2002, 85).

18. For useful surveys, see Kenen 1989; Cohen 1993; Willett 1999. Following Keohane 1984, cooperation is identified here with a mutual adjustment of national policy behavior, achieved through an implicit or explicit process of interstate bargaining. Practically speaking, cooperation may vary greatly in intensity, ranging from simple consultation or exchanges of information to partial or even full collaboration in the formulation and implementation of policy. Related terms such as "coordination" or "collective decision making" may be treated as essentially synonymous in meaning.

19. See, e.g., Coeuré and Pisani-Ferry 2000, 24.

20. See, e.g., Williamson 1985; Williamson and Miller 1987; Williamson and Henning 1994; Bergsten and Henning 1996. Mundell (2000a, 2001; also in IMF 2000a) goes further, calling for absolutely fixed exchange rates among the Big Three, though not as an end in itself but rather as a prelude to the establishment of his ultimate goal of a single world currency. Charles Goldfinger (2002, 113) suggests calling such a world currency the *geo*. Much the same approach is also

advocated by Kenichi Ohmae 2001, who argues for a consolidated transatlantic currency to be called the *doro* or *eullar*, together with a joint Asian currency to be called the *asea*, all of which would eventually be merged into a global currency known as the *esperanza*.

21. See, e.g., Reinhart and Reinhart 2002.

22. Corden 2002, 255. See also Salvatore 2000.

23. Bénassy-Quéré, Mojon, and Pisani-Ferry 1997. See also Kenen 1995. But for a stylized model suggesting an alternative conclusion, see Bénassy-Quéré and Mojon 2001.

24. For a specific proposal, see Coeuré and Pisani-Ferry 2000.

25. For citations, see chapters 2 and 5.

26. Articles of Agreement of the International Monetary Fund, Article I.

27. Articles of Agreement of the International Monetary Fund, Article IV, Section 3 (b); emphasis added.

28. Rogoff, formerly at Harvard University, is chief of the IMF's research department; Eichengreen, a Berkeley professor, is a frequent IMF consultant.

References

Abdelal, Rawi. 2001. *National Purpose in the World Economy* (Ithaca: Cornell University Press).

Adams, Charles, Donald J. Mathieson, Garry Schinasi, and Bankim Chadha. 1998. *International Capital Markets: Developments, Prospects, and Key Policy Issues* (Washington, D.C.: International Monetary Fund).

Adams, Charles, Donald J. Mathieson, and Garry Schinasi. 1999. *International Capital Markets: Developments, Prospects, and Key Policy Issues* (Washington, D.C.: International Monetary Fund).

Aggarwal, Raj, and Mbodja Mougoue. 1996. "Cointegration among Asian Currencies: Evidence of the Increasing Influence of the Japanese Yen." *Japan and the World Economy* 8: 291–308.

Aglietta, Michel. 2002. "Whence and Whither Money?" In *The Future of Money* (Paris: Organization for Economic Cooperation and Development), ch. 2.

Akin, David, and Joel Robbins, eds. 1999. *Money and Modernity: State and Local Currencies in Melanesia* (Pittsburgh: University of Pittsburgh Press).

Alesina, Alberto. 2001. "Interview." *IMF Survey*, 2 July, 223–25.

Alesina, Alberto, and Robert J. Barro, eds. 2001a. *Currency Unions* (Stanford: Hoover Institution Press).

———. 2001b. "Dollarization." *American Economic Review* 91, no. 2 (May): 381–85.

———. 2002. "Currency Unions." *Quarterly Journal of Economics* 117, no. 2 (May): 409–36.

Alesina, Alberto, Robert J. Barro, and Silvana Tenreyro. 2002. "Optimal Currency Areas." Working Paper 9072 (Cambridge, Mass.: National Bureau of Economic Research).

Alesina, Alberto, Vittorio Grilli, and Gian Maria Milesi-Ferretti. 1994. "The Political Economy of Capital Controls." In Leonardo Leiderman and Assaf Razin, eds., *Capital Mobility: The Impact on Consumption, Investment and Growth* (New York: Cambridge University Press), ch. 11.

Alexander, Volbert, and George M. von Furstenberg. 2000. "Monetary Unions— A Superior Alternative to Full Dollarization in the Long Run." *North American Journal of Economics and Finance* 11, no. 2 (December): 205–25.

Aliber, Robert Z. 2002. *The New International Money Game*. 6th ed. (Chicago: University of Chicago Press).

Alogoskoufis, George, and Richard Portes. 1997. "The Euro, the Dollar, and the International Monetary System." In Paul R. Masson, Thomas H. Krueger, and Bart G. Turtelboom, eds., *EMU and the International Monetary System* (Washington, D.C.: International Monetary Fund), ch. 3.

Alonso-Gamo, Patricia, Stefania Fabrizio, Vitali Kramarenko, and Qing Wang. 2002. "Lithuania: History and Future of the Currency Board Arrangement." Working Paper WP/02/127 (Washington, D.C.: International Monetary Fund).

Altbach, Eric. 1997. "The Asian Monetary Fund Proposal: A Case Study of Japanese Regional Leadership." *JEI Report* 47A (Washington, D.C.: Japan Economic Institute).

Ambrosi, Gerhard Michael. 2000. "The Prospects for Global Monetary Bilingualism." In Robert A. Mundell and Armand Cleese, eds., *The Euro as a Stabilizer in the International Economic System* (Boston: Kluwer Academic), ch. 13.

Anderson, Benedict. 1991. *Imagined Communities: Reflections on the Origins and Spread of Nationalism.* Rev. ed. (London: Verso).

Andrews, David M., and Thomas D. Willett. 1997. "Financial Interdependence and the State: International Monetary Relations at Century's End." *International Organization* 51, no. 3 (Summer): 479–511.

Angarski, Krassimir, and Emil Harsev. 1999. "The Project 'Euro 2000' " (*http://www.capital.bg/old/weekly/99–10/03–10–3.htm*).

Anthony, Myrvin L., and Andrew Hughes Hallett. 2000. "Is the Case for Economic and Monetary Union in the Caribbean Realistic?" *World Economy* 23, no. 1 (January): 119–44.

Ariyoshi, Akira, Karl Habermeier, Bernard Laurens, Inci Ötker-Robe, Jorge Iván Canales-Kriljenko, and Andrei Kirilenko. 2000. *Capital Controls: Country Experiences with Their Use and Liberalization* (Washington, D.C.: International Monetary Fund).

Arora, Vivek, and Olivier Jeanne. 2001. "Economic Integration and the Exchange Rate Regime: Some Lessons from Canada." Policy Discussion Paper PDP/01/1 (Washington, D.C.: International Monetary Fund).

Athukorala, Prema-chandra. 2001. *Crisis and Recovery in Malaysia: The Role of Capital Controls* (Northampton, Mass.: Edward Elgar).

Auerbach, Nancy Neiman. 2001. *States, Banks, and Markets: Mexico's Path to Financial Liberalization in Comparative Perspective* (Boulder: Westview Press).

Aykens, Peter A. 2002. "(Mis)Trusting Authorities: Distributed Authority Networks and a Social Theory of Currency Crises." Brown University. Typescript.

Baliño, Tomás J. T, and Charles Enoch. 1997. *Currency Board Arrangements: Issues and Experiences* (Washington, D.C.: International Monetary Fund).

Baliño, Tomás J. T., Adam Bennett, and Eduardo Borensztein. 1999. *Monetary Policy in Dollarized Economies* (Washington, D.C.: International Monetary Fund).

Bank for International Settlements. 1996. *Implications for Central Banks of the Development of Electronic Money* (Basle).

———. 2000. *Survey of Electronic Money Developments* (Basle).

———. 2002. *Triennial Central Bank Survey: Foreign Exchange and Derivatives Market Activity in 2001* (Basle).

Bank of Japan. 1994. "The Circulation of Bank of Japan Notes." *Quarterly Bulletin* (November): 90–118.

Barro, Robert J. 1995. "Inflation and Economic Growth." *Bank of England Quarterly Bulletin* 35, no. 2 (May): 166–76.

———. 1999. "Let the Dollar Reign from Seattle to Santiago." *Wall Street Journal*, 8 March, A18.

———. 2000. "The Dollar Club: Why Countries are So Keen to Join." *Business Week*, 11 December, 34.

Bayoumi, Tamim, and Paolo Mauro. 1999. "The Suitability of ASEAN for a Regional Currency Arrangement." Working Paper WP/99/162 (Washington, D.C.: International Monetary Fund).

Beddoes, Zanny Minton. 1999. "From EMU to AMU? The Case for Regional Currencies." *Foreign Affairs* 78, no. 4 (July/August): 8–13.

Begg, David. 2002. "Growth, Integration, and Macroeconomic Policy Design: Some Lessons for Latin America." *North American Journal of Economics and Finance* 13, no. 3 (December): 279–95.

Bénassy-Quéré, Agnès. 1996a. *Exchange Rate Regimes and Policies in Asia*. Document de Travail 96–07 (Paris: CEPII).

———. 1996b. *Potentialities and Opportunities of the Euro as an International Currency*. Document de Travail 96–09 (Paris: CEPII).

———. 1999a. "Exchange Rate Regimes and Policies: An Empirical Analysis." In Stefan Collignon, Jean Pisani-Ferry, and Yung Chul Park, eds., *Exchange Rate Policies in Emerging Asian Countries* (London: Routledge), ch. 3.

———. 1999b. "Optimal Pegs for East Asian Currencies." *Journal of the Japanese and International Economies* 13: 44–60.

Bénassy-Quéré, Agnès, and Benoît Coeuré. 2000. *Big and Small Currencies: The Regional Connection*. Document de Travail 2000–10 (Paris: CEPII).

———. 2002a. "On the Identification of De Facto Currency Pegs" (Paris: CEPII, unpublished).

———. 2002b. "The Survival of Intermediate Exchange Rate Regimes" (Paris: CEPII, unpublished).

Bénassy-Quéré, Agnès, and Amina Lahrèche-Révil. 1998. *Pegging the CEEC's Currencies to the Euro*. Document de Travail 98–04 (Paris: CEPII).

———. 1999. "L'euro comme monnaie de référence à l'Est et au Sud de l'Union européene." *Revue Économique* 50, no. 6: 1185–201.

———. 2000. "The Euro as a Monetary Anchor in the CEECs." *Open Economies Review* 11, no. 4: 303–21.

Bénassy-Quéré, Agnès, and Benoît Mojon. 2001. "EMU and Transatlantic Exchange Rate Stability." In Thomas Moser and Bernd Schips, eds., *EMU, Financial Markets and the World Economy* (Boston: Kluwer Academic), ch. 4.

Bénassy-Quéré, Agnès, Benoît Mojon, and Jean Pisani-Ferry. 1997. "The Euro and Exchange Rate Stability." In Paul R. Masson, Thomas H. Krueger, and Bart G. Turtelboom, eds., *EMU and the International Monetary System* (Washington, D.C.: International Monetary Fund), ch. 7.

Bénassy-Quéré, Agnès, Benoît Mojon, and Armand-Denis Schor. 1998. *The International Role of the Euro*. Document de Travail 98–03 (Paris: CEPII).

Berentsen, Aleksander. 1998. "Monetary Policy Implications of Digital Money." *Kyklos* 51, no. 1: 89–117.

Berg, Andrew, and Eduardo Borensztein. 2000a. "The Dollarization Debate." *Finance and Development* (March): 38–41.

———. 2000b. "The Pros and Cons of Full Dollarization." Working Paper WP/00/50 (Washington, D.C.: International Monetary Fund).

Berg, Andrew, Eduardo Borensztein, and Paolo Mauro. 2002. "An Evaluation of Monetary Regime Options for Latin America." *North American Journal of Economics and Finance* 13, no. 3 (December): 213–35.

Bergsten, C. Fred. 1997. "The Impact of the Euro on Exchange Rates and International Policy Cooperation." In Paul R. Masson, Thomas H. Krueger, and Bart G. Turtelboom, eds., *EMU and the International Monetary System* (Washington, D.C.: International Monetary Fund), ch. 2.

———. 1998. "Missed Opportunity." *International Economy* 12, no. 6 (November/December): 26–27.

———. 1999. "Dollarization in Emerging-Market Economies and its Policy Implications for the United States." *Official Dollarization in Emerging-Market Countries*. Hearings before the Subcommittee on Economic Policy and Subcommittee on International Trade and Finance, Committee on Banking, Housing, and Urban Affairs. U.S. Senate, 22 April, 58–61.

Bergsten, C. Fred, and C. Randall Henning. 1996. *Global Economic Leadership and the Group of Seven* (Washington, D.C.: Institute for International Economics).

Bergsten, C. Fred, Takatoshi Ito, and Marcus Noland. 2001. *No More Bashing: Building a New Japan-United States Economic Relationship* (Washington, D.C.: Institute for International Economics).

Berman, Sheri, and Kathleen McNamara. 1999. "Bank on Democracy." *Foreign Affairs* 78, no. 2 (March/April): 2–8.

Berrigan, John, and Hervé Carré. 1997. "Exchange Arrangements Between the EU and Countries in Eastern Europe, the Mediterranean, and the CFA Zone." In Paul R. Masson, Thomas H. Krueger, and Bart G. Turtelboom, eds., *EMU and the International Monetary System* (Washington, D.C.: International Monetary Fund), ch. 5.

Bhagwati, Jagdish. 1998. "The Capital Myth." *Foreign Affairs* 77, no. 3 (May/June): 7–12.

———. 2000. *The Wind of the Hundred Days* (Cambridge, Mass.: MIT Press).

Bird, Graham. 2002. "Where Do We Stand on Choosing Exchange Rate Regimes in Developing and Emerging Economies?" *World Economics* 3, no. 1 (January–March): 145–67.

Bird, Graham, and Ramkishen S. Rajan. 2002. *The Evolving Asian Financial Architecture*. Essay in International Economics 226 (Princeton: International Finance Section).

Bixler, Raymond W. 1957. *The Foreign Policy of the United States in Liberia* (New York: Pageant Press).

Bjorksten, Nils. 2001. "The Current State of New Zealand Monetary Union Research." *Reserve Bank of New Zealand Bulletin* 64, no. 4 (December): 44–55.

Blinder, Alan S. 1996. "The Role of the Dollar as an International Currency." *Eastern Economic Journal* 22, no. 2 (Spring): 127–36.

———. 1997. "Is Government Too Political?" *Foreign Affairs* 76, no. 6 (November/December): 115–26.

Bogetić, Zeljko. 2000a. "Full Dollarization: Fad or Future?" *Challenge* 43, no. 2 (March–April): 17–48.

———. 2000b. "Official Dollarization: Current Experiences and Issues." *Cato Journal* 20, no. 2 Fall: 179–213.

———. 2002. "Montenegro's Currency and Foreign Trade Reforms: A Brief Review." *Montenegrin Economic Papers* 1, no. 1 (January): 77–83.

Bordo, Michael D., and Lars Jonung. 1999. "The Future of EMU: What Does the History of Monetary Unions Tell Us?" Working Paper 7365 (Cambridge, Mass.: National Bureau of Economic Research).

Boughton, James M. 1993. "The Economics of the CFA Franc Zone." In Paul R. Masson and Mark P. Taylor, eds., *Issues in the Operation of Currency Unions* (Cambridge: Cambridge University Press), ch. 4.

Bowles, Paul. 2002. "Asia's Post-Crisis Regionalism: Bringing the State Back In, Keeping the (United) States Out." *Review of International Political Economy* 9, no. 2 (May): 230–56.

Brash, Don. 2000. "United We Stand? The Pros and Cons of Currency Union." *Policy* 16, no. 3 (Spring): 15–18.

Bratkowski, Andrzej, and Jacek Rostowski. 2001a. "The EU Attitude to Unilateral Euroization: Misunderstandings, Real Concerns and Ill-Designed Admission Criteria" (*www.eu-enlargement.org*).

———. 2001b. "Unilateral Adoption of the Euro by EU Applicant Countries: The Macroeconomic Aspect." In Lucjan J. Orlowski, ed., *Transition and Growth in Post-Communist Countries: The Ten-Year Experience* (Northampton, Mass.: Edward Elgar), ch. 8.

Brittan, Samuel. 1998. "The Capital Myth." *Financial Times*, 1 October.

Bruno, Michael, and William R. Easterly. 1996. "Inflation and Growth: In Search of a Stable Relationship." *Federal Reserve Bank of St. Louis Review* 78 (May–June): 139–46.

Bubula, Andrea, and İnci Ötker-Robe. 2002. "The Evolution of Exchange Rate Regimes Since 1990: Evidence from De Facto Policies." Working Paper WP/02/155 (Washington, D.C.: International Monetary Fund).

Buira, Ariel. 1999. *An Alternative Approach to Financial Crises*. Essay in International Finance 212 (Princeton: International Finance Section).

Buiter, Willem H. 1999a. "Alice in Euroland." *Journal of Common Market Studies* 37, no. 2 (June): 181–209.

———. 1999b. "The EMU and the NAMU: What is the Case for North American Monetary Union?" *Canadian Public Policy/Analyse de Politiques* 25, no. 3 (September): 285–305.

———. 2000. "Is Iceland an Optimal Currency Area?" In Már Gudmundsson, Tryggvi Thor Herbertsson, and Gylfi Zoega, eds., *Macroeconomic Policy: Iceland in an Era of Global Integration* (Reykjavík: University of Iceland Press), 33–55.

Bundesbank. 1995. "The Circulation of Deutsche Mark Abroad." *Monthly Report* 47, no. 7 (July): 65–71.

———. 1999. "Recent Developments in Electronic Money." *Monthly Report* 51, no. 6 (June): 41–57.

Calvo, Guillermo A. 1999. "On Dollarization." University of Maryland. Typescript.

———. 2000. "Testimony on Dollarization." *Monetary Stability in Latin America: Is Dollarization the Answer?* Hearings before the Subcommittee on Domestic and International Monetary Policy. Committee on Banking and Financial Services. U.S. House of Representatives, 22 June, 61–65.

Calvo, Guillermo A., and Carmen M. Reinhart. 2001. "Fixing for Your Life." In Susan M. Collins and Dani Rodrik, eds., *Brookings Trade Forum 2000* (Washington, D.C.: Brookings Institution), 1–57.

———. 2002. "Fear of Floating." *Quarterly Journal of Economics* 117, no. 2 (May): 379–408.

Calvo, Guillermo A., and Carlos A. Vegh. 1993. "Currency Substitution in High Inflation Countries." *Finance and Development* 30, no. 1 (March): 34–37.

Camard, Wayne. 1996. "Discretion with Rules? Lessons from the Currency Board Arrangement in Lithuania." Paper on Policy Analysis and Assessment PPAA/96/1 (Washington, D.C.: International Monetary Fund).

Camdessus, Michel. 2000. "Council on Foreign Relations Address." *IMF Survey*, 7 February, 33–36.

Capie, Forrest. 1999. "Monetary Unions in Historical Perspective: What Future for the Euro in the International Financial System." In Michele Fratianni, Dominick Salvatore, and Paolo Savona, eds., *Ideas for the Future of the International Monetary System* (Boston: Kluwer Academic), 77–95.

Carr, Jack L., and John E. Floyd. 2002. "Real and Monetary Shocks to the Canadian Dollar: Do Canada and the United States Form an Optimal Currency Area?" *North American Journal of Economics and Finance* 13, no. 1 (May): 21–39.

Carrera, Jorge. 2002. "Hard Peg and Monetary Unions: Main Lessons from the Argentine Experience." Paper prepared for a conference on The Euro and Dollarization. Fordham University, New York, 5–6 April.

Carrera, Jorge, and Federico Sturzenegger, eds. 2000. *Coordinación de Políticas Macroeconómicas en el Mercosur* (Buenos Aires: Fundacion Gobierno y Sociedad and Fondo de Cultura Económica).

Cassidy, John. 1998. "The New World Disorder." *New Yorker*, 26 October, 198–207.

Castellano, Marc. 1999. "Internationalization of the Yen: A Ministry of Finance Pipe Dream?" *JEI Report* 23A, 1–10.

———. 2000. "East Asia Monetary Union: More Than Just Talk?" *JEI Report* 12A, 1–9.

Castro, Jorge. 1999. "Basis of the Dollarization Strategy and a Treaty of Monetary Association." Working Paper Submitted by the Secretary of State for Strategic Planning (Buenos Aires: Secretariat of Strategic Planning).

Centre for Research and Information on Canada. 2002. *Portraits of Canada 2001* (Montreal).

Chang, Li Lin, and Ramkishen S. Rajan. 2001. "The Economic and Politics of Monetary Regionalism in Asia." *ASEAN Economic Bulletin* 18, no. 1 (April): 103–18.

Chang, Roberto, and Andrés Velasco. 2003. "Dollarization: Analytical Issues." In Eduardo Levy-Yeyati and Federico Sturzenegger, eds. *Dollarization: Debates and Policy Alternatives* (Cambridge, Mass.: MIT Press), ch. 2.

Chauffour, Jean-Pierre, and Loukas Stemitsiotis. 1998. *The Impact of the Euro on Mediterranean Partner Countries.* Euro Paper 24 (Brussels: European Commission).

Clément, Jean A. P., with Johannes Mueller, Stéphane Cossé, and Jean Le Dem. 1996. *Aftermath of the CFA Franc Devaluation*. Occasional Paper 138 (Washington, D.C.: International Monetary Fund).

Cline, William R. 1999. "International Capital Flows: Discussion." In Jane Sneddon Little and Giovanni P. Olivei, eds., *Rethinking the International Monetary System* (Boston: Federal Reserve Bank of Boston), 158–62.

Coeuré, Benoît, and Jean Pisani-Ferry. 2000. "The Euro, Yen, and Dollar: Making the Case against Benign Neglect." In Peter B. Kenen and Alexander K. Swoboda, eds., *Reforming the International Monetary and Financial System* (Washington, D.C.: International Monetary Fund), ch. 3.

Cohen, Benjamin J. 1965. "Capital Controls and the U.S. Balance of Payments." *American Economic Review* 55, no. 1 (March): 172–76.

———. 1971. *The Future of Sterling as an International Currency* (London: Macmillan).

———. 1977. *Organizing the World's Money: The Political Economy of International Monetary Relations* (New York: Basic Books).

———. 1986. *In Whose Interest? International Banking and American Foreign Policy* (New Haven: Yale University Press).

———. 1993. "The Triad and the Unholy Trinity: Lessons for the Pacific Region." In Richard Higgott, Richard Leaver, and John Ravenhill, eds., *Pacific Economic Relations in the 1990s: Cooperation or Conflict?* (Boulder: Lynne Rienner), 133–58.

———. 1994. "Beyond EMU: The Problem of Sustainability." In Barry Eichengreen and Jeffry A. Frieden, eds., *Political Economy of European Monetary Unification*. 1st ed. (Boulder: Westview Press), ch. 8.

———. 1996. "Phoenix Risen: The Resurrection of Global Finance." *World Politics* 48, no. 2 (January): 268–96.

———. 1998. *The Geography of Money* (Ithaca: Cornell University Press).

———. 1999. *Technology, Globalization, and the Future of Money*. Working Paper T99–1 (Atlanta: European Union Center of the University System of Georgia; available online at: www.inta.gatech.edu/eucenter/wpapers99/pdf/cohen.pdf).

———. 2000a. *Dollarization: Pros and Cons* (Munich: Center for Applied Policy Research; available online at: www.cap.uni-muenchen.de/transatlantic/papers/americas.html).

———. 2000b. *Life at the Top: International Currencies in the Twenty-First Century*. Essay in International Economics 221 (Princeton: International Economics Section).

———. 2000c. "Marketing Money: Currency Policy in a Globalized World." In Aseem Prakash and Jeffrey A. Hart, eds., *Coping with Globalization* (New York: Routledge).

———. 2000d. "Money in a Globalized World." In Ngaire Woods, ed., *The Political Economy of Globalization* (London: Macmillan).

———. 2000e. *Political Dimensions of Dollarization* (Dallas; Federal Reserve Bank of Dallas; available online at: *www.dallasfed.org/htm/dallas/pdfs/cohen/pdf*).

Cohen, Benjamin J. 2000f. "Taming the Phoenix? Monetary Governance After the Crisis." In Greg Noble and John Ravenhill, eds., *The Asian Financial Crisis and the Structure of Global Finance* (New York: Cambridge University Press).

———. 2001a. "Beyond EMU: The Problem of Sustainability." In Barry Eichengreen and Jeffry A. Frieden, eds., *Political Economy of European Monetary Unification*, 2d ed. (Boulder: Westview Press), ch. 8.

———. 2001b. "Electronic Money: New Day or False Dawn?" *Review of International Political Economy* 8, no. 2 (Summer): 197–225.

———. 2001c. "Monetary Governance and Capital Mobility in Historical Perspective." Paper prepared for a Workshop on Governance of International Financial Markets and Free Movement of Capital—Strategies and Prospects (Pforzheim: Protestant Academy Loccum, January).

———. 2002a. "Capital Controls: Why Do Governments Hesitate?" In Leslie Elliott Armijo, ed., *Debating the Global Financial Architecture* (Albany: State University of New York Press), ch. 3.

———. 2002b. "U.S. Policy on Dollarization: A Political Analysis." *Geopolitics* 7, no. 1 (Summer): 63–84.

———. 2003a. "Capital Controls: The Neglected Option." In Geoffrey R. D. Underhill and Xiaoke Zhang, eds., *International Financial Governance Under Stress: Global Structures versus National Imperatives* (New York: Cambridge University Press, forthcoming).

———. 2003b. "Monetary Governance in a World of Regional Currencies." In David A. Lake and Miles Kahler, eds., *Governance in a Global Economy* (Princeton: Princeton University Press, forthcoming).

———. 2003c. "Monetary Union: The Political Dimension." In Dominick Salvatore, James W. Dean, and Thomas D. Willett, eds., *The Dollarization Debate* (New York: Oxford University Press, forthcoming).

———. 2003d. "Are Monetary Unions Inevitable?" *International Studies Perspectives* 4, no. 3 (August): 275–92.

Coleman, Andrew. 2001. "Three Perspectives on an Australasian Monetary Union." Paper prepared for a conference, Future Directions for Monetary Policies in East Asia. Reserve Bank of Australia. Canberra, 24 July.

Collyns, Charles. 1983. *Alternatives to the Central Bank in the Developing World* (Washington, D.C.: International Monetary Fund).

Cooper, Richard N. 1974. "A Monetary System for the Future." *Foreign Affairs* 63, no. 1 (Fall): 166–84.

———. 1995. "One Money for How Many?" In Peter B. Kenen, ed., *Understanding Interdependence: The Macroeconomics of the Open Economy* (Princeton: Princeton University Press), 84–88.

———. 1998. "Should Capital-Account Convertibility be a World Objective?" In Stanley Fischer, Richard N. Cooper, Rudiger Dornbusch, Peter M. Garber, Carlos Massad, Jacques J. Polak, Dani Rodrik, and Savak S. Tarapore, *Should the IMF Pursue Capital-Account Convertibility?* Essay in International Finance 207 (Princeton: International Finance Section), 11–19.

———. 1999a. "Exchange Rate Choices." In Jane Sneddon Little and Giovanni P. Olivei, eds., *Rethinking the International Monetary System* (Boston: Federal Reserve Bank of Boston), 99–123.

———. 1999b. "Should Capital Controls be Banished?" *Brookings Papers on Economic Activity* 1: 89–141.

———. 2000. "Key Currencies after the Euro." In Robert A. Mundell and Armand Cleese, eds., *The Euro as a Stabilizer in the International Economic System* (Boston: Kluwer Academic), ch. 11.

Cooper, Scott B. 1999. "Regional Monetary Cooperation Beyond Western Europe." Ph.D. diss., Duke University.

Corbo, Vittorio, and Patricio Rojas. 1997. "Exchange Rate Volatility, Investment and Growth: Some New Evidence." In William C. Gruben, David M. Gould, and Carlos E. Zarazaga, eds., *Exchange Rates, Capital Flows, and Monetary Policy in a Changing World Economy* (Boston: Kluwer Academic), 55–77.

Corden, W. Max. 2002. *Too Sensational: On the Choice of Exchange Rate Regimes* (Cambridge, Mass.: MIT Press).

Coricelli, Fabrizio. 2001. "Exchange Rate Arrangements in the Transition to EMU: Some Arguments in Favor of an Early Adoption of the Euro" (www.eu-enlargement.org).

Corker, Robert, Craig Beaumont, Rachel van Elkan, and Dora Iakova. 2000. "Exchange Rate Regimes in Selected Advanced Transition Economies—Coping with Transition, Capital Inflows, and EU Accession." Policy Discussion Paper PDP/00/3 (Washington, D.C.: International Monetary Fund).

Costa, Cláudia, and Paul De Grauwe. 2001. "Monetary Policy in a Cashless Society." Paper prepared for a SUERF meeting. Brussels, Belgium, 25–27 October.

Council of Economic Advisers. 1999. *Annual Report* (Washington, D.C.: Government Printing Office).

Council on Foreign Exchange and Other Transactions. 1999. "Internationalization of the Yen for the 21st Century." Tokyo, 20 April; available at: *www.mof.go.jp/english/if/e1b064a.htm*.

Courchene, Thomas J. 1999. "Towards a North American Common Currency: An Optimal Currency Area Analysis." In Thomas J. Courchene, ed., *Room to Manoeuvre? Globalization and Policy Convergence* (Kingston, On.: Queens University), 271–334.

Courchene, Thomas J., and Richard G. Harris. 2000a. "From Fixing to Monetary Union: Options for North American Currency Integration." *C.D. Howe Institute Commentary* 127 (June): 1–28.

———. 2000b. "North American Monetary Union: Analytical Principles and Operational Guidelines." *North American Journal of Economics and Finance* 11, no. 1 (August): 3–18.

Craig, Ben. 1996. "Competing Currencies: Back to the Future?" *Federal Reserve Bank of Cleveland Economic Commentary*, 15 October.

Cronin, David, and Kevin Dowd. 2001. "Does Monetary Policy Have a Future?" *Cato Journal* 21, no. 2 (Fall): 227–44.

Crosby, Mark, and Glenn Otto. 2002. "An Australia-New Zealand Currency Union." In Gordon de Brouwer, ed., *Financial Markets and Policies in East Asia* (London: Routledge), ch. 14.

Cukierman, Alex. 1992. *Central Bank Strategy, Credibility, and Independence: Theory and Evidence* (Cambridge, Mass.: MIT Press).

Cukierman, Alex. 1998. "The Economics of Central Banking." In H.C. Wolf, ed., *Contemporary Policy Issues: Macroeconomics and Finance*, vol. 5 (London: Macmillan).

Danthine, Jean-Pierre, Francesco Giavazzi, and Ernst-Ludwig von Thadden. 2001. "European Financial Markets After EMU: A First Assessment." In Charles Wyplosz, ed., *The Impact of EMU on Europe and the Developing Countries* (Oxford: Oxford University Press), ch. 9.

D'Arista, Jane. 2000. "Dollarization: Critical U.S. Views." Paper prepared for a conference, To Dollarize or Not to Dollarize: Currency Choices for the Western Hemisphere. Ottawa, Canada, 4–5 October.

Dean, James W. 2001. "De Facto Dollarization in Latin America." Paper prepared for a Conference, To Dollarize or Not to Dollarize: Currency Choices for the Western Hemisphere. Ottawa, Canada, 4–5 October.

Dean, James W., and Kenneth Kasa. 2001. "Capital Flows in Euroland and Implications for Unilateral Adoption of the Euro in Eastern Europe." Paper prepared at the Seventh Dubrovnik Economic Conference. Dubrovnik, 28–29 June.

De Boissieu, Christian. 1988. "Concurrence entre monnaies et polycentrisme monétaire." In D. E. Fair and Christian De Boissieu, eds., *International Monetary and Financial Integration—The European Dimension* (Boston: Kluwer Academic), ch. 13.

de Brouwer, Gordon. 2000a. "ANZAC Dollar." *Agenda* 7, no. 3: 273–76.

———. 2000b. "Should Pacific Island Nations Adopt the Australian Dollar?" *Pacific Economic Bulletin* 15, no. 2: 161–69.

———. 2001. "Currency and Monetary Arrangements for East Timor." In Hal Hill and João M. Saldanha, eds., *East Timor: Development Challenges for the World's Newest Nation* (Canberra: Asia Pacific Press).

De Gregorio, José, Sebastian Edwards, and Rodrigo O. Valdés. 2000. "Controls on Capital Inflows: Do They Work?" *Journal of Development Economics* 63: 59–83.

De Grauwe, Paul. 2000. *Economics of Monetary Union*, 4th ed. (Oxford: Oxford University Press).

de Zamaróczy, Mario, and Sopanha Sa. 2002. "Macroeconomic Adjustment in a Highly Dollarized Economy: The Case of Cambodia." Working Paper WP/02/92 (Washington, D.C.: International Monetary Fund).

Dellas, Harris, and George S. Tavlas. 2001. "Lessons of the Euro for Dollarization: Analytic and Political Economy Perspectives." *Journal of Policy Modeling* 23, no. 3 (April): 333–45.

Detken, Carsten, and Philipp Hartmann. 2000. "The Euro and International Capital Markets." *International Finance* 3, no. 1 (April): 53–94.

———. 2002. "Features of the Euro's Role in International Financial Markets." *Economic Policy* 35 (October): 553–69.

Díaz-Alejandro, Carlos F. 1988. *Trade, Development and the World Economy: Selected Essays* (Oxford: Basil Blackwell).

Dietz, Raimund. 2001. "Unilateral Euroisation: A Misguided Idea" (www.euenlargement.org).

Dodd, Nigel. 1994. *The Sociology of Money* (New York: Continuum).

Dooley, Michael P. 1996. "A Survey of Literature on Controls over International Capital Transactions." *International Monetary Fund Staff Papers* 43, no. 4 (December): 639–87.

Dornbusch, Rudiger. 2000a. "Emerging Market Crises: Origins and Remedies." In Peter B. Kenen and Alexander K. Swoboda, eds., *Reforming the International Monetary and Financial System* (Washington, D.C.: International Monetary Fund), 148–54.

———. 2000b. *Keys to Prosperity: Free Markets, Sound Money, and a Bit of Luck* (Cambridge, Mass.: MIT Press).

———. 2001a. "Fewer Monies, Better Monies." Working Paper W8324 (Cambridge, Mass.: National Bureau of Economic Research).

———. 2001b. "Malaysia: Was It Different?" Working Paper W8325 (Cambridge, Mass.: National Bureau of Economic Research).

Dornbusch, Rudiger, Federico A. Sturzenegger, and Holger Wolf. 1990. "Extreme Inflation: Dynamics and Stabilization." *Brookings Papers on Economic Activity* 2: 2–84.

Douthwaite, Richard. 1999. *The Ecology of Money* (Totnes, U.K.: Green Books).

Dowd, Kevin, ed. 1992. *The Experience of Free Banking* (London: Routledge).

———. 2001. "The Emergence of Fiat Money: A Reconsideration." *Cato Journal* 20, no. 3 (Winter): 467–76.

Dowd, Kevin, and David Greenaway. 1993. "Currency Competition, Network Externalities and Switching Costs: Towards an Alternative View of Optimum Currency Areas." *Economic Journal* 103 (September): 1180–89.

Doyle, Brian M. 2000. " 'Here, Dollars, Dollars . . .' Estimating Currency Demand and Worldwide Currency Substitution." International Finance Discussion Paper 657 (Washington, D.C.: Federal Reserve Board of Governors).

Drew, Aaron, Viv Hall, John McDermott, and Robert St. Clair. 2001. "Would Adopting the Australian Dollar Provide Superior Monetary Policy in New Zealand?" Discussion Paper DP2001/03 (Wellington, N.Z.: Reserve Bank of New Zealand).

Duncan, R. C., and Xinpeng Xu. 2000. "Should Papua New Guinea Adopt a Stronger Exchange Rate Regime?" *Pacific Economic Bulletin* 15, no. 2, 36–45.

Dunn, Robert, Jr. 2002. "The Misguided Attractions of Foreign Exchange Controls." *Challenge* 45, no. 5 (September/October): 98–111.

Ebenstein, Alan. 2001. *Friedrich Hayek: A Biography* (New York: Palgrave).

The Economist. 1994. "Electronic Money: So Much for the Cashless Society." 26 November, 21–23.

———. 1998. "One World, One Money." 26 September, 80.

———. 1999. "Fiscal Flexibility." 27 November, 80.

———. 2000. "E-Cash 2.0." 19 February, 67–69.

———. 2002. "Remember Fiscal Policy?" 19 January, 64.

Edison, Hali J., and Carmen Reinhart. 2001. "Stopping Hot Money." *Journal of Development Economics* 66: 533–53.

Edison, Hali J., Michael Klein, Luca Ricci, and Torsten Sløk. 2002. "Capital Account Liberalization and Economic Performance: Survey and Synthesis." Working Paper WP/02/120 (Washington, D.C.: International Monetary Fund).

Edwards, Sebastian. 1998. "How About a Single Currency for Mercosur?" *Wall Street Journal*, 28 August, A11.

———. 1999a. "How Effective are Capital Controls?" *Journal of Economic Perspectives* 13, no. 4 (Fall): 65–84.

———. 1999b. "International Capital Flows and Emerging Markets: Amending the Rules of the Game?" In Jane Sneddon Little and Giovanni P. Olivei, eds., *Rethinking the International Monetary System* (Boston: Federal Reserve Bank of Boston), 137–57.

———. 2000. "Capital Flows, Real Exchange Rates, and Capital Controls: Some Latin American Experiences." In Sebastian Edwards, ed., *Capital Flows and the Emerging Markets: Theory, Evidence, and Controversies* (Chicago: University of Chicago Press), ch. 7.

———. 2001. "Dollarization: Myths and Realities." *Journal of Policy Modeling* 23, no. 3 (April): 249–65.

———. 2002. "The Great Exchange Rate Debate After Argentina." Working Paper 9257 (Cambridge, Mass.: National Bureau of Economic Research).

Edwards, Sebastian, and I. Igal Magendzo. 2001. "Dollarization, Inflation and Growth." Working Paper 8671 (Cambridge, Mass.: National Bureau of Economic Research).

Eichengreen, Barry. 1994. *International Monetary Arrangements for the 21st Century* (Washington, D.C.: Brookings Institution).

———. 1996. *A More Perfect Union? The Logic of Economic Integration*. Essay in International Finance 198 (Princeton: International Finance Section).

———. 1998. "Does Mercosur Need a Single Currency?" Working Paper 6821 (Cambridge, Mass.: National Bureau of Economic Research).

———. 1999. *Toward a New International Financial Architecture: A Practical Post-Asia Agenda* (Washington, D.C.: Institute for International Economics).

———. 2001. "What Problems Can Dollarization Solve?" *Journal of Policy Modeling* 23, no. 3 (April): 267–77.

———. 2002a. "The Globalization Wars." *Foreign Affairs* 81, no. 4 (July/August): 157–64.

———. 2002b. "When to Dollarize." *Journal of Money, Credit, and Banking* 34, no. 1 (February): 1–24.

———. 2003. *Capital Flows and Crises* (Cambridge, Mass.: MIT Press).

Eichengreen, Barry, and Tamim Bayoumi. 1999. "Is Asia an Optimum Currency Area? Can It Become One? Regional, Global, and Historical Perspectives on Asian Monetary Relations." In Stefan Collignon, Jean Pisani-Ferry, and Yung Chul Park, eds., *Exchange Rate Policies in Emerging Asian Countries* (London: Routledge), ch. 21.

Eichengreen, Barry, and Nathan Sussman. 2000. "The International Monetary System in the (Very) Long Run." *World Economic Outlook Supporting Studies* (Washington, D.C.: International Monetary Fund), ch. 2.

Eichengreen, Barry, Michael Mussa, and a Staff Team. 1998. *Capital Account Liberalization: Theoretical and Practical Aspects* (Washington, D.C.: International Monetary Fund).

Eijffinger, Sylvester C. W. and Jakob De Haan. 1996. *The Political Economy of Central Bank Independence.* Special Paper in International Economics 19 (Princeton: International Finance Section).

Ellis, Stephen. 1999. *The Mask of Anarchy: The Destruction of Liberia and the Religious Dimension of an African Civil War* (New York: New York University Press).

Enoch, Charles, and Anne-Marie Gulde. 1997. "Making a Currency Board Operational." Paper on Policy Analysis and Assessment PPAA/97/10 (Washington, D.C.: International Monetary Fund).

European Central Bank. 1999. "The International Role of the Euro." *ECB Monthly Bulletin* (August): 31–53.

———. 2000a. "The Eurosystem and the EU Enlargement Process." *ECB Monthly Bulletin* (February): 39–51.

———. 2000b. "Issues Arising from the Emergence of Electronic Money." *ECB Monthly Bulletin* (November): 49–60.

———. 2001. *Review of the International Role of the Euro* (Frankfurt).

———. 2002. "The Eurosystem's Dialogue with EU Accession Countries." *ECB Monthly Bulletin* (July): 51–63.

Evenett, Simon J. 2000. "Capital Controls: Theory, Evidence and Policy Advice." *International Finance* 3, no. 3 (November): 471–86.

Fatás, Antonio, and Andrew K. Rose. 2001. "Do Monetary Handcuffs Restrain Leviathan? Fiscal Policy in Extreme Exchange Rate Regimes." *International Monetary Fund Staff Papers* 47 (special issue): 40–61.

Feige, Edgar L. 1996. "Overseas Holdings of U.S. Currency and the Underground Economy." In Susan Pozo, ed., *Exploring the Underground Economy* (Kalamazoo: W. E. Upjohn Institute for Employment Research), 5–62.

———. 1997. "Revised Estimates of the Underground Economy: Implications of U.S. Currency Held Abroad." In Owen Lippert and Michael Walker, eds., *The Underground Economy: Global Evidence of its Size and Impact* (Vancouver: Simon Fraser Institute), 151–208.

Feige, Edgar, and James W. Dean. 2002. "Dollarization and Euroization in Transition Countries: Currency Substitution, Asset Substitution, Network Externalities and Irreversibility." Paper prepared for a conference, The Euro and Dollarization. Fordham University, New York, 5–6 April.

Feldstein, Martin. 1998. "Refocusing the IMF." *Foreign Affairs* 77, no. 2 (March/April): 20–33.

Fernández-Arias, Eduardo, and Ricardo Hausmann. 2000. "International Initiatives to Stabilize Financial Integration." In Eduardo Fernández-Arias and Ricardo Hausmann, eds., *Wanted: World Financial Stability* (Washington, D.C.: Inter-American Development Bank), 165–91.

Fischer, Stanley. 1982. "Seigniorage and the Case for a National Money." *Journal of Political Economy* 90, no. 2 (April): 295–313.

———. 1993. "The Role of Macroeconomic Factors in Growth." *Journal of Monetary Economics* 32 (December): 485–512.

———. 1998. "In Defense of the IMF." *Foreign Affairs* 77, no. 4 (July/August): 103–6.

Fischer, Stanley. 2001. "Exchange Rate Regimes: Is the Bipolar View Correct?" *Journal of Economic Perspectives* 15, no. 2 (Spring): 3–24.

Fontaine, Juan Andrés. 2000. "Official versus Spontaneous Dollarization." *Cato Journal* 20, no. 1 (Spring/Summer): 35–42.

Forbes, Steve. 1999. "Dollar Diplomacy." *Forbes*, 22 March, 31–32.

Frankel, Jeffrey A. 1999. *No Single Currency Regime is Right for All Countries or at All Times*. Essay in International Finance 215 (Princeton: International Finance Section).

————. 2000. "Impact of the Euro on Members and Non-Members." In Robert A. Mundell and Armand Cleese, eds., *The Euro as a Stabilizer in the International Economic System* (Boston: Kluwer Academic), ch. 7.

Frankel, Jeffrey A., and Andrew K. Rose. 2002. "Estimating of the Effect of Currency Unions on Trade and Output." *Quarterly Journal of Economics* 117, no. 2 (May): 437–67.

Frankel, Jeffrey A., and Shang-Jin Wei. 1998. " Regionalization of World Trade and Currencies: Economics and Politics." In Jeffrey A. Frankel, ed., *The Regionalization of the World Economy* (Chicago: University of Chicago Press), ch. 7.

Frankman, Myron. 2002. "Beyond the Tobin Tax: Global Democracy and a Global Currency." *ANNALS* 581 (May): 62–73.

Fratianni, Michele, and Andreas Hauskrecht. 2002. "A Centralized Monetary Union for Mercosur: Lessons from EMU." Paper prepared for a conference, The Euro and Dollarization. Fordham University, New York, 5–6 April.

Fratzscher, Marcel. 2001. "Financial Market Integration in Europe: On the Effects of EMU on Stock Markets." Working Paper 48 (Frankfurt: European Central Bank).

————. 2002. "The Euro Bloc, the Dollar Bloc and the Yen Bloc: How Much Monetary Policy Independence Can Exchange Rate Flexibility Buy in an Interdependent World?" Working Paper 154 (Frankfurt: European Central Bank).

Freedman, Charles. 2000. "Monetary Policy Implementation: Past, Present and Future—Will Electronic Money Lead to the Eventual Demise of Central Banking?" *International Finance* 3, no. 2 (July): 211–27.

Frenkel, Michael, and Jens Søndergaard. 2001. "How Does EMU Affect the Dollar and the Yen as International Reserve and Investment Currencies?" In Thomas Moser and Bernd Schips, eds., *EMU, Financial Markets and the World Economy* (Boston: Kluwer Academic), ch. 2.

Frick, Robert L. 1996. "Alternative Monetary Systems: The Ithaca HOUR." *Durell Journal of Money and Banking* 8, no. 2 (Spring): 29–35.

Frieden, Jeffry A. 1991. "Invested Interests: The Politics of National Economic Policies in a World of Global Finance." *International Organization* 45, no. 4 (Autumn): 425–51.

————. 1993. "The Dynamics of International Monetary Systems: International and Domestic Factors in the Rise, Reign, and Demise of the Classical Gold Standard." In Jack Snyder and Robert Jervis, eds., *Coping with Complexity in the International System* (Boulder: Westview Press), 137–62.

————. 1994. "Exchange Rate Politics: Contemporary lessons from American History." *Review of International Political Economy* 1, no. 1 (Spring): 81–103.

———. 2003. "The Political Economy of Dollarization: Domestic and International Factors." In Eduardo Levy-Yeyati and Federico Sturzenegger, eds. *Dollarization: Debates and Policy Alternatives* (Cambridge, Mass.: MIT Press), ch. 8.

Friedman, Benjamin M. 1999. "The Future of Monetary Policy: The Central Bank as an Army with Only a Signal Corps?" *International Finance* 2, no. 3 (November): 321–38.

———. 2000. "Decoupling at the Margin: The Threat to Monetary Policy from the Electronic Revolution in Banking." *International Finance* 3, no. 2 (July): 261–72.

Friedman, Milton, and Robert A. Mundell. 2001. "One World, One Money? A Debate." *Policy Options/Options Politiques* (May): 10–30.

Friedman, Thomas. 1999. *The Lexus and the Olive Tree: Understanding Globalization* (New York: Farrar, Straus and Giroux).

Furche, Andreas, and Graham Wrightson. 1996. *Computer Money: A Systematic Overview of Electronic Payment Systems* (Heidelberg: Verlag für digitale Technologie GmbH).

Gabrisch, Hubert. 2001. "The Shock of Unilateral Euroisation on EU Candidate Countries" (www.eu-enlargement.org).

Galati, Gabriele. 2001. "Why Has Global FX Turnover Declined? Explaining the 2001 Triennial Survey." *BIS Quarterly Review* (December): 39–47.

Garrett, Geoffrey. 2001. "The Politics of Maastricht." In Barry Eichengreen and Jeffry A. Frieden, eds., *Political Economy of European Monetary Unification*, 2d. ed. (Boulder: Westview Press), ch. 5.

Gavin, Michael. 2000. "Official Dollarization in Latin America." *Monetary Stability in Latin America: Is Dollarization the Answer?*, Hearings before the Subcommittee on Domestic and International Monetary Policy, Committee on Banking and Financial Services. U.S. House of Representatives, 22 June, 45–50.

Gelfond, Robert. 2001. "Toward Free-Market Money." *Cato Journal* 21, no. 2 (Fall): 245–54.

Ghosh, Atish R., and Steven Phillips. 1998. "Warning: Inflation May Be Harmful to Your Growth." *IMF Staff Papers* 45, no. 4 (December): 672–710.

Ghosh, Atish R., Anne-Marie Gulde, and Holger C. Wolf. 2000. "Currency Boards: More Than a Quick Fix?" *Economic Policy* 31 (October): 271–335.

Giambiagi, Fabio. 1999. "Mercosur: Why Does Monetary Union Make Sense in the Long-term?" *Integration and Trade* 3, no. 9 (December): 59–81.

Glasner, David. 1989. *Free Banking and Monetary Reform* (Cambridge: Cambridge University Press).

Glick, Reuven. 2002. "Fixed or Floating: Is It Still Possible to Manage in the Middle?" In Gordon de Brouwer, ed., *Financial Markets and Policies in East Asia* (London: Routledge), ch. 9.

Glick, Reuven, and Andrew K. Rose. 2002. "Does a Currency Union Affect Trade? The Time Series Evidence." *European Economic Review* 41, 1125–51.

Glover, Paul. 1995. "Communities Making Their Own Money." *Earth Island Journal* (Winter): 37.

Goff, Patricia. 2000. "Invisible Borders: Economic Liberalization and National Identity." *International Studies Quarterly* 44, no. 4 (December): 533–62.

Goldfajn, Ilan, and Gino Olivares. 2001. "Full Dollarization: The Case of Panama." *Economía* 1, no. 2 (Spring): 101–55.

Goldfinger, Charles. 2002. "Intangible Economy and Electronic Money." In *The
Future of Money* (Paris: Organization for Economic Cooperation and Development), ch. 4.

Goldstein, Morris. 1998. *The Asian Financial Crisis: Causes, Cures, and Systemic
Implications* (Washington, D.C.: Institute for International Economics).

———. 2002. *Managed Floating Plus* (Washington, D.C.: Institute for International Economics).

Goodhart, Charles A. E. 1995. "The Political Economy of Monetary Union." In
Peter B. Kenen, ed., *Understanding Interdependence: The Macroeconomics of
the Open Economy* (Princeton: Princeton University Press), ch. 12.

———. 1998. "The Two Concepts of Money: Implications for the Analysis of
Optimal Currency Areas." *European Journal of Political Economy* 14:
407–32.

———. 2000. "Can Central Banking Survive the IT Revolution?" *International
Finance* 3, no. 2 (July): 189–209.

Goodhart, Charles A. E., Ryon Love, Richard Payne, and Dagfinn Rime. 2002.
"Analysis of Spreads in the Dollar/Euro and Deutschemark/Dollar Foreign Exchange Markets." *Economic Policy* 35 (October): 535–52.

Grabel, Ilene. 1996a. "Financial Markets, the State, and Economic Development:
Controversies within Theory and Policy." International Papers in Political
Economy 3, no. 1 (London: University of East London).

———. 1996b. "Marketing the Third World: The Contradictions of Portfolio
Investment in the Global Economy." *World Development* 24, 1761–76.

Greco, Thomas H., Jr. 1995. "The Essential Nature of Money." *Earth Island Journal* (Winter): 35–36.

Green, Michael Jonathan. 2001. *Japan's Reluctant Realism: Foreign Policy Challenges in an Era of Uncertain Power* (New York: Palgrave).

Greenspan, Alan. 1998. "The Globalization of Finance." *Cato Journal* 17, no. 3
(Winter): 243–50.

———. 1999. "Remarks." *Official Dollarization in Emerging-Market Countries*.
Hearings before the Subcommittee on Economic Policy and Subcommittee on
International Trade and Finance, Committee on Banking, Housing, and Urban
Affairs. U.S. Senate, 22 April, 7–23.

Grimes, Arthur. 2000. "An Anzac Dollar: Does It Make Sense?" *Policy* 16, no. 3
(Spring): 10–14.

Grimes, Arthur, and Frank Holmes. 2000. *An ANZAC Dollar? Currency Union
and Business Development* (Wellington, N.Z.: Victoria University, Institute of
Policy Studies).

Grimes, William W. 2000. "Japan and Globalization: From Opportunity to Restraint." In Samuel S. Kim, ed., *East Asia and Globalization* (New York: Rowman and Littlefield), ch. 3.

———. 2001a. "Internationalization of the Yen and the New Politics of Monetary
Insulation." Boston University. Typescript.

———. 2001b. *Unmaking the Japanese Miracle: Macroeconomic Politics, 1985–
2000* (Ithaca: Cornell University Press).

Grubel, Herbert G. 1999. *The Case for the Amero: The Economics and Politics of a North American Monetary Union* (Vancouver: Simon Fraser Institute).

———. 2000. "The Merit of a Canada-U.S. Monetary Union." *North American Journal of Economics and Finance* 11, no. 1 (August): 19–40.

Guidotti, Pablo E., and Andrew Powell. 2001. "The Dollarization Debate in Argentina and Latin America." Universidad Torcuato Di Tella. Typescript.

Guidotti, Pablo E., and Carlos A. Rodriguez. 1992. "Dollarization in Latin America: Gresham's Law in Reverse?" *International Monetary Fund Staff Papers* 39, no. 3 (September): 518–44.

Guillaume, Dominique M., and David Stasavage. 2000. "Improving Policy Credibility: Is There a Case for African Monetary Unions?" *World Development* 28, no. 8 , 1391–1407.

Gulde, Anne-Marie. 1999. "The Role of the Currency Board in Bulgaria's Stabilization." Policy Discussion Paper PDP/99/3 (Washington, D.C.: International Monetary Fund).

Gulde, Anne-Marie, Juha Kähkönen, and Peter Keller. 2000. "Pros and Cons of Currency Board Arrangements in the Lead-up to EU Accession and Participation in the Euro Zone." Policy Discussion Paper PDP/00/1 (Washington, D.C.: International Monetary Fund).

Haggard, Stephan. 2000. *The Political Economy of the Asian Financial Crisis* (Washington, D.C.: Institute for International Economics).

Haggard, Stephan, and Sylvia Maxfield. 1996. "The Political Economy of Financial Internationalization in the Developing World." In Robert O. Keohane and Helen V. Milner, eds., *Internationalization and Domestic Politics* (New York: Cambridge University Press), ch. 9.

Haggard, Stephan, Chung H. Lee, and Sylvia Maxfield, eds. 1993. *The Politics of Finance in Developing Countries* (Ithaca: Cornell University Press).

Hale, David D. 1995. "Is it a Yen or a Dollar Crisis in the Currency Market?" *Washington Quarterly* 18, no. 4 (Autumn): 145–71.

———. 1998a. "The Hot Money Debate." *The International Economy* 12, no. 6 (November/December): 8–12, 66–69.

———. 1998b. "The IMF, Now More Than Ever." *Foreign Affairs* 77, no. 6 (November/December): 7–13.

Hamada, Koichi. 1999a. "The Choice of International Monetary Regimes in a Context of Repeated Games." In Michele Fratianni, Dominick Salvatore, and Paolo Savona, eds., *Ideas for the Future of the International Monetary System* (Boston: Kluwer Academic), 47–75.

———. 1999b. "From the AMF to the Miyazawa Initiative: Observations on Japan's Currency Diplomacy." *Journal of East Asian Affairs* 13, no. 1 (Spring/Summer): 33–50.

Hamada, Koichi, and David Porteous. 1992. "L'Intégration Monétaire dans Une Perspective Historique." *Revue d'Économie Financière* 22 (Autumn): 77–92.

Hampson, Rick. 2001. "Whatever They Think of America, People and Nations the World Over Prefer the Greenback." *USA Today*, 26 December.

Hanke, Steve H. 1996. "Don't Cry For Me." *The International Economy* (March/April): 46–51, 71.

Hanke, Steve H. 2002. "Currency Boards." *Annals of the American Academy of Political and Social Science* 579 (January): 87–105.

Hanke, Steve H., and Kurt Schuler. 2002. "What Went Wrong in Argentina?" *Central Banking* 12, no. 3 (February): 43–48.

Hargreaves, David, and John McDermott. 1999. "Issues Relating to Optimal Currency Areas: Theory and Implications for New Zealand." Reserve Bank of New Zealand *Bulletin* 62, no. 3 (September): 16–29.

Harris, Richard G. 2001. "Mundell and Friedman: Four Key Disagreements." *Policy Options/Options Politiques* (May): 34–36.

Hartley, Peter. 2001. *Monetary Arrangements for New Zealand* (Wellington, N.Z.: New Zealand Business Roundtable).

Hartmann, Philipp. 1998. *Currency Competition and Foreign Exchange Markets: The Dollar, the Yen and the Euro* (Cambridge: Cambridge University Press).

Hau, Harald, William Killeen, and Michael Moore. 2002a. "The Euro as an International Currency: Explaining Puzzling First Evidence from the Foreign Exchange Markets." *Journal of International Money and Finance* 21, no. 3 (June): 351–83.

———. 2002b. "How Has the Euro Changed the Foreign Exchange Market?" *Economic Policy* 34 (April): 149–91.

Haug, Alfred A. 2001. "Co-Movement Towards a Currency or Monetary Union? An Empirical Study for New Zealand." *Australian Economic Papers* 40, no. 3 (September): 307–17.

Hausmann, Ricardo. 1999a. "Should There Be Five Currencies or One Hundred and Five?" *Foreign Policy* 116 (Fall): 65–79.

———. 1999b. "Why the Interest in Reform?" In Jane Sneddon Little and Giovanni P. Olivei, eds., *Rethinking the International Monetary System* (Boston: Federal Reserve Bank of Boston), 94–96.

Hausmann, Ricardo, Ugo Panizza, and Ernesto Stein. 2001. "Why Do Countries Float the Way They Float?" *Journal of Development Economics* 66 (December): 387–414.

Hausmann, Ricardo, Michael Gavin, Carmen Pagés-Serra, and Ernesto Stein. 2000. "Financial Turmoil and the Choice of Exchange Rate Regime." In Eduardo Fernández-Arias and Ricardo Hausmann, eds., *Wanted: World Financial Stability* (Washington, D.C.: Inter-American Development Bank), 131–64.

Hayek, Friedrich A. 1976. *Choice in Currency: A Way to Stop Inflation.* Occasional Paper 48 (London: Institute of Economic Affairs).

———. 1990. *Denationalisation of Money—The Argument Refined.* 3d ed. (London: Institute of Economic Affairs).

Hefeker, Carsten. 1997. *Interest Groups and Monetary Integration: The Political Economy of Exchange Regime Choice* (Boulder: Westview Press).

Helleiner, Eric. 1994. *States and the Remergence of Global Finance: From Bretton Woods to the 1990s* (Ithaca: Cornell University Press).

———. 1998a. "Electronic Money: A Challenge to the Sovereign State?" *Journal of International Affairs* 51, no. 2 (Spring): 387–409.

———. 1998b. "National Currencies and National Identities." *American Behavioral Scientist* 41, no. 10 (August): 1409–36.

———. 1999. "Denationalising Money? Economic Liberalism and the 'National Question' in Currency Affairs." In Emily Gilbert and Eric Helleiner, eds., *Nation-States and Money: The Past, Present and Future of National Currencies* (London: Routledge), ch. 8.

———. 2000. "Think Globally, Transact Locally: Green Political Economy and the Local Currency Movement." *Global Society* 14, no. 1, 35–51.

———. 2002a. "Economic Nationalism as a Challenge to Economic Liberalism? Lessons from the 19th Century." *International Studies Quarterly* 46, no. 3 (September): 307–29.

———. 2002b. "Why Are Territorial Currencies Becoming Unpopular?" In David M. Andrews, C. Randall Henning, and Louis W. Pauly, eds., *Governing the World's Money* (Ithaca: Cornell University Press), ch. 8.

———. 2003a. *The Making of National Money: Territorial Currencies in Historical Perspective* (Ithaca: Cornell University Press).

———. 2003b. "Toward a North American Common Currency?" In W. Clement and L. Vosko, eds., *Changing Canada: Political Economy as Transformation* (Montreal: McGill-Queen's University Press, forthcoming).

Helweg, M. Diana. 2000. "Japan: A Rising Sun?" *Foreign Affairs* 79, no. 4 (July/August): 26–39.

Henckel, Timo, Alain Ize, and Arto Kovanen. 1999. "Central Banking Without Central Bank Money." Working Paper WP/99/92 (Washington, D.C.: International Monetary Fund).

Henning, C. Randall. 1999. *The Exchange Stabilization Fund: Slush Money or War Chest?* (Washington, D.C.: Institute for International Economics).

———. 2000. "U.S.-EU Relations after the Inception of the Monetary Union: Cooperation or Rivalry?" In C. Randall Henning and Pier Carlo Padoan, *Transatlantic Perspectives on the Euro* (Washington, D.C.: Brookings Institution), ch. 1.

———. 2002. *East Asian Financial Cooperation* (Washington, D.C.: Institute for International Economics).

Hernández, Leonardo, and Peter Montiel. 2001. "Post-Crisis Exchange Rate Policy in Five Asian Countries: Filling in the 'Hollow Middle'?" Working Paper WP/01/170 (Washington, D.C.: International Monetary Fund).

Higgott, Richard. 1998. "The Asian Economic Crisis: A Study in the Politics of Resentment." *New Political Economy* 3, no. 3, 333–56.

Hochreiter, Eduard, Klaus Schmidt-Hebbel, and Georg Winckler. 2002. "Monetary Unions: European Lessons, Latin American Prospects." *North American Journal of Economics and Finance* 13, no. 3 (December): 297–321.

Honohan, Patrick, and Philip Lane. 1999. "Pegging to the Dollar and the Euro." *International Finance* 2, no. 3 (November): 379–410.

———. 2001. "Will the Euro Trigger More Monetary Unions in Africa?" In Charles Wyplosz, ed., *The Impact of EMU on Europe and the Developing Countries* (Oxford: Oxford University Press), ch. 12.

Hoshi, Takeo, and Anil K. Kashyap. 2001. *Corporate Financing and Governance in Japan: The Road to the Future* (Cambridge, Mass.: MIT Press).

Hufbauer, Gary C., Jeffrey J. Schott, and Kimberly A. Elliott. 1990. *Economic Sanctions Reconsidered: History and Current Policy*, 2d ed. (Washington, D.C.: Institute for International Economics).

Hüfner, Martin. 2000. "Give the Euro Greater Currency." *The International Economy* (November/December): 24–25, 50.

Hughes, Christopher W. 2000. "Japanese Policy and the East Asian Currency Crisis: Abject Defeat or Quiet Victory?" *Review of International Political Economy* 7, no. 2 (Summer): 219–53.

Huizinga, John. 1994. "Exchange Rate Volatility, Uncertainty, and Investment: An Empirical Investigation." In Leonardo Leiderman and Assaf Razin, eds., *Capital Mobility: The Impact on Consumption, Investment and Growth* (Cambridge: Cambridge University Press), 185–213.

Ibarra, David, and Juan Carlos Moreno-Brid. 2001. "Currency Boards and Monetary Unions: The Road Ahead or a *Cul de Sac* for Mexico's Exchange Rate Policy?" In Martín Puchet Anyul and Lionello F. Punzo, eds., *Mexico Beyond NAFTA: Perspectives for the European Debate* (New York: Routledge), ch. 1.

Ingham, Geoffrey. 2002. "New Monetary Spaces?" In *The Future of Money* (Paris: Organization for Economic Cooperation and Development), ch. 5.

International Financial Institution Advisory Commission. 2000. *Report* (Washington, D.C.).

International Monetary Fund. 1999a. *Annual Report* (Washington, D.C.).

———. 1999b. "Dollarization: Fad or Future for Latin America?" Economic Forum, 24 June (*http:www.imf.org/external/np/tr/1999/tr990624.htm*).

———. 1999c. *Results of the 1997 Coordinated Portfolio Investment Survey* (Washington, D.C.).

———. 2000a. "One World, One Currency: Destination or Delusion?" Economic Forum, 8 November (*http://www.imf.org/external/np/tr/2000/tr001108.htm*).

———. 2000b. *World Economic Outlook* (Washington, D.C.).

———. 2001. *International Capital Markets: Developments, Prospects, and Key Policy Issues* (Washington, D.C.).

———. 2002a. "Lao People's Democratic Republic: Selected Issues and Statistical Appendix." Country Report 02/61 (Washington, D.C.).

———. 2002b. "Republic of Belarus: Selected Issues." Country Report 02/22 (Washington, D.C.).

Irving, Jacqueline. 1999. "For Better or For Worse: The Euro and the CFA Franc." *Africa Recovery* 12, no. 4 (April): 1, 25–29.

———. 2001. "The Pros and Cons of Expanded Monetary Union in West Africa." *Finance and Development* (March): 24–28.

Issing, Otmar. 2000. *Hayek, Currency Competition and European Monetary Union*. Occasional Paper 111 (London: Institute of Economic Affairs).

Itam, Samuel, Simon Cueva, Erik Lundback, Janet Stotsky, and Stephen Tokarick. 2000. *Developments and Challenges in the Caribbean Region* (Washington, D.C.: International Monetary Fund).

Ito, Takatoshi, and Michael Melvin. 2000. "The Political Economy of Japan's Big Bang." In Magnus Blomstrom, Byron Gangnes, and Sumner La Croix, eds., *Japan's New Economy: Continuity and Change in the Twenty-First Century* (New York: Oxford University Press), 162–74.

Jameson, Kenneth P. 2001. "Latin America and the Dollar Bloc in the Twenty-first Century: To Dollarize or Not?" *Latin American Politics and Society* 43, no. 4 (Winter): 1–35.

Johnson, Harry G. 1973. *Further Essays in Monetary Economics* (Cambridge, Mass.: Harvard University Press).

Johnston, R. Barry, and a Staff Team. 1999. *Exchange Rate Arrangements and Currency Convertibility: Developments and Issues* (Washington, D.C.: International Monetary Fund).

Joint Economic Committee. 2000a. *Basics of Dollarization.* Staff Report (Washington, D.C.).

———. 2000b. *Dollarization: A Guide to the International Monetary Stability Act.* Staff Report (*http://www.senate.gov/~jec/dollaract.htm*).

Jomo, K. S., ed. 2001. *Malaysian Eclipse: Economic Crisis and Recovery* (London: Zed Books).

Jones, Aaron. 2000. "The Future of Argentina's Quasi-Currency Board: Toward a Mercosur Monetary Union?" *Journal of Public and International Affairs* 11 (Spring): 52–68.

Judson, Ruth A., and Richard D. Porter. 2001. "Overseas Dollar Holdings: What Do We Know?" *Wirtschaftspolitische Blätter* 4 (April): 431–40.

Kaltenthaler, Karl, and Frank O. Mora. 2002. "Explaining Latin American Economic Integration; The Case of Mercosur." *Review of International Political Economy* 9, no. 1 (March): 72–97.

Kaminsky, Graciela, and Sergio Schmukler. 2001. "Short- and Long-Run Integration: Do Capital Controls Matter?" *Brookings Trade Forum 2000*, 125–78.

Kaplan, Ethan, and Dani Rodrik. 2001. "Did the Malaysian Capital Controls Work?" Working Paper 8142 (Cambridge, Mass.: National Bureau of Economic Research).

Kapur, Devesh. 1998. "The IMF: A Cure or a Curse?" *Foreign Policy* 111 (Summer): 114–29.

Katada, Saori N. 2001a. *Banking on Stability: Japan and the Cross-Pacific Dynamics of International Financial Crisis* (Ann Arbor: University of Michigan Press).

———. 2001b. "Determining Factors in Japan's Cooperation and Noncooperation with the United States: The Case of Asian Financial Crisis Management, 1997–1999." In Akitoshi Miyashita and Yoichiro Sato, eds., *Japanese Foreign Policy in Asia and the Pacific: Domestic Interests, American Pressure, and Regional Integration* (New York: Palgrave).

———. 2002. "Japan and Asian Monetary Regionalisation: Cultivating A New Regional Leadership after the Asian Financial Crisis." *Geopolitics* 7, no. 1 (Summer): 85–112.

Katzman, Julie T. 2000. "Dollarization." In Patrick J. DeSouza, ed., *Economic Strategy and National Security: A Next Generation Approach* (New York: Council on Foreign Relations), 203–15.

Kemmerer, Edwin. 1916. "A Proposal for Pan-American Monetary Unity." *Political Science Quarterly* 31: 66–80.

Kenen, Peter B. 1988. *Managing Exchange Rates* (New York: Council on Foreign Relations Press).

Kenen, Peter B. 1989. *Exchange Rates and Policy Coordination* (Ann Arbor: University of Michigan Press).

———. 1995. *Economic and Monetary Union in Europe: Moving Beyond Maastricht* (Cambridge: Cambridge University Press).

———. 2001. *The International Financial Architecture: What's New? What's Missing?* (Washington, D.C.: Institute for International Economics).

Keohane, Robert O. 1984. *After Hegemony: Cooperation and Discord in the World Political Economy* (Princeton: Princeton University Press).

Keohane, Robert O., and Stanley Hoffmann. 1991. "Institutional Change in Europe in the 1980s." In Robert O. Keohane and Stanley Hoffmann, eds., *The New European Community: Decisionmaking and Institutional Change* (Boulder: Westview Press), ch. 1.

King, Mervyn. 1999. "Challenges for Monetary Policy: New and Old." *Bank of England Quarterly Bulletin* 39: 397–415.

Kirshner, Jonathan. 1995. *Currency and Coercion: The Political Economy of International Monetary Power* (Princeton: Princeton University Press).

———. 1999. "Keynes, Capital Mobility and the Crisis of Embedded Liberalism." *Review of International Political Economy* 6, no. 3 (Autumn): 313–37.

Kiuchi, Takashi. 2000. "The Asian Crisis and Its Implications." In Karl Kaiser, John J. Kirton, and Joseph P. Daniels, eds., *Shaping a New International Financial System: Challenges of Governance in a Globalizing World* (Aldershot, U.K.: Ashgate), ch. 3.

Klein, Benjamin. 1974. "The Competitive Supply of Money." *Journal of Money, Credit, and Banking* 6, no. 4 (November): 423–53.

Klein, Benjamin, and Michael Melvin. 1982. "Competing International Monies and International Monetary Arrangements." In Michael B. Connolly, ed., *The International Monetary System: Choices for the Future* (New York: Praeger), ch. 9.

Klein, Lawrence R. 1993. "Some Second Thoughts on the European Monetary System." *Greek Economic Review* 15, no. 1 (Autumn): 105–14.

Knapp, George F. [1905]. 1924. *The State Theory of Money* (London: Macmillan).

Knöbl, Adalbert, Andres Sutt, and Basil Zavoico. 2002. "The Estonian Currency Board: Its Introduction and Role in the Early Success of Estonia's Transition to a Market Economy." Working Paper WP/02/96 (Washington, D.C.: International Monetary Fund).

Kobrin, Stephen J. 1997. "Electronic Cash and the End of National Markets." *Foreign Policy* 107 (Summer): 65–77.

———. 1998. "Back to the Future: Neomedievalism and the Postmodern Digital World Economy." *Journal of International Affairs* 51, no. 2 (Spring): 361–86.

Kopcke, Richard W. 1999. "Currency Boards: Once and Future Monetary Regimes?" *New England Economic Review* (May/June): 21–37.

Korhonen, Iikka, and Pekka Sutela. 2000. "Currency Boards in the Baltics." In Iliana Zloch-Christy, ed., *Economic Policy in Eastern Europe: Were Currency Boards a Solution?* (Westport, Conn.: Praeger), ch. 5.

Krasner, Stephen D. 1999. *Sovereignty: Organized Hypocrisy* (Princeton: Princeton University Press).

Krueger, Anne. 2002. *A New Approach to Sovereign Debt Restructuring* (Washington, D.C.: International Monetary Fund).

Krueger, Russell, and Jiming, Ha. 1996. "Measurement of Cocirculation of Currencies." In Paul D. Mizen and Eric J. Pentecost, eds., *The Macroeconomics of International Currencies: Theory, Policy and Evidence* (Brookfield, Vt.: Edward Elgar), ch. 4.

Krugman, Paul R. 1992. "The International Role of the Dollar." In Paul R. Krugman, *Currencies and Crises* (Cambridge, Mass.: MIT Press), ch. 10.

———. 1993. *What Do We Need to Know about the International Monetary System?* Essay in International Finance 190 (Princeton: International Finance Section).

———. 1998a. "The Confidence Game." *New Republic*, 5 October, 23–25.

———. 1998b. "Saving Asia: It's Time to Get Radical." *Fortune Magazine* 138, no. 5: 74–80.

———. 1999a. "Capital Control Freaks: How Malaysia Got Away with Economic Heresy." *Slate* (*http://slate.msn.com/Dismal/99–09–27/Dismal.asp*), 1–6.

———. 1999b. "Monomoney Mania: Why Fewer Currencies Aren't Necessarily Better." *Slate* (*http://slate.msn.com/Dismal/99–04–15/Dismal.asp*), 1–3.

———. 1999c. *The Return of Depression Economics* (New York: Norton).

———. 2001a. "A Latin Tragedy." *New York Times*, 15 July, WK15.

———. 2001b. "Other People's Money." *New York Times*, 18 July, A23.

Kwan, Chi Hung. 1998. "The Theory of Optimum Currency Areas and the Possibility of Forming a Yen Bloc in Asia." *Journal of Asian Economics* 9, no. 4 (Winter): 555–80.

———. 1999. "Towards a Yen Bloc in Asia." *NRI Quarterly* 8 (Summer): 2–13.

———. 2001. *Yen Bloc: Toward Economic Integration in Asia* (Washington, D.C.: Brookings Institution).

Laidler, David. 1999. "Canada's Exchange Rate Options." *Canadian Public Policy/Analyse de Politiques* 25, no. 3 (September): 324–32.

Lake, David A. 1993. "Leadership, Hegemony, and the International Economy: Naked Emperor or Tattered Monarch with Potential?" *International Studies Quarterly* 37, no. 4 (December): 459–89.

Lambert, Michael J., and Kristin D. Stanton. 2001. "Opportunities and Challenges of the U.S. Dollar as an Increasingly Global Currency: A Federal Reserve Perspective." *Federal Reserve Bulletin* 87, no. 9 (September): 567–75.

Lamfalussy, Alexandre. 2000. *Financial Crises in Emerging Markets* (New Haven: Yale University Press).

Larrain, Felipe, and Andrés Velasco. 2001. *Exchange-Rate Policy in Emerging-Market Economies: The Case for Floating*. Essay in International Economics 224 (Princeton: International Economics Section).

Laurence, Henry. 2002. "Japan and the New Financial Order in East Asia: From Competition to Cooperation." In Leslie Elliott Armijo, ed., *Debating the Global Financial Architecture* (Albany: State University of New York Press), ch. 8.

LeBaron, Blake, and Rachel McCulloch. 2000. "Floating, Fixed, or Super-Fixed? Dollarization Joins the Menu of Exchange-Rate Options." *American Economic Review* 90, no. 2 (May): 32–37.

Letiche, John M. 2000. "Lessons from the Euro Zone for the East Asian Economies." *Journal of Asian Economics* 11: 275–300.

Levy-Yeyati, Eduardo, and Federico Sturzenegger. 2000a. "Classifying Exchange Rate Regimes: Deeds vs. Words." CIF Working Paper 02/2000 (Buenos Aires: Universidad Torcuato Di Tella).

———. 2000b. "Is EMU a Blueprint for Mercosur?" *Latin American Journal of Economics* 110 (April): 63–99.

———. 2001. "Exchange Rate Regimes and Economic Performance." *International Monetary Fund Staff Papers* 47 (special issue): 62–98.

Lietaer, Bernard. 2001. *The Future of Money: Creating New Wealth, Work, and a Wiser World* (London: Century).

Lim, Linda. 1999. "Malaysia's Response to the Asian Financial Crisis." *Malaysia: Assessing the Mahathir Agenda*. Hearings before the Subcommittee on Asia and the Pacific, Committee on International Relations. U.S. House of Representatives, 16 June, 37–41.

Litfin, Karen. 1997. "Sovereignty in World Ecopolitics." *Mershon International Studies Review* 41, no. 2 (November): 167–204.

Little, Jane Sneddon, and Giovanni P. Olivei, eds. 1999. *Rethinking the International Monetary System* (Boston: Federal Reserve Bank of Boston).

Loedel, Peter H. 1999. *Deutsche Mark Politics: Germany in the European Monetary System* (Boulder: Lynne Rienner).

Lopez, Franklin A. 2002. "Dollarization in Vulnerable Economies: The Lessons from Ecuador." Paper prepared for a conference, The Euro and Dollarization. Fordham University, New York, 5–6 April.

López-Mejía, Alejandro. 1999. "Large Capital Flows: A Survey of the Causes, Consequences, and Policy Responses." Working Paper WP/99/17 (Washington, D.C.: International Monetary Fund).

Loriaux, Michael, Meredith Woo-Cumings, Kent E. Calder, Sylvia Maxfield, and Sofía A. Pérez. 1997. *Capital Ungoverned: Liberalizing Finance in Interventionist States* (Ithaca: Cornell University Press).

Lynch, Daniel C., and Leslie Lundquist. 1996. *Digital Money: The New Era of Internet Commerce* (New York: John Wiley & Sons).

Mack, Connie. 2000. "Dollarization." *Central Banking* 11, no. 1, 63–69.

Madrick, Jeff. 2001. "Economic Scene: The Mainstream Can't or Won't Recognize Some Basic Facts about World Poverty." *New York Times*, 2 August, C2.

Makinen, Gail E. 2000. "Euro Currency: How Much Could It Cost the United States?" CRS Report 98–998E, updated (Washington, D.C.: Congressional Research Service).

Mankiw, N. Gregory. 2000. "The Savers-Spenders Theory of Fiscal Policy." *American Economic Review* 90, no. 2 (May): 120–25.

Mann, Catherine. 1999. "Dollarization." *Official Dollarization in Emerging-Market Countries*. Hearings before the Subcommittee on Economic Policy and Subcommittee on International Trade and Finance, Committee on Banking, Housing, and Urban Affairs. U.S. Senate, 22 April, 55–57.

Martin, Lisa L., and Beth Simmons. 1999. "Theories and Empirical Studies of International Institutions." In Peter J. Katzenstein, Robert O. Keohane, and

Stephen D. Krasner, eds., *Exploration and Contestation in the Study of World Politics* (Cambridge, Mass.: MIT Press), 89–117.

Martin, William McChesney. 1970. *Toward a World Central Bank?* (Washington, D.C.: Per Jacobsson Foundation).

Masson, Paul R. 1999. "Monetary and Exchange Rate Policy of Transition Economies of Central and Eastern Europe after the Launch of EMU." Policy Discussion Paper PDP/99/5 (Washington, D.C.: International Monetary Fund).

Masson, Paul R., and Catherine Pattillo. 2001a. "Monetary Union in West Africa: An Agency of Restraint for Fiscal Policies?" Working Paper WP/01/34 (Washington, D.C.: International Monetary Fund).

———. 2001b. *Monetary Union in West Africa (ECOWAS): Is It Desirable and How Could It Be Achieved?* (Washington, D.C.: International Monetary Fund).

Masson, Paul R., and Mark P. Taylor. 1993. "Currency Union: A Survey of the Issues." In Paul R. Masson and Mark P. Taylor, eds., *Policy Issues in the Operation of Currency Unions* (New York: Cambridge University Press), ch. 1.

Matsuyama, Kiminori, Nobuhiro Kiyotaki, and Akihiko Matsui. 1993. "Toward a Theory of International Currency." *Review of Economic Studies* 60, no. 2 (April): 283–307.

Mattli, Walter. 2000. "Sovereignty Bargains in Regional Integration." *International Studies Quarterly* 2, no. 2 (Summer): 149–80.

Maxfield, Sylvia. 1990. *Governing Capital: International Finance and Mexican Politics* (Ithaca: Cornell University Press).

———. 1992. "The International Political Economy of Bank Nationalization: Mexico in Comparative Perspective." *Latin American Research Review* 27, no. 1: 75–103.

———. 1997. *Gatekeepers of Growth: The International Political Economy of Central Banking in Developing Countries* (Princeton: Princeton University Press).

McCallum, John. 1999a. "Seven Issues in the Choice of Exchange Rate Regime for Canada." *Current Analysis*. Royal Bank of Canada (February).

———. 1999b. "Theoretical Issues Pertaining to Monetary Unions." Working Paper 7393 (Cambridge, Mass.: National Bureau of Economic Research).

———. 2000. "Engaging the Debate: Costs and Benefits of a North American Common Currency." *Current Analysis*. Royal Bank of Canada (April).

McCauley, Robert N. 1997. *The Euro and the Dollar,* Essay in International Finance 205 (Princeton: International Finance Section).

McCaw, Sharon, and John McDermott. 2000. "How New Zealand Adjusts to Macroeconomic Shocks: Implications for Joining a Currency Area." Reserve Bank of New Zealand *Bulletin* 63, no. 1 (March): 35–51.

McKinnon, Ronald I. 1984. *An International Standard for Monetary Stabilization* (Washington, D.C.: Institute for International Economics).

———. 1997. *The Rules of the Game: International Money and Exchange Rates* (Cambridge, Mass.: MIT Press).

McLeod, Ross H. 2000. "Which Currency for East Timor?" *Pacific Economic Bulletin* 15, no. 1: 113–18.

McNamara, Kathleen R. 1998. *The Currency of Ideas: Monetary Politics in the European Union* (Ithaca: Cornell University Press).

McNamara, Kathleen R. 2002. "Rational Fictions: Central Bank Independence and the Social Logic of Delegation." *West European Politics* 25, no. 1 (January): 47–76.

McNamara, Kathleen R., and Sophie Meunier. 2002. "Between National Sovereignty and International Power: What External Voice for the Euro?" *International Affairs* 78, no. 4 (October): 849–68.

Melvin, Michael. 1988. "Monetary Confidence, Privately Produced Monies, and Domestic and International Monetary Reform." In Thomas D. Willett, ed., *Political Business Cycles: The Political Economy of Money, Inflation, and Unemployment* (Durham: Duke University Press), ch. 18.

Mill, John Stuart. [1848] 1871. *Principles of Political Economy* (London: Longman, Green)

Ministry of Finance. 2000. "Japanese Big Bang" (*www.mof.go.jp/english/bigbang/ebb37.htm*).

Moggridge, Donald, ed. 1980a. *The Collected Writings of John Maynard Keynes*, Vol. 25, *Activities, 1940–1944: Shaping the Post-war World, the Clearing Union* (Cambridge: Cambridge University Press).

———. 1980b. *The Collected Writings of John Maynard Keynes*, Vol. 26, *Activities, 1941–1946: Shaping the Post-war World, Bretton Woods and Reparations* (Cambridge: Cambridge University Press).

Molano, Walter T. 2000. "Addressing the Symptoms and Ignoring the Causes: A View from Wall Street on Dollarization." *Monetary Stability in Latin America: Is Dollarization the Answer?*, Hearings before the Subcommittee on Domestic and International Monetary Policy, Committee on Banking and Financial Services, U.S. House of Representatives, 22 June, 51–60.

Montiel, Peter, and Carmen M. Reinhart. 1999. "Do Capital Controls and Macroeconomic Policies Influence the Volume and Composition of Capital Flows? Evidence from the 1990s." *Journal of International Money and Finance* 18 (August): 619–35.

Moravcsik, Andrew. 1998. *The Choice for Europe* (Ithaca: Cornell University Press).

Moreno-Villalaz, Juan Luis. 1999. "Lessons from the Monetary Experience of Panama: A Dollar Economy with Financial Integration." *Cato Journal* 18, no. 3 (Winter): 421–44.

Morgan, E. Victor. 1965. *A History of Money* (Baltimore: Penguin).

Mourmouras, Alex, and Steven H. Russell. 2000. "Smuggling, Currency Substitution and Unofficial Dollarization: A Crime-Theoretic Approach." Working Paper WP/00/176 (Washington, D.C.: International Monetary Fund).

Mulgan, Aurelia George. 2000. "Japan: A Setting Sun?" *Foreign Affairs* 79, no. 4 (July/August): 40–52.

Mundell, Robert A. 1961. "A Theory of Optimum Currency Areas." *American Economic Review* 51, no. 3 (September): 657–65.

———. 1968. "A Plan for a World Currency." *Next Steps in International Monetary Reform*, Hearings before the Subcommittee on International Exchange and Payments, the Joint Economic Committee of the Congress, 9 September, 14–28.

———. 1993. "EMU and the International Monetary System: A Transatlantic Perspective." Working Paper 13 (Vienna: Austrian National Bank).

———. 2000a. "Currency Areas, Exchange Rate Systems and International Monetary Reform," *Journal of Applied Economics* 3, no. 2 (November): 217–56.

———. 2000b. "The Euro and the Stability of the International Monetary System." In Robert A. Mundell and Armand Cleese, eds., *The Euro as a Stabilizer in the International Economic System* (Boston: Kluwer Academic), ch. 5.

———. 2000c. "Exchange Rate Arrangements in Central and Eastern Europe." In Sven Arndt, Heinz Handler, and Dominick Salvatore, eds., *Eastern Enlargement: The Sooner, the Better?* (Vienna: Ministry for Economic Affairs and Labor), 158–65.

———. 2000d. "A Reconsideration of the Twentieth Century." *American Economic Review* 90, no. 3 (June): 327–40.

———. 2001. "Guitián Memorial Lecture." *IMF Survey*, 5 March, 75–76.

Murray, John. 2000. "Why Canada Needs a Flexible Exchange Rate." *North American Journal of Economics and Finance* 11, no. 1 (August): 41–60.

Mussa, Michael. 2002. *Argentina and the Fund: From Triumph to Tragedy* (Washington, D.C.: Institute for International Economics).

Mussa, Michael, Alexander K. Swoboda, Jeromin Zettelmeyer, and Olivier Jeanne. 2000. "Moderating Fluctuations in Capital Flows to Emerging Market Economies." In Peter B. Kenen and Alexander K. Swoboda, eds., *Reforming the International Monetary and Financial System* (Washington, D.C.: International Monetary Fund), ch. 4.

Mussa, Michael, Paul Masson, Alexander Swoboda, Esteban Jadresic, Paolo Mauro, and Andrew Berg. 2000. *Exchange Rate Regimes in an Increasingly Integrated World Economy* (Washington, D.C.: International Monetary Fund).

Nadal-De Simone, Francisco, and Piritta Sorsa. 1999. "A Review of Capital Account Restrictions in Chile in the 1990s." Working Paper WP/99/52 (Washington, D.C.: International Monetary Fund).

Neely, Christopher J. 1999. "An Introduction to Capital Controls." *Federal Reserve Bank of St. Louis Review* 81, no. 6 (November/December): 13–30.

Negroponte, Nicholas. 1996. "Being Local." *Wired* 11 April, 286.

Nenovski, Nikolay, Kalin Hristov, and Boris Petrov. 2000. "Transition from Lev to Euro—Early Steps to the EU" (*http://www.capital.bg/old/weekly/00–06/17.6.htm*).

Nicholls, Shelton, Anthony Birchwood, Philip Colthrust, and Earl Boodoo. 2000. "The State of and Prospects for the Deepening and Widening of Caribbean Integration." *The World Economy* 23, no. 3 (September): 1161–94.

Nicolas, Françoise. 1999. "Is There a Case for a Single Currency Within ASEAN?" *Singapore Economic Review* 44, no. 1, 1–25.

———. 2000. "Post-Crisis Exchange Rate Policies in East Asia: Options and Challenges." *Asia Pacific Journal of Economics and Business* 4, no. 1 (June): 4–27.

Niskanen, William A. 2000. "Dollarization for Latin America?" *Cato Journal* 20, no. 1 (Spring/Summer): 43–47.

Noble, Gregory W., and John Ravenhill, eds. 2000. *The Asian Financial Crisis and the Architecture of Global Finance* (Cambridge: Cambridge University Press).

Nurkse, Ragnar. 1944. *International Currency Experience: Lessons from the Inter-War Period* (Geneva: League of Nations).

Nuti, Mario. 2000. "The Costs and Benefits of Euro-Isolation in Central-Eastern Europe before or instead of EMU Membership." In Sven Arndt, Heinz Handler, and Dominick Salvatore, eds., *Eastern Enlargement: The Sooner, the Better?* (Vienna: Ministry for Economic Affairs and Labor), 171–94.

Nye, Joseph S., Jr. 1990. "Soft Power." *Foreign Policy* 80 (Fall): 153–71.

Oatley, Thomas H. 1997. *Monetary Politics; Exchange Rate Cooperation in the European Union* (Ann Arbor: University of Michigan Press).

Obstfeld, Maurice, and Kenneth Rogoff. 1996. *Foundations of International Finance* (Cambridge, Mass.: MIT Press).

O'Grady, Mary Anastasia. 1999. "Mexican CEOs are Talking Up Dollarization." *Wall Street Journal*, 12 February, A17.

Ohmae, Kenichi. 2001. "Globalization, Regions, and the New Economy." Working Paper 1 (Los Angeles: UCLA Center for Globalization and Policy Research).

O'Keefe, Thomas Andrew. 2000. "Speaking with One Voice: Prospects for Mercosur Currency." *Latin American Law and Business Report*, 8, no. 2 (29 February): 21–23.

Okun, Arthur M. 1975. *Equality and Efficiency: The Big Tradeoff* (Washington, D.C.: Brookings Institution).

Orléan, Andre. 1989. "Mimetic Contagion and Speculative Bubbles." *Theory and Decision* 27, nos. 1–2, 63–92.

Osband, Kent, and Delano Villanueva. 1993. "Independent Currency Authorities." *International Monetary Fund Staff Papers* 40, no. 1 (March): 202–16.

Overturf, Stephen F. 1997. *Money and European Union* (New York: St. Martin's Press).

Padoan, Pier Carlo. 2000. "The Role of the Euro in the International System: A European View." In C. Randall Henning and Pier Carlo Padoan, *Transatlantic Perspectives on the Euro* (Washington, D.C.: Brookings Institution), ch. 2.

Park, Yung Chul, and Yunjong Wang. 2000. "Reforming the International Financial System: Prospects for Regional Financial Cooperation in East Asia." In Jan Joost Teunissen, ed., *Reforming the International Financial System: Crisis Prevention and Response* (The Hague: Forum on Debt and Development), 70–83.

Pastor, Manuel, and Carol Wise. 2001. "From Poster Child to Basket Case." *Foreign Affairs* 80, no. 6 (November/December): 60–72.

Pauly, Louis W. 1988. *Opening Financial Markets: Banking Politics on the Pacific Rim* (Ithaca: Cornell University Press).

———. 1997. *Who Elected the Bankers? Surveillance and Control in the World Economy* (Ithaca: Cornell University Press).

———. 1999. "Good Governance and Bad Policy: The Perils of International Organizational Overextension." *Review of International Political Economy* 6, no. 4 (Winter): 401–24.

Payer, Cheryl. 1974. *The Debt Trap: The International Monetary Fund and the Third World* (New York: Monthly Review Press).

Pempel, T. J., ed. 1999. *The Politics of the Asian Economic Crisis* (Ithaca: Cornell University Press).

Peterson, Erik R. 1988. *The Gulf Cooperation Council: Search for Unity in a Dynamic Region* (Boulder: Westview Press).

Porter, Richard D., and Judson, Ruth A. 1996. "The Location of U.S. Currency: How Much Is Abroad?" *Federal Reserve Bulletin* 82, no. 10 (October): 883–903.

Portes, Richard. 1999. "Global Financial Markets and Financial Stability: Europe's Role." Discussion Paper 2298 (London: Centre for Economic Policy Research).

Portes, Richard, and Hélène Rey. 1998. "The Emergence of the Euro as an International Currency." In David Begg, Jürgen von Hagen, Charles Wyplosz, and Klaus F. Zimmermann, eds., *EMU: Prospects and Challenges for the Euro* (Oxford: Blackwell), 307–43.

Posen, Adam S. 2001. "Japan 2001—Decisive Action or Financial Panic." International Economic Policy Brief PB01–4 (Washington, D.C.: Institute for International Economics).

Pou, Pedro. 1999. "Is Globalization Really to Blame?" In Jane Sneddon Little and Giovanni P. Olivei, eds., *Rethinking the International Monetary System* (Boston: Federal Reserve Bank of Boston), 243–50.

Powell, Andrew, and Federico Sturzenegger. 2003. "Dollarization: The Link Between Devaluation and Default Risk." In Eduardo Levy-Yeyati and Federico Sturzenegger, eds. *Dollarization: Debates and Policy Alternatives* (Cambridge, Mass.: MIT Press), ch. 6.

Prati, Alessandro, and Garry J. Schinasi. 1997. "European Monetary Union and International Capital Markets: Structural Implications and Risks." In Paul R. Masson, Thomas H. Krueger, and Bart G. Turtelboom, eds., *EMU and the International Monetary System* (Washington, D.C.: International Monetary Fund), ch. 11.

Przeworski, Adam, and James R. Vreeland. 2000. "The Effect of IMF Programs on Economic Growth." *Journal of Development Economics* 62: 385–421.

Radelet, Steven, and Jeffrey Sachs. 1998. "The East Asian Financial Crisis: Diagnosis, Remedies, Prospects." *Brookings Papers on Economic Activity* 1: 1–74.

———. 2000. "The Onset of the East Asian Financial Crisis." In Paul Krugman, ed., *Currency Crises* (Chicago: University of Chicago Press), ch. 4.

Rajan, Ramkishen. 2001. "Financial and Macroeconomic Co-operation in ASEAN: Issues and Policy Initiatives." In Mya Than, ed., *ASEAN Beyond the Regional Crisis: Challenges and Initiatives* (Singapore: Institute of Southeast Asian Studies), 126–47.

Reinhart, Carmen M., and Vincent Raymond Reinhart. 1998. "Some Lessons for Policy Makers Who Deal with the Mixed Blessing of Capital Inflows." In Miles Kahler, ed., *Capital Flows and Financial Crises* (Ithaca: Cornell University Press), ch. 4.

———. 2002. "Is a G-3 Target Zone on Target for Emerging Markets?" *Finance and Development* (March): 17–19.

Reinhart, Carmen M., and Kenneth S. Rogoff. 2002. "The Modern History of Exchange Rate Arrangements: A Reinterpretation." Working Paper 8963 (Cambridge, Mass.: National Bureau of Economic Research).

Reti, Steven P. 1998. *Silver and Gold: The Political Economy of International Monetary Conferences, 1867–1892* (Westport, Conn.: Greenwood Press).

Ries, Christine P. 1997. "Introduction and Overview." In Christine P. Ries and Richard J. Sweeney, eds., *Capital Controls in Emerging Economies* (Boulder: Westview Press), 1–12.

Ritter, Joseph A. 1995. "The Transition from Barter to Fiat Money." *American Economic Review* 85, no. 1 (March): 134–49.

Robertson, James. 1990. *Future Wealth* (London: Cassell).

Robson, William B. P. 2001. "New Currency Regimes: How Green the Grass? How High the Fence?" *Policy Options/Options Politiques* (May): 45–50.

Robson, William B. P., and David Laidler. 2002. "No Small Change: The Awkward Economics and Politics of North American Monetary Integration." *C. D. Howe Institute Commentary* 167 (July): 1–29.

Rodrik, Dani. 1999. "Governing the Global Economy: Does One Architectural Style Fit All?" In Susan M. Collins and Robert Z. Lawrence, eds., *Brookings Trade Forum 1999* (Washington, D.C.: Brookings Institution), 105–39.

Rogoff, Kenneth. 1998. "Blessing or Curse? Foreign and Underground Demand for Euro Notes." In David Begg, Jürgen von Hagen, Charles Wyplosz, and Klaus F. Zimmerman, eds., *EMU: Prospects and Challenges for the Euro* (Oxford: Blackwell), 261–303.

——— 2001. "Why Not a Global Currency?" *American Economic Review* 91, no. 2 (May): 243–47.

——— 2002a. "Managing the World Economy." *The Economist*, 3 August, 62–64.

——— 2002b. "An Open Letter to Joseph Stiglitz." *IMF Survey*, 8 July, 209–11.

Rojas-Suarez, Liliana. 2000. "What Exchange Rate Arrangement Works Best for Latin America?" Paper prepared for a conference, To Dollarize or Not to Dollarize: Currency Choices for the Western Hemisphere. Ottawa, Canada, 4–5 October.

Rose, Andrew K. 2000. "One Money, One Market: The Effect of Common Currencies on Trade." *Economic Policy* 30 (April): 7–45.

———. 2001. "Currency Unions and Trade: The Effect is Large." *Economic Policy* 33 (October): 449–57.

———. 2002. "The Effect of Common Currencies on International Trade: A Meta-Analysis." Paper prepared for a conference, The Euro and Dollarization. Fordham University, New York, 5–6 April.

Rose, Andrew K., and Charles M. Engel. 2002. "Currency Unions and International Integration." *Journal of Money, Credit, and Banking* 34, no. 4 (November): 1067–89.

Rose, Andrew K., and Eric van Wincoop. 2001. "National Money as a Barrier to International Trade: The Real Case for Currency Union." *American Economic Review* 91, no. 2 (May): 386–90.

Rosecrance, Richard. 2000. "The International Political Implications of the Euro." In Robert A. Mundell and Armand Cleese, eds., *The Euro as a Stabilizer in the International Economic System* (Boston: Kluwer Academic), ch. 4.

Roubini, Nouriel. 1998. "The Case Against Currency Boards: Debunking 10 Myths about the Benefits of Currency Boards (*http://www.stern.nyu.edu/globalmacro/CurrencyBoardsRoubini.html*).

Rowley, Anthony. 1997. "International Finance: Asian Fund, R.I.P." *Capital Trends* 2, no. 14 (December): 1–3.

Ruggie, John G. 1983. "International Regimes, Transactions, and Change: Embedded Liberalism in the Postwar Economic Order." In Stephen D. Krasner, ed., *International Regimes* (Ithaca: Cornell University Press), 195–231.

Sachs, Jeffrey, and Felipe Larrain. 1999. "Why Dollarization is More Straitjacket than Salvation." *Foreign Policy* 116 (Fall): 80–92.

Salvatore, Dominick. 2000. "The Present International Monetary System: Problems, Complications, and Reforms." *Open Economies Review* 11 (August): 133–48.

————. 2001. "Which Countries in the Americas Should Dollarize?" *Journal of Policy Modeling* 23, no. 3 (April): 347–55.

Samuelson, Robert J. 1999. "Dollarization—A Black Hole." *Washington Post*, 12 May, A27.

Santillán, Javier, Marc Bayle, and Christian Thygesen. 2000. "The Impact of the Euro on Money and Bond Markets." Occasional Paper 1 (Frankfurt: European Central Bank).

Santiprabhob, Veerathai. 1997. "Bank Soundness and Currency Board Arrangements: Issues and Experiences." Paper on Policy Analysis and Assessment PPAA/97/11 (Washington, D.C.: International Monetary Fund).

Savastano, M.A. 1996. "Dollarization in Latin America: Recent Evidence and Policy Issues." In Paul D. Mizen and Eric J. Pentecost, eds., *The Macroeconomics of International Currencies: Theory, Policy and Evidence* (Brookfield, Vt.: Edward Elgar), ch. 12.

Schaede, Ulrike. 2000. "After the Bubble: Evaluating Financial Reform in Japan in the 1990s." University of California at San Diego. Typescript.

Schmitt-Grohé, Stephanie, and Martín Uribe. 1999. "Dollarization and Seigniorage: How Much Is at Stake?" University of Pennsylvania. Typescript (*http://www.econ.upenn.edu/~uribe*).

Schuldt, Jürgen. 2003. "Latin American Official Dollarization: Political Economy Aspects." In Dominick Salvatore, James W. Dean, and Thomas D. Willett, eds., *The Dollarization Debate* (New York: Oxford University Press, forthcoming).

Schuler, Kurt. 1999. *Encouraging Official Dollarization in Emerging Markets.* Staff Report (Washington, D.C.: Joint Economic Committee).

Schuler, Kurt, and Robert Stein. 2000. "The International Monetary Stability Act: An Analysis." Paper prepared for a conference, To Dollarize or Not to Dollarize: Currency Choices for the Western Hemisphere. Ottawa, Canada, 4–5 October.

Schulze, Günther G. 2000. *The Political Economy of Capital Controls* (New York: Cambridge University Press).

Schwartz, Anne J. 1993. "Currency Boards: Their Past, Present, and Possible Future Role." *Carnegie Rochester Conference Series on Public Policy* 39 (December): 147–87.

Scrimgeour, Dean. 2002. "Exchange Rate Volatility and Currency Union: New Zealand Evidence" (Wellington, N.Z.: Reserve Bank of New Zealand, typescript).

Seidman, Lawrence. 2001. "Reviving Fiscal Policy." *Challenge* 44, no. 3 (May/June): 17–42.

Seitz, Franz. 1995. "The Circulation of Deutsche Mark Abroad." Discussion Paper 1/95 (Frankfurt: Deutsche Bundesbank).

Shelton, Judy. 1994. *Money Meltdown: Restoring Order to the Global Currency System* (New York: Free Press).

———. 1999. "Prepared Statement." *Official Dollarization in Emerging-Market Countries*. Hearings before the Subcommittee on Economic Policy and Subcommittee on International Trade and Finance, Committee on Banking, Housing, and Urban Affairs. U.S. Senate, 22 April, 47–53.

Shlaes, Amity. 1997. "Loving the Mark." *New Yorker*, April 28, 188–93.

Singleton, Andrew. 1995. "Cash on the Wirehead." *BYTE* 20, no. 6 (June): 71–78.

Sinn, Hans-Werner, and Frank Westermann. 2001a. "The Deutschmark in Eastern Europe, Black Money and the Euro: On the Size of the Effect." *CESifo Forum* 3: 35–40.

———. 2001b. "Why Has the Euro Been Falling? An Investigation into the Determinants of the Exchange Rate." Working Paper 8352 (Cambridge, Mass.: National Bureau of Economic Research).

Solomon, Elinor Harris. 1997. *Virtual Money: Understanding the Power and Risks of Money's High-Speed Journey into Electronic Space* (New York: Oxford University Press).

Solomon, Lewis D. 1996. *Rethinking Our Centralized Monetary System: The Case for a System of Local Currencies* (Westport, Conn.: Praeger).

Sörg, Mart, and Vello Vensel. 2000. "The Currency Board in Estonia." In Iliana Zloch-Christy, ed., *Economic Policy in Eastern Europe: Were Currency Boards a Solution?* (Westport, Conn.: Praeger), ch. 6.

Soros, George. 1998. *The Crisis of Global Capitalism* (New York: PublicAffairs).

———. 2002. "Don't Blame Brazil." *Financial Times*, 13 August, 13.

Spencer, Peter. 2001. "Regulation of the Payments Market and the Prospect for Digital Money." In *Electronic Finance: A New Perspective and Challenges*, BIS Paper 7 (Basle: Bank for International Settlements), 69–79.

Starr, Pamela K. 1997. "Government Coalitions and the Viability of Currency Boards: Argentina Under the Cavallo Plan." *Journal of Interamerican Studies and World Affairs* 39, no. 2 (Summer): 83–133.

———. 2001. "Dollars for Pesos? The Politics of Dollarization in Latin America." *Revista de Economia Política* (Brazilian Journal of Political Economy) 21, no. 1 (January–March): 62–77.

———. 2002. "Dollarization in Mexico: Does It Make Sense and Is It Likely?" Paper prepared for a conference, Dollarization and Latin America. Florida International University, Miami, 4 March.

Stewart, David C. 1997. "Picking Winners and Losers in Digital Cash." *Bank Technology News* 7, no. 9 (October): 28–39.

Stiglitz, Joseph. 1998. "Central Banking in a Democratic Society." *The Economist* 146: 199–226.

———. 2002. *Globalization and Its Discontents* (New York: Norton).

Stix, Helmut. 2001. "Survey Results about Foreign Currency Holdings in Five Central and Eastern European Countries." *CESifo Forum* 3: 41–48.

Stone, Randall W. 2002. *Lending Credibility: The International Monetary Fund and the Post-Communist Transition* (Princeton: Princeton University Press).

Strange, Susan. 1971a. "The Politics of International Currencies." *World Politics* 23, no. 2 (January): 215–31.

———. 1971b. *Sterling and British Policy: A Political Study of an International Currency in Decline* (London: Oxford University Press).

Streeten, Paul. 1991. "Global Prospects in an Interdependent World." *World Development* 19, no. 1, 123–33.

Summers, Lawrence H. 1999a. "Reflections on Managing Global Integration." *Journal of Economic Perspectives* 13, no. 2 (Spring): 3–18.

———. 1999b. "Statement." *Official Dollarization in Emerging-Market Countries*. Hearings before the Subcommittee on Economic Policy and Subcommittee on International Trade and Finance, Committee on Banking, Housing, and Urban Affairs. U.S. Senate, 22 April, 4–7.

Swoboda, Alexander. 1968. *The Euro-Dollar: An Interpretation*. Essay in International Finance 64 (Princeton: International Finance Section).

Szapáry, György. 2000. "Maastricht and the Choice of Exchange Rate Regime in Transition Countries during the Run-Up to EMU." Working Document 153 (Brussels: Centre for European Policy Studies).

———. 2001. "Transition Countries' Choice of Exchange Rate Regime in the Run-Up to EMU Membership." *Finance and Development* (June): 26–29.

Takagi, Shinji. 1999. "The Yen and Its East Asian Neighbors, 1980–1995: Cooperation or Competition?" In Takatoshi Ito and Anne O. Krueger, eds., *Changes in Exchange Rates in Rapidly Developing Countries: Theory, Practice, and Policy Issues* (Chicago: University of Chicago Press), ch. 7.

Tavlas, George S. 1993. "The 'New' Theory of Optimum Currency Areas." *World Economy* 16, no. 6 (November): 663–85.

———. 1994. "The Theory of Monetary Integration." *Open Economies Review* 5: 211–30.

Taylor, Lance. 2000. "The Consequences of Capital Liberalization." *Challenge* 43, no. 6 (November–December): 38–57.

Thacker, Strom C. 1999. "The High Politics of IMF Lending." *World Politics* 52, no. 1 (October): 38–75.

Thrift, Nigel, and Andrew Leyshon. 1999. "Moral Geographies of Money." In Emily Gilbert and Eric Helleiner, eds., *Nation-States and Money: The Past, Present and Future of National Currencies* (New York: Routledge), ch. 9.

Thygesen, Niels et al. 1995. *International Currency Competition and the Future Role of the Single European Currency*. Final Report of a Working Group on European Monetary Union-International Monetary System (London: Kluwer Law International).

Tiebout, Charles M. 1956. "A Pure Theory of Local Expenditures." *Journal of Political Economy* 64, no. 5 (October): 416–24.

Timberlake, Richard H. 1987. "Private Production of Scrip Money in the Isolated Community." *Journal of Money, Credit, and Banking* 19, no. 4 (November): 437–47.

———. 1992. "Scrip Money." In Peter Newman, Murray Milgate, and John Eatwell, eds., *The New Palgrave Dictionary of Money and Finance*. Vol. 3 (London: Macmillan), 401–2.

Trejos, Alberto, and Randall Wright. 1996. "Search-Theoretic Models of International Currency." *Federal Reserve Bank of St. Louis Review* 78 (May/June): 117–32.

Tsygankov, Andrei P. 2000. "Defining State Interests After Imperial Disintegration: National Identity, Domestic Structures and Foreign Trade Policies of Latvia and Belarus." *Review of International Political Economy* 7, no. 1 (Spring): 101–37.

———. 2001. *Pathways After Empire: National Identity and Foreign Economic Policy in the Post-Soviet World* (New York: Rowman and Littlefield).

Tumin, Zachary. 2002. "The Future Technology of Money." In *The Future of Money* (Paris: Organization for Economic Cooperation and Development), ch. 3.

Twinham, Joseph Wright. 1992. *The Gulf, Cooperation and the Council: An American Perspective* (Washington, D.C.: Middle East Policy Council).

Ulan, Michael K. 2002. "Should Developing Countries Restrict Capital Inflows?" *ANNALS* 579 (January): 249–60.

Ul Haque, Nadeem, and Mohsin S. Khan. 1998. "Do IMF-Supported Programs Work? A Survey of the Cross-Country Empirical Evidence." Working Paper WP/98/169 (Washington, D.C.: International Monetary Fund).

Ungerer, Horst. 1997. *A Concise History of European Monetary Integration: From EPU to EMU* (Westport, Conn.: Quorum Books).

United States Treasury. 2000. *The Use and Counterfeiting of United States Currency Abroad* (Washington, D.C.).

van Beek, Frits, José Roberto Rosales, Mayra Zermeño, Ruby Randall, and Jorge Shepherd. 2000. *The Eastern Caribbean Currency Union: Institutions, Performance, and Policy Issues.* Occasional Paper 195 (Washington, D.C.: International Monetary Fund).

van Ham, Peter. 2001. "The Rise of the Brand State." *Foreign Policy* 80, no. 5 (September/October): 2–6.

Vaubel, Roland. 1977. "Free Currency Competition." *Weltwirtschafliches Archiv* 113, no. 3: 435–61.

———. 1984. "The Government's Money Monopoly: Externalities or Natural Monopoly?" *Kyklos* 37, no. 1, 27–57.

———. 1990. "Currency Competition and European Monetary Integration." *Economic Journal* 100 (September): 936–46.

Velde, François R., and Marcelo Veracierto. 2000. "Dollarization in Argentina." *Economic Perspectives* (Federal Reserve Bank of Chicago) 24, no. 1 (First Quarter): 24–35.

Vernengo, Matias, and Louis-Philippe Rochon. 2000. "Exchange Rate Regimes and Capital Controls." *Challenge* 43 n. 6 (November–December): 76–92.

———. 2001. "Financial Openness and Dollarization: A Skeptical View." Paper prepared for a conference, The Role of the Central Bank under Dollarization. Quito, Ecuador, 22–23 March.

Vogel, Steven K., ed. 2002. *U.S.-Japan Relations in a Changing World* (Washington, D.C.: Brookings Institution).

Volcker, Paul, and Toyoo Gyohten. 1992. *Changing Fortunes: The World's Money and the Threat to American Leadership* (New York: Times Books).

von Furstenberg, George M. 2000a. "Can Small Countries Keep Their Own Money and Floating Exchange Rates?" In Karl Kaiser, John J. Kirton, and Joseph P. Daniels, eds., *Shaping a New International Financial System* (Aldershot, U.K.: Ashgate), ch. 11.

———— 2000b. "A Case Against U.S. Dollarization." *Challenge* 43, no. 4 (July/August): 108–20.

———— 2000c. "US-Dollarization in Latin America: A Second-Best Monetary Union for Overcoming Regional Currency Risk." *Economia, Societa e Istituzioni* 12, no. 3 (September): 281–318.

———— 2001a. *One Region, One Money: Implications of Regional Currency Consolidation for Financial Services*, 25th Annual Lecture (Geneva: International Association for the Study of Insurance Economics).

———— 2001b. "Pressures for Currency Consolidation in Insurance and Finance: Are the Currencies of Financially Small Countries on the Endangered List?" *Journal of Policy Modeling* 23, no. 3 (April): 321–31.

———— 2002a. "One Region, One Money?" *The Annals of the American Academy of Political and Social Science* 579 (January): 106–22.

———— 2002b. "One Region, One Money: The Need for New Directions in Monetary Policies." In Michele Fratianni, Paolo Savona, and John J. Kirton, eds., *Governing Global Finance: New Challenges, G7 and IMF Contributions* (Aldershot, U.K.: Ashgate), ch. 7.

von Furstenberg, George, and Michele Fratianni. 1996. "Monetary Union: Still Coming in Europe and North America?" *Challenge* (July/August): 34–39.

Wade, Robert. (1998–1999). "The Coming Fight Over Capital Controls." *Foreign Policy* 113 (Winter): 41–54.

Wade, Robert, and Frank Veneroso. 1998a. "The Gathering Support for Capital Controls." *Challenge* 41, no. 6, 14–26.

————. 1998b. "The Resources Lie Within." *The Economist*, 7 November, 19–21.

Wallace, Mark. 2001. "Hour Town." *Harper's Magazine*, November, 54–55.

Walter, Norbert. 1998. "An Asian Prediction." *The International Economy* 12, no. 3 (May/June): 49.

————. 2000. "The Euro and Its Consequences for Global Capital Markets." In Robert A. Mundell and Armand Cleese, eds., *The Euro as a Stabilizer in the International Economic System* (Boston: Kluwer Academic), ch. 6.

————. 2002. "Europe Tomorrow: Political Union Will be Sustained." *International Economy* (Spring): 39.

Wang, Yunjong. 2003. "Instruments and Techniques for Financial Cooperation." In Gordon de Brouwer, ed., *Financial Arrangements in East Asia* (London: Routledge, forthcoming).

Weatherford, Jack. 1997. *The History of Money* (New York: Three Rivers Press).

————. 1998. "Cash in a Cul-de-Sac." *Discover* (October): 100.

Weishaar, Wayne, and Wayne Parrish. 1933. *Men Without Money* (New York: Putnam's).

West Indian Commission. 1992. *Time for Action: Report of the West Indian Commission* (Black Rock, Barbados: West Indian Commission Secretariat).

Whalen, Christopher. 2001. "Mexican Meltdown?" *International Economy* (September/October): 30–33, 49.

Wheatley, Jonathan. 2001. "The Mercosur Marriage is in Trouble." *Business Week*, 29 January, 25.

White, Lawrence H. 1989. *Competition and Currency* (New York: New York University Press).

Willett, Thomas D. 1999. "Developments in the Political Economy of Policy Coordination." *Open Economies Review* 10: 221–53.

———. 2000. *International Financial Markets as Sources of Crises or Discipline: The Too Much, Too Late Hypothesis*, Essay in International Finance 218 (Princeton: International Finance Section).

———. 2001. "Truth in Advertising and the Great Dollarization Scam." *Journal of Policy Modeling* 23, no. 3 (April): 279–89.

———. 2002. "Fear of Floating Needn't Imply Fixed Rates: An OCA Approach to the Operation of Stable Intermediate Currency Regimes." *Open Economies Review* (forthcoming).

Williamson, John. 1985. *The Exchange Rate System*, rev. ed. (Washington, D.C.: Institute for International Economics).

———. 1990. "What Washington Means by Policy Reform." In John Williamson, ed., *Latin American Adjustment: How Much Has Happened?* (Washington, D.C.: Institute for International Economics), 5–20.

———. 1995. *What Role for Currency Boards?* (Washington, D.C.: Institute for International Economics).

———. 2000. *Exchange Rate Regimes for Emerging Markets: Reviving the Intermediate Option* (Washington, D.C.: Institute for International Economics).

———. 2002. "The Evolution of Thought on Intermediate Exchange Rate Regimes." *Annals of the American Academy of Political and Social Science* 579 (January): 73–86.

Williamson, John, and C. Randall Henning. 1994. "Managing the Monetary System." In Peter B. Kenen, ed., *Managing the World Economy: Fifty Years After Bretton Woods* (Washington, D.C.: Institute for International Economics), 83–111.

Williamson, John, and Molly Mahar. 1998. *A Survey of Financial Liberalization*. Essay in International Finance 211 (Princeton: International Finance Section).

Williamson, John, and Marcus Miller. 1987. *Targets and Indicators: A Blueprint for the International Coordination of Economic Policy* (Washington, D.C.: Institute for International Economics).

Wójcik, Cezary. 2000. "A Critical Review of Unilateral Euroization Proposals: The Case of Poland." *Focus on Transition* 2 (Vienna: Austrian National Bank): 48–76.

Wolf, Martin. 1998. "Flows and Blows." *Financial Times*, 3 March.

Woo, Wing Thye, Jeffrey D. Sachs, and Klaus Schwab, eds. 2000. *The Asian Financial Crisis: Lessons for a Resilient Asia* (Cambridge, Mass.: MIT Press).

Woodford, Michael. 2000. "Monetary Policy in a World Without Money." *International Finance* 3, no. 2 (July): 229–60.

Worrell, Keith. 1995. "A Note on the Null-Case for a Common CARICOM Currency." *Social and Economic Studies* 44, no. 1 (March): 184–90.

Wriston, Walter B. 1998. "Dumb Networks and Smart Capital." *Cato Journal* 17, no. 3 (Winter): 333–44.

Wyplosz, Charles. 1999. "An International Role for the Euro?" In Jean Dermine and Pierre Hillion, eds., *European Capital Markets with a Single Currency* (Oxford: Oxford University Press), ch. 3.

Xu, Xinpeng. 1999. "The Exchange-Rate Regime in Papua New Guinea—Getting It Right." *Pacific Economic Bulletin* 14, no. 2: 48–60.

Yuen, Hazel. 2000. "Is Asia an Optimum Currency Area?" National University of Singapore. Typescript.

Zaidi, Iqbal. 1990. "Monetary Coordination Among the Gulf Cooperation Council Countries." *World Development* 18, no. 5, 759–68.

Zelizer, Viviana A. 1994. *The Social Meaning of Money* (New York: Basic Books).

Zimbalist, Andres, and John Weeks. 1991. *Panama at the Crossroads: Economic Development and Political Change in the Twentieth Century* (Berkeley: University of California Press).

Zloch-Christy, Iliana. 2000. "The Currency Board in Bulgaria: Is It a Solution or the Economic Consequences of Failed Reforms?" In Iliana Zloch-Christy, ed., *Economic Policy in Eastern Europe: Were Currency Boards a Solution?* (Westport, Conn.: Praeger), ch. 7.

Index

Abdelal, Rawi, 50
afghani, 138, 235n. 42
Afghanistan, 138, 234n. 21. *See also* afghani
Africa, 55, 175, 178. *See also* East Africa; West Africa; sub-Saharan Africa; specific African countries
African Financial Community, 43–44
African Union, 175
Aglietta, Michel, 243n. 27
Aliber, Robert, 99, 100
alitononfo, 244n. 12
Ambrosi, Gerhard Michael, 91
American Economics Association, 212
amero, 163, 165
Andes, the, 84, 137, 150
Andorra, 43, 91–92, 131
Andrews, David M., 238n. 4
Anwar Ibrahim, 115
ANZAC dollar ("Zac"), 166
Arab Cooperation Council, 241n. 58
Arab Maghreb Union, 241n. 58
archbishop of Canterbury, 129
Argentina, 40, 43, 82, 120, 126, 128, 134–35, 142, 143, 145, 149, 171–72; Argentine central bank, 236n. 55; and barter currencies, 242n. 10; and Brazil, 147–48; and the Contingent Repurchase Facility, 129; and the Convertibility Plan, 145, 147, 148, 236n. 54; LETS systems in, 182; Quasi-Currencies in, 237n. 67. *See also* peso (Argentine)
Aridor, Yoram, 134
asea, 245n. 20
ASEAN + 3, 97
Asia, 94, 116
Asian financial crisis of 1997–1998, 96, 108, 117–18, 146, 169; key contributing factor, 119; and Latin America, 133
Asian Monetary Fund (AMF), 96, 97, 230n. 49
Association of Southeast Asian Nations (ASEAN), 41, 58, 60, 169–71, 178; members of, 225n. 16
Australia, 151, 177, 190; lack of interest in forming a monetary union with New

Zealand, 167–68; LETS programs in, 181. *See also* dollar (Australian)
Aykens, Peter, 101, 189, 238n. 5
Azerbaijan, 14, 16

Bahamas, 43, 45, 149, 173
Bahrain, 176
baht, 96, 114
Balassa-Samuelson effect, 229n. 36
balboa, 16, 43, 225n. 21
Balkans, 13–14, 91, 92, 138, 149, 150, 158, 218
Bank for International Settlements (BIS), 11–12, 200, 242n. 16
Bank of China, 117
Bank of Japan, 13, 198, 223n. 9
Banque Central des Etats de l'Afrique de l'Ouest (BCEAO), 174
Barbados, 173
Barro, Robert, 81, 136
barter, 2, 9
barter clubs, 183
barter fairs, 183
Beenz, 188, 198
Belarus, 177; and a possible monetary union with Russia, 168. *See also* rubel
Belgium, 44, 160
Belgium-Luxembourg Economic Union (BLEU), 44, 45
Berg, Andrew, 236n. 50
Bergsten, Fred, 83
Berk-Shares program, 181
Berman, Sheri, 210
bezant, 68
Bhagwati, Jagdish, 108, 109
Bhutan, 43, 45, 151
bimonetarism, xvii, xviii, 43, 45, 48, 150, 152
bimonetary countries, 63 (table)
Blinder, Alan, 209, 210
Bolivia, 14, 16, 113, 137
Borensztein, Eduardo, 236n. 50
Bosnia and Herzegovina, 43, 92, 145, 146, 151, 237n. 61
Botswana, 69, 227n. 3

Brazil, 68, 119, 120, 147–48, 150, 171–72, 240n. 43. *See also* real
Bretton Woods, 106–7, 220
Britain, 38, 67–68, 92, 160; and the Bank Charter Act (1844), 6; development of the first currency boards, 143–44; history of money in, 6; LETS programs in, 181; protection of the sterling area, 23; rejection of the euro, 9, 161. *See also* pound
Brittan, Samuel, 104
Brunei, 43, 141, 144, 146, 236n. 58
Buiter, Willem, 55, 137, 164
Bulgaria, 43, 45, 92, 145, 148
Bundesbank, 13, 200, 243n. 8

Calvo, Guillermo, 88, 206
Cambodia, 14, 16, 150, 170, 234nn. 15, 21
Camdessus, Michel, 31
Canada, 57, 68, 177, 181, 183, 238n. 12; LETS programs in, 181; and a possible monetary union with the United States, 162–66. *See also* loonie
Canada-U.S. Free Trade Agreement (1989), 238n. 13
Canadian Tire Stores, 181
Cape Verde, 240n. 52
capital controls, 104, 205–6, 230n. 5; benefits and costs of, 109–12; "curative" controls, 114; and the element of time, 112–14, 118–21; legitimacy of, 104–9; and "preventive" controls, 114. *See also* coercion
capital mobility, 34–35; Bhagwati's criticism of "myth" of beneficence of, 108; and critical efficiency benefits, 110
Cardoso, Fernando, 172
Caribbean, the, 56, 84, 137, 150, 162, 173–74, 175, 178; and currency substitution, 13
Caribbean Community and Common Market (CARICOM), 173, 240n. 48; members of, 240n. 48; and the West Indian Commission, 240n. 49
Caribbean Monetary Union (CMU), 173
Central African Economic and Monetary Community (CAEMC), 43–44; franc of, 226n. 24; members of, 226n. 24
Central America, 56, 84, 137, 149–50
central bank, 6, 45, 49, 80, 125, 127, 140, 193–94; autonomy, 195, 198–99; control, 195, 198–99; and "credibility in a bottle," 127; impact of deterritorialization on, 194–96; impact of electronic money on, 192–93, 196–97, 199–202; impact of local money on, 185–86; and independence, 207–8; in Latin America, 81; as lender of last resort, 129; and reliance on open-market operations, 142; and world central bank idea, 211–14
CFA Franc Zone, 41, 43–44, 45, 56, 57, 58, 94, 156, 159, 174, 175, 177; what "CFA" stands for, 225n. 13
Chang, Roberto, 233n. 9
Chiang Mai Initiative, 97; and the ASEAN + 3 formula, 171
Chile, 119–21, 126, 225n. 10, 232n. 43, 243n. 8; and the unremunerated reserve requirement (URR), 119–20, 121. *See also* peso (Chilean)
China, 68, 98, 137, 171, 181; as illustration of the disadvantages of preventive controls, 117–18; and opposition to the AMF, 230n. 54. *See also* Bank of China; yuan
Choice Diagram, 52–54, 123, 211, 218, 219; for Canada, 162, 164; and dollarization (DL) curve, 53–54, 122, 132, 134, 150, 153; and domestic politics, 59; for East Asia, 169; and economic linkages, 57; and Ecuador and El Salvador, 84; and monetary alliance (MA) curve, 53–54, 122, 153, 163, 178; and national currency (NC) curve, 53–54, 99, 103, 112, 114, 118, 121, 132, 134, 145, 151, 153, 178; and political linkages, 58; and small states, 56; for South America, 171
Choice in Currency (Hayek), 30
Clark, Helen, 167
Cline, William, 120–21
Closer Economic Relations (CER) Agreement (1983), 166
coercion, xvii, 39, 103–4, 121; benefits and costs of, 109–12; historical perspective on, 106–9; and political values, 104–6; and restraints on inflows, 118–21; and restraints on outflows, 112–14
Cohen, Benjamin J., xiii–xiv, 33, 95, 105, 203, 224n. 3, 232n. 28
coinage, 3–4; dominant international coins, 4; petty coins, 3; specie, 3
Colombia, 119

colon, 134
Common Market. *See* European Union
Common Monetary Area (CMA), 44–45, 46, 48, 49, 58, 177
common tender, 190
Comoros Islands, 43
complementary currency. *See* local money
computer money. *See* electronic money
confidence game, 39, 99, 100, 102, 103, 115, 121, 205, 207, 224–25n. 8
Congo, 234n. 21
Contraction Contention, xiii, xiv, 1, 26, 31, 41–42, 179, 212; Cohen's critique of, 31–32
Convergence Council, 174, 177
Cooper, Richard, 73, 110–11, 113, 114, 212
Cooper, Scott, 238n. 5
cooperation, 244n. 18; conditions for, xviii; policy-optimizing approach to, 217; regime-preserving approach to, 217
Corden, Max, 216
Costa Rica, 126, 134, 137
Costello, Peter, 168
Countdown, 235n. 43
Courchene, Thomas, 163
Croatia, 14
currency. *See* money
currency bloc, 41, 78; formation of, xvi, 74; and market leader's status/prestige, 80
currency board, xvii, xviii, 7–8, 43, 45, 50, 139, 152; future prospects of, 145–51; key features of, 139–40; pros and cons of, 139–43; recent experience, 143–45
currency-board countries, 63 (table)
currency internationalization, 8–9, 36; and the global foreign-exchange market, 11–12; motivation for, 9–10
Currency Pyramid, xiv, 61, 214; the Big Three, xvi–xvii, 67–68, 79, 196, 214–18 (*see also* dollar/United States; euro/Euroland; yen/Japan); Elite Currency, 15, 68; full dollarization's formalization of, 130; and "junk currencies," 27, 40, 212; and Patrician Currency, 15; and Permeated Currency, 16, 43, 137; and Plebian Currency, 15; and Pseudo-Currency, 16, 43, 131; and Quasi-Currency, 16, 43, 137; and shifts in relative standing among the Big Three, xvi, 68–74; and Top Currency, 14–15, 223n. 13

currency substitution, 8–9, 36, 76, 113, 127, 149, 195; areas of the world concentrated in, 13–14; motivation for, 10; signal of rapid growth of, 13
currency union, 8
CyberCoin, 187
Cybergold, 242n. 19
Cyprus, 69
Czechoslovakia, 55

Danthine, Jean-Pierre, 73
Danzig, 144
D'Arista, Jane, 82–83
Dayton accord (1995), 145, 237n. 61
Dean, James W., 235n. 37
decolonization, 7, 44, 58, 144; and abandonment of colonial-era currency boards, 55
default risk, 125–26
de Gaulle, Charles, 75
Deli-Dollars, 181
Denationalisation of Money (Hayek), 30, 224n. 19
Denmark, 9, 44, 92, 160
"denomination rents," 85, 125
dependent territories, 65–66 (table), 225n. 20
deterritorialization of money, xiii, 1, 3, 8, 13–14, 78, 103, 113; impact on macroeconomic management, 20–21; impact on monetary insulation, 23–24; impact on the role of money as a political symbol, 22–23; impact on seigniorage, 21–22; implications of, 194–96; libertarian view of, 104–6
Detken, Carsten, 73
deutsche mark (DM), 9, 12, 13, 161, 223n. 8
devaluation risk, 125–26
Díaz, Porfirio, 150
Diebold, William, 228n. 23
DigiCash, 187, 188, 200
digital money. *See* electronic money
diplomatic influence. *See* money, as an instrument of diplomatic influence
disinflation, 102
Djibouti, 43, 58, 144, 146
Doe, Samuel, 132
Doe dollars, 132
dollar (Australian), 13, 15
dollar (U.S.), xv, xvi, 9, 40–41; as favored vehicle for currency exchange

dollar (U.S.) (*cont.*)
  worldwide, 12; as favored vehicle for the
    invoicing of international trade, 12;
    notes of in circulation abroad, 13; as sup-
    planting the pound sterling, 67; as Top
    Currency, 15, 68, 73, 75, 77; and use of
    $100 bills, 13
dollarization, xvii, xviii, 8, 40, 42–43, 48,
    50–51, 79–80, 123–24, 154; costs of,
    79, 127–30; definition of, 223n. 3; and
    full dollarization, 123–30, 153; future
    prospects, 135–39; and interest savings
    for the U.S. government, 76; and mone-
    tary clientele, 80; and near-dollarization,
    123, 131–32; purported benefits of,
    124–27; in recent experience, 132–35;
    U.S. views on, 81–87
Dooley, Michael, 111
Dornbusch, Rudiger, 27–28, 31, 116, 140,
    148–49, 231n. 15, 236n. 48
doro, 245n. 20
Dostum, Abdurrashid, 138
Dowd, Kevin, 29–30
Doyle, Brian M., 223n. 8
Duhalde, Eduardo, 148

East Africa, 58
East Asia, 95, 97, 98, 107, 108, 137, 144,
    150, 169–71, 207; "tiger" economies
    in, 171
East-Central Europe, 13–14, 91, 92, 138,
    149, 150, 158, 207, 218; and the adop-
    tion of the euro, 40; and currency substi-
    tution, 57
East Timor, 91, 138, 151
Eastern Caribbean Common Market, 173
Eastern Caribbean Currency Union
    (ECCU), 41, 42, 51, 56, 57, 58, 60, 156,
    159, 173–74, 177; and the Eastern Carib-
    bean Central Bank (ECCB), 45; members
    of, 240n. 48
eCash, 187
Economic and Monetary Union (EMU),
    41, 49, 51, 57, 58, 60, 70–72, 75–76,
    156, 158–62, 177, 217; conditions for
    membership in, 92–93; and ERM 2,
    150, 229n. 34; and the European Cen-
    tral Bank (ECB), 12, 45, 71, 76, 91, 93,
    159, 198, 242nn. 14, 21; as model for
    West Africa, 240–41n. 55
Economic Community of West African
    States (ECOWAS), 174–75

Economist, The. See The Economist
Ecuador, 40, 43, 45, 56, 83, 84, 89, 124,
    126, 131, 133–34, 135, 137, 145, 156,
    159. *See also* sucre
Edwards, Sebastian, 114, 120, 127, 243n. 5
Eichengreen, Barry, 30, 34, 41, 120, 221,
    228n. 18, 245n. 28
El Salvador, 40, 43, 56, 83, 84, 124, 131,
    134, 135, 145, 156, 159, 225n. 10. *See
    also* colon
electronic money, 186, 200; approaches to,
    186–89; and confidentiality, 189, 199–
    200; and consequences for monetary pol-
    icy, 192–93; critical issues for, 189–92;
    "e-cash version 1.0," 187, 188; "e-cash
    version 2.0," 187, 188; and frequent-
    flyer miles, 187–88, 242n. 22; and less
    competitive currencies, 196–97; and the
    market leaders, 197–99; and network
    money, 186–87; and portability, 189;
    and reliability, 189; and security, 189;
    and smart cards, 186–87
e-money. *See* electronic money
esperanza, 245n. 20
Estonia, 43, 92, 93, 145, 146, 151
eullar, 245n. 20
euro, xv, xvi, 9, 12, 13, 40–41, 42, 70–74,
    75–76, 83, 91–94, 229n. 31; high-de-
    nomination notes of, 76, 227n. 12; and
    international bonds and notes issuance,
    227n. 9; as Patrician Currency, 15; trans-
    actions costs and, 71–72, 73–74; as "vir-
    tual" currency, 9
euroization, 40, 91, 138–39
Euroland, 70, 227n. 6. *See also* Economic
    and Monetary Union
Euronext, 72
Europe, xvii, 6, 42, 91–94, 107, 181, 196,
    198; dollarized enclaves of, 57. *See also*
    Economic and Monetary Union; Euro-
    pean Union; specific countries of Europe
European Community (EC). *See* European
    Union
European Monetary System (EMS) (1979),
    160, 177; and ERM 1, 229n. 34
European System of Central Banks, 243n. 8
European Union (EU), 9, 57, 71, 91, 159–
    60; candidates for entry to, 229n. 33;
    Council of Ministers, 71, 93; discourage-
    ment of early euroization, 150; Euro-
    pean Commission, 71, 93, 160; Euro-
    pean Parliament, 93; former names of,

160; new members of, 229n. 33. *See also* Economic and Monetary Union

Eurosystem, 75, 227n. 6

exchange rate, 17; and the exchange-rate peg, 7–8, 33, 34; and exchange-rate targeting, 216; fixed versus flexible forms of, 33; floating, 206–7; IMF focus on, 219

exchange-rate union, 8, 42

Fátas, Antonio, 126

Federal Reserve Board, 6, 13, 85, 86–87, 198, 211, 243n. 8; highest note denominations issued by, 228n. 15

financial markets, 11, 102, 111; in Europe, 71–72; in Japan, 69–70

fiscal policy. *See* macroeconomic management, fiscal policy as core tool of

Fischer, Stanley, 128

Flooz, 187, 188, 198

Food and Drug Administration (FDA), 210

foreign-domestic currency use. *See* currency substitution

Fox, Vicente, 136

Fraga, Arminio, 240n. 43

franc (Swiss), 13, 15

France, 44, 160, 238n. 10; dislike of the term "Euroland," 227n. 6

Frankel, Jeffrey, 34, 86, 127, 234n. 32

Franklin, Benjamin, 153, 178

Freedman, Charles, 192, 200, 201, 243n. 26

Frieden, Jeffrey, 35, 59, 226n. 33

Friedman, Benjamin, 192, 195, 198–99

Friedman, Thomas, 103

Frost, David, 23

fully dollarized countries, 62 (table)

Gambia, 144, 174, 241n. 55

Gavin, Michael, 81, 235n. 34

geo, 244n. 20

geography of money, xiv, 1; and benefits of territorial money, 17–19; Westphalian Model of, 5, 7, 27, 144, 179. *See also* Currency Pyramid

Geography of Money, The (Cohen), xiii–xiv, 95, 105, 203, 224n. 3; and the Two S's, 7

Germany, 38, 160, 190; adoption of the euro by, 38, 161; as hegemon state, 159. *See* Bundesbank; deutsche mark

Ghana, 144, 174, 175, 241n. 55

Ghosh, Atish R., 147

ghost monies, 4

Giavazzi, Francesco, 73

global financial wealth, 12

Glover, Paul, 182–83, 184, 241n. 6

gold standard, 140

Goldberg, Whoopi, 187

Goldfinger, Charles, 244n. 20

Goldstein, Morris, 129

Goodhart, Charles, 192, 199–200, 201, 243n. 26

Greater East Asia Co-Prosperity Sphere, 171

Greece, 44, 159, 227n. 12

green money. *See* local money

Green Mountain Hours, 183

Greenaway, David, 29

Greenpoints, 242n. 19

Greenspan, Alan, 84, 86–87, 110, 199

Gresham's Law, 4, 132

Gresham's-Law-in-reverse, 4, 9, 28

Grimes, Arthur, 166, 167

Grubel, Herbert, 163, 164–65, 166

Guatemala, 136, 149

Guinea, 174

Gulde, Anne-Marie, 147

Gulf Cooperation Council (GCC), 176; and the Unified Economic Agreement, 176

Gutierrez, Lucio, 134

Guyana, 173

Ha, Jiming, 13

Haiti, 149, 173

Hale, David, 78, 104

Hanke, Steve, 140, 142, 147

Hartmann, Philipp, 73

Hausmann, Ricardo, 41, 124, 136

Hayek, Friedrich, 30, 224n. 20

Helleiner, Eric, 19, 50, 164, 184, 192, 199, 200, 201, 223n. 2, 225n. 9, 231n. 8, 236n. 48, 238n. 12

Henning, Randall, 94

Higgott, Richard, 97

Hoffmann, Stanley, 158

Holmes, Frank, 166, 167

Hong Kong, 43, 118, 141, 142, 144, 146–47; and the Exchange Fund, 142, 236n. 55

Honohan, Patrick, 39

Hüfner, Martin, 91

hysteresis, 29

India, 68
Indonesia, 100, 118, 151. *See also* rupiah
inflation, 10, 18, 195; Hayek's solution to,
    30; and negative relationship between in-
    flation and growth, 102
inflation tax, 101, 205
information technology, 113
Institute for International Economics, 216
integrationist interests, 59, 85, 135
International Currency Experience (League
    of Nations), 107
international currency use. *See* currency in-
    ternationalization
International Monetary Conference
    (1867), 211–12
International Monetary Fund (IMF), xix,
    12, 14, 48, 109, 113, 212, 230–31n. 7;
    as counsel to countries with troubled cur-
    rencies, 102; and a country's political re-
    lationship with Washington and IMF
    credit, 230n. 48; and the 1997 approval
    of a plan to amend the Fund's charter,
    108, 231n. 14; original design of, 106–7;
    possible use of as mediator, 218–21; and
    promotion of the Washington Consen-
    sus, 107; and restrictions on capital-ac-
    count transactions, 231n. 13; and the
    United States as the institution's largest
    member, 96–97
International Monetary Stability Act, 89–91
intor, 214, 244n. 17
iPoints, 242n. 19
Iran, 176
Iran-Iraq War, 176
Ireland, 144, 236n. 57
Iron Law of Economic Controls, 232n. 28
Isla Vista Community Currency, 183
Israel, 15, 58, 134. *See also* shekel
Issing, Otmar, 199, 202
Italy, 44, 160, 183, 227n. 3, 238n. 10
Ithaca Hours, 182–83
Ito, Takatoshi, 70

Jamaica, 173
Japan, xvii, 6, 38, 69–70, 75, 76–77, 94–
    98, 107, 137, 171, 196, 198, 207, 217,
    227n. 3; and the Big Bang program, 70,
    77; and Council on Foreign Exchange
    and Other Transactions, 77; credit rating
    of, 69; financial system of, 69–70; and
    Healthcare Currency, 183. *See also* Bank
    of Japan; yen

Katzman, Julie, 82
Kemmerer, Edwin, 244
Kenen, Peter, 217
Keohane, Robert O., 158, 244n. 18
Keynes, John Maynard, 18, 107, 109,
    244n. 17
Kiguel, Miguel, 232n. 4, 234n. 32
King, Mervyn, 200–201, 202
Kiribati, 43, 151
Kirshner, Jonathan, 24, 51
Klein, Benjamin, 30, 230n. 1
Klein, Lawrence, 130, 134
Knapp, George, 189, 200
Kobrin, Stephen, 192, 198
Kohl, Helmut, 38
Koizumi, Junichiro, 95
Kosovo, 229n. 31, 235n. 44
Krasner, Stephen, 7
Krueger, Anne, 109
Krueger, Russell, 13
Krugman, Paul R., 31, 39, 47, 67–68, 99,
    102, 103, 117, 148, 225n. 8; on "Plans
    A and B," 109, 114
Kuwait, 15, 176

Lake, David, 158
Lane, Philip, 39
Laos, 16, 150, 170
Latin America, 16, 58, 91, 94, 107, 119,
    196, 207; and the Asian financial crisis
    of 1997–1998, 133; and the blocking of
    capital flight in the 1980s, 113; Bush ad-
    ministration policy toward monetary de-
    velopments in, 87, 228n. 24; and cur-
    rency substitution, 13, 57; and
    dollarization, 40, 136, 149; evidence of
    monetary followership in, 228n. 16; and
    monetary relations with the United
    States, 81–84, 85, 87. *See also* specific
    Latin American countries
Latin Monetary Union (LMU), 44, 45–46,
    177; and the Banque de France, 46
Latvia, 69, 91
"Left Behind" series, 244n. 14
legacy currency, 71, 227n. 8
legal tender, 6
lender of last resort (LOLR), 128, 129, 174
Lesotho, 44, 45, 49
Leyshon, Andrew, 184–85
Liberia, 174
Liechtenstein, 42, 45, 131
Lietaer, Bernard, 242n. 11

Lim, Linda, 116
Linton, Michael, 181
Litfin, Karen, 39, 142–43
Lithuania, 43, 92, 142, 145, 146, 151
Local-Exchange Trading System (LETS), 181–82; names of monies, 182
local money, 180, 203; barter-based systems, 181–84, 241n. 4; consequences, 185–86; motivations, 184–185; objectives of, 184; scrip-based systems, 180–81
loonie, 163, 164
Lukashenko, Aleksandr, 168
Luxembourg, 44, 45, 160

Maastricht Treaty (1992), 41, 71, 92–93, 159, 160, 161, 239n. 37, 243n. 8; and the Exchange-Rate Mechanism (ERM 2), 93, 229n. 34
Mack, Connie, 89
Mack Bill, 89, 128, 137. See also International Monetary Stability Act
macroeconomic management, 18, 47–48, 205; benefits of, 79; and currency regionalization, 47–48; effects of deterritorialization on, 20–21; fiscal policy as core tool of, xix; 208–10; and "sound" macroeconomic management, 100–101
macroeconomics, 33–36: and broader political considerations, 35–36
Madrid, Arnulfo Arias, 225n. 21
Mahuad, Jamil, 133
Malayan Currency Board, 236n. 58
Malaysia, 170, 171, 236n. 58; as illustration of the advantages of curative controls, 114–17, 119. See also ringgit
Mann, Catherine, 82
market alliance, xv, xviii, 37, 38, 217. See also cooperation; monetary union
market followership, xv, xvii–xviii, 37, 39, 51, 79, 217, 218, 228n. 16; and Latin America, 81. See also bimonetarism; currency board; dollarization
market leadership, xv, 36, 37–38; benefits of, 37; formal leadership in, xvi–xvii, 74, 78–81; informal leadership in, xvi, 74, 75–78; and "soft power," 80. See also Currency Pyramid, euro; dollar (U.S.); yen
market preservation, xv, xvii, 36, 39, 50, 99, 112–13, 179, 217; as default strategy, 51. See also coercion; persuasion
Marshall Islands, 60, 130
Martin, William McChesney, 212

Marx, Groucho, 137
Mathathir Mohamad, 115, 116, 137, 169
Mauritania, 240n. 52
Mauritius, 69, 143
McCallum, John, 165–66
McKinnon, Ronald, 216
McNamara, Kathleen, 210, 238n. 5
Mediterranean, the, 58, 94, 139, 149, 150; and the adoption of the euro, 40
Meltzer, Allen, 218
Melvin, Michael, 70
Menem, Carlos, 40, 81, 125, 134, 135, 147, 171–72, 240n. 47
Mercosur, 41, 58, 60, 171–73, 177, 178; associate members of, 240n. 42; members of, 225n. 15; what "Mercosur" stands for, 225n. 15. See also "mini-Maastricht"
Mexico, 57, 82, 96, 113, 120, 128, 129, 136, 149, 150, 181, 232n. 29, 238–39n. 14; and the "tequila effect," 147
Micronesia, 42, 45
Middle East, 13, 94, 196
Mill, John Stuart, 211
mimesis, 29
"mini-Maastricht," 172, 177
Miyazawa, Kiichi, 97
Molano, Walter, 82
Monaco, 60, 91, 131
Mondex, 187, 188, 200
mondo, 244n. 17
monetary aggregates, 141, 193: and M0 (base money or central-bank currency), 141, 193; and M1 (demand deposits), 141, 193; and M2 (reservable deposits or broad money supply), 141, 193, 223n. 11; and M3, 141; and M4, 141
"monetary evangelicals," 140
monetary policy, 17–18; and autonomy, 195, 198–99; and control, 195, 198–99; function of, 48; goal of, 193; how monetary policy works, 193–94; outsourcing of, 39, 47, 127, 179; transmission mechanism of, 194; usurping of, 204–8
monetary union, 8, 43–45, 153–54; effects of, 154–55; European resistance to, 160–61; main advantage of, 153; main disadvantage of, 153; obstacles to, 155–58; sustainability of, 156–57. See also CFA Franc Zone; Common Monetary Area; Eastern Caribbean Currency Union; Economic and Monetary Union

monetary unions, 64 (table)
money: capital certainty of, 11; exchange
    convenience of, 11; future value of, 10–
    11; history of, 3–7; and inertia, 29–30,
    67–68, 72, 113; invention of, 2; as an in-
    strument of diplomatic influence, 51, 80;
    as medium of exchange, 1, 4, 9–10, 78;
    as political symbol, 18–19, 22–23, 50–
    51, 80, 100, 101, 129–30, 140; as social
    institution, 190; stock of, 17; as store of
    value, 1, 10, 78; territorial conception
    of, 2; transactional network of, 2, 11,
    28, 29; as unit of account, 1, 4, 9–10,
    78. *See also* coinage; deterritorialization
    of money; electronic money; geography
    of money; local money
Montenegro, 92, 228n. 31, 235n. 44
Morgan Stanley Capital International,
    115–16
Morocco, 151
Mundell, Robert, 27, 28, 80, 138–39, 169,
    192, 213–14, 223n. 16, 244nn. 16, 20
Mundell-Fleming model, 33
Mussa, Michael, 237n. 65
Myanmar, 170

Namibia, 44, 45, 49
National Bank of Switzerland, 243n. 8
national identity, 18–19, 50. *See also*
    money, as political symbol
nation-state, 2; as the basic unit of mone-
    tary authority, 5
Nauru, 151
near-dollarized countries, 43, 45, 62 (table)
NetCash, 187
Netherlands, the, 160
network theory, 28–29; and infostructure,
    28; and infrastructure, 28
New Miyazawa Initiative, 97, 230n. 50
New Zealand, 177, 243n. 8; and a possible
    monetary union with Australia, 166–68
Nicaragua, 14, 134, 137
Nigeria, 174, 175, 241n. 55
Niskanen, William, 83
Noriega, Manuel, 130
North America, 207
North American Free Trade Agreement
    (NAFTA), 162, 164, 238n. 13
North American Monetary Union
    (NAMU), 162–66
Norway, 15, 44, 92, 160
Nye, Joseph, 80

Obstfeld, Maurice, 232n. 23
Ohmae, Kenichi, 245n. 20
Okun, Arthur, 105
oligopoly, xiv, 36, 99–100, 215; and infor-
    mal leadership, xvi, 74; and industrial oli-
    gopoly, 99; and interdependence of deci-
    sion making, 74; state as, 25–26, 99
Oman, 176
One Nation/One Money principle, 2–3, 5,
    7, 142
One Person/One Vote principle, 105
optimization, 34
optimum currency area (OCA) theory, 27,
    34, 156–57, 223–24n. 16, 226n. 28;
    country characteristics stressed in, 34,
    54; criteria approach to, 224n. 16; key
    underlying assumptions of, 46–47
Organization of African Unity, 175
Organization of Eastern Caribbean States, 173
oro, 244

Pacific, the, 57
Padoan, Pier Carlo, 92, 227n. 10
Palestine, 151
Panama, 42–43, 45, 55, 89, 125, 126, 130,
    131, 133. *See also* balboa
Papua New Guinea, 151
Pauly, Louis, 220
Payer, Cheryl, 220
PayPal, 187, 188
Peace of Westphalia (1648), 5
Persian Gulf, 162, 176, 178, 241n. 59
persuasion, xvii, 39, 99–103, 121; cost of,
    xvii. *See also* confidence game
Peru, 14, 16, 113, 128, 137, 232n. 29
peso (Argentine), 145, 147, 172
peso (Chilean), 120
Poland, 69, 93
political symbolism. *See* money, as political
    symbol
Portes, Richard, 72, 74, 77, 91, 228n. 27
Pou, Pedro, 234–35n. 32
pound, 15, 67–68
private currency. *See* electronic money;
    local money
private sector, xviii–xix, 18; as alternative
    source of money, 31–32; and benefits
    from deterritorialization, 24–25; increas-
    ing leverage of, 204; as major producer
    of money, 179; and U.S. policy regarding
    dollarization, 86. *See also* electronic
    money; local money

Project Euro 2000, 93
public receivability, 6

Qatar, 176

rand, 13, 44–45
ratchet effects, 29
Reagan administration, 130
real, 133, 172
recession, 103, 195
regionalization, xv–xvi; and currency issue,
    42–45; and decision making, 45–46; and
    horizontal regionalization (*see* market al-
    liance); and maximum acceptable region-
    alization, 51–54; and vertical regionaliza-
    tion (*see* market followership)
Reinhart, Carmen M., 206
renminbi. *See* yuan
Rey, Hélène, 72, 74, 91, 228n. 27
ringgit, 115
Rodrik, Dani, 103
Rogoff, Kenneth, 76, 212, 221, 223n. 9,
    232n. 23, 245n. 28
Rome Treaty (1957), 160, 239n. 37
"root-canal" economics, 102–3, 205
Rose, Andrew K., 47, 126, 226n. 26
Roubini, Nouriel, 143
Ruá, Fernando de la, 148, 225n. 11
rubel ("bunny"), 168
Rubin, Robert, 96, 117
Ruggie, John, 107
rupiah, 100
Russia, 177; lack of interest in forming a
    monetary union with Belarus, 168
Ryan, Paul, 90

Samuelson, Robert, 82–83
San Marino, 43, 91, 131
Santa Barbara Hours, 183
Saudi Arabia, 15, 176
Scandinavian Monetary Union (SMU), 44,
    46, 177; and the Swedish Rijksbank, 46
Scaruffi, Gaspara, 243–44n. 12
Schaede, Ulrike, 70
Scotland, 190
Schuler, Kurt, 90
Schwartz, Anna, 144
scrip issues, 180–81
Second Pan-American Scientific Conference
    (1915), 244
Securities and Exchange Commission, 210

seigniorage, 18, 35, 37, 140, 155, 205; ben-
    efits of, 79–80; and currency regionaliza-
    tion, 49; and depreciation of a money's
    value, 101; effects of deterritorialization
    on, 21–22; effects of dollarization on,
    127–28; electronic seigniorage, 189; as
    "inflation tax," 18; and international sei-
    gniorage, 21
Shakespeare, 11
shekel, 134
Shelton, Judy, 81, 99–100
Sierra Leone, 144, 174, 234n. 21, 241n. 55
Silva, Luiz Inácio Lula da, 172
silver dollar (Mexican), 68
Singapore, 118, 144, 145, 170, 171,
    236n. 58
Slovenia, 93
Smith, Adam, 185
"snake in the tunnel" initiative, 160, 177
social money. *See* local money
Solomon, Elinor Harris, 242n. 14
Somalia, 234n. 21
Soros, George, 109, 115, 205
South Africa, 44, 89. *See also* rand
South America, 162, 171. *See also* Mercosur
South Asia, 151
South Korea, 15, 116, 117, 137–38
South Pacific, 151, 168, 242n. 12
Southeast Asia, 13, 16, 162
Soviet Union/Soviet bloc (former), 13, 16,
    55, 58, 196
stagnation, 103, 195
Starr, Pamela, 137
state, the: the hegemon state, 157–58; as
    oligopolist, 25–26, 99; power of in deter-
    ritorialized monetary geography, 31; un-
    avoidable role of in the governance of
    money, 203; in the Westphalian model,
    106. *See also* nation-state
state branding, 100
state monetary strategy choice, 54; and
    country size, 55–56; and domestic poli-
    tics, 58–59; and economic linkages, 56–
    57; the empirical record, 54–55; as an in-
    herently tripartite choice, xvi; and politi-
    cal linkages, 57–58; and sharing, 8, 40;
    sovereignty bargain and, 39, 123; and
    subordination, 7–8, 40
state preferences. *See* state monetary strat-
    egy choice
state theory of money, 189, 200
Stein, Gertrude, 2

Stein, Robert, 90
Stiglitz, Joseph, 103, 221
Strange, Susan, 223n. 13
Streeten, Paul, 212
sub-Saharan Africa, 58, 94, 139, 149, 150, 174, 232n. 12
sucre, 133
Sudan, 234n. 21
Summers, Lawrence, 84
Suriname, 173
Sussman, Nathan, 41
Swaziland, 44, 45
Sweden, 9, 15, 44, 92, 160
Switzerland, 44, 68, 92, 160. *See also* franc (Swiss); National Bank of Switzerland

Taiwan, 15, 118
Tavlas, George S., 226n. 28
Taylor, Lance, 112
Tesco Clubcard, 242n. 19
Thailand, 96, 116, 117, 119, 170, 171. *See also* baht
The Economist, 96, 133, 147–48, 168, 187, 188, 191, 208, 212
Thrift, Nigel, 184–85
Thygesen, Niels, 12
Tiebout, Charles, 226n. 27
Timberlake, Richard, 190
Tortoriello, Frank, 181
transactions costs, 2, 28, 157; and currency regionalization, 46–47; and institutional design, 157; savings of, 78–79; and territorial currency, 17
Treaty of Chaguaramas (1973), 240n. 48
Trinidad and Tobago, 173
trust development: stage 1: momentary trust, 101–2; stage 2: reputational trust, 102; stage 3: affective trust, 102
Turkey, 94
Tuvalu, 43, 151

"Unholy Trinity," 33, 205, 206
United Arab Emirates, 15, 176
United States (U.S.), xvii, 77–78, 177, 196, 198, 208–9, 217, 227n. 3; anti-dollarization views in, 82–83; benign neglect of dollarization policy in, 83–85; and euroization, 93–94; and the Federal Reserve System, 6; history of money in, 6; its lack of interest in forming a monetary

union with Canada, 165–66; pro-dollarization views in, 81–82; and seigniorage-sharing, 87–89. *See also* dollar; Federal Reserve Board
Uruguay, 14
U.S. State Department, 86
U.S. Treasury, 13, 86–87, 88

Vatican, the, 91, 131
Vaubel, Roland, 28, 30
vehicle currency, 223n. 5
Velasco, Andrés, 233n. 9
"virtual" money. *See* electronic money
Visa Buxx, 187
Visa Cash, 187
Volcker, Paul, 213
von Furstenberg, George, 42, 155, 158, 224n. 22
von Thadden, Ernst-Ludwig, 73

Washington Consensus, 107, 231n. 12
Weatherford, Jack, 191
Werner, Pierre, 244n. 17
West Africa, 58, 162, 174–75, 177
West African Currency Board, 144
West African Economic and Monetary Union (WAEMU), 43, 174; franc of, 226n. 23; members of, 226n. 23. *See also* Banque Central des Etats de l'Afrique de l'Ouest
West African Monetary Institute, 174, 177, 240n. 55
Western Europe, 207
Willett, Thomas, 232n. 26, 238n. 4
Williamson, John, 121, 140, 231n. 12
Wolf, Holger C., 147
Wolf, Martin, 231n. 15
Woodford, Michael, 192, 201, 243n. 26
World Bank, 107
World Economic Forum, 231n. 15
world economy, globalization of, xiii
Wriston, Walter, 103, 105, 191
Wyplosz, Charles, 76, 94

yen, xv, xvi, 9, 12, 69–70, 76–77, 94–98, 226n. 1, 227n. 2; as Patrician Currency, 15
yenization, 95, 137, 150
yuan, 68, 117, 118
Yugoslavia, 55

DATE DUE

GAYLORD			PRINTED IN U.S.A.